D0635741

The Adolescent
as Decision-maker

Educational Psychology

Allen J. Edwards, Series Editor
Department of Psychology
Southwest Missouri State University
Springfield, Missouri

Judith Worell and Fred Danner (eds.). The Adolescent as Decision-maker: Applications to Development and Education

Marvin J. Fine (ed.). The Second Handbook on Parent Education: Contemporary Perspectives

Claire E. Weinstein, Ernest T. Goetz, and Patricia A. Alexander (eds.). Learning and Study Strategies: Issues in Assessment, Instruction, and Evaluation

Gary D. Phye and Thomas Andre (eds.). Cognitive Classroom Learning: Understanding, Thinking, and Problem Solving

Gilbert R. Austin and Herbert Garber (eds.). Research on Exemplary Schools

Louise Cherry Wilkinson and Cora B. Marrett (eds.). Gender Influence in Classroom Interaction

Leo H. T. West and A. Leon Pines (eds.). Cognitive Structure and Conceptual Change

Catherine T. Best (ed.). Hemispheric Function and Collaboration in the Child

Charles D. Holley and Donald F. Dansereau (eds.). Spatial Learning Strategies: Techniques, Applications, and Related Issues

John R. Kirby (ed.). Cognitive Strategies and Educational Performance

Penelope L. Peterson, Louise C. Wilkinson, and Maureen Hallinan (eds.). The Social Context of Instruction: Group Organization and Group Processes

Michael J. A. Howe (ed.). Learning from Television: Psychological and Education Research

Ursula Kirk (ed.). Neuropsychology of Language, Reading, and Spelling

The Adolescent as Decision-maker

Applications to Development and Education

Edited by

Judith Worell
Fred Danner

Educational and Counseling Psychology
College of Education
University of Kentucky
Lexington, Kentucky

Academic Press, Inc.
Harcourt Brace Jovanovich, Publishers
San Diego   New York   Berkeley   Boston
London   Sydney   Tokyo   Toronto

ℒℙ

Academic Press, Inc.
San Diego, California 92101

United Kingdom Edition published by
Academic Press Limited
24–28 Oval Road, London NW1 7DX

Library of Congress Cataloging-in-Publication Data

The Adolescent as decision-maker : applications to development and
    education / edited by Judith Worell and Fred Danner.
        p.   cm. -- (Educational psychology)
    Includes bibliographies and index.
    ISBN   0-12-764052-5   (alk. paper)
    1. Adolescence. 2. Adolescent psychology. 3. Educational
psychology. 4. Educational sociology.   I. Worell, Judith, Date.
II. Danner, Fred, Date. III. Series.
LB1135.A35   1989
370.15--dc20   89-53
                                                                  CIP

Printed in the United States of America
89   90   91   92   9   8   7   6   5   4   3   2   1

09/09/91

Contents

Part II. Journey through Adolescence

Part III. Transitions to Adulthood

Contributors

Numbers in parentheses indicate the pages on which the authors' contributions begin.

CAROLE AMES (181), Institute for Child Behavior and Development, University of Illinois at Urbana-Champaign, Champaign, Illinois 61820

RUSSELL AMES (181), University High School, University of Illinois at Urbana-Champaign, Champaign, Illinois, 61801

ARMANDO DE ARMAS (83), Department of Psychiatry and Human Behavior, University of Mississippi Medical Center, Jackson, Mississippi 39216

ANDREW BOXER (209), Michael Reese Hospital and Medical Center, and the University of Chicago, Chicago, Illinois 60637

FRED DANNER (3, 51), Department of Education and Counseling Psychology, University of Kentucky, Lexington, Kentucky 40506

ROBERT D. ENRIGHT (111), Department of Educational Psychology, University of Wisconsin, Madison, Wisconsin 53706

JEFFREY A. KELLY (83), Department of Psychiatry and Human Behavior, University of Mississippi Medical Center, Jackson, Mississippi 39216

DANIEL K. LAPSLEY (111), Department of Psychology, University of Notre Dame, South Bend, Indiana 46556

RUTH ANDREA LEVINSON (209), Orthogenic School, The University of Chicago, Chicago, Illinois 60637

GARY B. MELTON (281), Department of Psychology, University of Nebraska, Lincoln, Nebraska 68588

PATRICIA H. MILLER (13), Department of Psychology, University of Florida, Gainesville, Florida 32611

ANNE C. PETERSEN (209), The Pennsylvania State University, University Park, Pennsylvania 16802

RONALD C. SERLIN (111), Department of Educational Psychology, University of Wisconsin, Madison, Wisconsin 53706

JERRY SULS (143), Department of Psychology, State University of New York at Albany, Albany, New York 12222

JUDITH WORELL (3, 245), Department of Educational and Counseling Psychology, University of Kentucky, Lexington, Kentucky 40506

Preface

This book represents the third in a series of reviews relating current theory and research in human development to educational practice. The first two volumes covered the preschool and elementary school years (Holm & Robinson, 1977; Worell, 1982). The present volume extends the reviews of development within educational contexts to a consideration of the adolescent years, approximately twelve through eighteen. The focus of each chapter is on an important aspect of adolescence, summarizing relevant theory and research from approximately the past decade. Each chapter then considers the relevance of this review for applications to teacher behavior, instructional design, curriculum management, school administration, and educational policy. The text is most appropriate for upper undergraduate or graduate courses in psychology, human development, educational psychology, and the secondary school curriculum.

The target audience is expected to have a background in both psychology and education, and to be familiar with the basic concepts and principles in learning and human development. The reader will appreciate in each chapter the careful balance of attention to important conceptual issues within an area, as well as a more technical review and evaluation of recent research. The emphasis on contemporary research will necessarily omit important contributions from the past, and authors have, for the most part, handled the integration of present and past research with general summation and review. Thus, readers will be guided through both the history and the present status of the most significant topics relevant to contemporary adolescence.

The selection of chapters for this book was guided by the authors' frame of reference in considering the significance of adolescence for both development and education. We chose to view adolescence as a time of increased pressure for problem-solving and personal decision. Within this broad framework, we begin with a consideration of major theories about adolescent development, recognizing the contributions of alternative viewpoints to our understanding of contemporary research. The remaining chapters were designed to explore major areas in which the developing person might be arriving at important life decisions, and the contributions of current research to our understanding of the processes within which these decisions take place. We hope that the contributions of these chapters will be not only for update and review, but will serve to stimulate discussion and debate.

We wish to express our appreciation to those individuals who contributed their time, expertise, and efforts to the completion of the book. First, we would like to congratulate one another for maintaining a productive working relationship that remained open, communicative, and supportive despite our very considerable differences in theoretical outlook and professional expertise. We next wish to express our delight and admiration for the chapter authors, who worked within deadlines and editorial revisions with good humor and cooperative effort. A special thanks is also due to our colleagues and students whose helpful comments and suggestions contributed to the development of our own chapters: Dr. Margaret Gardner, Connie Christian, and Deborah Danner. Finally, we are grateful to the efforts of the professional staff at Academic Press, especially the support and encouragement given by Allen J. Edwards and Joe Ingram.

Judith Worell
Fred Danner

I

Concepts of Development in Adolescence

1

Adolescents in Contemporary Context

Judith Worell
Fred Danner

How does adolescence differ from other major periods of the life span, and of what significance are these differences for the educational community? We are not the first to observe that Western society has created an adolescent community by segregating our young people into educational units that prepare them with public ritual to fulfill unarticulated goals (Lasch, 1985; Lipsett, 1980). Our adolescent community is set apart as a group of individuals with few responsibilities, many restrictions, and a complex legal status that maintains a dependency on adults for privilege and access to resources. Having created this population, we now spend time and effort attempting to discover what these young people are all about. We have designed this book to explore in depth some of the major issues that face the early and middle adolescent person who is entering puberty, coping with transitions in many areas of personal and social functioning, and seeking to maintain a comfortable balance between the needs of self and those of society.

A View of Adolescence

We view adolescence as a time of increased pressure for problem solving and personal decision. As young persons grow toward autonomy and adulthood, they experience increased expectations from self and others for independence of thought, choice, and action. For each individual, the choices that are made during the high school years in self-discipline, social relationships, sexual behavior, academic commitment, and work–career–family planning may influence the course of future life development. Although transformation from childhood compliance to mature autonomy develops gradually across the teenage years, the young person is increasingly aware of the personal mandate to arrive at important life decisions.

This decision-making view of adolescence guided our selection of content areas in which the progression of self-development might be explored through theory and research. Although there are many internal and external influences on human development over which the adolescent lacks direct control, each experience provides an opportunity for individual choice. What are the most useful and important areas of development to consider in examining these choices?

Theories of adolescence contain useful guidelines for considering the adolescent in the context of the "developmental tasks" to be mastered on the road to maturity. In Chapter 2, Miller points out that these major tasks include developing a sense of identity, adjusting to major body changes, developing abstract thought, acquiring interpersonal skills, establishing autonomy, acquiring a personal value system, and setting goals for future achievement in career and family settings. For each of these developmental tasks, the adolescent is faced with a demand that cannot be ignored, thus setting the stage for complex decisions about what to believe, how to feel, and what can be done to accomplish the set of tasks.

The remaining eight chapters consider content areas that are relevant to these tasks. These chapters are divided into two parts: "Journey through Adolescence" and "Transitions to Adulthood." "Journey through Adolescence" covers five major areas of adolescent development that influence the decisions of both adolescents and the people who care about them: cognition, social relationships, moral development, self-awareness, and motivation. The section on "Transitions to Adulthood" extends the range of student concerns to topics that are essential for mature, effective adult functioning: sexuality, sex roles, and legal status.

JOURNEY THROUGH ADOLESCENCE

Each of the five chapters in this section discusses recent research on aspects of adolescent development that are relevant for decision making. The chapter on cognitive development considers the empirical status of the Piagetian notion of a dramatic improvement in cognitive ability during adolescence. Of particular importance for decision making is the claim that adolescents develop the ability to reflect upon their own thinking, systematically test hypotheses, and think about their futures. Understanding the development of social relationships is also critical for decision making since effective relationships with the peer group enable the adolescent to practice arriving at personal decisions that are independent of parents and teachers. The chapter by de Armas and Kelly looks at the adolescent who fails to establish satisfying social contacts and discusses school-based interventions designed to remediate deficits in developmentally critical social skills.

The chapter on moral and social education focuses on attempts to explain and influence the growth of moral reasoning. These attempts are clearly relevant for parents and educators who are committed to supporting the development of ethical decision making. The chapter on self-awareness and self-identity highlights the special vulnerability of adolescents as they face difficult and potentially dangerous choices. This topic is critical because the development of a sense of identity is the center around which all other adolescent decisions revolve. And finally, the chapter on motivation and achievement directly considers adolescent decision making in the context of school achievement.

TRANSITIONS TO ADULTHOOD

The three chapters in this section focus on transitions to mature adult functioning. The chapter on sexuality explores the biological, social, and psychological dimensions of adolescent sexual development and examines the effectiveness of school-based interventions in helping the adolescent to arrive at wise personal decisions in this critical area. The transition to adulthood also confronts the adolescent with important life–career choices that have been traditionally related to the separate roles of women and men in our society. The sex-roles chapter examines changes in sex-role attitudes and behaviors during adolescence and the relationship of contemporary sex-role decisions to personal well-being.

The chapter on the legal status of adolescents provides a fascinating account of our ambivalence concerning the ability and right of adolescents to make their own decisions. When does a person become mature enough to make critical life decisions?

The Roles of Parents and Teachers

One of the tasks of the parent and educator is to assist in the decision process by relaxing external supervision; providing stimulation, challenge, and advanced information; ensuring attention to desirable social models; and encouraging a commitment to meaningful life goals and values.

Clearly, many adolescents fail to experience the variety of social and intellectual encouragements that might facilitate effective problem-solving processes and satisfying decisions. As the developing person struggles to understand and adjust to the changes that are taking place both within the self and in the contemporary social community, choices may be influenced by immediate stimuli and pressing personal needs. In the absence of clear and effective adult standards and structures, students may select a lifestyle that responds to the seduction of media manipulation and peer pressure. Parents and educators are understandably concerned about those adolescents who fail to confront the difficult choices required by an adult-status attainment and instead opt out of this responsibility by random pleasure seeking or withdrawal. We are, however, impressed with the fact that the majority of high school students are declaring clear goals and facing their futures with confidence and commitment (Herzog & Bachman, 1982). The confusion and identity diffusion that characterize a small minority of today's youth should not be the dominant theme of a psychology of adolescence.

The message that the psychology of development can bring to the educational community is this: We are teaching not only subjects but also developing persons. It is critical for their optimal transition to the world of adults that adolescents learn to manage the process of effective decision making in relation to their physical and social selves, their progress through the educational sequence, and their plans for future life functioning. We believe that a thorough understanding of the developmental process in adolescence will facilitate both effective interaction with students and competent management of the instructional environment. We believe it is particularly important that the curriculum in high schools emphasizes the ubiquity of choice in life, helping students to understand how to evaluate the consequences of alternative choices and how to arrive at personally and socially productive solutions.

In addition to learning from positive experiences, students may also learn to grow from mistakes and failure. Part of the developmental and educative process is to encourage a productive confrontation with failure and to integrate failure experiences into renewed effort and coping. Thus, one of the lessons of a decision-making model is that concerned with effective coping when the outcomes of our decisions are not satisfying. Viewing and helping students to view the negative outcomes in their lives as additional challenges for renewed decision making seems to us to be a facilitative feature of a decision model for adolescence. Further, this approach may encourage parents and teachers not to blame students for their failures and mistakes but rather to help students use these experiences as building materials for constructive remediation.

Social Contexts of Adolescence

The self-direction suggested by a decision-making approach to individual development provides the adolescent opportunities for both freedom and responsibility. During these developing years, the adolescent is learning to set realistic goals, consider alternatives, and to select personally meaningful choices. The outcomes of these decisions are influenced by the totality of the developmental facts in each individual's life space, as well as by the current social and cultural–historical environment. We can conceptualize the influences of social factors on adolescent development as constituting two broad categories, proximal and distal.

At the proximal level, adolescents are contending with the values and goals of parents, the pressures and pleasures derived from peers, and the learning environment provided by the educational community. We know that parental patterns of influence that emphasize autonomy, explanation of rules, and active sharing of decision-making processes lead to increased independence, feelings of both freedom and responsibility, and self-esteem in adolescents (Baumrind, 1975; Martin, 1975).

Armed with some of the tools required for effective decision processes, the adolescent from a "democratic" and autonomy-giving family is prepared to contend with the multiple stresses engendered by a heterogeneous peer and educational community that communicates conflicting messages and demands. School personnel are in a particularly advantageous position to reinforce the efforts of the supportive family by continuing the patterns of shared communication and avoidance of coercive power. In addition, schools are designed to provide resources for information-seeking activities. It should be the explicit goal of the high school to encourage an information-seeking attitude in the developing person, providing evidence to the adolescent that mature decisions are frequently derived from resolutions of conflicting polarities and discrepant points of view. The information-seeking stance can be utilized effectively at many points in the adolescent's high school career, including curriculum selection, attendance policies, social and sexual behavior, and career–family planning. From our knowledge of the effects of modeling on observer behavior, we can anticipate that teachers and administrators who demonstrate in their own behavior the patterns and attitudes they wish to encourage will be rewarded with a similar role adoption in many of their students.

At the broader distal or cultural level, today's adolescent is faced, as never before in history, with immediate stimulation, and opportunities for intense gratification and equally intense anxiety. The impact of the information explosion, the multiple messages sent by the media, especially television, and the rapid societal change are only beginning to be examined and understood by the psychological community. It is certainly clear to the parent and teacher that much of what contemporary adolescents learn and understand is out of the control of the adults who care most intimately about what happens to their children. Given this fact, it becomes even more critical that we provide our youth with the foundations for coping with a world that none of us can fully control or anticipate. With a future largely unknown and a present in constant flux, the admonitions of the life-span theorist are especially important: That decisions made at one point in life may not necessarily hold us for a lifetime, and that life plans and outcomes may be as discontinuous as they are stable (Baltes, Reese, & Lipsett, 1980). Acceptance of the life-span position can throw us into a sense of anxiety about the unknown or a feeling of strength and anticipation of challenge. Take a look at today's adolescents and understand that this is the position in which they now find themselves. We hope that parents and schools will help the adolescent to choose challenges and will encourage the development of those attitudes and skills that are required to meet them.

Decision-making Limitations

We would be remiss in our position if we failed to point out the pitfalls in adopting a decision approach to adolescence. Three points should be considered. First, we will be faced with students who live in and return to homes where parents are overpermissive, punitive, controlling, or neglectful. Thus, not all students will have the prerequisite skills for participating in a shared decision-making experience. These students will provide a particular challenge to teachers who themselves accept and practice a democratic process. We offer no easy solutions here, but we recognize that preparation and groundwork may be necessary for students who have few autonomy and decision-making skills.

Second, we may want to be cautious about the responses of communities where influential factions may support indoctrination and traditional "truths" over inquiry and freedom of thought. Whenever school systems are out of step with prevailing community values, some conflict seems inevitable. Without suggesting solutions again, we are concerned that schools remain sensitive to community values without compromising their responsibility to encourage independence and maturity of action and thought in the developing individual. The content of possible school–community conflict may vary across regions, ranging from beliefs about appropriate dress, social and sexual behavior, access to information that some believe is objectionable, and strategies of teaching that encourage free inquiry and exploration. Policies concerning these issues should be developed across the entire school community and supported by consensus and communication within the educational system.

Finally, we should point out that a decision-making model is limited by the extent to which options and alternatives are more open to some students than to others. Teachers who fail to help students consider these limitations may anticipate that students will frequently make decisions that are below their potential or unrealistic in terms of societal opportunities. Some of these limitations on free decision-making include considerations of economic sufficiency, racial and ethnic group membership, and gender. We point out in Chapter 9 the discrepancies in girls' and boys' career choices and the apparent continued traditionality of employment planning in young women. Schools can help to counteract the societal limitations in free choice and opportunity by raising student awareness of these constraints on individual choice and can help students generate alternatives for training, goal-selection, and self-preparation. We are not suggesting that students limit their aspirations or set their sights lower than they desire, but that they become fully aware and thus able to cope with the internal and external barriers to the process of open and unbiased choice.

What Do We Know About Adolescence?

Our approach involves a dual focus on developments that are enduring features of adolescence, such as changes in physical, cognitive, and social status and the changing social contexts in which these nearly universal shifts occur. It is surprisingly difficult to maintain this dual focus, as everyone knows who teaches a course on adolescence. The authors of most texts on adolescence expend a great deal of effort trying to keep up with the latest preoccupations of the current adolescent cohort. The painful result of 2-year publication lags is that the descriptions of who is doing what at what age and which drugs are causing problems are already out-of-date by the time one assigns the text.

We seem to need constant reminders from life-span developmental psychologists, such as Baltes *et al.* (1980), and Schaie (1965), to be cautious in making firm conclusions about developments at any point in life that are strongly affected by changes in social contexts. The message is not that some things never change and others change too quickly for us to measure, but rather that one must simultaneously consider the relatively enduring aspects of individual development and the changes in families, schools, and the wider social environment that affect this development.

The mix of chapters in this volume reflects this dual focus on individual development in a shifting social context. The fact that one can make any sense out of this dynamic set of forces is a tribute both to the integrative powers of the chapter authors and to the inherent wisdom of human development. Despite the dire warnings of each generation of adult observers and the enormous number of barriers to successful development, most adolescents weather the transition to adulthood. Perhaps Erikson (1968) described it best when he characterized development as a series of "normative crises" or challenges, each fraught with danger but most successfully resolved by a majority of people.

As educators, however, we cannot be content to simply allow adolescents to survive the transition to adulthood. We have a responsibility to assist them. Too often our only response to this need for guidance and sensitivity is to insist upon high achievement—a response that creates both anxiety and apathy (Covington & Beery, 1976) and does not speak to the tremendous variations in developmental status that adolescents present (Lipsitz, 1977).

Exemplary schools and programs for young adolescents such as those described by Lipsitz (1984) and Wigginton (1985) seem to have found a way to be sensitive to the developmental needs of adolescents *as a first priority* without sacrificing academic achievement. They not only take seriously the adolescent's current developmental status but also consider the needs of the adult community that he or she is about to enter. Wigginton's now-famous *Foxfire* books, for example, were written and produced by his high school students. These students pursued the history and customs of their community, organized their findings in a highly engaging manner, and were immensely proud of themselves when adults were interested enough to buy the books. Wigginton used his students' pressing concerns about their current status and immediate future in the community to encourage them to observe, to think, and to write. In so doing, he helped them grow by looking outside of themselves.

This focus on others is too often neglected in both the education and the study of adolescents. Adolescents are often viewed as self-centered and immature, preoccupied with trivial aspects of themselves, and showing little concern for the welfare of others. Critics of our educational systems, such as Urie Bronfenbrenner (1979) and Maurice Gibbons (1974), attribute a great deal of this immaturity to the fact that we segregate children by age levels and provide them with very little responsibility either for themselves or others. This age segregation and lack of meaningful responsibilities discourage the development of helping and caring relationships across age groups, thereby cutting off one of the certain routes to maturity. Although there is no single definition of maturity that everyone would accept, it is generally agreed that maturity is not simply a function of age—it takes hard work and personal growth and is reflected most directly in a person who genuinely cares about the growth of others.

How mature are adolescents capable of being? One implication of our problem-solving model for enhancing adolescent development is that we need accurate information about adolescents. How do they think? What are they capable of understanding? What are the long-term consequences of their educational and social experiences during adolescence? Answers are difficult to find for several reasons. One that we have already mentioned is the preoccupation of much of the available research with the more superficial aspects of adolescents, such as their tastes, recreational preferences, and behavior in public places. Since these characteristics change so rapidly, even the most careful descriptive accounts offer little hope of improving secondary education.

A second limitation on our knowledge is more philosophical. Over 20 years ago, Adelson (1964) observed that the adolescent serves as a projective figure in the American mind. There are certain qualities, such as a heightened idealism and a purposeful striving for a better society, that we attribute to that figure, and it is extraordinarily difficult for us to believe evidence to the contrary when we find it. Adelson's subsequent studies of the development of social and political awareness provide many sobering examples of the painfully slow intellectual awakening of the typical adolescent. In fact, in one summary of his careful work in this area, Adelson (1975) likened the pursuit of adolescent idealism to the search for the Loch Ness monster: a search that may tell us more about what we want to believe about adolescents than about what they are really like.

And finally, our knowledge about adolescents is limited by the fragmented nature of the research on this stage of life. Until very recently, most of the available information on adolescence came from studies only incidentally concerned with adolescents, was conducted cross-sectionally, and was difficult to integrate with the research of other interested psychologists and educators. Two recent developments in the field of developmental psychology are beginning to change this picture. One is the resurgence of interest in the educational implications of basic developmental research. Researchers such as Lawson (1985), Selman (1980), and Nucci (1982) have taken their interests in science, interpersonal understanding, and morality, respectively, and systematically applied them to education. The second promising development is the creation of the Society for Research in Adolescent Development. This new organization brings together a small but growing band of researchers who have been studying adolescents in relative isolation.

These developments lead us to hope that 10 years from now the task of integrating what we know about adolescents and drawing out the implications for education will be both easier and more difficult than it is today. Easier because more researchers will be conducting long-term programmatic research with the ultimate goal of improving the education of adolescents, and more difficult because there will be a much larger body of good research to review.

References

Adelson, J. (1964). The mystique of adolescence. *Psychiatry, 27,* 1–6.

Adelson, J. (1975). The development of ideology in adolescence. In S. Dragastin & G. Elder (Eds.), *Adolescence in the life cycle: Psychological change and social context* (pp. 63–78). New York: Wiley.

Baltes, P. B., Reese, H. W., & Lipsett, L. P. (1980). Life-span developmental psychology. In M. R. Rosenzweig & L. W. Porter (Eds.), *Annual Review of Psychology, 31,* 65–110.

Baumrind, D. (1975). Early socialization and adolescent competence. In S. E. Dragastin & G. H. Elder (Eds.), *Adolescence in the life cycle: Psychological change and social context.* New York: Wiley.

Bronfenbrenner, U. (1979). *The ecology of human development.* Cambridge, MA: Harvard University Press.

Covington, M., & Berry, R. (1976). *Self-worth and school learning.* New York: Holt.

Erikson, E. (1968). *Identity: Youth and crisis.* New York: Norton.

Gibbons, M. (1974). Walkabout: Searching for the right passage from childhood and school. *Phi Delta Kappan, 55,* 576–602.

Herzog, A., & Bachman, J. (1982). *Sex-role attitudes among high school seniors: Views about work and family roles.* Ann Arbor, MI: Institute for Social Research, University of Michigan.

Lasch, C. (1985). "Excellence" in education: Old refrain or new departure? *Issues in Education, 3,* 1–12.

Lawson, A. (1985). A review of research on formal reasoning and science teaching. *Journal of Research in Science Teaching, 22,* 569–617.

Lipsett, J. S. (1980). The age group. In M. Johnson (Ed.), *Toward adolescence: The middle school years.* Seventy-ninth yearbook of the National Society for the Study of Education. Chicago: University of Chicago Press.

Lipsitz, J. (1977). *Growing up forgotten.* Lexington, MA: Heath.

Lipsitz, J. (1984). *Successful schools for young adolescents.* New Brunswick, NJ: Transaction Books.

Martin, B. (1975). Parent–child relations. In F. D. Horowitz (Ed.), *Review of child development research* (Vol. 4). Chicago: University of Chicago Press.

Nucci, L. (1982). Conceptual development in moral and conventional domains: Implications for values and education. *Review of Educational Research, 52,* 93–122.

Schaie, K. (1965). A general model for the study of developmental problems. *Psychological Bulletin, 64,* 92–107.

Selman, R. (1980). *The growth of interpersonal understanding.* New York: Academic Press.

Wigginton, E. (1985). *Sometimes a shining moment: The foxfire experience.* New York: Anchor Press.

2

Theories of Adolescent Development

Patricia H. Miller

Introduction

> Youth awakes to a new world and understands neither it nor himself. . . .
> Never has youth been exposed to such dangers of both perversion and arrest
> as in our land and day. Urban life has increased temptations, prematurities,
> sedentary occupations, and passive stimuli, just when an active, objective
> life is most needed. (Hall, 1904, Vol. I, p. xv)

G. Stanley Hall's description of adolescence sounds remarkably contemporary. Adolescents' attempts to understand themselves and the world
and make intelligent personal decisions are the concern of the various
theories of adolescence proposed since the beginning of this century.
These theories, despite their diversity, all address two central questions.
First, is adolescence an inevitable, universal, unique stage of life or is it a
cultural creation of the recent history of the Western world? Second, is
adolescence necessarily a turbulent, traumatic time? Some theories
explicitly concern themselves with these questions, whereas the position
of other theories is more implicit. We first will examine each of these
questions and will then consider a set of developmental tasks faced by the
adolescent that provide a context for these questions because they
identify potential sources of difficulty during adolescence.

From the viewpoint of society, adolescence did not really exist until
almost the 20th century. For many centuries adolescents, and even
children, fully entered the adult work force—often as early as age 6 or 7.
The Roman Emperor Claudius married at 12 and became a high priest at
13. Even when children attended school rather than worked, they did not
romp in a bucolic setting. Rather, they faced adult problems. In the 1300s
and 1400s boys of elementary-school age often had to carry sabers to

school for protection. A societally recognized period of adolescence began to arise out of a series of social changes. As the Western world became more technological, there was a need for a literate, educated population. Free public schooling became widespread in the late nineteenth century. At about the same time there were social reforms that protected children and young adolescents from being sent to war or working long hours in factories. More recently adolescence has become even more extended as most teenagers finish high school and the majority attend college.

This history might be interpreted to show that adolescence as a universal, unique time of development was "invented" shortly before the automobile. However, it could be the case that stepping into socially defined adult roles during childhood merely created a superficial appearance of adulthood that masked the same psychological turmoil felt by adolescents today. This issue is still unresolved.

Today, most developmental theories view adolesence as an important time during development, a phase that is not merely a cultural invention. However, there is sharp disagreement as to whether adolescence is actually a "stage" that is qualitatively different from earlier development or is a more gradual continuation of earlier development. Those positing discontinuity differ in whether the causes lie in sexual development, new social expectations, the need to unlearn well-established behaviors, the adolescent's ambiguous social status, cognitive reorganization, or some other factor.

The second question, concerning whether adolescence is necessarily a stormy, stressful time, was raised early in this century by G. Stanley Hall. His influential two-volume treatise bore the overwhelming title *Adolescence: Its Psychology and Its Relations to Physiology, Anthropology, Sociology, Sex, Crime, Religion and Education* (1904). He pictured adolescence as a time of *Sturm und Drang* (storm and stress), a phrase referring to a period of German literary history at the turn of the 18th century characterized by emotionality, idealism, pain, and a revolt against the old. Hall believed that because of the rapid and drastic physical changes of puberty, adolescents necessarily face difficult times. Families must try to weather the contradictions in adolescents as they swing from a frenzied state of energy to appalling apathy, from selfishness to altruism, from good humor to depression. This concept of adolescence is held by many theorists and many more parents but has been challenged by Margaret Mead and others. The degree of conflict may vary from culture to culture or may vary from person to person within a culture due to one's combination of biological inheritance and social circumstances.

These two questions concerning the nature of adolescence can be translated into a more specific set of developmental tasks faced by adolescents. This list is a composite drawn from various psychologists (e.g., Havighurst, 1957; Hill, 1980). Some of these tasks begin during childhood and thus point to the continuity of development, whereas other tasks are primarily a concern of adolescence and therefore point to discontinuity. Attempts to master these tasks can involve a great deal of stress or little stress and result in favorable or unfavorable outcomes, depending on a host of factors identified by the theories in this chapter. Each task involves some sort of problem solving and personal decision making.

The developmental tasks of adolescence include the following:

1. Develop a sense of identity—a concept of one's unique combination of values, attitudes, beliefs, and behaviors. All of the other developmental tasks contribute to this personal identity.

2. Adjust to a changing body. The many physical changes during puberty require perceptual–motor and psychological adjustment. In particular, an adolescent's gender identity crystalizes as a result of sexual maturity.

3. Develop abstract thought. Adolescents acquire more complex and abstract forms of reasoning that they apply to both the physical world of objects and events and to the social world of people, social events, and social structures.

4. Acquire interpersonal skills. Emerging sexuality and the value placed on the peer group make it critical to develop skills for interacting with and building relationships with same- and cross-sex peers.

5. Establish a new relationship with one's family. Adolescents' growing need for autonomy and their lessening emotional dependence on the family require a new relationship with family members who, however, are still needed for psychological and financial support.

6. Formulate a value system. Both adolescents' development of abstract thought and their greater penetration into society catalyze the development of a personal moral philosophy concerning why acts are right or wrong and what values are most important.

7. Set goals for future achievement. Adolescents set tentative goals concerning higher education, preparation for a career, marriage, and so on. Their testing out of their abilities in various academic, social, athletic, and artistic settings facilitates the formation of realistic goals.

These tasks obviously are interrelated, with progress within one task propelling development in another task. For example, cognitive development may help youths imagine themselves in various possible careers, infer what others are feeling and thinking during social interaction, and understand abstract moral philosophies. The interrelationships can also be negative. Failure to develop appropriate interpersonal skills can lead to a negative self-concept, a turbulent relationship with the family, and pessimism regarding one's future achievements.

Theories of adolescence differ in the particular developmental tasks they emphasize. For example, biological theories emphasize adjustment to a changing body, psychosocial theories focus on interpersonal skills and on emerging self-identity, and cognitive theories address the development of abstract thinking and a value system. As each theory is described, it can be related back to this set of developmental tasks.

The theories introduced in this chapter are organized into six groups: biological, psychoanalytic, psychosocial, social–cultural, field, and cognitive theories. In general, the first four groups move in order from an emphasis on internal biological influences to an emphasis on external environmental influences. These four groups share a concern with the emotional–social–personality facets of adolescence. In contrast, the final group of theories—cognitive theories—pays much less attention to these areas. Work on the cognitive structures underlying adolescents' perceptions of themselves and the world is the most active area of theorizing concerning adolescence in recent years. Field theory is a blend of cognitive, social, and biological forces.

The above characterization of the theories as internal versus external and emotional versus cognitive in focus is, of course, an oversimplification. All of the theories address all four areas; they differ in their emphasis.

Biological Theories

HALL

The dramatic physical changes at puberty are the most easily observed changes of adolescence. There is a close tie between physical and psychological development in a relatively direct sense, as hormonal changes affect emotions and behavior, and in a more indirect sense, as the adolescent and society react to the physical changes. All of this underlies G. Stanley Hall's (1904) notion that this is a period of storm and stress. Hall even referred to adolescence as a "second birth." He considered adolescence important not only because of rapid and far-reaching physical changes but also because adolescents are more amenable to the civilizing influences of society than are younger children. In Hall's view, a teenager is somewhere between an uncivilized savage with uncontrolled impulses and a responsible member of modern society: "The forces of sin and those of virtue never struggle so hotly for possession of the youthful soul'' (Hall, 1904, Vol. 2, p. 83).

Hall's maturationist view was quite influential. More broadly, he was the main proponent of the idea that adolescence is a special stage of development and a legitimate field of study. As the first PhD in psychology in the United States, he began work that established him as the father of a scientific psychology of adolescence, or "the Columbus of adolescence" (Sprinthall & Collins, 1984).

GESELL

The maturationist tradition was carried on by Arnold Gesell. He viewed development as the unfolding of physical structures and behaviors according to a biological blueprint. Gesell's interest in sequences, patterns, and organization can be seen in his general conclusion that the organism becomes more differentiated and integrated during development. Within the genetically controlled changes, environmental factors such as home and school can modulate this development. However, "acculturation can never transcend maturation" (Gesell & Ilg, 1943, p. 41). Gesell's main contribution was his careful and detailed observational work, which led to a normative description of development. In *Youth: The Years From Ten to Sixteen* (Gesell, Ilg, & Ames, 1956), there appears a description of "the twelve year old," "the thirteen year old," and so on for each year. For example, "No twelve-year-old party can be guaranteed immune from some sort of kissing game—a most natural expression for Twelve" (p. 122) and "The tight, withdrawn ways of Thirteen have loosened up at Fourteen" (p. 182).

EVALUATION

The spirit of the biological theories can be seen in the current research on hormonal changes during adolescence and the effects of early versus late maturation. For example, investigators report correlations between hormone levels and psychological adjustment, such as higher levels of adrenal androgens and lower levels of sex steroids associated with obsessive–compulsive, hyperactive and delinquent behaviors in boys (Nottelmann, Susman, Blue, Inoff-Germain, Dorn, Loriaux, Cutler, & Chrousos, 1986). Although biological theories have contributed to our understanding of adolescence by emphasizing the universal physical changes that influence behavior, these theories are limited in that they do not account for social and cultural factors that can underlie the stress of adolescence. For example, high school students whose ethnic or socioeconomic group is in the minority at their school are more likely to have self-image problems than those who are in the majority (Rosenberg,

1975). More generally, Hall's claim that adolescent stress is universal is clearly false. For instance, the majority of adolescents accept their parents' religious, educational, and social values (Bachman, Johnston, & O'Malley, 1981). In addition, the individual differences noted throughout this volume show that the behavior of adolescents is not as tied to particular ages or levels of physical maturation as Gesell proposed.

EDUCATIONAL IMPLICATIONS

Theories such as Hall's and Gesell's that emphasize genetically controlled maturation have implications for educational settings involving adolescents. Although the environment certainly can influence adolescent development, there are limits to this influence—limits set by a biological clock. Many problems will simply be outgrown and do not need the intervention of parents or teachers. The ideal educator knows when not to meddle. Hall believed that a certain amount of uncivilized behavior must be tolerated by society until children "evolve" to the point that they can be trained. Although Gesell's norms for each age are useful for identifying early and late developers, it is important not to consider these individual differences as abnormal simply because they deviate from the average.

Perhaps the main message of biological theories for educators is that they should be sensitive to when all children as individuals, directed by their own innate growth potential, have reached a state of readiness for acquiring new behaviors (e.g., interacting with the other sex) or concepts (democracy and social responsibility) via training. In other words, "Gesell maintains that the school curriculum should be founded on a psychology of development rather than a psychology of learning" (Muus, 1982, p. 174).

Psychoanalytic Theories

FREUD

Psychoanalytic theory, founded by Freud, also emphasizes biological influences. Because Freud held a unique conception of personality and his work spawned a number of later theories, psychoanalytic theory will be discussed separately from the above biological theories.

In Freud's view, the goal of the genital stage of adolescence is to develop the capacity to form healthy, mature heterosexual relationships during adulthood. As a result of puberty, sexual impulses, which were repressed during the latency period, reappear but at an even more intense level. Consequently, the previously achieved balance between the id, ego, and superego, unable to take the added strain, is upset, and the adolescent experiences psychological conflict and emotional turmoil—Hall's storm and stress. For this reason, the defense mechanisms, unconscious processes for controlling anxiety by distorting reality in some way, take on added importance. They can help the adolescent mature into an adult if they are not relied on too heavily. The ego has many defense mechanisms to draw on, including repressing anxiety-arousing thoughts, disguising an unacceptable emotion by transforming it into its opposite (for example, hate into love), "projecting" by attributing anxiety-arousing thoughts to others rather than the self, and temporarily regressing to a less stressful period of development.

Anna Freud (1946) spotlights two more defenses as particularly important during adolescence. Because of a fear that they may lose control over their sexual impulses, adolescents resort to asceticism, marked by the denial of any type of pleasure: "Every time the instinct says, 'I will,' the ego retorts, 'Thou shalt not,' much after the manner of strict parents in the early training of little children" (p. 168). Because of the newly acquired ability to think abstractly, the adolescent now can make greater use of a second defense—intellectualization. In intellectualization, the adolescent transforms emotional conflicts into abstract philosophical arguments, stripped of emotion. These two defenses can be illustrated by an adolescent male who greatly desires to establish close relationships with females but has been unsuccessful at doing so. In asceticism, he may renounce these desires and other pleasure seeking and throw himself into a demanding, disciplined schedule of studying, sports training, or religious training and even deny himself favorite foods or adequate sleep. In extreme cases, "Ascetic teenagers will join a cult, give away all their possessions to the leader, shave their heads, learn to chant, often experiment with strange drugs, and beg at airports" (Sprinthall & Collins, 1984). Or, using intellectualization, he may develop the argument that emotional relationships would hinder his search for truth or self realization, or he may discuss at length the philosophical basis of sexual promiscuity or rape.

One important process during adolescence involves identification. An identification with the same-sex parent, established when the Oedipal conflict was resolved around age 5, changes its form as the Oedipal conflict reemerges in adolescence. Some conflict with parents is necessary as adolescents withdraw emotionally from their parents. This emotional void is filled by identification with people outside the family, particularly people of the other sex. These attachments may at first be directed toward a mature "father figure" in the case of girls or a "mother figure" in boys, as in "I want a girl just like the girl that married dear old dad" (Muus, 1982, p. 47).

BLOS

Many later theorists expanded and elaborated Freud's theory, but the theorist most interested in adolescence was Peter Blos. In contrast to Freud's emphasis on the first five years of life, Blos stresses the "second individuation process" at adolescence as critical for forming a permanent personality structure. The stronger sexual drives and new social expectations, along with the accompanying anxiety, inevitably lead to rebellion, conflict, and experimentation—a temporary regression in the service of ego development. If adolescents successfully resolve this crisis, they achieve a newly reorganized personality with a stronger, more independent ego. An essential part of this individuation process is pulling away from the psychological dependence on parents and establishing closer ties with peers. Blos (1979) observes that "the formation of a conflict between generations and its subsequent resolution is the normative task of adolescence" (p. 11). The peer group helps the child disengage from the family by giving a sense of security. This process has its psychological dangers, namely, that the youth may become too dependent on the peer group or may be rejected by the peer group.

EVALUATION

Adolescents' identification with peers, emotional disengagement from parents, and use of defense mechanisms are common forms of adolescent problem solving, the theme of this book. What is challenged by the literature, however, is whether these changes are best understood by the psychoanalytic framework. Criticism (e.g., Miller, 1989) has been directed at the weak methodology (e.g., adults' potentially biased recollections of childhood and adolescence) and the uncertain testability of hypotheses because of the distance between, and variable relationship between, psychological constructs and overt behaviors. With respect to content, research also challenges the psychoanalytic claim that adolescence necessarily involves a crisis with one's parents (e.g., Douvan & Adelson, 1966).

EDUCATIONAL IMPLICATIONS

Although biology thrusts the adolescent into the genital stage, the degree of conflict and the degree of success at reestablishing a satisfactory, newly equilibrated personality depend partly on social influences, including the school setting. Anxiety, rebellion, rapidly changing emotions, and contradictory behavior should be tolerated because they are necessary for developing a stronger, mature personality that can cope with adult life. Educators can help by not making rules or expectations more frustrating than necessary and by discouraging heavy reliance on defense mechanisms. Educators also can look beyond a problem behavior to the underlying psychological conflict and encourage teenagers to talk about and try to understand their feelings.

Psychosocial Theories: Ego Development and the Search for Identity

ERIKSON

Erik Erikson's life span theory probably has had more influence on research and theorizing on adolescence than any other theory. Although he accepted many of the psychoanalytic assumptions concerning drives, psychological structures, the conscious and unconscious, and stages of development, he modified the theory in several important ways. First, he added a psychosocial dimension to the psychosexual stages of psychoanalytic theory. The biologically based sexual drives mesh with the beliefs, expectations, and institutions of society. This emphasis reflects Erikson's awareness of the vast influence of one's culture on one's development. He had moved away from the psychoanalytic narrow perspective of the therapy session with middle class or upper middle-class European and urban American clients to a broader perspective based on diverse groups. He studied childrearing among the Yurok along the Pacific Coast and the Sioux in South Dakota, the play both of disturbed and of normal children, social behavior in India, and combat crises in "shell-shocked" American soldiers in World War II. Worried about the effects of rapid social changes in America, he has written about racial tensions, changing gender roles, the generation gap, the threat of nuclear war, and the identity problems of immigrants. He recognized that the usual growing pains of adolescence can intensify when society is going through difficult times.

A second modification of psychoanalytic theory is Erikson's emphasis on ego development, particularly his view that the central crux of development is a life-long search for identity. Identity, for Erikson, means "a conscious sense of individual identity . . . an unconscious striving for a continuity of personal character . . . a maintenance of an inner solidarity with a group's ideals and identity" (Erikson, 1959, p. 102). Identity includes a sense of continuity between what one has been and what one will become. A person asks "Who am I?" in each stage and forms an answer based on personal experience in that stage and all previous stages.

The search for identity is most critical during adolescence as a youth tries to integrate previous identities into a new coherent whole and prepare for future developmental tasks requiring a solid sense of self. Erikson coined the term "identity crisis" to describe the disorientation and loss of identity he observed both in World War II soldiers and in certain troubled adolescents who were out of touch with their culture. As an immigrant to the United States when facism loomed in Europe, Erikson knew first hand the threat of unfamiliar social landscapes to one's identity.

Erikson's concerns with cultural influences and the development of identity can be seen in his "eight ages of man": trust versus mistrust, autonomy versus shame and doubt, initiative versus guilt, industry versus inferiority, identity versus identity diffusion (adolescence), intimacy versus isolation, generativity versus self-absorption, and integrity versus despair. In each stage there is a critical issue to be resolved, but each issue appears in some degree in all stages. Ideally, by the end of each stage, the person will have achieved a favorable balance of the two extremes of the critical dimension, with the positive aspect dominating the negative. For example, an adolescent will achieve a basic sense of identity but maintain a bit of healthy identity diffusion in order to be open to later identity development. If a stage-defined crisis is not handled successfully, it will haunt the person during later stages and make development more difficult.

The spirit of the adolescent stage is captured in a saying that hangs in a cowboys' bar in the West: "I ain't what I ought to be, I ain't what I'm going to be, but I ain't what I was" (Erikson, 1959, p. 93). Part of the thrust of a concern with identity is the rapid physical change brought by puberty. This new body with its sexual urges is not the old self the youth knew. The pressure for a changed identity is intensified by society's expectations that adolescents will begin to make decisions about schooling and careers. The adolescent attempts to define the self by trying out many different roles—serious student, athlete, artist, and musician—and different personality types—clown, introverted philosopher, leader, and angry young man. No detail of one's identity is unimportant: Erikson describes an adolescent girl who had three distinctly different handwriting styles. If young people can integrate the various facets of their personalities and talents into a meaningful whole, they have successfully achieved a sense of identity. Healthy heterosexual relationships can be formed only after a person has a solid enough identity that it is not lost in such a relationship.

To illustrate identity diffusion, Erikson (1959, p. 91) quotes the aimless and lost Biff, the son in *Death of a Salesman*: "I just can't take hold, Mom. I can't take hold of some kind of life." Diffusion is more likely if there are threats to identity such as homosexual feelings, minority-group status, pressures from parents to enter a particular occupation, and inadequate interaction with peers. Peers are particularly important because feedback from peers while one is trying out various roles helps to define the self and pinpoint personal strengths and weaknesses. An extremely diffused identity can lead to drug use, delinquency, and even suicide because the despairing adolescent "would rather be nobody or somebody bad, or indeed, dead . . . than be not-quite-somebody" (Erikson, 1959, p. 132).

It may be helpful to relate Erikson's theory back to the questions raised at the beginning of the chapter. First, it is clear that adolescence is a unique time because the issue of identity takes on particular importance. Second, adolescence always involves some turmoil because of the new biological and social pressures, but the degree of turmoil depends on a host of cultural, sociohistorical, and interpersonal factors. Ideally, there is a "fit" between the needs of the person in each stage and the society with its patterns of child care, schools, social organizations, values, and so on. In reality, however, the institutions that meet the needs of one generation may be inadequate for the next and thus create additional storm and stress for the adolescent. The degree of turmoil involved in establishing an identity also depends on how successfully the youth has resolved the earlier stages. A confident, secure adolescent has roots in the sense of trust developed in the first stage; a self-conscious or dependent teenager may result from a failure of autonomy in the second stage and feelings of inferiority in the third.

MARCIA

One of the many researchers influenced by Erikson's work on identity versus identity diffusion is James Marcia. He expanded two of Erikson's notions—crisis and commitment: "Crisis refers to times during adolescence when the individual seems to be actively involved in choosing among alternative occupations and beliefs. Commitment refers to the degree of personal investment the individual expresses in an occupation or belief" (Marcia, 1967, p. 119). The presence or absence of crisis or commitment forms the following four potential "identity statuses":

1. *Identity-diffused* youths have experienced neither an identity crisis nor a commitment. There is no active search for an identity. Being easily influenced by others, they rapidly change from one belief to another and change their behavior to fit with the group they happen to be with. One consequence is that their self-esteem easily rises or falls, depending on how others react to them.

2. *Foreclosure* youths have made commitments without experiencing an identity crisis. They have accepted beliefs, attitudes, and an occupation from others, especially their parents, without question. They over-identify with and conform to their peer group or parents. At its extreme, this status can be seen in the Hitler Youth of Nazi Germany (Muus, 1982). The lack of psychological conflict comes at a high price, for the person is somewhat defensive and rigid and essentially is an extension of other people, remaining somewhat dependent on them. Unlike identity diffusion, there is consistency in the person's beliefs and goals.

3. *Moratorium* youths are in a severe state of identity crisis with a great deal of anxiety but cannot yet make a commitment. They make several tentative commitments as they try out roles and experiments. Erikson himself spent a great deal of time in a moratorium state as he explored art, psychology, education, and other interests.

4. *Identity-achieved* youths have experienced an identity crisis and resolved it by making personal commitments. As Erikson concluded, this identity is a synthesis of one's past, present, and future and involves self-acceptance, ego strength, and the ability to achieve heterosexual intimacy.

Although these four identity statuses may form a developmental sequence, the only necessary sequence is that moratorium must be experienced before identity achievement. Identity diffusion, foreclosure, and moratorium are normal phases of adolescence and become problematic only if they extend into adulthood. Some people never develop through all four steps. It should be noted that a person may be in one status with respect to one area of life and in another status in another area. A person may have established an identity concerning personal values and relationships with other people but still be searching for the right college major.

Marcia's theory is based primarily on open-ended interviews with college students. Ages 18 to 21 do in fact appear to form a crucial period for progressing toward the identity-achieved status. There is a sharp increase in the proportion of students in the identity-achieved status from the freshman to the senior year of college (Waterman, Geary, & Waterman, 1974). However, even by the senior year, about one third are still in a state of identity diffusion.

There is extensive research on the personality correlates of each of the four statuses and on how the family influences the statuses (see Marcia, 1980, for a review). One consistent finding is that males and females show different personality correlates for the four statuses. For example, the greatest "fear of success" was found among identity-achieved and moratorium females but among foreclosure and identity-diffused males (Howard, 1975; Orlofsky, 1978).

EVALUATION

There is considerable research support for the centrality of identity development during adolescence (Siegel, 1982). However, the empirical support for Erikson's and Marcia's specific claims concerning the developmental course of the achievement of identity is somewhat shaky. For example, resolving the identity crisis increases the likelihood of resolving the crisis of intimacy in the following stage, but some people appear to resolve the two crises at the same time (Orlofsky, Marcia, & Lesser, 1973). Marcia (1980) himself has noted some of the limitations of his work. Most of the research has been limited to college students and they may not generalize to adolescents who start working after high school or are unemployed. In addition, identity development appears to differ between white males and minority or female adolescents (McGuire, McGuire, Child, & Fujioka, 1978). Researchers also have criticized Erikson's personal interviews and Marcia's self-descriptive questionnaires, noting that evidence from adolescents' self-perceptions (those they are willing to reveal) should be supplemented by information from parents, teachers, peers, and behavioral observations (e.g., Mischel, 1981).

EDUCATIONAL IMPLICATIONS

The ego-identity theories suggest that schools can facilitate the adolescent's task of defining the self. Schools, by providing a variety of academic and extracurricular settings, permit adolescents to try out various roles and test their abilities. Inspiring teachers can challenge adolescents' beliefs and values with new ideas or problems. It is critical that honest, but constructive, feedback from educators and peers accompany these experiences. The educator's role as a sounding board is not easy:

> In their search for a new sense of continuity and sameness, adolescents have to refight many of the battles of earlier years, even though to do so they must artificially appoint perfectly well-meaning people to play the roles of adversaries; and they are ever ready to install lasting idols and ideals as guardians of a final identity. (Erikson, 1950, p. 261)

Schools have been criticized for encouraging foreclosure by rewarding conformity, submission to authority, and unquestioned acceptance of certain values. This may help maintain order and facilitate passive academic learning in large, structured classrooms, but at the expense of stifling creativity and identity development.

One continuing controversy is to what extent, if at all, the curriculum should foster emotional–social development via classes in family living, interpersonal relations, drug abuse, career planning, and so on. Psychosocial identity and academic goals need not be incompatible. For example, in English courses students could read and discuss the problems of adolescents as illustrated in literature (Muus, 1982).

Social–Cultural Theories

ANTHROPOLOGY (MEAD, BENEDICT)

Carrying the psychosocial perspective one step further leads us to a set of theories that stress the social influences on adolescent development. This view has its roots in early anthropological work, especially that of Margaret Mead. Mead observed adolescents in Samoa in the 1920s and saw little of the storm and stress believed by social scientists of the times to be an inevitable part of adolescence. Instead, society encouraged continuity between childhood and adulthood. Children were exposed to the great events of life such as birth, death, and sex that usually are hidden from children in the modern Western world. Even young children had responsibilities in the economy of the island. Thus, children were not acquiring roles that they would have to unlearn later. Subsequent work by a number of anthropologists revealed a great range in the nature of adolescence in various societies, a finding that plays down the role of biological influences.

One clear example of cultural differences in the role of the adolescent is the varying reactions of societies to the onset of menstruation (Benedict, 1950; Mead, 1952). Northern California Indian tribes believed that a menstruating girl threatened the survival of the tribe because she could dry up the water supply and scare off the game. In contrast, the Yuki Indians of California believed that a girl could improve the food supply by lying quietly while menstruating.

SOCIAL LEARNING

Within the field of developmental psychology the most influential theory of social influences is social learning theory. The theory stresses learned behaviors, particularly behaviors learned by watching others or by having one's behavior reinforced by others, although biological factors are also considered important. Via social learning, children and adolescents acquire sex-typed behavior, learn to obey rules concerning morality, and learn skills for interacting with others. Thus, social learning theory emphasizes the *processes* of learning rather than the changes in personality structure that are of interest to the psychoanalytic and psychosocial theorists.

The environment, by providing models, stimuli, and reinforcements, exerts control over an adolescent's behavior. It should be noted, however, that to some extent adolescents create the very environment that influences them. An attractive, pleasant, early maturing teenage male may encounter an adult environment that both responds positively to him and has high expectations of him because of his mature appearance. He may not be allowed to show the juvenile behavior of a younger looking boy of the same age. The kinds of settings an adolescent chooses to enter also influence what models and reinforcements are experienced. The teenager who attends school dances and joins many school clubs has a different set of learning experiences than the teenager who avoids the social anxiety of these situations and retreats to the security of home.

One implication of these principles of learning is that an adolescent probably will behave in different ways in different settings because different behaviors have been reinforced or punished in these settings. An adolescent may be obedient and conforming at home around parents but rebellious and challenging of authority at school because the latter behavior is applauded by peers but punished by parents. This emphasis on situational determinants contrasts sharply with the "trait" theories, a category that includes most of the theories described thus far. Trait theories describe traits such as conformity, identity, and aimlessness, or, more generally, personality structures, that a person "has" and expresses in various settings. Thus, trait theories predict that a person behaves similarly in different settings.

Bandura's (1977) account of how observational learning occurs is much more cognitive than earlier versions of social learning. Whether observational learning occurs depends on whether the person attends carefully to the model, the behavior, uses feedback to improve his attempted modeling, and is motivated to learn. The growing ability to manipulate mental symbols greatly advances observational learning. Via "abstract modeling," the adolescent can abstract a general rule, for example, a moral rule, or the rules of a game, from observing specific behaviors.

One way that social learning theory differs from psychoanalytic and psychosocial theories is that it does not see adolescence as a developmental stage, qualitatively different from other times in development. The same general principles of learning operate throughout development. What changes is the types of models available, the expectations of others, the ability to symbolize the behavior to be learned, strategies for self-control and self-management, and so on.

The concept within social learning theory that is closest to identity formation is self-efficacy, especially as studied by Bandura. As adolescents receive feedback concerning their attempts to use a skill, they are building a self-concept concerning their abilities. Others' reactions to the adolescent's social, academic, athletic, and artistic endeavors help shape self-efficacy. Work by Dweck and Bush (1976) suggests that the effect of this feedback depends on the age of the evaluator and the sex of the child. Among fifth-grade girls, failure feedback from peers led to much greater improvement in performance than feedback from adults. For boys, the opposite was true.

EVALUATION

Research has revealed both similarities and differences in adolescent behavior across various cultures. For example, Barry, Bacon, and Child (1957) found that nearly all cultures studied tend to socialize girls to be nurturant and obedient and boys to be self-reliant and achieving. Still, some cultures do not differentially socialize the two sexes with respect to these traits. Whether universal changes in behavior during adolescence reflect universal biological changes, universal socialization, or both is an unanswered question. Furthermore, because cultural influences can only be observed, and not directly manipulated, it is difficult to test the claims of anthropological theories.

Social learning theories, in contrast, are probably the most testable theories of adolescence. They generally make specific predictions about observable behaviors and lend themselves to controlled laboratory experimentation. Hundreds of studies have documented the influence of models, reinforcement, and punishment on child and adolescent behaviors as diverse as sex-appropriate actions, conformity to moral rules, and judgments concerning quantity (Miller, 1989). Two examples of this research will be presented. First, Patterson (1981) has identified a chain of interaction between parents and their aggressive adolescent sons that rapidly escalates toward aggression as each family member manipulates the other by aversive behavior. For example, a girl teases her adolescent brother, then he hits her, which causes his parents to punish him, which in turn increases the adolescent's aggression. Patterson finds that helpful interventions may involve writing a contract between the parents and child that spells out what behaviors will be reinforced or punished by access to or withdrawal of rewards.

A second example of confirming research is work on prosocial actions such as sharing and helping. Grusec (1982) finds that altruism can be increased in a number of ways—by providing altruistic models, reinforcing altruistic behavior, attributing sharing to internal desires and values, and telling children they ought to share and directly instructing them to donate.

Social learning theory does, however, have its limitations. Although the theory recently has been modified to include cognitive aspects of observational learning, there still is not a specific account of exactly how adolescents' level of cognitive development facilitates or limits their observational learning. The dramatic changes in thinking from preadolescence to late adolescence surely interact with social learning in important ways.

EDUCATIONAL IMPLICATIONS

All of the social–cultural theories assign great responsibility for adolescents' development to peers and adults, including teachers, for they provide feedback, serve as models, and shape behavior. What the models do is as important as what they say. If these models and schedules of reinforcement are similar to those in the youth's developmental history, then adolescence should be smooth and continuous with childhood. If new models or expectations emerge, such as when joining a tough, rebellious peer group at the beginning of high school, then coping with life is more difficult for the adolescent.

The type of models is also a concern to educators in other ways. In early adolescence, boys begin to pull ahead of girls in math performance. Although it is not clear what causes this phenomenon, it is suspected that social learning plays a role. Causes may include male math teachers as models, the tendency for fathers rather than mothers to help with math homework, the attribution of girls', but not boys', success at math to great effort and their failure to poor ability, and girls' and their parents' expectation that girls do not do well in math (Meece, Parsons, Kaczala, Goff, & Futterman, 1982).

Another concern of school personnel is that the desirable behaviors modeled by parents and teachers may be offset by undesirable behavior, such as substance abuse and violence, modeled by popular entertainers via the mass media or by actors in television programs or movies. Because research shows that high-status models are especially likely to be imitated, this is an area of particular concern.

Field Theory

LEWIN

Kurt Lewin depicted development as changes in one's "life space," defined as all the factors that influence a person's behavior at a given time. These factors are the physical environment, the social environment, and one's physical and psychological makeup, including needs, motives, and goals. The person psychologically organizes the world into positive-attracting and negative-repelling features of and barriers to certain goals. Lewin expressed the life space with maplike geometrical representations— a line drawing of an oval divided into sections with dividing lines representing barriers and pluses and minuses representing valences of goals.

During development this life space becomes more differentiated into regions. The person (age, talents, etc.) and the environment (relationships with family and friends, school structure, etc.) keep changing simultaneously. Because the two are so interdependent, a change in one causes a change in the other. If this change is gradual there is little stress because people can adjust by changing their psychological organization slightly. If, as during adolescence, there is more rapid change due to sudden physical changes and new social pressure, there is storm and stress. In addition, there is conflict if there are two positive goals in the environment, such as making money now and finishing high school, or if a goal has both a positive and negative valence such as wanting to date someone but fearing one's social ineptitude.

Lewin sees adolescents as marginal members of society, living in a poorly defined area between two worlds, a "social no man's land" (Lewin, 1939, p. 881). They must give up the behaviors and goals of childhood but do not yet have the status and skills of an adult. In other words, adolescents enter a cognitively unstructured region, not unlike moving into a strange town. Their ambiguous role as they change their group membership carries a great deal of stress. Since the perceptual structure is unstable, behavior is unstable. The adolescent is "oversensitive, easily shifted from one extreme to the other, and particularly sensitive to the shortcomings of younger fellows" (Lewin, 1939, pp. 882–883). At the same time, adults vacillate in whether they treat the adolescent as a child or an adult.

Adolescents' life space differs from that of children in the following ways: (1) an increased scope (e.g., more areas of their environment are open to them, the time span stretches into a more distant past and future); (2) a greater differentiation into various social relations and areas of activities; (3) an increased organization which allows them to coordinate behaviors to achieve a goal; (4) an increase in the strength of the boundaries between the various regions; and (5) an increase in realism. For example, as adolescents move into new areas of their psychological field, such as their first dance, they define and structure those areas, and identify new goals and how to achieve them.

EVALUATION

Children's perceptions of themselves in relation to their social world clearly change during adolescence. What is less clear, however, is exactly how these perceptions relate both to life events and to behavior. The relationship appears to be complex. For example, a longitudinal study of the transition from sixth to seventh grade revealed that self-image problems were most prevalent in girls who, during the same year, went through puberty, began dating, and changed schools (Simmons, Blyth, Van Cleave, & Bush, 1979). Girls low in self-esteem to start with were especially vulnerable. There also is evidence that changes in behavior can lead to, rather than simply result from, changes in self-concept (Mischel, 1981). There are obvious methodological difficulties inherent in measuring a construct as complex and vague as "life space" and specifying its temporal relationship to biological and social changes, on the one hand, and behavior, on the other.

EDUCATIONAL IMPLICATIONS

Lewin's theory influenced many areas of psychology, especially what came to be known as "ecological psychology," particularly as seen in the work of Roger Barker and Herbert Wright and their colleagues. In *Big School, Small School*, Barker and Gump (1964) examined the influence of an environmental variable, high school size, on students' behavior. In terms of the ratio of the number of students to the number of "behavior settings," for example, clubs, school athletic teams, and student council meetings, behavior settings in small schools are more likely to be understaffed than those in large schools. Thus, students in small schools face a different environment than in large schools. Students in small schools encounter greater encouragement to participate in activities (because a certain number of people are needed to keep these settings going) and participate in a wider variety of activities. In other words, the student in a small school is needed by the environment. One outcome is that these students have the opportunity to try out many different roles and assume positions of responsibility that might be closed to them in a larger school. On the negative side, there is less opportunity to specialize and develop one talent, such as music, to a high level, and a smaller variety of courses and activities are available. Barker and Gump report different kinds of satisfactions in the two sizes of schools. Small-school students mentioned satisfaction related to direct participation, such as improved competence, meeting challenges, cooperating with peers, and a sense of importance: "It gave me more confidence" and "This gave me a chance to see whether or not I am a good salesman." Students in large high schools mentioned more derived satisfactions, such as belonging to something larger than themselves and observing others: "I like the companionship of mingling with the rest of the crowd."

Cognitive Theories

PIAGET

The theories presented thus far portray the adolescent as a feeling social being, under biological and social pressure, searching for emotional stability and a meaningful sense of self. In stark contrast, Jean Piaget saw a logical scientist–philosopher, striving for an understanding of the physical world of time, space, quantity, and physical causality. Even when Piaget studied concepts concerning the social world, he was more interested in the logic of perceiving social relationships than the youth's emotional reaction to these relationships. Piaget did not deny the importance of emotion but simply had little interest in studying it.

Cognitive change during adolescence can be summarized in terms of Piaget's general formula of development: development = physical maturation + experience with the physical environment + social experience + equilibration (elimination of a mild cognitive storm and stress due to cognitive contradiction). Neurological changes in early adolescence, combined with the new experiences possible in adolescence and the driving force of equilibration, create a new form of thinking. Thus, innate and environmental factors are in constant interaction.

Early adolescence, roughly 11 to 15 years, is the period of formal operational thought. This stage was prepared for by the earlier stages in which the world was understood in terms of physical actions (sensorimotor), symbolic thought (preoperational), and concrete thought (concrete operational thought). As earlier, the adolescent constructs knowledge rather than simply records information like a passive camera taking pictures of reality. Children enter the period of formal operations with an organized set of mental operations that can be applied to concrete events and objects. For example, the mental operations of addition, subtraction, multiplication, and division form an organized network. Another operation, mentally reversing an event, has facilitated the knowledge that the amount of a liquid is conserved when it is poured into a taller, thinner container even though it looks like there is an increase.

These operations are carried one step further after cognitive reorganization gradually occurs during the formal operational period. There now can be operations on operations as children reflect on their own thinking or mentally manipulate concepts that refer to the abstract as well as to the concrete, the possible and hypothetical as well as the real. In Piaget's (1947) words, the adolescent "is an individual who thinks beyond the present and forms theories about everything, delighting especially in consideration of that which is not" (p. 148). In a sense, "reality is now secondary to possibility" (Inhelder & Piaget, 1958, p. 251). Adolescents love to think about philosophical, ethical, and political issues.

Adolescents think like a scientist. They identify the possibly relevant variables in a problem, mentally generate all possible outcomes of combinations of the variables, formulate a hypothesis concerning the most likely outcome, and test the hypothesis by systematically manipulating these variables. Piaget's focus is on the problem-solving process rather than whether the answer is correct. A concrete operational child might obtain a correct answer but would have arrived at this answer in basically a trial-and-error fashion. For example, when given colorless liquid X and told that combining it with a certain combination of four unknown colorless liquids produces a yellow color, the concrete operational child proceeds haphazardly, trying combinations more-or-less randomly. In contrast, the formal operational adolescent systematically tries out all possible combinations of the liquids until a yellow liquid is produced.

The adolescent acquires a logical system of propositional logic, based on all combinations of logical possibilities, that underlies the thinking about many different content areas. This logical system and the tasks used to study it are described in Piaget's main book on adolescence, *The Growth of Logical Thinking from Childhood to Adolescence* (Inhelder & Piaget, 1958). Some of the problems used by Piaget include determining what variable governs how fast a pendulum swings, how proportionality is calculated, what law governs the relationship between the angle at which a billiard ball hits the side of the table and the angle at which it rebounds, and what variables determine how far down a suspended rod bends. By the end of the formal operational period, these problems are approached by thinking that is abstract, flexible, and complex. The formal operational period truly involves "the conquest of thought" (Elkind, 1967, p. 1029).

Piaget held the now controversial position that the cognitive structure is applied to both the physical and social world. Just as adolescents can experiment with the physical and social world, they can experiment with various possible roles for themselves. Their newly formed ability to derive all possible combinations of a set of numbers or chemicals also allows them to imagine various possibilities for their future. The frequent bull sessions of teenagers cover abstract moral and social issues such as abortions, affirmative action, and the death penalty. The ability to consider these issues from different perspectives and derive the implications of each issue for other social issues is an advance over the previous stage. In addition, the new ability to think about thought processes now permits the adolescent to have thoughts such as "I'm thinking that I'm thinking about him thinking about me."

Adolescents' thinking about the social world, however, still is naive in some ways. They overestimate the possibility of solving social problems and personal problems through logical thinking. This, combined with their awareness of the difference between possibility and actuality, can make them highly critical and intolerant of the deficiencies of their parents and the current social order. They later will become aware of the practical problems of achieving an ideal society.

Although the stage of formal operations brings the last structural change in thinking by approximately age 15, there is further development in that one's formal operations are applied to more and more content areas as one gains a greater variety of experiences. It appears, however, that even adults draw on their formal operational abilities only part of the time. Although this issue is far from settled, some studies show that only about one-third of adolescents and adults pass most formal operational tasks (Capon & Kuhn, 1979; Keating, 1980). It is argued (Piaget, 1972) that people use their formal operational thought in areas in which they have the most experience, such as their occupation and hobbies.

ELKIND

Piaget's views of adolescence have been elaborated on by several researchers, particularly David Elkind. In Elkind's view, the cognitive structures of early adolescence lead to certain misperceptions of the self and others that in turn lead to certain emotional experiences and behaviors.

Piaget's research has shown that young children tend to be egocentric, that is, they do not know that other people's viewpoints can be different from their own. Although adolescents usually are not egocentric in this way, Elkind discovered another type of lingering egocentrism that arises because adolescents now have the ability to conceptualize the thinking of other people. Because of their own preoccupation with their appearance and behavior, children entering adolescence often assume that others also are constantly observing them and evaluating them. If an adolescent male notices a small grease spot on his shirt just as he arrives at a party, he will spend the evening imagining that everyone has noticed the spot and is talking about it and considering him socially inept. An imaginary audience notices whether one's jeans have the right designer label or whether one's hair curls in the right direction. Teenagers constantly are on stage, playing to this audience and anticipating its reactions to their appearance and behavior. Thus, there is a cognitive basis to the self-consciousness of adolescence.

Because adolescents greatly value the opinions of their peers, these perceived constant evaluations by the imaginary audience are of great concern. In fact, however, when teenagers are together the probable outcome is that they actually observe each other very little:

> The boy who stands in front of the mirror for 2 hours combing his hair is probably imagining the swooning reactions he will produce in the girls. Likewise, the girl applying her makeup is more likely than not imagining the admiring glances that will come her way. When these young people actually meet, each is more concerned with being the observed than with being the observer. (Elkind, 1967, p. 1030)

Elkind assesses imaginary audience behavior, especially the willingness to reveal various facets of oneself to an audience, with the Imaginary Audience Scale (Elkind & Bowen, 1979). For example, one item is the following:

> You have been looking forward to your friend's party for weeks, but just before you leave for the party your mother tells you that she accidentally washed all your good clothes with a red shirt. Now all your jeans are pink in spots. The only thing left to wear are your jeans that are too big and too baggy. Would you go to the party or would you stay home?

The subject can answer: (1) Go to the party but buy a new pair of jeans to wear, (2) Stay home, or (3) Go to the party in either the pink or baggy jeans. It appears that 13-year-olds are less willing to reveal themselves (expose themselves to possible ridicule) than are younger or older subjects.

Adolescent egocentrism also leads to the "personal fable." This is the belief that the self is unique, special, indestructible, and immortal. Adolescents believe that because of their uniqueness as an individual, nobody can ever understand how they feel. Elkind cites Salinger's Holden Caulfield in *Catcher in the Rye* as a prime example of these personal torments. Adolescents may even construct melodramatic stories about themselves that they partially believe. For example, one might fantasize that one was adopted and actually has famous biological parents. Teenagers also may believe that they will not become pregnant even if birth control devices are not used or believe that they can drink and drive without having an accident. These things only happen to other people. As formal operations solidify and adolescents continually test their imaginary audiences against reality, they gradually replace the imaginary audience with a realistic audience that is not preoccupied with the adolescent. The personal fable diminishes after the adolescent establishes close interpersonal relationships with peers and discovers that they also "suffer with such agonized intensity, or experience such exquisite rapture" (Elkind, 1967, p. 1031). As Elkind predicts, self-consciousness, egocentrism, the imaginary audience, and the personal fable peak during early adolescence and decline thereafter (Elkind & Bowen, 1979; Enright, Lapsley, & Shukla, 1979). It is probable, however, that the imaginary audience and the personal fable never completely disappear even during adulthood.

SELMAN

The differentiation of the cognitive self from the cognitive other also is a main theme of Robert Selman's (1980) work on interpersonal understanding. Like Piaget and Elkind, Selman views the development of social cognition as movement through an invariant sequence of stages or levels of perspective taking. Up to the preadolescent years, children have differentiated the self from the other while confusing the psychological and physical aspects of the social world, for example, between what one says and what one feels (Level 0); differentiated the social perspectives (interpretations of social events, thoughts, feelings) of the self and the other (Level 1); and coordinated the two viewpoints by reflecting on one's own thoughts and feelings from another person's perspective (Level 2). At this point the child knows that people are aware of each other's perspectives and are evaluating these perspectives. In Level 3, during preadolescence, roughly 10 to 12 years, children realize that reciprocal perspectives can form an infinite chain. They can step outside of the interaction and thereby objectively view it and simultaneously coordinate the perspectives of each person. Finally, in Level 4, the adolescent realizes that there are various levels of mutuality between people, for example, a superficial level, the level of common interests, and the level of deep, unspoken feelings. They know that the perspectives among people form a social system that can be generalized into a legal or societal moral point of view. The development of formal operations is necessary (but not sufficient) for this most advanced level of interpersonal understanding, and some adults never reach it. These stages, as applied to four domains, appear in Table 2.1.

Selman assesses a person's stage by posing an interpersonal dilemma in the context of a story. For example, in Selman's most commonly used

Table 2.1 Selman's Developmental Stages of Social Cognition

Social Perspective	Domains of Interpersonal Understanding			
	Individuals	Close friendship	Peer group organization	Parent–child relationship
0: Egocentric or undifferentiated	Physical entity	Momentary physical playmate	Physicalistic connections	Egocentric–pragmatic
1: Subjective or differentiated	Intentional subject	One-way assistance	Unilateral relations	Authoritarian
2: Self-reflective or reciprocal	Introspective self	Fairweather cooperation	Bilateral partnerships	Emotional understanding
3: Third-person or mutual	Stable personality	Intimate-mutual sharing	Homogeneous community	Individual personalities
4: Societal or in-depth	Complex self-systems	Autonomous interdependence	Pluralistic organization	

Note. Adapted from R. Selman (1979). *Assessing interpersonal understanding: An interview and scoring manual in five parts constructed by the Harvard–Judge Baker Social Reasoning Project*, p. 7. Reprinted by permission.

story a boy is trying to decide whether to give, as a birthday present to his friend, a puppy to replace the one that ran away. The dilemma is intensified when the upset friend says that he never wants to look at another dog. Subjects are asked a series of questions intended to assess how aware they are of the character's conflicting feelings, the discrepancy between how one feels and what one says, and awareness of one's own feelings.

The person's reasons for why the boy should or should not buy the puppy reveal the underlying structure of thought. An adolescent still in Level 2 might believe that the child has conflicting feelings about getting a new puppy, but these feelings would occur one after the other. In contrast, in Level 3, the child knows that these conflicting feelings can occur at the same time and, in Level 4, knows that a new feeling of ambivalence can arise out of this conflict.

Each of the domains is concerned with several issues. For example, for the concept of the individual, the issues are subjectivity (awareness of thoughts, feelings, and emotions), self-awareness (awareness that the self can reflect on its own thoughts and actions), personality (perception of stable traits), and personality change (knowledge of how and why people change).

Like Piaget, Selman believes that social cognitive development is stimulated by appropriate interactions with others, especially peers. Selman found that a group of emotionally disturbed boys aged 7 to 12 was similar to a normal group on tests of logic and physical concepts but was lower in interpersonal understanding. Thus, interpersonal reasoning and personality are related, though the causal direction is not clear. Pathological social interaction could hinder social cognitive development, or immature social cognition could lead to abnormal social interaction. In one case study, 14-year-old Charlie had a number of suspensions from school because of his disruptive behavior. His mother felt that the neighborhood children made a scapegoat of him. In fact, he was provoking the attacks by antagonizing his peers with his inappropriate methods of trying to interact with them. By helping him reflect on his behavior and view it from a variety of perspectives, a therapist was able to stimulate progress in his social behavior. This restructuring of social perspectives during therapy shares Freud's emphasis on the patient's increased understanding of his thinking and feelings, but it stresses cognitive change more than emotional realignment. It is interesting that the notion of the unconscious, so critical for psychoanalysis, arises during Selman's last stage: "He might not be aware of his deeper feelings. . . . He may not want to admit to himself that another dog could take Pepper's place. . . . He may feel guilty about it. He doesn't want to face these feelings, so he says, no new dog" (Selman, 1980, p. 106).

Selman's theoretical model is just one of the many recent minitheories that fall under the heading of "social cognition." Although they differ in various ways, what they have in common is the assumption that people develop an underlying cognitive structure or set of cognitive skills that allow them (1) to infer what other people are thinking, feeling, intending, and seeing, and what they are like as a person (Shantz, 1975) and (2) to understand social relationships or social institutions such as group organization or the economic system. In different ways, these theories propose a developmental change from reasoning about others in terms of observable behavior and physical appearance to reasoning in terms of inferred, unobservable thoughts, feelings, intentions, and personality. Although most of these theories aim for a description of stagelike developmental changes, some focus on the processes, such as memory, attention, and comprehension, underlying the gradual development of this knowledge. A main controversy is whether these structures or skills are the same or different for various domains such as friendship, parent–child relations, and politics.

With respect to the "self," the work of Piaget, Elkind, and Selman contrasts with that of the psychoanalysts, ego psychologists, and social psychologists in a central way. The former group, the cognitive psychologists, focuses on the growing degree of complexity of the cognitive structure underlying the understanding of the self in a context of human relationships. The latter group focuses on "ego strength," on the positive or negative view of the self, and on the emotional reaction to this self-evaluation. The two general approaches, then, are complementary more than contradictory. Neither one alone gives a full view of the emerging self in adolescence.

KOHLBERG

Because adolescents achieve new levels of thinking such as formal operations, advanced perspective-taking skills, and a multifaceted concept of the self, they now are compelled to question the values instilled during their socialization. They reason about the morality of issues ranging from the right to wear one's hair like a favorite rock star to the right to have an abortion. The most influential theory of the development of moral reasoning during adolescence is that of Kohlberg (1969). In his view, a child of any age is a moral philosopher with definite beliefs as to why an act is right or wrong. Much like Piaget, Kohlberg saw stagelike changes but, unlike Piaget, thought that these stages can continue to develop well beyond the time of achievement of formal operations in adolescence. The stages are based on the type of reasoning underlying the course of action rather than the action itself. As Carroll and Rest (1982) point out, the same stage of reasoning could underlie the behavior of a

Catholic nun, Nazi storm trooper, Russian Bolshevik, Indian peasant, and Mississippi Boy Scout.

Kohlberg proposes three levels with two stages per level. By adolescence, most people in the Western world have completed Stage 1, when judgments are based on punishment and obedience, and Stage 2, when judgments are based on satisfying one's own needs and desires. Next, at the conventional level, usually during adolescence, the person takes a societal perspective. The "good boy–good girl" orientation of Stage 3 dictates that one should do what meets the approval of significant others. Having good motives, obeying rules, and conforming are all important, and mutual expectations and caring are more important than individual desires. During Stage 4, law and order prevail. One should obey laws and do one's duty in order to maintain the social order for its own sake. Finally, at the postconventional level during late adolescence or adulthood, there is a social contract orientation. One generally should follow agreements made in social or legal contracts. Rules are arbitrary and sometimes wrong but generally serve to maintain the will of the majority and human rights. A sixth stage involves universal ethical principles, such as justice, inalienable human rights, and logical consistency, that are above the laws of society.

These stages are universally developed in an invariant order with each stage encompassing more factors and considering more of the complexities of human interaction than the earlier stages. However, some people never reach these more advanced stages. Because the rate of development is influenced by social factors such as the "moral atmosphere" of one's environment and cultural factors such as length and type of schooling, there can be striking individual differences between individuals of the same age in the same culture or in different cultures. Also, depending on one's experiences, one can be in different stages of moral reasoning for different domains such as the value of human life and property rights.

It is interesting to note that Kohlberg's stages are somewhat related to Erikson's stages of ego identity. Podd (1972) found that college students with identity-achievement status had significantly higher moral judgment scores than those with identity-diffusion and foreclosure statuses.

EVALUATION

Surely the pervasive changes in adolescent thought described by cognitive theorists are both caused by, and a cause of, the social and personality changes emphasized by noncognitive theories. However, cognitive theories have tended to ignore the role of critical features of adolescence such as changes in emotions, expectations of society, and relationships with the family. One critical question here is how the emerging formal operational structures actually are applied in a sociohistorical context by an adolescent in a particular emotional state. The observed unevenness in the application of one's highest level of reasoning may reflect differences in an adolescent's motivation in different domains or in his emotional instability.

Although Piaget's theory began a revolution in the way psychologists viewed the thinking of children and adolescents, it inevitably faced criticism as well. With respect to adolescence, research has questioned whether the inconsistent use of formal operations by adults merely shows the incomplete application of an underlying formal operational structure. Instead, perhaps the structural-stage notion is damaged. The general problem with testing Piaget's theory of formal operations is that the connection between overt performance and the underlying logical competence is not adequately described (see Keating, 1980, for a discussion of these challenges to Piaget's theory). For example, there appear to be several types of logical structures that would predict the same set of cognitive judgments (Osherson, 1975).

Elkind and Selman have advanced the general Piagetian framework in important ways. Their inclusion of peer relationships and role taking increases the usefulness of cognitive theory for understanding the period of adolescence. But the empirical base of both approaches is still too thin to permit an adequate evaluation.

Kohlberg's theory has been quite influential, generating an enormous literature not only on his own stages of moral development but also on children's and adolescents' conceptions of social conventions such as dress codes and manners (e.g., Turiel, 1978) and on prosocial reasoning (e.g., Eisenberg-Berg & Mussen, 1978). His claims regarding sequences and the nature of reasoning at each level generally are supported by longitudinal studies (Colby, Kohlberg, Gibbs, & Lieberman, 1983; Nisan & Kohlberg, 1982).

Criticisms and limitations, some of which have been raised by Kohlberg himself, include the following: First, because most adults never reach the highest level of moral reasoning, Kohlberg essentially has dropped this final stage. Second, the theory's applicability to women and to other cultures has been challenged. Gilligan (1982), for example, has proposed that females, because they are taught to be empathic and concerned about the needs of others, are more sensitive to the moral issue of one's obligations to others and the conflict between one's own needs and those of others. In contrast, males emphasize the right of the individual, justice, and moral dilemmas based on conflicts of interest. The evidence for sex differences on Kohlberg's measure is inconsistent, with some studies showing males more advanced, but most showing no sex difference (Walker, 1984). It should be noted that Kohlberg developed his theory on the basis of studies with males. A similar argument is based on the fact that in certain cultures, such as those of a Kibbutz or a socialistic country, one's commitment to the collective is an important issue to which Kohlberg's scoring system is not sensitive (Snarey, 1985). Third, although there is some relationship between moral reasoning and moral behavior, this relationship is far from perfect (Blasi, 1980). Other factors, such as available models and rewards, as suggested by social learning theory, appear to be involved. Finally, Kohlberg's moral dilemmas may not be relevant to the concerns of adolescents. In one study, adolescents' descriptions of moral dilemmas of personal interest to them were quite unlike those used by Kohlberg (Yussen, 1977).

EDUCATIONAL IMPLICATIONS

If cognitive theorists gave a word of advice to school personnel it would probably be "look at the situation from the child's point of view." One role of the teacher is to assess whether each child is cognitively ready to learn a new concept; there must be a cognitive structure that can assimilate the new concept or accommodate to it. The material must be at an appropriate level because the child's thinking can develop only in small steps, not great leaps. An adolescent must adequately master precalculus material before entering a calculus class. Young adolescents in transition from concrete to formal operations may be only beginning to grasp the scientific method and may still need physical props or the guidance of teachers to support their fragile mental manipulation of variables in the science laboratory or history class.

Once it is clear that adolescents are ready to learn and all the materials are appropriate, they can learn best by actively becoming involved in the material. For example, the ability and need to imagine and evaluate alternative life styles and future roles and to take the perspective of society can be nurtured in literature classes by arguing particular points of view or by role playing. As learning proceeds, a good teacher is always vigilant for misacquisitions—learning the correct answer but not understanding the underlying concept. Finally, educators should be mindful that an objectively minor mistake during class can seem catastrophic to adolescents who feel that everyone's eyes are upon them, judging their worth as a person.

As adolescents achieve new levels of abstract thinking, they are ready to develop a more advanced moral philosophy. Several studies have demonstrated that this development can be fostered by moral training via discussions about moral dilemmas (e.g., Hersch, Paolitto, & Reimer, 1979). Instructors encourage students to verbalize their reasons for a particular moral choice, ask clarifying questions, and challenge them to consider others' reasons. They thereby clarify and stimulate adolescents' moral reasoning. Role playing at the next stage of moral reasoning can also help stimulate the cognitive reorganization necessary for moving to the next stage. Similarly, in accordance with the ideas of Selman and Elkind, early adolescents who have been trained in perspective-taking skills are more able to solve interpersonal problems (Marsh, Serafica, & Barenboim, 1980).

Kohlberg notes that schools have a "hidden moral curriculum"— instilling values such as obeying the teacher and working quietly without disturbing others. He believes that many schools actually encourage lower levels of moral reasoning such as fear of punishment and blind obedience of rules.

Summary

The theories can be summarized by returning to the two questions of the introduction regarding the unique, stagelike nature of adolescence and the necessity of the storm and stress of adolescence. The biologically and psychoanalytically oriented theories view adolescence as a unique and universal period of change, usually somewhat stressful because of the rapid physical changes, especially hormonal changes. Psychosocial theories recognize the uniqueness of adolescence and the biologically based potential for conflict but stress the role of social experiences in determining the amount of conflict and the positive or negative outcome of this conflict. Social–cultural theories emphasize even more the environmental influences on the nature of adolescence. Although adolescence is different from other age periods in certain ways, the degree of difference and the extent of the turmoil depend greatly on social factors. Field theorists contend that the effect of this environment greatly dpeends on how the person perceives it in terms of goals, barriers, and valences. This perception influences the degree of discontinuity and stress during adolescence. Although cognitive-stage theories see adolescence as a unique time in that it is qualitatively different from middle childhood, they do not consider it a more conflictful time than other developmental stages.

The theories differ primarily in what aspect of the adolescent (e.g., thinking versus feeling) and what types of influences (e.g., biological versus environmental) they choose to emphasize. Clearly, no one theory by itself gives a complete view of the developing adolescent in a social context.

References

Bachman, J., Johnston, L., & O'Malley, P. (1981). *Monitoring the future: Questionnaire responses from the nation's high school seniors 1980.* Ann Arbor, MI: Institute of Social Research, University of Michigan.

Bandura, A. (1977). *Social learning theory.* Englewood Cliffs, NJ: Prentice-Hall.

Barker, R. G., & Gump, P. V. (1964). *Big school, small school: High school size and student behavior.* Stanford, CA: Stanford University Press.

Barry, H., III, Bacon, M. K., & Child, I. L. (1957). A cross-cultural survey of some sex differences in socialization. *Journal of Abnormal and Social Psychology, 55,* 327–332.

Benedict, R. (1950). *Patterns of culture.* New York: New American Library.

Blasi, A. (1980). Bridging moral cognition and moral action: A critical review of the literature. *Psychological Bulletin, 88,* 1–45.

Blos, P. (1979). *The adolescent passage: Developmental issues.* New York: International Universities Press.

Capon, N., & Kuhn, D. (1979). Logical reasoning in the supermarket: Adult females' use of a proportional reasoning strategy in an everyday context. *Developmental Psychology, 15,* 450–452.

Carroll, J. L., & Rest, J. R. (1982). Moral development. In B. B. Wolman (Ed.), *Handbook of developmental psychology* (pp. 434–451). Englewood Cliffs, N.J.: Prentice-Hall.

Colby, A., Kohlberg, L., Gibbs, J., & Lieberman, M. (1983). A longitudinal study of moral judgment. *Monographs of the Society for Research in Child Development, 48* (Nos. 1–2, Serial No. 200).

Douvan, E., & Adelson, J. (1966). *The adolescent experience.* New York: Wiley.

Dweck, C. S., & Bush, E. S. (1976). Sex differences in learned helplessness: I. Differential debilitation with peer and adult evaluators. *Developmental Psychology, 12,* 147–156.

Eisenberg-Berg, N., & Mussen, P. H. (1978). Empathy and moral development in adolescence. *Developmental Psychology, 14,* 185–186.

Elkind, D. (1967). Egocentrism in adolescence. *Child Development, 38,* 1025–1034.

Elkind, D., & Bowen, R. (1979). Imaginary audience behavior in children and adolescents. *Developmental Psychology, 15,* 38–44.

Enright, R., Lapsley, D., & Shukla, D. (1979). Adolescent egocentrism in early and late adolescence. *Adolescence, 14,* 687–695.

Erikson, E. H. (1950). *Childhood and society.* New York: Norton.

Erikson, E. H. (1959). Identity and the life cycle. *Psychological issues, Monograph 1.* New York: International Universities Press.

Freud, A. (1946). *The ego and the mechanisms of defense.* New York: International Universities Press.

Gesell, A., & Ilg, F. L. (1943). *Infant and child in the culture of today.* New York: Harper.

Gesell, A., Ilg, F. L., & Ames, L. B. (1956). *Youth: The years from ten to sixteen.* New York: Harper.

Gilligan, C. (1982). *In a different voice: Psychological theory and women's development.* Cambridge, MA: Harvard University Press.

Grusec, J. E. (1982). The socialization of altruism. In N. Eisenberg (Ed.), *The development of prosocial behavior* (pp. 139–166). New York: Academic Press.

Hall, G. S. (1904). *Adolescence* (Vols. 1–2). New York: Appleton.

Havighurst, R. J. (1957). *Developmental tasks and education.* New York: Longmans, Green.

Hersch, R., Paolitto, D., & Reimer, J. (1979). *Developmental moral education: Kohlberg's theory in practice.* New York: Longmans, Green.

Hill, J. P. (1980). *Understanding early adolescence: A framework*. Chapel Hill, NC: Center for Early Adolescence.

Howard, M. R. (1975). *Ego identity status in women, fear of success, and performance in a competitive situation*. Unpublished doctoral dissertation, State University of New York at Buffalo.

Inhelder, B., & Piaget, J. (1958). *The growth of logical thinking from childhood to adolescence*. New York: Basic Books.

Keating, D. P. (1980). Thinking processes in adolescence. In J. Adelson (Ed.), *Handbook of adolescent psychology* (pp. 211–246). New York: Wiley.

Kohlberg, L. (1969). Stage and sequence: The cognitive-developmental approach to socialization. In D. A. Goslin (Ed.), *Handbook of socialization theory and research* (pp. 347–480). Chicago: Rand McNally.

Lewin, K. (1939). Field theory and experiment in social psychology: Concepts and methods. *American Journal of Sociology*, **44**, 868–896.

Lewin, K. (1946). Behavior and development as a function of the total situation. In L. Carmichael (Ed.), *Manual of child psychology* (pp. 918–970). New York: Wiley.

Marcia, J. E. (1967). Ego identity status: Relationship to change in self-esteem, "general maladjustment," and authoritarianism. *Journal of Personality*, **35**, 118–133.

Marcia, J. E. (1980). Identity in adolescence. In J. Adelson (Ed.), *Handbook of adolescent psychology* (pp. 159–187). New York: Wiley.

Marsh, D. T., Serafica, F. C., & Barenboim, C. (1980). Effect of perspective-taking training on interpersonal problem solving. *Child Development*, **51**, 140–145.

McGuire, W., & McGuire, C., Child, P., & Fujioka, T. (1978). Salience of ethnicity in self-concept as a function of one's ethnic distinctiveness in the social environment. *Journal of Personality and Social Psychology*, **36**, 511–520.

Mead, M. (1952). Adolescence in primitive and modern society. In G. E. Swanson, T. M. Newcomb, & E. L. Hartley (Eds), *Readings in social psychology* (rev. ed.). New York: Holt.

Meece, J. L., Parsons, J. E., Kaczala, C. M., Goff, S. B., & Futterman, R. (1982). Sex differences in math achievement: Toward a model of academic choice. *Psychological Bulletin*, **91**, 324–348.

Miller, P. H. (1989). *Theories of developmental psychology*. (2nd ed.). New York: Freeman.

Mischel, W. (1981). *Introduction to personality*. New York: Holt.

Muus, R. E. (1982). *Theories of adolescence* (4th ed.). New York: Random House.

Nisan, M., & Kohlberg, L. (1982). Universality and variation in moral judgment: A longitudinal and cross-sectional study in Turkey. *Child Development*, **52**, 865–876.

Nottelman, E. D., Susman, E. J., Blue, J. H., Inoff-Germain, G., Dorn, L. D., Loriaux, D. L., Cutler, G. B., & Chrousos, G. P. (1986). Gonadal and adrenal hormone correlates of adjustments in early adolescence. In R. Lerner & T. Foch (Eds.), *Biological-psychosocial interactions in early adolescence*. Hillsdale, NJ: Erlbaum, 1986.

Orlofsky, J. L. (1978). Identity formation, achievement, and fear of success in college men and women. *Journal of Youth and Adolescence*, **7**, 49–62.

Orlofsky, J. L., Marcia, J., & Lesser, I. (1973). Ego identity status and the intimacy versus isolation crisis of young adulthood. *Journal of Personality and Social Psychology*, **27**, 211–219.

Osherson, D. N. (1975). *Logical abilities in children* (Vol. 3). Hillsdale, NJ: Erlbaum.

Patterson, G. R. (1981). *Coercive family processes*. Eugene, OR: Castala.

Piaget, J. (1947). *The psychology of intelligence*. New York: Harcourt, Brace.

Piaget, J. (1972). Intellectual evolution from adolescence to adulthood. *Human Development*, **15**, 1–12.

Podd, M. H. (1972). Ego identity status and morality: The relationship between two developmental constructs. *Developmental Psychology,* **6,** 497–507.

Rosenberg, M. (1975). The dissonant context and the adolescent self-concept. In S. Dragastin & G. Elder, Jr. (Eds.), *Adolescence in the life cycle* (pp. 97–116). Washington, DC: Hemisphere.

Selman, R. L. (1980). *The growth of interpersonal understanding: Developmental and clinical analyses.* New York: Academic Press.

Shantz, C. U. (1975). The development of social cognition. In M. F. Hetherington (Ed.), *Review of child development research* (Vol. 5, pp. 257–323). Chicago: University of Chicago Press.

Siegel, O. (1982). Personality development in adolescence. In B. B. Wolman (Ed.), *Handbook of developmental psychology* (pp. 537–548). Englewood Cliffs, NJ: Prentice-Hall.

Simmons, R., Blyth, D., Van Cleave, E., & Bush, D. (1979). Entry into early adolescence: The impact of school structure, puberty, and early dating on self-esteen. *American Sociological Review,* **44,** 948–967.

Snarey, J. (1985). The cross-cultural universality of social-moral development: A critical review of Kohlbergian research. *Psychological Bulletin,* **97,** 202–232.

Sprinthall, N. A., & Collins, W. A. (1984). *Adolescent psychology: A developmental view.* Reading, MA: Addison-Wesley.

Turiel, E. (1978). Social regulations and domains of social concepts. In W. Damon (Ed.), *New directions for child development* (Vol. 1, pp. 45–74). San Francisco: Jossey-Bass.

Walker, L. J. (1984). Sex differences in the development of moral reasoning: A critical review. *Child Development,* **55,** 677–691.

Waterman, A. S., Geary, P. S., & Waterman, C. K. (1974). Longitudinal study of changes in ego identity status from the freshman to senior year at college. *Developmental Psychology,* **10,** 387–392.

Yussen, S. (1977). Characteristics of moral dilemmas written by adolescents. *Developmental Psychology,* **13,** 162–163.

II

Journey through Adolescence

Overview

The chapters in Part II cover five major areas of adolescent development that influence the growth of autonomous functioning. They provide a basis for understanding the developmental forces and contexts that affect the psychological growth of adolescents. A desirable outcome of this growth and the unifying theme of all of the chapters is the development of effective decision-making skills. Therefore, each chapter reviews recent research in a domain that is relevant for the development of skills that are important for effective adult functioning.

Prior to adolescence, children are generally not considered cognitively mature enough to make responsible choices. A few years later, they are faced with many critical decisions. What happens during this brief time span to prepare the adolescent for these decisions? In the cognitive domain, the skills relevant for effective decision making include the ability to generate and test hypotheses, reflect upon one's own thought, and consider the likely future consequences of current choices. These are precisely the skills that Piaget claimed are spontaneously developed during adolescence. In Chapter 3, Danner critically evaluates Piaget's account of adolescent intellectual development and how it has influenced educational practice. He concludes that Piaget overestimated the pace of intellectual growth during adolescence but his views on the process by which this growth proceeds provide many useful suggestions for secondary educators.

While cognitive growth provides the intellectual basis for decision making, most important decisions are played out in the social arena. Therefore, the development of appropriate social skills is another critical task for adolescents. Adolescents who fail to establish effective social relationships are denied an important avenue for the development of autonomous decision making. Since peers provide an opportunity for social comparison, feedback, and practice in personal decision making, interpersonal-skill deficits can seriously retard healthy psychological development. In Chapter 4, de Armas and Kelly review recent research on this developmental problem and discuss school-based interventions designed to alleviate it.

While it is useful for analytical purposes to separate intellectual and social development, actual decision making draws upon skills from both domains. The development of moral reasoning in adolescence provides a good example of this blend of intellectual and social skills. In Chapter 5, Lapsley, Enright, and Serlin critically examine recent advances in moral and social education that have their roots in Kohlberg's theory of moral development. Kohlberg's influential and controversial theory provides a perspective from which to view the difficult social and moral choices that adolescents face. The power and limits of this theory and the variety of educational interventions it has encouraged are discussed. The authors conclude that moral curricula can be effective especially when students are given decision-making responsibilities within a democratic framework.

Adolescents' most basic decisions concern their developing sense of self and all other decisions are influenced by their progress in this domain. In Chapter 6, Suls considers a broad range of "self" issues, effectively synthesizing recent research on adolescent self-concept, self-esteem, and identity formation. He concludes that many of the phenomena that are typically thought to be a part of adolescence, such as self-consciousness, introspection, and confusion, do not necessarily occur simultaneously. Instead, they are manifested and worked out at different times during the period from age 12 to 21. With respect to identity formation, he concludes that the intense questioning and decision making that lead to identity achievement occur most often after the high school years rather than during high school.

The final chapter in this section concerns adolescent decisions in the area of motivation for school achievement. In this chapter, Ames and Ames present a qualitative view of motivation and use it to explain how the goals, values, and beliefs of adolescent students affect their decisions and behaviors in school settings. They conclude that many common educational practices encourage adolescents to focus too exclusively on the question "How smart am I?" This focus leads many students to adopt decision-making strategies that maintain a sense of dignity and self-worth at the expense of actual task involvement and learning.

The five chapters in this section, then, provide both a summary of recent research and a basic framework within which to view the decision-making capabilities of the developing adolescent. The picture that emerges is of a slow and difficult journey toward self-confidence and mastery. Intellectual, social, and physical changes propel adolescents forward but also put them at considerable psychological risk. The task for those of us who work with and care about adolescents is to be sensitive to the challenges they face and to provide them with the support and guidance they need.

3

Cognitive Development in Adolescence

Fred Danner

What can we say with confidence about changes in intellectual abilities during adolescence and how might knowledge of these changes be usefully applied to the education of adolescents? These seem like simple enough questions. Unfortunately, not much has changed since Hill (1973) claimed that

> much of the presently available information about development during adolescence is only incidentally related to the period, focuses on males instead of females, is cross-sectional rather than longitudinal, does not take seriously the diversity of adolescent setting and experiences, and is done in discrete "chunks" rather than programmatically. (p. 182)

Similarly, in the aptly titled book *Growing Up Forgotten*, Lipsitz (1977) observed that studies of cognitive development in adolescence represent only a small fraction of the total number of studies on mental growth.

There is, however, a fairly extensive recent literature based upon Piaget's view of intellectual development during adolescence and it is this literature that is the primary source for this chapter. To make the task more manageable, I decided to ignore two interesting areas of work—cognitive-skills training (Chipman, Segal, & Glaser, 1985; Segal, Chipman, & Glaser, 1985) and sex differences in cognitive functioning (Halpern, 1986; Wittig & Petersen, 1979).

I chose to focus primarily on the Piagetian view of adolescent development both because it has stimulated much of the recent work on adolescent cognitive development and because it provides a coherent framework within which to consider isolated findings in the literature. However, there are general problems in extrapolating from any psychological theory of development to educational practice and specific problems with doing so from Piaget's theory. The general problems are that educational practices are rarely direct products of theories of learning and development, are not uniquely prescribed by any one theory, and are valid only insofar as they solve the problems to which they are addressed (Murray, 1980). Furthermore, the usefulness of a theory of learning and development for educators depends upon the degree to which it leads them to think and act more effectively, but no one theory captures all or even most of the relevant variables which influence instructional effectiveness. Therefore, a single theory is unlikely to dramatically improve educational practice—even Piaget's comprehensive theory of cognitive development.

The specific problems of applying Piaget's theory to education have been pointed out by many authors whose evaluations range from strong endorsements of its value to educators (Elkind, 1981; Kamii, 1973) to more cautious endorsements (Duckworth, 1979; Ginsburg, 1981; Karplus, 1981; Kuhn, 1979) to scathing attacks on its inability to capture the complexity of educational problems (Egan, 1983). A common theme in most of the critiques of Piaget's impact on education is that there is a fundamental discrepancy between his concern for typical, spontaneous, and universal intellectual achievements and educators' concern for individual differences, specific content areas, and context effects (Lovell & Shayer, 1978; Zimmerman, 1983). This is a difference in focus that Piaget readily acknowledged when he was repeatedly pressed to make specific recommendations for educational practice (Piaget, 1970b).

Despite the controversy surrounding the educational implications of Piaget's theory, there are several reasons to base a review of adolescent cognitive development on this theory. First, whatever one thinks of the Piagetian approach, it is a powerful force in the field that, as Beilin (1980) points out, has few major adversaries and is in little immediate danger of being superseded. Second, it has stimulated a kind of grass-roots movement among secondary educators, particularly those involved in math and science education. There is now enough work in this area to draw some conclusions about promising and not so promising approaches to adolescent instruction. And finally, the difficulties experienced in the translation of Piagetian ideals into practice have led to revisions and alternatives to the theory that have the potential for improving instruction.

This chapter is divided into two sections. The first section briefly describes Piaget's picture of the intellectual developments occurring during adolescence, considers the empirical status of this picture, and describes four major ways in which it might influence secondary education. The specific areas of influence include educational goals, assessment methods, matching curricula to students, and instructional methods. The second section considers in more detail how the Piagetian approach is actually being used and might more profitably be used.

Piaget's Description of Adolescent Development

The primary source for Piaget's description of adolescent intellectual development is *The Growth of Logical Thinking from Childhood to Adolescence,* which he coauthored with Barbel Inhelder (Inhelder & Piaget, 1958). There are also many good secondary sources that provide a synopsis and critique of Piaget's description (e.g., Brainerd, 1978; Ennis, 1977; Ginsburg & Opper, 1979). This section will consider what develops during adolescence according to Piaget, the accuracy of this picture for adolescent development, and how the theory has influenced educational practice.

In order to provide a context for describing adolescent development, it is important to consider some of the unique features of Piaget's revolutionary approach to intellectual development. First, he asserted that knowledge is constructed by the activity of the child. This emphasis on the personal, subjective, and constructive aspects of learning is a dominant theme in Piaget's writings, which comes across very clearly in statements such as "what is taught is effectively assimilated only when it gives rise to an active reconstruction or even reinvention by the child" (Piaget, 1970a, p. 721). Second, he insisted that intellectual growth is a form of adaptation that, like biological growth, has an inherent structure and developmental trajectory. Thus, for Piaget, the sophisticated mental operations of a mature adult have their roots in the simple sensorimotor coordinations of the developing infant. Furthermore, the elaboration of these sensorimotor coordinations impels the child through an invariant sequence of progressively more adequate mental structures.

The picture Piaget paints is of a highly active child who begins with a very simple structure (or organization of the mind), uses this structure to confront the world, assimilates new information into the structure, which then affords the opportunity for new attempts to understand and operate on the world. For an excellent and deliberately mundane example of this bootstrapping process see Flavell (1985, p. 7). This process is both encouragingly positive and irritatingly slow—positive in the sense that almost any minimally adequate human environment can provide sufficient stimulation for growth (Sameroff, 1975; Scarr-Salapatek, 1976), and slow in that attempts to accelerate it are presumed to be largely ineffective.

In other words, each stage of cognitive development reflects a particular mode of operating on information that carries with it both the seeds for change and a resistance to it. Change comes about as children become more and more aware of inadequacies and inconsistencies in their thought (Piaget, 1970a), but this change occurs very slowly. Piaget referred to this conservative aspect of development as assimilation, the process of incorporating information into an existing structure and even distorting it if necessary to make it fit. Anyone who teaches can give many examples of this faulty assimilation of information. No matter how clearly you think you have presented some new information, it is often solemnly returned to you in dramatically altered form, sometimes replete with completely inaccurate quotations attributed to you.

Such misunderstandings indicate that one has not hit the right instructional level. While Piaget was certainly not the first to highlight what is sometimes called the problem of the match, he was particularly vehement in his insistence that what children are capable of learning depends upon their developmental level. If this is true, then an assessment of cognitive levels would be a necessary first step in appropriately matching instruction to students. More will be said on this later, but I should note here that there is now considerable evidence that many Piagetian concepts can be taught to children at earlier ages than Piaget deemed possible or proper (Brainerd, 1983).

The success of training studies designed to teach Piagetian concepts has led to vigorous disputes between those who seek to accelerate development and those who view it as nearly impossible to do so in any meaningful way. The debate has taken on a decidedly personal tone as evidenced by this statement from a critic of Piaget:

> That learning is constrained by development seems almost a definitional matter to Piagetians; that is, learning effects are identified by their following the development of a particular cognitive structure. The idea of testing to see whether this is the case seems to strike them as bizarre, and as prima facie evidence that such experimenters cannot understand the theory. (Egan, 1983, p. 82)

Perhaps all of us can be accused of not understanding the theory. The sheer volume and complexity of Piaget's writings, the nearly mystical quality of his insights concerning the relationship between biology and knowledge, and the legion of true believers each with his or her own bias have made it nearly impossible to evaluate Piaget's ideas. In the brief description of adolescent development that follows, I shall attempt to be as clear as possible about Piaget's claims without delving into the details of the mathematical logic that he favored. For detailed critiques of this logic see Brainerd (1978) and Ennis (1977).

What Develops During Adolescence?

According to Piaget, a major and final shift in intellectual organization begins in early adolescence and is achieved to some degree by late adolescence in all normal individuals (Piaget, 1972). This transition from childlike, concrete modes of thought to abstract operations is called the development of formal operations. He seemed to view this development as the virtually inevitable consequence of an active mind trying to make sense out of the world. To borrow Howard Gardner's metaphor, Piaget asserted that the development of formal operations, like the fundamental stages that precede them, is like a giant cognitive wave that spontaneously spreads its ways of knowing across all important domains of cognition (Gardner, 1983).

What are the features of this dramatic shift? Inhelder and Piaget (1958) focused on three major differences between formal-operational intelligence and concrete-operational intelligence. First, formal-operational intelligence is hypothetico–deductive, that is, it involves deducing conclusions from previously given premises. The striking aspect of this form of reasoning for Piaget was that the individual with formal operations can reason at a purely symbolic level about hypotheses rather than facts. That is, he or she can represent and reason about propositions that have no basis in fact. In a very real sense, adolescents can now project themselves beyond the concrete world and grapple with ideas of the possible, the probable, and the ideal.

Second, formal operations are reflective, that is, they can operate on themselves to produce new information. The term "formal" is itself an attempt to capture this feature of the operations that develop during adolescence—formal operations are operations on operations. By way of contrast, concrete operations allow the child to manipulate only directly verifiable information. That is, the products of concrete-operational thought are limited to generalizations derived from everyday experience. Conservation, for example, is one of the classic intellectual achievements of the concrete-operations stage. Yet clearly, the principle that certain properties of objects remain constant despite changes in appearance is an empirical fact that can be directly observed and verified. What formal operations presumably allow one to do is to go beyond this simple cataloging of physical correspondences to generate and systematically test hypotheses. Piaget referred to this process of reflecting upon information and generating testable hypotheses as reflective abstraction.

And finally, Piaget claimed that formal operations were essential for inductive or "scientific" reasoning—the process of inferring general principles from specific instances. For Piaget, the embodiment of this process was the scientist conducting a series of experiments. A good scientist generates hypotheses, plans a series of systematic tests of these hypotheses, and then makes appropriate inferences. This ability to act like a scientist was studied by Inhelder and Piaget (1958) in a series of tasks involving physical laws that they presented to children and adolescents. One such task, the bending of rods, provides a good illustration of the different problem-solving styles of children and adolescents. Subjects were provided both with rods that differed in length, diameter, and material and with weights that could be attached to the rods. They were then asked to find out what makes a difference in bending and to justify their responses. Children below the age of 11 or 12 simply guessed and/or conducted a few haphazard tests of bending by hanging weights on different rods. When pressed for justifications of their conclusions, the children frequently presented confounded tests as proof, for example, they would demonstrate that a long, thin, copper rod bent more than a short, thick, steel rod and confidently conclude that this proved that long rods bend more than short rods.

Adolescent subjects performed differently. They began by describing in advance what might make a difference in bending and proceeded to test the effects of these potentially important variables one at a time. That is, they isolated each variable and directly tested for its effects by holding all other variables constant. To test for the effects of length, for example, they selected for comparison long and short rods that were alike in every other respect. This systematic isolation and testing of variables is one of the crowning achievements of the formal-operational stage and indicated to Piaget that adolescents have the ability to construct and test elaborate theories of how the world operates.

In summary, Piaget asserted that adolescents develop the ability to generate hypotheses, reflect upon their own thought, and rigorously apply logic to the problems they face. This characterization does not match descriptions of adolescents that focus on their sometimes chaotic emotional and social lives, and it obviously reflects Piaget's preoccupation with science and epistemology. It has, therefore, probably turned off many people who have a greater interest in the affective and interpersonal domains of development. In fact, Piaget was keenly aware of the importance of the emotional and social context of intellectual development. However, it simply made no sense to him to ask whether affective developments cause cognitive developments, or vice versa, since he viewed affect and intelligence as inseparable aspects of the same psychological phenomenon (Mischel, 1971). As Flavell stated, "We only have a single head, after all, and it is firmly attached to the rest of the body'' (Flavell, 1985, p. 3).

Piaget's emphasis on logic, therefore, does not preclude a consideration of the emotional side of adolescence. In fact, understanding the intellectual structures that individuals of any age bring to bear on the problems of daily living should help us account for how they experience these problems. This is precisely the premise that guides much of the research in the area now known as social cognition (see Fiske & Taylor, 1984; Flavell & Ross, 1981; Shantz, 1983), and it is reflected in the chapters on moral development, self-concept, and achievement that appear elsewhere in this volume.

But is the Piagetian description of adolescent cognitive development correct? Is there a fundamental and nearly universal shift in cognitive ability during adolescence that allows the adolescent to deal more effectively with the abstract world of ideas? If so, the nature and timing of this shift should be extremely important for educators. It is to these questions we now turn.

Is the Piagetian Description Correct?

Piaget's description of the development of formal operations has been attacked on both logical and empirical grounds. Incorrect inferences regarding the logical abilities presumed to underlie performance on formal tasks (Ennis, 1977) and inconsistent performance across tasks (Martorano, 1977) have led some observers to conclude that Piaget's description of adolescent development is neither accurate nor useful (Brainerd, 1978). I am not a logician, but I find Ennis's criticisms rather compelling. Nevertheless, it is every bit as important to describe accurately how adolescents perform as it is to argue about why they perform as they do. Here the evidence is clear—performance on reasoning tasks is much more uneven than a straightforward interpretation of Piaget would lead one to expect (Neimark, 1981; Shaklee, 1979).

Why is there this mismatch? Did Piaget sample poorly? Did he overinterpret his results and/or ignore incompatible data? The problem is both conceptual and practical. Conceptually, the notion of stages of intellectual development implies a rapid and simultaneous shift across all domains of thought (Flavell, 1971, 1985). In his zeal to counteract what he felt were simplistic quantitative models of development, Piaget put tremendous emphasis on qualitative differences between the thinking of younger and older children. Practically, this qualitative emphasis, coupled with his case-history style of reporting has led most readers to a stair-step metaphor of intellectual growth. That is, virtually every individual Piaget described was unambiguously "in" one stage or substage of development and therefore transitions between stages must have been both rapid and complete. As for adolescents, every child over the age of 12 whose performance was described by Inhelder and Piaget (1958) appeared to have developed formal operations.

Subsequent replications of Inhelder and Piaget's experiments indicate that a substantial proportion of older adolescents and even adults do not perform well on formal tasks. Since Piaget viewed formal operations as the virtually universal achievement of all adolescents, he was moved to comment on this threat to his assertions. In a rare concession to his critics, he acknowledged that formal abilities might develop somewhat later than he had originally reported and that they might be limited to each individual's areas of personal interest or professional specialization (Piaget, 1972). In other words, the logical abilities are still universally achieved but their full expression is limited (at least initially) by familiarity with particular content.

A few attempts have been made to test this hypothesis that performance on more familiar tasks will indicate that a higher proportion of adolescents and adults have formal skills. Sinnot (1975) and deLisi and Staudt (1980), for example, found that adults evidence formal operations more readily when tasks match their interests and/or academic specializations. Similarly, Danner and Day (1977) and Neimark (1981) argued that the typical presentation format for formal operations tasks is so ambiguous that many intelligent adolescents and adults fail to demonstrate the logical abilities that they possess.

Clearly, there is a problem with criteria. What does it mean to "have" formal operations? If you use Piaget's tasks with adolescents and accept his rather strict criteria, "the thinking described by Piaget as characteristic of adolescence is a development only found in about the upper third" (Shayer, 1980, p. 705). If you use more familiar tasks, provide assistance, or lower memory demands (Case, 1978; Danner & Day, 1977), more people demonstrate formal abilities at an earlier age. But do they have these abilities in any educationally useful sense? A review by Shayer (1980) suggests that many if not most adolescents do not. This problem is compounded by the astonishingly wide range of intellectual functioning that characterizes adolescence. "Among the children of 12 can be found every Piagetian level of behavior ranging from that of the average 6/7-year-old to that of the top 10 percent of 16-year-olds" (Shayer, 1980, p. 705).

Given this dispute, it is not surprising that many people have concluded that formal operations are not universally attained and do not adequately characterize typical adult thinking (Riegel, 1973). It is ironic, therefore, that a growing number of researchers is moving in precisely the opposite direction. These researchers, such as Kitchener and King (1981) and Sternberg and Downing (1982), are devising tests of abilities that build upon and reach considerably beyond formal operations. For recent reviews of this research on advanced stages of thinking, see Commons, Richards, and Armon (1984) or Mines and Kitchener (1986).

It is unfortunate that a simplified version of Piaget's description of cognitive development during adolescence is not accurate. A relatively rapid, universal, and easily measured shift in intellectual competence during adolescence would surely make life easier for secondary educators. The fact that these developments are more gradual, uneven, and uncertain makes the translation to education more difficult. Adolescents are simply too complicated for our conceptual vehicles to carry. Nevertheless, even a flawed picture of development can provide us with educationally relevant insights. Zimiles (1981) expressed this notion well in his comments on the relevance of Piaget's theory for reading instruction.

> There are a host of methodological and theoretical values and perspectives that owe their widespread currency to the Piagetian movement. They have been incorporated into the conceptual and methodological frameworks of many developmental psychologists who are not necessarily committed to the substantive details of the Piagetian framework. The situation is not unlike the large number of people influenced by the Judeo-Christian ethical code who do not however adhere to the specific theology. In the case of learning to read, it is the Piagetian surround, the ways of thinking about children's cognition, and not the specific theoretical constructs that seem to be helpful. (p. 283)

Implications for the Education of Adolescents

What, then, does this Piagetian surround—these ways of thinking about cognition—imply for education? If taken seriously, it provides a challenge to our fundamental ideas about educational goals, methods of assessment, timing and content of curricula, and teaching methods. How well this challenge is being met will be considered later. Here I will simply describe the most obvious implications of a Piagetian approach to adolescent education. Before doing so, it is important to note that Piaget made a distinction between three different types of knowledge, all of which are important in school settings (Piaget, 1970b). One he called social arbitrary knowledge because it involves culturally dependent information, such as vocabulary, which is simply memorized. He acknowledged that this form of knowledge could be acquired through direct instruction and relatively passive rote-learning techniques. While this type of learning is important, Piaget was not interested in it and was convinced that schools overemphasize it.

Piaget was more interested in the two types of knowledge that he called physical and logicomathematical. Physical knowledge is directly learned from experience with the environment. For example, physical properties of objects, such as their size, shape, and color, are directly abstracted from sensory input. Logicomathematical knowledge, on the other hand, is acquired by reflecting upon actions exerted on objects rather than from objects themselves. Piaget's favorite example of this type of knowledge was that of a mathematician friend who told him of a discovery he had made as a child. He was counting some pebbles he had set out in a line. He counted from left to right and got 10. Then he counted from right to left and also got 10. Fascinated, he kept rearranging and counting them until he concluded that no matter how he arranged them, he would always get 10. He had discovered that number is independent of order. Clearly, this fundamental principle is not a property of pebbles.

To Piaget, this logicomathematical type of knowledge is a personal construction that can neither be directly taught nor simply experienced. It requires both action and reflection upon that action. This bias toward forms of knowledge that require active, self-directed learning must be kept firmly in mind when considering the educational implications of Piaget's theory.

EDUCATIONAL GOALS. As Kuhn (1979) points out, behaviorist accounts of learning and cognitive development do not specify educational goals. They suggest techniques by which specific objectives can be obtained, but they are neutral with regard to the adequacy of these objectives. Piaget's theory of cognitive development, on the other hand, clearly assumes that development is universal, sequential, and stagelike. It therefore becomes possible to argue that the overall aim of education is to assist the child to make progress through this naturally occurring sequence (Kohlberg & Mayer, 1972). Since Piaget claimed that formal operations represent the last and most adequate stage of cognitive development, one obvious implication is to establish the development of formal operations as an explicit goal for secondary education. The problems in trying to implement this goal will be considered later. The point here is simply that a Piagetian perspective leads one to consider adopting a stage of development as an educational goal. This is a radical departure from thinking in terms of specific subject matter objectives.

ASSESSMENT. In a report delivered to the National Commission on Excellence in Education, Resnick and Resnick (1985) claim that "American school children are the most tested in the world and the least examined" (p. 17). While this may be a bit of an overstatement, it is clear that standardized tests strongly influence the placement of students, the content of curricula, and our judgments of individual schools and teachers. Piaget's approach to assessment, sometimes referred to as the clinical method, presents a challenge to our preoccupation with the efficient sorting of children. As early as 1929, Piaget was pointing out how difficult it is to avoid the dual traps of too harshly judging a child's "wrong" answers and too quickly accepting as correct answers that mimic a typical adult's response (Piaget, 1929). His solution was to utilize a clinical interview procedure, a nonstandardized, focused interview in which each child is individually encouraged to think aloud while solving problems and to thoroughly explain the reasons behind his or her answers.

This emphasis on individual assessment is too impractical for widespread use (Duckworth, 1979) and relies very heavily on linguistic facility (Brainerd, 1973). Nevertheless, it can provide valuable insights into the reasoning abilities of students. At the very least, it can serve as a reminder to us that much of our current testing focuses on superficial and/or easily testable items rather than on genuine understanding. A recent analysis of 12 standardized tests in science highlights this concern. Morgenstern and Renner (1984) report that 90% of the items on all 12 tests were based on simple recall. None of the questions required students to compare, imagine, or analyze.

If we truly believe that education involves something more than the acquisition of factual information, then our assessment procedures ought to reflect that something more. Piaget's approach to assessment encourages us to look more carefully at children's reasoning. As Nucci and Gordon (1979) stated, "Good testing should be viewed as an extension of listening" (p. 98). We might learn more about our students by listening to them as did Piaget.

CURRICULA. Piaget's description of the development of formal operations and his procedures for assessing them offered the hope that curriculum materials could be better matched to adolescents' levels of cognitive functioning. We could certainly use some help in this area. Shayer (1980) and Nucci and Gordon (1979), for example, claim that to understand many high school texts requires a level of cognitive sophistication that most adolescents do not possess. They base this claim on analyses of the demands of curriculum materials and assessments of formal operational thinking in large numbers of adolescents. Identifying the problem is relatively easy; constructively responding to it is quite another. If students do not possess the logical abilities that the curriculum requires, we must either lower our demands, encourage the development of the missing abilities, or do both. Each of these approaches has been attempted. Their success rests upon our ability to specify clearly both the cognitive levels of our students and the logical structure of our materials. Unfortunately, we cannot do either very well. Students operate on many levels depending on the context of a task, and most tasks can be solved in more than one way. Therefore, a Piagetian approach to matching curricula to students is no panacea. Its value in the long run may rest on its persistent focus on whether material has been understood and how it is understood.

INSTRUCTIONAL METHODS. The kinds of instructional methods advocated by Piagetians are quite sensible if you accept the primacy of logicomathematical knowledge and the overall goal of development as the aim of education. If you do not accept these premises (Egan, 1983), then the methods seem hopelessly misguided. Specifically for adolescents, you would see your task as facilitating the development of formal reasoning. And, believing that this goal is primarily achieved by the students' personal efforts at mental construction, you would emphasize methods that are highly active and largely student-directed and that maximize opportunities for cognitive conflict.

Some variation of these three emphases—high levels of activity, self-direction, and cognitive conflict—is present in virtually every educational program that has looked to Piagetian theory for support. The uses and effects of these methods will be described later. The important point here is that many of Piaget's followers have taken his suggestions about the natural course of spontaneous intellectual development as clear guidelines for all school instruction. Statements such as "each time one prematurely teaches a child something he could have discovered for himself, that child is kept from inventing it and consequently from understanding it completely" (Piaget, 1970a, p. 715) are taken as commandments against direct instruction that we violate at the students' peril.

Exaggerations such as these are unfortunate because they diminish the credibility of Piagetians in the eyes of practically minded educators and therefore lower the probability that any of his ideas will receive a fair test. The very strong bias against direct instruction, for example, runs counter to most teachers' view of their primary task, which is to transmit to students the skills and accumulated wisdom of their culture. The sheer magnitude of this task necessitates an emphasis on efficiency, sometimes at the expense of high student involvement and interest. Yet the Piagetian alternative, with its emphasis on individual discovery and invention, seems terribly inefficient, especially in some subject matter areas. As Piaget (1973b) himself acknowledged, "neither Latin nor history can be reinvented, nor is it possible to make experiments (in order to 'see for oneself'—i.e., of an heuristic nature, or to verify explanatory hypotheses) with Greek civilization" (p. 34). Obviously, which aspects of school learning might best profit from Piaget-inspired methods is an empirical question. Ironically, this is an empiricism that Piaget fully supported (Piaget, 1973a).

Piaget's Influence on the Education of Adolescents

This section considers in more detail how the Piagetian account of adolescent intellectual development has influenced educational practice and how it might continue to do so. It is important to note that different psychologists and educators, starting from the same Piagetian base, often reach very different conclusions regarding educational practice (Pascual-Leone, Goodman, Ammon, & Subelman, 1978). This diversity of educational recommendations has been blamed on misinterpretations of the theory (DeVries, 1978) and/or inconsistencies and ambiguities in the theory (Pascual-Leone *et al.*, 1978). A third possibility is that Piaget was correct when he emphasized the personal constructive aspect of learning; even highly intelligent individuals are constrained by the process of assimilation and will therefore distort complex new ideas to fit their current preferred modes of thinking.

I suspect that all three forces have operated to produce the diversity that we now see in recommended "Piagetian" approaches to secondary education. To provide some order to this variety of interpretations, this section is organized like its predecessor. Educational practices are divided into the four categories of goals, assessment, curricula, and methods.

Education Goals

If one believes that the overall aim of education is to help children move through a naturally occurring sequence of development (Kohlberg & Mayer, 1972), it is necessary to be very clear about the characteristics of this sequence. Unfortunately, as the number of studies of Piaget's stages of development have increased, support for the distinct character and essential cohesiveness originally attributed to these stages has decreased. As Flavell (1985) concluded,

> developmental psychologists have become increasingly skeptical in recent years about the theoretical utility of the construct of "cogntive-developmental stage." In particular, Piaget's concrete-operational and formal-operational "stages" have been sharply criticized. The structures used to model concrete- and formal-operational thinking appear inadequate; the state-to-state developmental changes not quite so exclusively qualitative if you look at underlying processes; the within-stage changes more gradual, important and extended in time than originally believed, and the same-stage developments less concurrent than Piagetian theory seemed to require. (p. 295)

Therefore, neither the goal of achieving formal operations nor the means to assist adolescents in reaching this goal are clear.

Kuhn (1979) also points out that "the stage of formal operations, if it is to survive as a useful construct, must be operationally defined in its broadest and most comprehensive form. To the extent that it is defined only in terms of responses to a few problems in physics, or any other specific subject, it can have no broad theoretical or practical significance" (p. 347). In fact, Piaget did rather broadly define formal operations as a set of operations that enable the adolescent to systematically pursue and generate knowledge much like a scientist does. Thus, the educational goal of achieving formal operations has become a rather lofty one that is mingled with equally broad goals such as improving critical thinking and inquiry skills.

The goal of inducing students to become critical thinkers through inquiry training exercises has become a model for those in science education who, like Renner and Lawson (1975) and Karplus (1981), look to Piagetian theory for guidance. It is assumed that this goal can be reached by exposing students to a series of experiments involving exploration, discovery, and invention. It is interesting to note that similar claims for the power of certain kinds of exercises to radically improve thinking have been advanced by some computer scientists. Papert (1980), for example, claims that the use of computer languages such as LOGO, which are highly accessible to children, both requires and helps to induce systematic, hierarchically integrated thinking. Papert believes that these programming experiences will therefore empower thinking as students transfer their newly developed abilities to other problem-solving contexts.

D. N. Perkins (1985) refers to this empowering hypothesis as the "fingertip effect." When we have new and more powerful vehicles for thinking at our fingertips, we will seize the opportunity for better thinking and learning and transfer these new abilities to other contexts. This is precisely why formal operations are such a tantalizing goal. As a powerful and generalized set of mental operations, they are, by definition, content free, a vehicle for thought that once attained in any narrow domain will rapidly spread to other domains of knowledge. In short, the theory proposes that students become better thinkers (Lawson, 1982, 1985).

If only it were that easy. The evidence to date does not support the fingertip hypothesis (Perkins, 1985). Kurland, Clement, Mawby, and Pea (1986), for example, studied the transfer of LOGO programming skills to other planning tasks and found virtually no transfer. Similarly, even Piaget reluctantly conceded that the range of application of formal operational skills might be severely limited by an individual's interests and occupational specializations (Piaget, 1972). In other words, new ways of thinking are not acquired in an all-or-nothing fashion. There is more resistance to change and difficulty in transfer than an optimistic reading of Piaget would lead one to expect. Kuhn (1979), for example, carefully studied subjects as they made the gradual transition from concrete to formal levels of problem solving over a period of several months. She concluded that the most difficult obstacle confronting the students was not their mastery of new strategies but their ability to give up less adequate ones.

What do these findings imply for educational goals? Since formal operations are themselves such an ill-defined goal, it is perhaps not surprising that many educators have seized upon the Inhelder and Piaget tasks as the means to the end of promoting intellectual growth. By doing so, however, they are repeating a mistake that has frequently been made by early childhood educators. They are failing to distinguish the tasks that Piaget devised as indices of conceptual growth from the growth itself (DeVries, 1978). While performance on the tasks may reflect important aspects of intellectual adaptation, they are still just tasks, and somewhat bizarre tasks at that. Therefore, to the extent that would-be Piagetian educators attempt to teach adolescents to solve specific formal operations tasks in hopes of broad transfer, they are on very shaky ground.

Perhaps it is time to abandon our more lofty, generalized, mind-expanding goals and return to the more tractable problem of specifying sequences of development within subject matter domains. This seems to be the direction of much current work in cognitive psychology that is concerned with the development of high degrees of expertise in very limited domains (Chi, Glaser, & Rees, 1982; Feldman, 1980; Glaser, 1986). At the very least, if we remain convinced that formal-operational skills are worth encouraging (Lawson, 1985), we should try to enhance transfer by providing multiple opportunities for transfer to new contexts (Wollman & Lawson, 1978) or, better yet, by explicitly teaching a transfer procedure (Wollman, 1984).

Assessment

There are three major ways in which Piaget's ideas about assessment have been applied to education. All three rest upon the assumption that Piaget's description of intellectual development provides an accurate picture of the sequence of development of highly generalizable cognitive competencies. If this assumption is valid, then his indices of intellectual development—his tasks—might (1) provide a means for matching children to appropriate levels of the school curriculum, (2) be used to directly assess Piagetian stages of development, or (3) be translated into a standardized format for administration to large numbers of children. All three approaches have been taken and none has been particularly successful. The first approach, matching children to curricula, will be discussed in a later section on curricula.

The second approach, directly assessing Piagetian stages of development using the clinical method, hasn't been very helpful to educators for several reasons. First, it is very time consuming to interview children individually, and, as Piaget himself pointed out, it is extremely difficult to avoid influencing the child's performance by talking too much or misinterpreting his or her statements (Piaget, 1929). Second, success or failure on Piaget's tasks depends very heavily on the child's verbal explanations. Therefore, one might incorrectly conclude that a child does not "have" a particular concept because he or she cannot adequately explain or justify answers (Brainerd, 1973). In other words, the ability to describe one's knowledge may lag considerably behind the acquisition of the knowledge itself. And finally, the developments that Piaget's tasks were designed to uncover are simply not seen as central to most educator's concerns. Unless your explicit goal is to teach conservation, for example, it is difficult to see how the timing of its acquisition is directly relevant to understanding particular academic content.

Because of these drawbacks, a third approach to applying Piagetian assessment to education has been gaining favor. This approach involves assembling and standardizing several Piagetian tasks and converting them to a paper-and-pencil format so that they can be administered to groups of children rather than individuals. By doing so, one can begin to attack the problem of relevance. That is, one can assess the Piagetian levels of large numbers of children and relate these levels to their achievement in traditional subject matter areas (Shayer, 1980). Unfortunately, standardized group-administered Piagetian tests are generally of poor quality and do not allow one to obtain detailed information about student's thought processes (Nagy & Griffiths, 1982).

Although some of the newer group tests demonstrate a higher degree of reliability and validity than earlier tests (Texley & Norman, 1984), there are large variations in existing group tests with respect to test formats (diagrams, words, concrete materials), response formats (multiple choice, essay, completion), scoring systems (right–wrong, scales), and the difficulty of the language employed. These variations significantly affect performance (Staver, 1984; Staver & Pascarella, 1984) and reflect either confusion regarding appropriate group tests or faith that almost anything that looks like a paper-and-pencil analogue of a Piagetian task is a good item to include on a test battery. Until these confusions are cleared up, it is not likely that group-administered Piagetian tests will provide educationally useful diagnostic information.

There is a paradox here: Group tests are supposed to help us measure intellectual growth more efficiently than individual assessments, yet the validity of group tests rests on comparisons with already accepted tests, that is, individual interviews. We hold up individual interviews as the standard and then eliminate the very features, flexibility and unique tailoring, that make them so effective for eliciting thought processes. What we gain in efficiency, we lose in sensitivity. Perhaps Ginsburg (1981) was correct when he wrote that "the major gain for standardization is a false sense of scientific respectability" (p. 318).

Curricula

The hope that Piaget's description of intellectual development would provide a better means to match curricula to students has yet to be realized. This hope was based upon a deceptively simple application of Piaget's claim that learning depends on developmental level, that is, that the ability to profit from instruction is intimately related to the child's current general level of intellectual development. Since Piaget provided both a description of developmental levels and a set of procedures for assessing them, many educators hoped that simultaneous assessments of children and curricula would allow the provision of a better match between them.

While Piaget's claim that learning depends upon developmental level is intuitively appealing, its implications for education are far from clear. In its weaker form, the claim amounts to little more than the obvious assertion that certain basic understandings facilitate later learning. In its stronger form, the claim leads to a frustrating paradox. If learning awaits development, how do you facilitate development? Eleanor Duckworth (1979) deftly highlights this paradox in an article titled "Either we're too early and they can't learn it or we're too late and they know it already: The dilemma of 'applying Piaget.' "

The heart of the problem is Piaget's insistence that cognitive growth is not simply a gradual accumulation of information, a quantitative affair, but rather it is an active series of qualitatively different transactions between a growing organism and its environment. For Piaget, this process of intellectual growth was clearly tied to biological maturation, but he was not able to specify the exact nature of the linkage. So we are left with a model of intellectual development that contains biologically based limitations on both the form and levels of development. These maturational limits on development, in the strong form of Piaget's argument, determine the child's ability to profit from any given instruction. This maturation hypothesis

> puts the educator in the rather awkward position of not being able to do anything to help until some innate prewiring of the nervous system is complete. This is a most uncomfortable position for educators to be placed in and is perhaps one reason why Piaget's work tends to so easily polarize psychologists and educators alike. (Lawson, 1985, p. 572)

Many critics of the relevance of Piaget's theory for education have pointed out the potential danger of taking this maturational hypothesis too literally. Egan (1983), for example, claims that it leads to a systematic underestimation of what children can do, and Driver (1978) worries that adolescents who are labeled as not yet capable of abstract logical thought "may be relegated to the science laboratory's equivalent of the sand tray and water play" (p. 59).

These are not trivial worries. In view of the rather sorry history of the uses and abuses of testing, we must be careful not to establish yet another means for denying children access to instruction. However well-intentioned the testing program—in this case the goal is to optimize the match between students and curricula—there is the danger that valuable instruction may be withheld from students who do poorly on the tests.

Furthermore, these worries are not limited to the areas of math and science. Similar debates about the appropriate timing of instruction are taking place in the social sciences. Studies of children's understanding of history, for example, indicate that historical thinking develops slowly, seems to require a level of formal thinking not attainable in the early years of schooling, and is only rarely observed even in high school (Levstik, 1986). Therefore, some have suggested that the study of history be modified to emphasize concrete experiences (Lello, 1980) or even postponed entirely until college (Elton, 1974).

What are we to make of these debates? Does it make sense to apply some form of developmental screening prior to offering instruction or should instruction be so simplified that all children achieve very basic mastery? If we take the former approach, we run the risk of underestimating and understimulating large numbers of children. In fact some specialists in measurement and evaluation despair that we are already doing too much of this and will soon be giving tests "to see who gets to go to the zoo" (E. Kifer, personal communication, August, 1985). If we take the second approach and simplify instruction to insure mastery, we may deprive children of the opportunity to develop the very skills we think they lack. Niaz and Lawson (1985), for example, in their study of college students' ability to learn how to balance chemical equations, concluded that it was a disservice to students to simply teach them algorithmic solution strategies. While such strategies allowed students to correctly balance equations without the need for any formal reasoning, it also deprived them of a good opportunity for developing such reasoning.

There is even the possibility that in our attempts to match curricula to the presumably low levels of students, we may thwart spontaneous growth. Carpenter, Hiebert, and Moser (1979) report a fascinating example of this in their study of first graders' understanding of addition and subtraction. Prior to any formal instruction, most of the children confidently and correctly applied a variety of self-generated strategies for solving addition and subtraction problems. After a year of formal instruction, performance was not as good! A typical response was to look at the experimenter and plaintively ask "Is this a 'take-aways'?" (J. Hiebert, personal communication, 1982).

Clearly, curricula should provide appropriate challenge without overwhelming the learner. However, vigorous attempts to eliminate student frustration by developmental screening or excessive simplification are likely to eliminate the challenge as well. One can take seriously the claims of Shayer (1980) and others who assert that much of the high school curriculum is above the typical adolescent's intellectual level without going to either extreme. To assume that only a few are capable or that all must be taught in an extremely concrete manner reflects a fundamental lack of respect for children's thinking. If the Piagetian approach to learning tells us anything, it is that children already have ideas and need a stimulating and supportive environment that allows them to freely express them. Premature emphases on adult levels of thinking and "correct" responses undermine self-confidence and help to create the passive, dependent learners we so quickly relegate to slower tracks in the curriculum.

Instructional Methods

As noted earlier, instructional methods inspired by Piaget emphasize student activity, self-direction, and cognitive conflict. Each of these emphases will be considered in turn. Then a current approach to science instruction will be presented that attempts to incorporate all three.

ACTIVE LEARNING. According to Piaget, knowledge is constructed by the activity of the child. It is neither given by experience nor directly passed from teacher to learner. While the teacher may serve as a stimulator and guide, any learning that takes place is a function of the child's active attempts to understand. This emphasis on the activities of the learner is, of course, not uniquely Piagetian. And, as Ginsburg (1981) points out, the corresponding appeal for active methods of education is just that—an exhortation that solves no educational problems.

It is easy to get the impression from reading the Piaget-for-teachers literature that what is being promoted is an instructional model based upon playtime in the preschool. I think that this unfortunate caricature has developed for two reasons. First, there has been and continues to be a heavy reliance on preschool examples in most discussions of active learning. Secondly, Piaget has himself made statements that contribute to an overemphasis on hands-on experience with concrete materials. In 1973, for example, in a forward to an influential book concerning Piagetian theory and education, he wrote "It is absolutely necessary that learners have at their disposal concrete material experiences (and not merely pictures), and that they form their own hypotheses and verify them (or not verify them) themselves through their own active manipulations" (Piaget, 1973a, p. x).

But what does it mean to actively manipulate? Must one literally be handling concrete materials to be active? Of course not. You are actively engaged in the complex task of abstracting meaning from the marks on this page right now. And surely some of your most important personal growth has occurred as a result of lively conversations and arguments or during periods of private but highly active reflection. This was so clear to Piaget (1970b) that he wrote, with some exasperation," it has finally been understood that an active school is not necessarily a school of manual labor" (p. 68). Unfortunately, I am not so sure it has been understood. Ask any of your colleagues about a "Piagetian classroom" and they are likely to describe a chaotic roomful of undisciplined preschoolers or a bunch of adolescents running amok in a science lab.

SELF-DIRECTED LEARNING. Closely related to the notion of active learning is the concept of self-directed learning. The self-directed nature of cognitive growth is at the center of Piaget's constructivist account of development. It reflects his conviction that children have major responsibility for their own cognitive development and provides theoretical support to those who advocate instructional methods based on discovery and student-initiated experimentation. While it is easy to demonstrate that young children spontaneously learn a tremendous amount of information without any formal instruction, we know surprisingly little about the efficacy of self-directed learning in school settings. Skeptics charge that discovery approaches do not compare favorably with direct instruction (Ausubel, Novak, & Hanesian, 1978) even on Piagetian tasks (Brainerd, 1983). Advocates of self-directed learning claim it is highly effective especially for the teaching of science (Kuhn, 1981; Lawson, 1985; Renner, Abraham, & Birnie, 1985).

There is another possibility that is only recently receiving serious attention: Some students may profit more from self-directed activities than others. Lawson and Bealer (1984), for example, found a link between cultural diversity and formal operations and suggested that adolescents from relatively isolated rural areas need the challenge of a good inquiry-based science program more than do culturally advantaged adolescents. Similarly, Lawrenz (1985) found that adolescents who were initially low in reasoning ability gained more from an inquiry-based science program than did those who were initially high reasoners.

It should come as no surprise that adolescents with their diversity of experiences, abilities, and preferences will not all respond similarly to any given instructional method. Therefore, the search for best methods through piecemeal comparisons of Method A to Method B is not very illuminating. The most practically significant instructional advances may ultimately come from aptitude by treatment interaction studies and from studies of the basic processes involved in self-regulated activity (e.g., Kuhn, 1981).

COGNITIVE CONFLICT. If cognitive growth is conceptualized as a highly active and self-directed process, then what motivates growth in the first place? Piaget attempted to account for motivation within his complex notions of equilibration and cognitive conflict. According to this formulation, cognitive growth occurs because of the child's intense interest in resolving discrepancies between what he or she already knows and understands about the world and new information that does not fit this understanding (Appel & Goldberg, 1977; Piaget, 1977). Furthermore, it is the nature of the match between children's existing knowledge structures and new information that determines both their ability to integrate the new information and their interest in doing so (Hunt, 1965; Mischel, 1971). Once again, we are talking about matching curricula to students. Only those tasks that present a realistic challenge to a child, relative to his or her cognitive level, are likely to engage persistent interest (Harter, 1978). If this premise is true, then how does one design instruction to maximize cognitive conflict?

Critics claim that reliance on cognitive conflict as a motivator—a kind of "Mr. Wizard" approach—is extraordinarily inefficient compared to direct instruction (Egan, 1983). Even those who are more sympathetic to the idea of cognitive conflict as a motivator point out that the cognitive-conflict process is itself poorly understood (Flavell, 1985; Kuhn, 1979). Why, for example, should a student who has just observed some unexpected event be dramatically affected? What if he or she does not notice the conflict, does not care about it, or does not know how to begin to resolve it? Similarly, does it really require some kind of perfectly matched push from the outside to initiate cognitive growth, or is such growth more appropriately characterized as a succession of internal reorganizations that are only indirectly related to environmental experiences?

This seemingly esoteric theoretical dispute has important practical implications. If cognitive conflict is caused by a discrepancy between what is presented and what is currently understood, then the search for optimal matching should proceed. If it is a highly personalized and internalized aspect of self-regulation, then matching may be superfluous. We simply do not know which of these alternative views is more accurate.

Implicit in the optimal-matching formulation is the familiar hypothesis that children are attracted to moderately discrepant or moderately complex stimuli. Unfortunately, this intuitively appealing hypothesis has been difficult to test because of problems in specifying degrees of discrepancy and complexity from the subject's point of view. A stringent test of the hypothesis requires a set of tasks with a clearly established developmental sequence of difficulty so that one can determine where individual children stand in the sequence and how much discrepancy exists between their level of understanding and the cognitive requirements of each task. Fortunately, the development of classification skills provides just such a task sequence. Danner and Lonky (1981) used a developmentally ordered series of classification tasks to test the hypothesis that children would choose to work on and find most interesting those tasks that are just beyond their current cognitive levels. Children aged 4 to 10 were divided into three cognitive-ability groups on the basis of their performance on a battery of classification tasks. When allowed to choose among learning centers that differed in the level of understanding of classification required, children from all three cognitive-ability groups spent the most time in the centers that were just beyond their initial ability levels, and they rated these centers as most interesting and moderately difficult. Similarly, Danner, Hiebert, and Winograd (1984) found that when the readability of material presented to children was carefully controlled, elementary school children indicated that they would chose materials that were slightly above their current reading-ability level.

These findings provide at least some support for the notions of optimal matching and cognitive conflict, that is, children view tasks that are just slightly "ahead" of their current cognitive levels as appropriately challenging and interesting. The theoretical significance of such findings is that they support a cognitive approach to the crucial educational problem of enhancing motivation for intellectual growth. This approach suggests that motivation and interest reside neither in tasks nor in individuals but in the distance between task demands and current abilities. As a practical matter, however, it is clear that teachers have neither the time nor the assessment devices to be the perfect diagnosticians that such an approach to motivation requires. But that is not as depressing as it seems, for the results also suggest that children can sometimes be trusted to choose tasks of appropriate difficulty for themselves. Given a choice of tasks, they overwhelmingly chose those that were slightly ahead of them developmentally—precisely the tasks that the perfect diagnostician would have selected.

Certainly there is more to motivation than the match between cognitive ability and task demands, but it is significant that children chose to work on those tasks that in theory provide optimal stimulation for cognitive growth. These findings suggest that we offer a wider range of tasks to students and let them sort themselves on the basis of interest. If this sounds like a blanket prescription for transferring important curriculum decisions from informed teachers to the fickle whims of student interest, it is not my intention.

Obviously, we need to determine when and under what conditions students can be trusted to make appropriate choices. This is an important area for research because very little is known about the development of children's interests and the cognitive consequences of their choices of activity (Malkus, Feldman, & Gardner, 1988). One hint as to the importance of the conditions under which choices are made is provided by Danner *et al.* (1984). They report that when children were asked to choose reading materials that they would be required to read aloud, they chose materials that were significantly below the level of those that they chose for private reading. Apparently, the potential for public embarrassment encouraged them to play it safe.

Ideally, most of us who teach see ourselves as inspiring students to challenge themselves, and we at least occasionally appeal to their current interests. But too often the cognitive conflict that students face in our classrooms has more to do with threats to their self-esteem than it does with supportive challenges to their intellectual growth (Covington, 1984; Covington & Beery, 1976). One way to foster a more supportive environment for growth may be to allow students to make more choices than we usually permit regarding the level of instruction and the nature of the tasks they must complete. Careful monitoring of the choices offered, the choices made, the effort expended, and the intellectual gains related to those choices would contribute greatly to our understanding of motivation in the classroom.

This appeal for more student choices and careful study of the consequences of those choices is not new. We already know that academically talented students enjoy and benefit from the freedom afforded to them by special enrichment and acceleration programs (Cox, Daniel, & Boston, 1985). Gifted students who work on self-chosen tasks at their own pace and without constant outside evaluation often work extraordinarily hard and cover astounding amounts of material in short periods of time. How much of these gains are due to the students' intellectual prowess and how much can we attribute to the energizing effects of an appropriately paced curriculum? Given the persistent problem of motivation in our high schools, it is certainly worth some careful study to see if children with more modest talents would also be energized by the opportunity to have a larger choice in the nature and pace of their work (Gibbons, 1974; Wang & Walberg, 1985).

THE LEARNING CYCLE APPROACH. The learning cycle approach to instruction, first introduced as part of the *Science Curriculum Improvement Study* (1970–1974), is a good example of an attempt to combine the three Piagetian emphases described earlier, that is, it encourages student activity and self-direction and also provides cognitive challenge. Originally designed for elementary science instruction, the approach has also been used with high school and college students. The term "learning cycle" refers to a three-step procedure. The three steps are exploration, concept introduction, and concept application.

During exploration, students work with new materials, ideas, or relationships with little interference or direct assessment of outcomes.

They work both alone and in small groups, which presumably increases the number of questions and ideas they generate. By observing the students during this phase, the teacher can gauge their initial levels of understanding and can suggest additional topics for exploration. Ideally, this open-ended exploration raises questions that the students cannot answer thus making them more receptive to the second step of the learning cycle.

The second step begins with the introduction of a new concept or principle that is directly related to the questions raised during the exploration phase. Karplus (1981) illustrates this procedure using the concepts of density and ratio as examples. Only after considerable exploration of the mass and volume of various objects are students formally presented with the concepts of density and ratio. This presentation might be in the form of a lecture and demonstration by the teacher of the relationship between weight, volume, and density, or it might consist of a demonstration film or textbook assignment.

The last step of the learning cycle requires that the student apply the new concept to additional examples. In the case of density, this might involve additional laboratory work in which the densities of various solids, liquids, and gases are computed. The reason for this phase of the learning cycle is to increase the generalizability of the concept. For those students who understood the concept when it was introduced, this application phase helps them to consolidate their knowledge by extending its range of application. For slower students, it provides additional opportunities for understanding on their own or seeking help from their peers or teacher.

This learning cycle approach to science instruction has been compared to more traditional lecture–demonstration approaches in a number of studies at both the high school and college level. Results on both content achievement posttests and assessments of formal reasoning following instruction generally favor the learning cycle approach (Renner & Lawson, 1975; Renner & Paske,1977; Schneider & Renner, 1980), but occasionally no significant differences in performance are found (Blake & Norland, 1978).

While some have argued that the learning cycle approach has thus proved to be an effective means to promote advances in reasoning (Lawson, 1985), many questions remain. Which students, for example, profit most from the learning cycle approach? Are there those who do not profit? Renner and Paske (1977) reported that students who already demonstrated some formal abilities actually gained more in reasoning from a more traditional course in physics than from a course based on the learning cycle approach.

Although the learning cycle approach was clearly inspired by Piaget's theory, one can easily criticize these procedures for not living up to one or another Piagetian tenet. Despite the stated emphasis on student autonomy, for example, the major goal of the learning cycle is to introduce key concepts, and the nature and timing of this introduction is entirely controlled by the teacher. On the other hand, the learning cycle approach has developed a kind of orthodoxy of its own. We are told, for example, that concept introduction "should always follow exploration" (Karplus, 1981, p. 305). Must this be so? Exploration could conceivably be valuable at any point in the sequence.

A related question involves transfer. What evidence is there that gains in reasoning ability attributed to a particular method of science instruction (Piagetian or not) will transfer to other subject matter domains? Many science educators such as Karplus (1981) view this as a critical question. They feel that it makes more sense to classify the applications of reasoning patterns rather than the developmental levels of individuals. That is, they do not expect individuals to perform at the same reasoning level across a wide range of tasks as Piagetian theory predicts. The task for educators, then, is to find ways to facilitate the transfer of newly acquired reasoning skills.

In the end, it won't matter whether or not the most effective means to promote intellectual growth among adolescents turn out to be in accord with Piaget's initial insights about cognitive development. It is clear, however, that his provocative ideas about development continue to challenge us to try to better understand both our students and ourselves.

References

Appel, M. & Goldberg, L. (Eds.) (1977). *Topics in cognitive development: Vol. 1. Equilibration: Theory research and application.* New York: Plenum.

Ausubel, D., Novak, J., & Hanesian, H. (1978). *Educational psychology: A cognitive view.* New York: Holt.

Beilin, H. (1980). Piaget's theory: Refinement, revision, or rejection? In R. Kluwe & H. Spada (Eds.), *Developmental models of thinking* (pp. 245–261). New York: Academic Press.

Blake, A., & Norland, F. (1978). Science instruction and cognitive growth in college students. *Journal of Research in Science Teaching, 15,* 413–419.

Brainerd, C. (1973). Judgments and explanations as criteria for the presence of cognitive structures. *Psychological Bulletin, 79,* 172–179.

Brainerd, C. (1978). *Piaget's theory of intelligence.* Englewood Cliffs, NJ: Prentice-Hall.

Brainerd, C. (1983). Modifiability of cognitive development. In S. Meadows (Ed.), *Developing thinking: Approaches to children's cognitive development* (pp. 26–66). London: Methuen.

Carpenter, T., Hiebert, J., & Moser, J. (1979). *The effect of problem structure on first-graders' initial solution processes for simple addition and subtraction problems* (Tech. Rep. No. 516). Madison, WI: University of Wisconsin, Research and Development Center for Individualized Schooling.

Case, R. (1978). Intellectual development from birth to adulthood: A neo-Piagetian approach. In R. S. Siegler (Ed.), *Children's thinking: What develops?* (pp. 37–71). Hillsdale, NJ: Erlbaum.

Chi, M., Glaser, R., & Rees, E. (1982). Expertise in problem solving. In R. Sternberg (Ed.), *Advances in the psychology of human intelligence* (Vol. 1). Hillsdale, NJ: Erlbaum.

Chipman, S., Segal, J., & Glaser, R. (1985). *Thinking and learning skills. Vol. 2: Research and open questions.* Hillsdale, NJ: Erlbaum.

Commons, M., Richards, F., & Armon, C. (1984). *Beyond formal operations: Late adolescent and adult cognitive development.* New York: Praeger.

Covington, M. (1984). The self-worth theory of achievement motivation: Findings and implications. *Elementary School Journal, 85,* 5–20.

Covington, M., & Beery, R. (1976). *Self-worth and school learning.* New York: Holt.

Cox, J., Daniel, N., & Boston, B. (1985). *Educating able learners: Program and promising practices.* Austin, TX: University of Texas Press.

Danner, F., & Day, M. (1977). Eliciting formal operations. *Child Development, 48,* 1600–1606.

Danner, F., Hiebert, E., & Winograd, P. (1984). *Children's understanding of text difficulty.* Paper presented at the American Educational Research Association, New Orleans.

Danner, F., & Lonky, E. (1981). A cognitive-developmental approach to the effects of rewards on intrinsic motivation. *Child Development, 52,* 1043–1052.

DeLisi, R., & Staudt, J. (1980). Individual differences in college students; performance on formal operations tasks. *Journal of Applied Developmental Psychology, 1,* 201–208.

DeVries, R. (1978). Early education and Piagetian theory. In J. Gallagher & J. Easley (Eds.), *Knowledge and development: Vol. 2. Piaget and education* (pp. 75–92). New York: Plenum.

Driver, R. (1978). When is a stage not a stage? A critique of Piaget's theory of cognitive development and its application to science education. *Educational Research, 21,* 54–61.

Duckworth, E. (1979). Either we're too early and they can't learn it or we're too late and they know it already: The dilemma of "applying Piaget." *Harvard Educational Review, 49,* 297–312.

Egan, K. (1983). *Education and psychology: Plato, Piaget, and scientific psychology.* New York: Teachers College Press.

Elkind, D. (1981). *Children and adolescents.* New York: Oxford Univresity Press.

Elton, G. (1974). What sort of history should we teach? In M. Ballard (Ed.), *New movements in the study and teaching of history* (pp. 221–230). Bloomington, IN: Indiana University Press.

Ennis, R. (1977). Conceptualization of children's logical competence: Piaget's propositional logic and alternative proposals. In L. S. Siegel & C. J. Brainerd (Eds.), *Alternatives to Piaget: Critical essays on the theory* (pp. 201–260). New York: Academic Press.

Feldman, D. (1980). *Beyond universals in cognitive development.* Norwood, NJ: Ablex.

Fiske, S., & Taylor, S. (1984). *Social cognition.* Reading, MA: Addison-Wesley.

Flavell, J. H. (1971). Stage-related properties of cognitive development. *Cognitive Psychology, 2,* 421–453.

Flavell, J. H. (1985). *Cognitive development* (2nd ed.). Englewood Cliffs, NJ: Prentice-Hall.

Flavell, J. H., & Ross, L. (1981). *Social cognitive development.* New York: Cambridge University Press.

Gardner, H. (1983). *Frames of mind: The theory of multiple intelligences.* New York: Basic Books.

Gibbons, M. (1974). Walkabout: Searching for the right passage from childhood and school. *Phi Delta Kappan,* **55,** 576–602.

Ginsburg, H. (1981). Piaget and education: The contributions and limits of genetic epistemology. In I. Siegel, D. Brodzinsky, & R. Golinkoff (Eds.), *New directions in Piagetian theory and practice* (pp. 315–330). Hillsdale, NJ: Erlbaum.

Ginsburg, H., & Opper, S. (1979). *Piaget's theory of intellectual development: An introduction* (2nd ed.). Englewood Cliffs, NJ: Prentice-Hall.

Glaser, R. (1986). On the nature of expertise. In C. Schooler & W. Schaie (Eds.), *Cognitive functioning and social structure over the life course.* Norwood, NJ: Ablex.

Halpern, D. (1986). *Sex differences in cognitive abilities.* Hillsdale, NJ: Erlbaum.

Harter, S. (1978). Pleasure derived from challenge and the effects of receiving grades on children's difficulty level choices. *Child Development,* **49,** 788–799.

Hill, J. (1973). *Some perspectives on adolescence in American society.* Paper prepared for the Office of Child Development, Washington, D.C.: U.S. Department of Health, Education, and Welfare.

Hunt, J. (1965). Intrinsic motivation and its role in psychological development. In D. Levine (Ed.), *Nebraska symposium on motivation.* Lincoln, NE: University of Nebraska Press.

Inhelder, P., & Piaget, J. (1958). *The growth of logical thinking from childhood to adolescence.* New York: Basic Books.

Kamii, C. (1973). Pedagogical principles derived from Piaget's theory: Relevance for educational practice. In M. Schwebel & J. Raph (Eds.), *Piaget in the classroom* (pp. 199–215). New York: Basic Books.

Karplus, R. (1981). Education and formal thought: A modest proposal. In I. Sigel, D. Brodzinsky, & R. Golinkoff (Eds.), *New directions in Piagetian theory and practice* (pp. 285–314). Hillsdale, NJ: Erlbaum.

Kitchener, K., & King, P. (1981). Reflective judgment: Concepts of justification and their relationship to age and education: *Journal of Applied Developmental Psychology,* **2,** 89–116.

Kohlberg, L., & Mayer, R. (1972). Development as the aim of education. *Harvard Educational Review,* **42,** 449–496.

Kuhn, D. (1979). The application of Piaget's theory of cognitive development to education. *Harvard Educational Review,* **49,** 340–360.

Kuhn, D. (1981). The role of self-directed activity in cognitive development. In I. Sigel, D. Brodzinsky, & R. Golinkoff (Eds.), *New directions in Piagetian theory and practice* (pp. 353–357). Hillsdale, NJ: Erlbaum.

Kurland, M., Clement, C., Mawby, R., & Pea, R. (1986). Mapping the cognitive demands of learning to program. In J. Bishop, J. Lochhead, & D. Perkins (Eds.), *Thinking: Progress in research and teaching.* Hillsdale, NJ: Erlbaum.

Lawrenz, F. (1985). Aptitude treatment effects of laboratory grouping method for students of differing reasoning ability. *Journal of Research in Science Teaching,* **22,** 279–287.

Lawson, A. (1982). Formal reasoning, achievement, and intelligence: An issue of importance. *Science Education,* **66,** 77–83.

Lawson, A. (1985). A review of research on formal reasoning and science teaching. *Journal of Research in Science Teaching,* **22,** 569–617.

Lawson, A., & Bealer, J. (1984). Cultural diversity and differences in formal reasoning ability. *Journal of Research in Science Teaching,* **21,** 735–743.

Lello, J. (1980). The concept of time, the teaching of history, and school organization. *History Teacher,* **13,** 341–350.

Levstik, L. (1986). Teaching history in the elementary school: A definitional and developmental dilemma. In V. Atwood (Ed.), *Elementary school social studies: Research as a guide to practice* (pp. 68–84). Washington, DC: National Council for the Social Studies.

Lipsitz, J. (1977). *Growing up forgotten*. Lexington, MA: Heath.

Lovell, K., & Shayer, M. (1978). The impact of the work of Piaget on science curriculum development. In J. Gallagher & J. Easley (Eds.), *Knowledge and development: Vol. 2. Piaget and education* (pp. 93–138). New York: Plenum.

Malkus, U., Feldman, D., & Gardner, H. (1988). Dimensions of mind in early childhood. In A. Pellegrini (Ed.), *The psychological bases of early education*. New York: Wiley.

Martorano, S. (1977). A developmental analysis of performance on Piaget's formal operations tasks. *Developmental Psychology, 13*, 666–672.

Mines, R., & Kitchener, K. (1986). *Adult cognitive development: Methods and models*. New York: Praeger.

Mischel, T. (1971). Cognitive conflict and the motivation of thought. In T. Mischel (Ed.), *Cognitive development and epistemology* (pp. 311–355). New York: Academic Press.

Morgenstern, C., & Renner, J. (1984). Measuring thinking with standardized science tests. *Journal of Research in Science Teaching, 21*, 639–648.

Murray, F. (1980). The generation of educational practice from developmental theory. In S. Modgil & C. Modgil (Eds.), *Toward a theory of psychological development*. Windsor, Berk: NFER Publishing.

Nagy, P., & Griffiths, A. (1982). Limitations of recent research relating Piaget's theory to adolescent thought. *Review of Educational Research, 52*, 513–556.

Neimark, E. (1981). Confounding with cognitive style factors: An artifact explanation for the apparent nonuniversal incidence of formal operations. In I. Sigel, D. Brodzinsky, & R. Golinkoff (Eds.), *New directions in Piagetian theory and practice* (pp. 177–189). Hillsdale, NJ: Erlbaum.

Niaz, M., & Lawson, A. (1985). Balancing chemical equations: The role of developmental level and mental capacity. *Journal of Research in Science Teaching, 22*, 41–51.

Nucci, L., & Gordon, N. (1979). Educating adolescents from a Piagetian perspective. *Journal of Education, 161*, 87–101.

Papert, S. (1980). *Mindstorms: Children, computers, and powerful ideas*. New York: Basic Books.

Pascual-Leone, J., Goodman, D., Ammon, P., & Subelman, I. (1978). Piagetian theory and neo-piagetian analysis as psychological guides in education. In J. Gallagher & J. Easley (Eds.), *Knowledge and development: Vol. 2. Piaget and education* (pp. 243–289). New York: Plenum.

Perkins, D. (1985). The fingertip effect: How information-processing technology shapes thinking. *Educational Researcher, 14*, 11–17.

Piaget, J. (1929). *The child's conception of the world*. New York: Harcourt, Brace.

Piaget, J. (1970a). Piaget's theory. In P. H. Mussen (Ed.), *Carmichael's manual of child psychology* (Vol. 1, 3rd ed., pp. 703–732). New York: Wiley.

Piaget, J. (1970b). *The science of education and the psychology of the child*. New York: Orion.

Piaget, J. (1972). Intellectual evolution from adolescence and adulthood. *Human Development, 15*, 1–12.

Piaget, J. (1973a). Forward. In M. Schwebel & J. Raph (Eds.), *Piaget in the classroom* (pp. ix–x). New York: Basic Books.

Piaget, J. (1973b). *To understand is to invent: The future of education*. New York: Grossman.

Piaget, J. (1977). Problems of equilibration. In M. Appel & L. Goldberg (Eds.), *Topics in cognitive development: Vol. 1. Equilibration: Theory research and application.* New York: Plenum.

Renner, J., Abraham, M., & Birnie, H. (1985). The importance of the form of student acquisition of data in physics learning cycles. *Journal of Research in Science Teaching, 22,* 303–325.

Renner, J., & Lawson, A. (1975). Intellectual development in preservice elementary school teachers: An evaluation. *Journal of College Science Teaching, 5,* 89–92.

Renner, J., & Paske, W. (1977). Comparing two forms of instruction in college physics. *American Journal of Physics, 45,* 851–859.

Resnick, D., & Resnick, L. (1985). Standards, curriculum, and performance: A historical and comparative perspective. *Educational Researcher, 14,* 5–20.

Riegel, K. (1973). Dialectic operations: The final period of cognitive development. *Human Development, 16,* 346–370.

Sameroff, A. (1975). Early influences on development: Fact or fantasy? *Merrill-Palmer Quarterly, 21,* 267–294.

Scarr-Salapatek, S. (1976). An evolutionary perspective on infant intelligence: Species patterns and individual variations. In M. Lewis (Ed.), *The origins of intelligence: Infancy and early childhood* (pp. 165–197). New York: Plenum.

Schneider, L., & Renner, J. (1980). Concrete and formal teaching. *Journal of Research in Science Teaching, 17,* 503–518.

Science Curriculum Improvement Study (1970–1974). Chicago: Rand McNally.

Segal, J., Chipman, S., & Glaser, R. (1985). *Thinking and learning skills. Vol. 1: Relating instruction to research.* Hillsdale, NJ: Erlbaum.

Shaklee, H. (1979). Bounded rationality and cognitive development: Upper limits on growth? *Cognitive Psychology, 11,* 327–345.

Shantz, C. (1983). Social cognition. In J. Flavell & E. Markman (Eds.), *Handbook of child psychology: Cognitive development* (Vol. 3). New York: Wiley.

Shayer, M. (1980). Piaget and science education. In S. Modgil & C. Modgil (Eds.), *Toward a theory of psychological development* (pp. 699–731). Windsor, Berks: NER Publishing.

Sinnot, J. (1975). Everyday thinking and piagetian operativity in adults. *Human Development, 18,* 430–443.

Staver, J. (1984). Effects of method and format on subjects' responses to a control of variables reasoning problem. *Journal of Research in Science Teaching, 21,* 517–526.

Staver, J., & Pascarella, E. (1984). The effect of method and format on the responses of subjects to a piagetian reasoning problem. *Journal of Research in Science Teaching, 21,* 305–314.

Sternberg, R., & Downing, C. (1984). The development of higher-order reasoning in adolescence. *Child Development 53,* 209–221.

Texley, J., & Norman, J. (1984). The development of a group test of formal operational logic in the content area of environmental science. *Journal of Research in Science Teaching, 21,* 589–598.

Wang, M., & Walberg, H. (1985). *Adapting instruction to individual differences.* Berkeley, CA: McCutchan.

Wittig, M., & Petersen, A. (1979). *Sex-related differences in cognitive functioning.* New York: Academic Press.

Wollman, W. (1984). Models and procedures: Teaching for transfer of pendulum knowledge. *Journal of Research in Science Teaching, 21,* 399–415.

Wollman, W., & Lawson, A. (1978). The influence of instruction on proportional reasoning of seventh graders. *Journal of Research in Science Teaching, 15,* 227–232.

Zimiles, H. (1981). Commentary on David Elkind: Stages in the development of reading. In

I. Sigel, D. Brodzinsky, & R. Golinkoff (Eds.), *New directions in Piagetian theory and practice* (pp. 281–284). Hillsdale, NJ: Erlbaum.

Zimmerman, B. (1983). Social learning theory: A contextualist account of cognitive functioning. In C. Brainerd (Ed.), *Recent advances in cognitive-developmental theory* (pp. 1–50). New York: Springer-Verlag.

4

Social Relationships in Adolescence: Skill Development and Training

Armando de Armas
Jeffrey A. Kelly

Adolescence is a developmental period characterized by change across many different areas of functioning. Certainly, one of the most visible and important areas where change takes place involves an adolescent's social relationships. Whether those relationships are with parents, siblings, same-sex peers, or different-sex persons, teenagers are called upon to interact with others in a different manner than they did during childhood.

In the early childhood years, the majority of a youngster's time is ordinarily spent with family members and in a social role that can best be described as supervised and subordinate. While parents may, to a greater or lesser degree, include their children in family decisionmaking, control and direction are matters that rest largely with the parent and not the child. Even when young children spend time outside the family home (as in preschool or daycare), the same pattern of close adult supervision over the child is usually maintained.

The social interactions of preschool and school-age children are not limited to parents, and youngsters also develop relationships with other children. As a number of investigators have pointed out, the social behavior of children with peers is centered heavily around play activities (Moore, Evertson, & Brophy, 1974). Studies of children's popularity, for example, rather consistently demonstrate associations between effective, reinforcing play skills and popularity with peers, and between the absence of those skills and social isolation (Hartup, Glazer, & Charlesworth, 1967; Gottman, Gonso, & Rasmussen, 1975). Social interactions among children, then, are dominated largely by play activity, although the forms of this activity appear to change depending on the age of the child (Berler, Kelly, & Romanczyk, 1980).

By early adolescence, several factors operate to alter the manner in which the young person interacts with both parents and peers. Developmental changes within the individual occur; these include more advanced cognitive-verbal skills, reasoning abilities, and growth and maturational changes associated with puberty. Adolescence ordinarily entails exposure to a range of new social interaction situations and social roles; dating, working with others in a part-time job, or spending time with peers in the absence of adult supervision are social activities not typically encountered until adolescence. Finally, there are different conduct expectations of adolescents compared to children. Teenagers are progressively permitted and expected to behave in a more adultlike, independent manner across a variety of social interactions.

In this chapter, we will consider the issue of how adolescents acquire the skills needed to function effectively in these new social situations. First, we will review research on the frequency and the nature of social skill deficits observed in adolescents, considering also the learning mechanisms that may account for the naturalistic development of socially skilled (or unskilled) behavior. In the next section of the chapter, several general intervention strategies that have proved useful for remediating social interaction problems will be discussed. Finally, we will review and evaluate the outcomes of research interventions that have specifically attempted to enhance the social skill behavior of adolescents.

The Frequency, Nature, and Development of Social Difficulties in Adolescence

Since adolescence entails exposure to new social situations; occupation of new roles in relationships with peers, parents, and others; and maturational change, one would expect that it is also a period of social interaction difficulty for many teenagers. This appears to be the case. Zimbardo (1977) reported that 54% of a large sample of seventh- and eighth-graders label themselves as excessively shy. Even older adolescents who have had several additional years of experience interacting with agemates appear to commonly have peer relationship problems. Thirty-one percent of older adolescents cite hetersocial interactions (e.g., social contacts with different-sex persons) as problematic for them, and 50% feel they would benefit from intervention to decrease their hetersocial anxiety (Arkowitz, Hinton, Perl, & Himadi, 1978). These findings confirm earlier survey-based research indicating that from 11.5 to over 50% of adolescents consider shyness, social anxiety, and social inhibition to be significant personal problems (Borkovec, Stone, O'Brien, &

Kaloupek, 1974; Bryant & Trower, 1974; Zimbardo, Pilkonis, & Norwood, 1975).

While transitory and situation-specific feelings of social awkwardness are probably common and "normal" among virtually all teenagers, there is evidence that some individuals experience more longstanding, persistent social interaction difficulties. Longitudinal data obtained by Kagan and Moss (1983), for example, demonstrate the stability of certain social interaction characteristics between the early school years and adulthood. In particular, social inhibition and apprehensiveness with peers during grade school were significantly predictive of adult social anxiety for both males and females. Patterns of persistent social interaction difficulties have also been established within adolescent-only populations; Russell, Peplau, and Ferguson (1978) found that approximately two-thirds of a sample of students scoring as lonely on the UCLA Loneliness Scale showed little change in their reports of social difficulties seven months after the initial assessment.

There have been, over the past 20 years, a number of other studies relating early-life social interaction problems to various adjustment difficulties in adulthood. Delinquency (Roff, Sells, & Golden, 1972), bad-conduct discharges from the military (Roff, 1961), poor school adjustment (Gronlund & Anderson, 1963), and the utilization of mental health services (Cowen, Pederson, Babigan, Izzo, & Trost, 1973) have been found to occur disproportionately often among persons considered socially isolated as children.

Based on findings such as these, there is evidence that (1) self-reports of loneliness, social anxiety, and other interpersonal difficulties are quite common among both young and older adolescents; (2) while transitory feelings of social awkwardness are probably normal and dissipate with experience in new social roles for many teenagers, some individuals exhibit much more persistent patterns of social anxiety, isolation, and loneliness; and (3) individuals with early-life social interaction problems, especially isolation, are at risk for adjustment difficulties later in life.

Labels such as "loneliness," "shyness," and "socially deficient" have been used quite commonly in the literature on adolescent social development. Unfortunately, these are relatively imprecise descriptors, and researchers have not always identified or operationalized the behavioral, cognitive, and affective variables that constitute inadequate social functioning among adolescents. However, recent research has established differences between teenagers who exhibit social interaction problems (such as self-reported loneliness, social anxiety, and antisocial conduct) and adolescents who appear better adjusted socially. These include differences in levels of social skill, cognitive and attributional processes, and participation in activities with peers.

SOCIAL SKILL FACTORS. An extensive body of research with young children has demonstrated that the frequency and quality of a child's social interaction skill predicts his or her sociometric status within a classroom and correlates with behavioral measures of social activity–withdrawal (see reviews by Combs & Slaby, 1978; Foster & Ritchey, 1979; and Van Hasselt, Hersen, Whitehill, & Bellack, 1979). Presumably, children with a well-developed repertoire of social interaction skills are able to initiate and maintain play behavior and are reinforcing agents with whom peers can interact. In contrast, children who lack appropriate social skill behaviors are more apt to be ignored or rejected by their classmates.

The same type of formulation has been applied to adolescents, and a number of investigations have found that teenagers who have social relationship problems also exhibit identifiable social skill deficits. Jones, Hobbs, and Hockenbury (1982), for example, identified highly lonely and nonlonely college students using scores on the UCLA Loneliness Scale. The students were then asked to engage in videotaped, 14-minute dyadic interactions. Subsequent ratings of the interactions revealed that the high lonely subjects made fewer partner references, asked fewer questions, emitted fewer partner attention statements, and continued the topic discussed by the partner less often than did nonlonely subjects. In an interesting experimental manipulation, Jones *et al.* (1982) then taught lonely students to practice and use the skills that were identified as deficient in the first part of the study. The investigators found significant decreases in self-reported loneliness, shyness, and self-consciousness two weeks later relative to lonely students who had received no training.

In a related area of research, older teenagers with complaints of heterosocial anxiety and infrequent dates have been found to exhibit deficient skills when placed in role plays requiring extended conversation with a different-sex partner. Such behaviors as extended silences (Bander, Steinke, Allen, & Mosher, 1975), speech dysfluencies (Heimberg, Madsen, Montgomery, & McNabb, 1980), negative-opinion statements (Twentyman & McFall, 1975), affective "flatness" (Bander *et al.* 1975; Heimberg *et al.*, 1980), and less reinforcing conversational content (Curran, 1977; Kupke, Hobbs, & Cheney, 1979) have been identified as specific deficits of heterosocially anxious and isolated teenagers.

Another source of support for the hypothesis that shy, lonely adolescents lack appropriate behavioral–social skills is the research that evaluates social skill treatment. Franco, Christoff, Crimmins, and Kelly (1983), for example, assessed a shy 14-year-old male by having him engage in 8-minute interactions with unfamiliar persons. Rated videotapes of those conversations revealed that the subject rarely asked conversational questions, rarely made speech acknowledgers ("really," "oh yeah," "sure," etc.), showed flat emotionality, and made little eye contact. Following a social skills-training program, the subject learned to exhibit these conversational behaviors and was evaluated, by a panel of popular peer judges who watched the tapes, to be much more friendly, likable, and intelligent. Similar patterns of pretreatment verbal and nonverbal social skill deficits have been reported in other investigations that required shy, socially inactive teenagers to role-play conversational interactions (cf. Christoff, Scott, Kelley, Schlundt, Baer, & Kelly, 1985; Rhodes, Redd, & Berggren, 1979).

To summarize, adolescents who report that they are shy, lonely, or anxious may lack the social skills needed to effectively and comfortably converse with others. Both verbal (e.g., conversational content, handling of silences, question asking, speech acknowledging) and nonverbal (e.g., eye contact, affect, voice quality) deficits have been observed in the role-plays of unskilled adolescents relative to their less anxious and more socially active counterparts.

COGNITIVE AND ATTRIBUTIONAL PROCESSES. A somewhat different line of research has examined cognitive and attributional factors that differentiate lonely versus nonlonely adolescents. Two aspects of cognitive functioning have received particular attention with this age group. They are self- and other-appraisals and social problem-solving skills.

Jones, Freeman, and Goswick (1981) conducted a series of studies examining cognitive correlates of loneliness among freshmen college students. In the first study, Jones *et al.* (1981) correlated scores on the UCLA Loneliness Scale with several self-report personality measures including the FIRO-B, the Rathus Assertiveness Scale, and the Coopersmith Self-Esteem Scale. For both male and females, reported loneliness was positively correlated with shyness, social anxiety, public self-consciousness; negatively correlated with self-esteem; and, for males only, negatively correlated with assertiveness scores.

To evaluate potential psychological mechanisms accounting for the lower self-evaluations of lonely students, Jones *et al.* (1981) had 70 students, varying by sex and by high- or low-lonely status on the UCLA Loneliness Scale, engage in 15-minute dyadic interactions. Members of each dyad were instructed simply to become acquainted during their conversation. Immediately after the interaction, each member of the dyad completed measures of interpersonal attraction, esteem, the FIRO-B as each subject thought his or her partner would answer, evaluations of partner attractiveness, and adjective ratings of the partner's behavior during the interaction.

In general, Jones *et al.* (1981) found little support for the hypothesis that lonely students would be judged negatively *by* their partners. Instead, lonely students generally attributed less favorable characteristics *to* their partners. For example, lonely men liked their partners less well than nonlonely men, while lonely women had less esteem for their partners and rated them lower in honesty and affection than did nonlonely women. The investigators suggest that lonely individuals may have a negative outlook about other people that interferes with the formation of relationships. Unfortunately, the antecedents of such attitudinal negativism are difficult to determine. An important question, not yet well-explored, is whether lonely, isolated, or anxious adolescents receive more negative social–behavioral responses from others. If they have a history of behavioral rejection by others, a pattern of negative self-evaluations and negative evaluations towards others might be expected.

In a different line of research, the social problem-solving skills of adolescents have been examined in several projects. Platt, Spivack, Altman, Altman, and Peizer (1974) and Horowitz, French, and Anderson (1982) each presented scenarios of social conflicts to adolescents exhibiting social and adjustment difficulties (e.g., loneliness, social anxiety, and emotional disorders). These investigators found that, relative to "normally" adjusted teenagers, adolescents with interpersonal difficulties were able to verbalize fewer solutions to social problems, to anticipate fewer obstacles, and to offer less step-by-step detail about how they would implement solutions to the interpersonal problems presented in the scenarios. Similar deficits in cognitive problem-solving skills have been reported by Sarason and Sarason (1981) for behavior-disordered high school students, Christoff *et al.* (1985) for socially withdrawn and "friendless" junior high school students, and Plienis, Hansen, Ford, Smith, Stark, and Kelly (1987) for teenagers with emotionally and socially disordered behavior. Thus, there is evidence that interpersonally-deficient adolescents not only lack effective social skills but may also be less skilled in the ability to generate solutions to interpersonal problems, conflicts, and dilemmas.

PARTICIPATION IN PEER SOCIAL ACTIVITIES.   Almost by definition, we would expect that teenagers who are evaluated (or who evaluate themselves) as lonely, shy, and socially anxious participate less frequently in social activities with peers. This appears to be true. Brennan (1982) and

Russell, Peplau, and Cutrona (1980) found that students scoring high in self-reported loneliness spend more time alone, date less often, and participate in fewer social and extracurricular activities than peers who do not report feelings of loneliness. Indirect support for the hypothesis that shy adolescents are socially inactive is based on the results of several intervention projects that reported increases in the frequency of peer interactions following treatment to alleviate shyness (Christoff *et al.*, 1985; Franco *et al.*, 1983). However, several investigations (Chelune, Sultan, & Williams, 1980; Jones 1981) found differences not in the *frequency* of self-monitored social interactions of lonely students relative to their nonlonely counterparts but instead in the *quality* of those interactions. High-lonely students reported fewer warm interactions with "intimate others" than students who did not describe themselves as lonely (Jones, 1981). In addition, the nature of peer social interactions influences feelings of loneliness. Consistently for females, but less consistently for males, self-disclosure with peers has been associated with lessened feelings of loneliness (Franzoi & Davis, 1985; Solano, Batten, & Parish, 1982). The second role as peer comforter or confidante has been especially related to social adjustment in adolescence (Marcoen & Brumagne, 1985).

Social Skill Difficulties in Adolescence: Some Conclusions

Based on the research reviewed here, it is possible to conclude that teenagers who experience social problems involving inadequate relationships with others (including isolation, loneliness, and insufficient friendships) may differ from their socially betteradjusted peers in several respects. First, social skill deficits, especially in conversational situations, have been frequently identified among socially isolated adolescents. The presence of these behavioral deficits would suggest that lonely teenagers may lack the behavioral repertoire to establish and maintain relationships. Second, adolescents with poor relationships exhibit less effective social problem-solving skills, more negative self-appraisals, and perhaps more negative appraisals of others than their peers. Finally, adolescents with relationship difficulties appear to spend less time in social situations with peers, especially peers with whom they feel close, than their socially betteradjusted counterparts.

Exactly how these factors contribute to the development of social inadequacies has received little research attention. It is possible that longstanding isolation from peers, perhaps beginning in childhood (Kagan & Moss, 1983), prevents the individual from naturalistically learning, practicing, and refining new social skills and social problem-solving abilities. Alternatively, the failure to develop effective social skills may be responsible for such later problems as social avoidance, social anxiety, and the labeling of oneself as socially incompetent. More cognitively oriented theorists might argue that negative patterns of self- and other-appraisals give rise to, or at least interfere with, effective social functioning with peers.

Perhaps because the existing data on adolescents' social difficulties are consistent with several different causal interpretations, there have also been several different approaches to the remediation of social relationship problems. These intervention strategies stress (1) the direct teaching of effective social skills; (2) increasing the individual's exposure to social interactions, either by exposure-based practice or by self-management approaches; or (3) increasing the individual's social problem-solving and cognitive coping repertoire. In the next section, we will consider briefly the basic rationale and components for each intervention strategy. Then, the application of these remediation approaches to the social difficulties of adolescents will be specifically discussed.

General Intervention Approaches

Social Skills Training

Skills-training interventions are based on the assumption that some adolescents encounter difficulties in social interactions because they have not yet acquired the competencies needed to handle social interactions effectively. The interaction difficulties can involve excessive shyness, isolation, anxiety, or inappropriate conduct. In any case, a skills-training model postulates that these types of social relationship problems are due to an individual's lack of the skills necessary for successful social interaction.

Efforts to define socially skilled behavior focus on the individual's ability to exhibit verbal skill components (e.g., asking conversational questions, maintaining appropriate topics of conversation) and nonverbal skill elements (voice quality, posture, eye contact, facial expressiveness, affect, and other nonverbal behaviors) during social interactions (see reviews by Eisler, Miller, & Hersen, 1973; Kelly, 1982; Twentyman & Zimering, 1979). Other elements of social skill include the individual's style or pacing of conversation (Hollandsworth, Glazeski, & Dressel, 1978) and the "molar" impression of competence created by the person's overall social demeanor during interactions with others (McFall, 1982).

The social skills-training model assumes that the socially inept individual has had a history of ineffective naturalistic skills learning, including limited exposure to skillful models, limited opportunities for social behavior rehearsal, and contingencies that failed to produce adequate skills learning. Interventions derived from this model attempt to use social learning principles in the skills-training session to directly teach the client more effective social behavior. These principles ordinarily include instruction, observation of skillful models, behavior rehearsal or role playing, feedback and shaping, and then assignments to practice newly acquired skills in the natural environment.

The types of social skills taught using this training model are quite varied and include assertiveness, conversational skills, heterosocial (dating initiation) skills, and other situationally defined competencies. Social skills training has also been reported with a wide range of client populations (see reviews by Combs & Slaby, 1978; Kelly, 1982; Twentyman & Zimering, 1979).

Practice-based (Exposure) Interventions

Practice-based interventions are derived from a conditioned-anxiety model of social withdrawal. The anxiety model does not postulate that socially isolated individuals lack appropriate social skills. Instead, the model is based on the notion that socially isolated individuals experience anxiety, awkwardness, and avoidance of social situations as the result of either vicarious or direct classical conditioning experiences (Arkowitz *et al.*, 1978). Thus, cues indicating the approach of social situations are associated with anxiety, and the socially anxious individual learns to avoid social situations which are anxiety producing. Anxiety-based models of social isolation presume that socially withdrawn individuals may actually possess adequate social skills and that anxiety experienced in social situations can diminish with exposure or practice. The conditioned-anxiety model has evolved from research studies demonstrating the effectiveness of systematic desensitization in cases of social withdrawal (Curran & Gilbert, 1975).

The anxiety model of social isolation has led to the development of practice-based interventions, especially for the reduction of anxiety. In general, a practice-based intervention progressively places the socially isolated, anxious individual in interpersonal situations that carry low probabilities of negative outcomes. With a history of increased exposure and decreased negative outcomes, the individual gradually becomes desensitized to social situations and is able to perform more skillfully in those situations. Thus, practice-based interventions rely on the assumption that socially inactive individuals often have adequate social skill repertoires (e.g., they know how to initiate and maintain conversations), but they lack (and need) additional practice using those skills.

Practice- and exposure-based interventions have been widely used with socially anxious college students. For example, Arkowitz and his colleagues have conducted a number of research studies designed to develop and to evaluate the efficacy of a practice-based treatment for anxiety that is related to dating (Arkowitz *et al.*, 1978; Christensen & Arkowitz, 1974; Christensen, Arkowitz, & Anderson, 1975). While this research attention has focused primarily on heterosocial anxiety and isolation, similar repeated-exposure interventions have been used to improve individuals' skill in same-sex interactions (Royce & Arkowitz, 1978).

Cognitive Problem Solving

A third general form of intervention that has been used to remediate social relationship difficulties is based on cognitive problem-solving principles. In contrast to social skills training (which presumes an absence of social–behavioral competence) or practice-based training (which presumes the existence of anxiety owing to insufficient exposure to social interactions), this model suggests that inadequate social relationships may be due to the individual's deficient problem-solving skills. Persons who successfully adapt to their social environment are seen as individuals who perceive a large number of behavioral options from which they can draw when facing a problem, who are more capable of thinking in terms of step-by-step methods of reaching interpersonal goals, and who are able to see situations from the perspective of others (Sarason & Sarason, 1981).

Training based on this model is directed towards teaching the individual how to plan, think through, and evaluate courses of action for handling social difficulties. Interventions typically present the skill-deficient person with hypothetical social problems and, using an instruction–modeling–shaping procedure, train him or her to verbalize the desired outcome to the problem, the possible methods or means to reach the outcome, and the specific steps needed to bring about the desired outcome (D'Zurilla & Goldfried, 1971; Platt *et al.*, 1974; Sarason & Sarason, 1981). As individuals learn these general problem-solving steps, they will presumably become able to apply them to a range of specific social relationship problems.

Behavioral Self-management

Behavioral self-management interventions are drawn from an operant perspective of human behavior. Self-management or self-control procedures are based on the assumption that although one's environment plays a critical role in the determination of behavior, one can instrumentally arrange environmental aspects to make certain behavioral responses more probable (Brigham, 1978). From an operant view, some individuals whose attempts at social interaction have not met with appropriate external reinforcement have not yet "learned" that social interactions can be rewarding and, therefore, will be less likely to engage in social activities again in the future. Through self-management, individuals are taught to rearrange environmental conditions to make the likelihood of their own appropriate social responses more likely. Researchers such as Rachlin and Green (1972), Karoly and Kanfer (1982), and Brigham (1978) have been major researchers of behavioral self-management.

Situations suitable for a behavioral self-management intervention typically involve a temporal component, a choice between immediate versus long-term consequences. In the example of social withdrawal, the isolated individual is seen as choosing to avoid the short-term aversive consequences of meeting social partners and thereby experiencing the long-term consequences of isolation and loneliness. In theory, the isolated person would perhaps agree that the long-term positive consequence of positive social relationships outweighs the short-term aversive aspects of meeting social partners. However, the immediate negative consequence exerts more behavioral control, and the individual remains socially withdrawn.

Derived from a radical behavioral perspective, behavioral self-management interventions teach individuals to purposefully analyze their environment in order to learn how to control and arrange different aspects of their surroundings to make a desired behavior more likely. With socially withdrawn individuals, this approach entails training to self-arrange a social environment so that increases in social activity will lead to positive reinforcement.

Social skills training, practice-based interventions, social problem-solving training, and behavioral self-management all represent general approaches to the treatment of social relationship difficulties. We will now consider how each intervention has been applied to the specific difficulties of adolescents.

Research Applications with Adolescents

Representative Research on Social Skills Training

Social skills training that utilizes a modeling, rehearsal, and feedback format has been used with disruptive adolescents (Filipczak, Archer, &

Friedman, 1980); with unassertive adolescents (Rhodes *et al.*, 1979); with adolescents exhibiting high dropout and delinquency rates (Sarason & Sarason, 1981); and with extremely shy and lonely adolescents (Franco *et al.*, 1983; Jones *et al.*, 1982). In the following section, several of these projects will be reviewed in detail.

Rhodes *et al.* (1979) reported on a project to improve the social skills of an unassertive 15-year-old male attending a residential facility for adolescents with social and/or educational problems. The adolescent in this study was an only child who had been reared by overly protective parents. Throughout his childhood, the parents had not allowed him to play with children his age as they feared he would be hurt. Thus, for a number of years, his only social contact with peers occurred at school. Eventually, as a result of a schoolyard fight, the young adolescent was removed from school by his parents. For 2 years before being placed in the residential center, he had virtually no social contact with other children.

During initial in-class observations and in a formal role-play assessment, the researchers found the adolescent to exhibit little or no eye contact, an inabiity to make requests of others, almost inaudible speech, and general unassertiveness. These components were selected as target behaviors and intervention was initiated. A series of scenes representative of typical adolescent interactions was developed to aid in training; each scene described a social situation and required the adolescent to act towards a role-play partner as he would if he were in that situation. A typical scene was of the following kind:

> Pretend you are sitting in front of the television. You have been waiting all day or a picture to come on and it is finally about to begin. But Doug (male confederate) comes in and changes the TV channel: "I don't want to watch that junk; I want to see something else!"

Training consisted of presenting the adolescent with one of the 10 scenes and asking him to respond to the partner as if he were actually in that situation. After responding, the participant was given feedback by the therapist on his performance. The feedback focused on the importance of changing his behavior. Next, the target behavior being taught in that particular session (eye contact, speech loudness, or verbal content) was modeled by an assistant, and the participant was given specific instructions on how to perform the target response. The adolescent was asked to practice the behavior again, and the cycle was repeated until his skill level became more socially appropriate; training then advanced to a new scene. This procedure was followed sequentially for each of the four target responses.

Rhodes *et al.* (1979) evaluated the social skills-training intervention using a multiple-baseline design across three target behaviors: frequency of requests for new behaviors from others, ratio of eye contact to speech duration, and loudness of speech. In 5 days of training, behavioral increases were shown on frequency of requests for new behaviors and on eye contact. Independent ratings of overall assertiveness gradually increased during training sessions and remained at higher levels during generalization testing as well. In addition, teacher reports of the adolescent's in-class behavior revealed that he was behaving more assertively with his classmates by the end of the intervention.

While the participant in the Rhodes *et al.* (1979) study was an extremely shy and withdrawn adolescent in a residential educational facility, similar social skills-training programs have been used with less severely withdrawn teenagers as well. Franco *et al.* (1983) conducted a social skills-training program with a shy 14-year-old male referred to a clinic by his parents, who were concerned about his longstanding shyness.

To evaluate baseline conversational behavior, the adolescent was asked to carry on several 10-minute ''get acquainted'' conversations with different training partners. From this assessment it was determined that the adolescent lacked effective conversational skills. Asking questions, making reinforcing–acknowledging comments, frequency of eye contact, and affective warmth were selected as target behaviors for training as a result of the role-play observations.

Franco *et al.* (1983) employed a 22-session skills-training approach similar to that described previously in this section. Sessions began with a presentation of the rationale for the skill behavior receiving attention that day. The therapist then provided examples of the behavior and modeled correct use of that skill. Finally, the shy adolescent participant was asked to rehearse the behavior targeted in the session. After each training session, the adolescent was introduced to a new conversational partner and asked to engage in a 10-minute conversation.

Throughout training, the therapists provided feedback concerning stylistic aspects of the adolescent's conversational skill and stressed the importance of adopting general conversational strategies. For example, during sessions that focused on asking questions, the shy adolescent was encouraged to adopt the strategy of ''finding out about the other person's interests'' rather than memorizing questions to ask. Similarly, he was encouraged to initiate and elaborate on conversational themes rather than to ask a series of unrelated questions.

Utilizing a multiple-baseline design, the researchers found socially significant improvement in each target behavior selected for training. Additionally, teachers, parents, and the adolescent himself reported post-training improvements on social adjustment, ease of interacting with friends, extracurricular activities, ability to carry on conversations with peers, and academic performance.

The skills-training programs discussed so far have been shown efficacious with skill-deficient adolescents individually. Skills-training programs in the schools have also been conducted using a group format, and procedures for applying skills training with groups have been presented by Kelly (1982). One large-scale group-training program was described by Filipczak *et al.* (1980) concerning their work in the Preparation through Responsive Educational Programs (PREP) project. PREP is a multidimensional program for the education of students in public junior high schools. One of the components of PREP is a social skills-training curriculum. This curriculum consists of over 200 instructional units that follow a standard format containing performance objectives, a teacher's guide, class and homework materials, and pre- and postmeasures. The training includes a wide range of teaching approaches such as lectures, discussions, role playing, and other simulations.

The PREP social skills curriculum follows the same general procedures described earlier in this section, but with the training techniques adapted to a group intervention format; skill assessment, modeling, skill rehearsal, feedback, and reinforcement are major components of the program. The social skills curriculum is divided into units, each focusing on a different social skill component. Units begin with a preassessment of student skill, conducted either by role playing, testing, or some type of game playing. Next, a social skill or concept is presented; the skill is presented through modeling by the teacher or through an audiovisual presentation. Skill rehearsal is provided using a variety of student tasks or activities designed to provide sufficient skill practice. Finally, a quiz or other measure of individual skill mastery is conducted, and feedback regarding each student's performance is provided orally or through classroom data postings.

Filipczak *et al.* (1980) report that PREP has been used with over 500 adolescents in urban, rural, and suburban settings over a 5-year period. The results indicate that students in the social skills curriculum became more skillful in dealing with specific interpersonal situations measurable in the school setting, such as working well with other students, showing courtesy and consideration, and exercising self-control.

EVALUATION AND CRITIQUE.   Social skills training is perhaps the most widely employed behavioral intervention for remediating such problems as unassertiveness, deficient conversational skills, and hetersocial deficits. While social skills training has been used most extensively with skills-deficient children and adults, a number of studies have established its efficacy with adolescents as well.

Social skills training seeks to improve a client's competence during role-plays or other interaction simulations. While there is convincing evidence that skills-deficient adolescents can learn to exhibit more effective social skills during such practice simulations, empirical evidence of generalization to "real-life" in vivo interactions is less impressive. Practice assignments, discrimination training to teach the young person when and where to use newly trained skills, and reinforcement of in vivo skill use may be essential generalization-enhancement strategies (Kelly, 1982).

At present, there exists relatively little normative data on what specific behaviors one *should* teach skills-deficient adolescents. While studies have compared popular versus unpopular young children to determine social–behavior correlates of peer acceptance (cf. Gottman *et al.*, 1975), there remains the need to better define such correlates among adolescents. In this way, we can ensure that interventions teach the skills-deficient adolescent socially valid skills that will, in fact, produce more satisfactory outcomes in various peer relationship situations.

Representative Research on Practice-based Interventions

The major proponents of practice-based interventions for social anxiety reduction have been Arkowitz and his colleagues (Christensen & Arkowitz, 1974; Arkowitz *et al.*, 1978). Their research has focused on minimal dating behavior and has evaluated the effect of providing heterosocially anxious adolescents and young adults with the opportunity to engage in practice dates.

An initial practice dating study (Christensen & Arkowitz, 1974) was designed as a treatment of heterosocial anxiety. In it, college students of both sexes volunteered to participate in a series of weekly practice dates designed to increased their dating effectiveness. Twenty-eight college students, 14 females and 14 males, completed assessment measures during a 12-day period before treatment and during a 12-day period after treatment. Among the measures completed during assessment periods were the Social Anxiety and Distress scale (SAD, Watson & Friend, 1969), the Fear of Negative Evaluation scale (FNE, Watson & Friend, 1969), the S-R Inventory of Anxiousness (Endler, Hunt, & Rosenstein, 1961), self-monitored frequencies of dating and nondating interactions, and ratings of self-perceived anxiety and skill.

Each participant was paired with 6 different-sex participants over a 5-week period. Participants received the names, addresses, and phone numbers of their social partners and were told to arrange the details of the dates (e.g., time, place, and activity) themselves. The students were aware that the other volunteers would always accept the dates and were assured that the purpose of each date was solely practice. Thus, not only was the initial fear of rejection removed, but the pressure to perform was also alleviated. The intervention was intended to help the students gain experience and ease in the role of dating as a result of the practice interactions.

Results from the Christensen and Arkowitz (1974) study were generally positive. Two of the self-report scales, the SAD and S-R Inventory of Anxiousness, showed significant pre–post reductions, all of the self-monitored measures improved significantly, and frequencies of dating increased not only with other experimental participants but also with students uninvolved in the research project. Self-perceptions of anxiety and skill improved significantly as well. Follow-up projects (Christensen *et al.,* 1975) have utilized more rigorous comparison groups and experimental controls and have supported the findings of the initial study.

In a later study, an exposure–practice intervention with same-sex peers was used to reduce interpersonal anxiety and increase activity in same-sex friendship interactions of students reporting loneliness and isolation. In it, Royce and Arkowitz (1978) recruited 28 male and 26 female college students to participate in a program designed to increase social activity and comfort in same-sex friendship interactions. Participants were randomly assigned to either of two treatment groups or two control groups. One treatment group received 12 "real-life" practice sessions plus 9 hours of social skills training, while the other treatment group received the 12 practice sessions alone. One control group received 6 weeks of group counseling and the other was a waiting-list, delayed-treatment control.

The interventions were evaluated in a multimodal fashion with a variety of self-report, self-monitoring, peer-rating, and behavioral skill measures. The results indicated that both treatment groups improved significantly compared to the control groups on measures of social anxiety and social activity, while no differences were found between control groups. Perhaps more important was the absence of significant differences between treatment groups. The treatment group receiving practice interactions alone did as well as the group receiving practice plus 9 hours of social skills training, with results maintained at 3- and 15-month follow-ups. The authors interpret these results as a strong indication that practice interactions may serve an in vivo desensitization function, reducing social anxiety and promoting increased social activity.

EVALUATION AND CRITIQUE.   While most of the research conducted by Arkowitz and and his colleagues has focused on the social interactions of older adolescents (i.e., college students), the practice-based model carries implications for adolescents of any age who must learn to cope with novel situations. Practice-based interventions could be used in middle and high schools with a wide range of social skills such as dating, conversing with same- or different-sex peers, and meeting new friends.

It is important to note that practice-based programs may not be the appropriate intervention in all cases of social withdrawal. Although there has been little research to directly address the issue, it is logical to assume that practice alone should be most effective with individuals who already have adequate levels of social skills. A practice-based program would help adequately skilled individuals overcome problems of anxiety and avoidance regarding social interaction, especially when training empha- sizes attending to positive or successful aspects of social performance (Haemmerlie, 1983). A practice-based approach, however, is not likely to be appropriate for individuals exhibiting exceptionally low levels of social skill. Individuals who are socially withdrawn due to a lack of adequate social skill may need a skills-training program as a primary intervention. Only after an adequate repertoire of social skill is developed would a practice-based program be indicated.

Representative Research on Social Problem-solving Training

As we discussed earlier, problem-solving training posits the existence of deficits in an individual's ability to anticipate and handle relationship problems. With adolescent populations, researchers have found evidence that socially maladjusted teenagers are less able to verbalize effective strategies to handle interpersonal difficulties (Platt *et al.*, 1974) and that training directed to improving social problem-solving skills can produce more adequate social adjustment (Christoff *et al.*, 1985; Sarason & Sarason, 1981).

Most research in this area has relied on assessment and training of means–end thinking. Means–End Problem Solving (MEPS) is a proce- dure developed by Shure and Spivack (1972) to judge the quality of problem-solving cognitions. In the MEPS procedure, individuals are presented with a situation describing a social problem, followed by a brief comment indicating that the problem was resolved. The respondents are asked to fully elaborate exactly how they could get from the problem situation to the successful outcome. A number of these situations are presented, and the solutions to each are judged on a formal rating scale. An example of a MEPS-format scene—taken from Sarason and Sarason (1981), who conducted social problem-solving training with high school tudents—is the following:

> You noticed that your friends seemed to be avoiding you. But you want to have friends and be well liked. The story ends with your friends liking you again. Begin where you first noticed your friends avoiding you.

The number of means, obstacles, and references to time, together with a global rating of the effectiveness of the respondent's solutions, are typically used as scoring criteria. Platt *et al.* (1974) define a "mean" as a plan or strategy for reaching the solution. Obstacles are forseeable impediments to reaching the goal, and references to time involve the respondent's ability to take advantage of an opportune moment to act on his or her proposed solution. Finally, an effectiveness rating is usually made for the final solution or mean. Ratings of effectiveness are typically made using Likert-type scales.

In a relatively early study, Platt *et al.* (1974) examined differences in problem-solving responses between adolescents hospitalized for emotional disturbance and high school students. Platt *et al.* (1974) hypothesized that the normal adolescents would perform better on problem-solving tasks including the MEPS, a role-taking task, and an optional-thinking task. The normal adolescents performed significantly better on tasks evaluating optional thinking, social means–ends thinking, and role taking.

Given the differences in social problem-solving cognitions between normal adolescents and emotionally disturbed adolescents found by Platt *et al.* (1974) and by Spivack and Levine (1963), more recent investigators have evaluated the efficacy of teaching cognitive problem-solving skills to socially deficient adolescents, examining the impact of training on measures of social functioning.

Christoff *et al.* (1985) reported a school intervention program combining social skills and problem-solving training for socially deficient adolescents. Christoff *et al.* (1985) conceptualized effective social functioning in terms of two related competencies: having the social skills repertoire needed to initiate social interactions effectively, carry on conversations, and behave assertively; and planning ways to apply those skills. Social problem-solving skills, as defined as these investigators, included being able to plan practical ways to meet others, develop strategies for increasing the number of people one meets during the day, discriminate when (and with whom) to initiate conversations, generate effective methods for resolving interpersonal conflicts, and similar skills.

Christoff *et al.* (1985) implemented their program with a group of shy junior high school students. The students ranged in age from 12 to 14 years and were recommended for treatment by the school's guidance counselor and by a teacher familiar with most of the school's students.

Training was conducted in group fashion at the school and consisted of eight training sessions. The first intervention phase was four problem-solving skills-training sessions. In the first session, students were presented with a rationale for using problem-solving skills, were instructed on the components of problem solving, and practiced applying the skills to an interpersonal problem situation. During remaining sessions, the components of problem solving were reviewed, and the students verbalized how they would apply the skills to a range of interpersonal problems. The components of problem solving practiced in the sessions were (1) recognizing a situation as a problem, (2) defining the problem completely, (3) generating as many solutions to problems as possible, (4) describing the probable negative and positive consequences of each solution, (5) determining the best solution or combination of solutions based on predicted consequences, and (6) developing a specific plan for implementing the chosen solution(s). Conversational skills training was the focus of the remaining four sessions, using a conventional skills-training approach such as that described in the social skills-training section of this chapter.

Christoff *et al.* (1985) employed a range of assessment devices and strategies in their assessment of treatment efficacy. These included means–ends problem-solving stories, a social-interaction anxiety survey developed by the authors, a self-esteem measure (Rosenberg, 1965), and a conservation self-monitoring diary. Using a multiple-baseline-across-target-behaviors design, the group of adolescents was found to improve in the ability to verbalize appropriate steps needed to handle a range of everyday social problems and in the effectiveness and likely success ratings of generated solutions. In addition, increases in self-esteem inventory scores indicated positive change in the ability to converse with others, and evidence of more frequent day-to-day social interactions was obtained. Similar outcomes were obtained in a school-based project that used the same training procedures with adolescents who were socially unskilled and had a history of severe emotional disturbance (Plienis *et al.*, 1987).

A larger scale cognitive problem-solving interventioin has been employed with students attending a high school with high rates of delinquency and dropout (Sarason & Sarason, 1981). The primary focus of this training was to teach students to handle everyday interpersonal problems that might occur with other adolescents and adults. Again, the intervention procedure was modeled after that developed by Spivack, Shure, and their colleagues (Platt *et al.*, 1974; Spivack and Shure, 1974) and entailed the direct training of means–end problem solving. After treatment, Sarason and Sarason (1981) found that students in the training condition exceeded no-treatment control group students in their posttreatment ability to verbalize how they would handle problems with others. Students receiving the problem-solving intervention also had lower rates of tardiness, fewer school absences, and less frequent conduct-problem referrals through a 1-year follow-up period.

EVALUATION AND CRITIQUE.   Normal and socially deficient adolescents appear to differ in the quality of their social problem solving as assessed by MEPS-like measures. Several interventions have successfully taught problem-solving steps to skills-deficient adolescents, and there is evidence that training can produce increases in social activity and self-esteem (Christoff *et al.*, 1983) and interpersonal conduct (Sarason & Sarason, 1981).

Just as social skills training uses change in performance during role-played interactions as a primary measure of skill acquisition, researchers of problem solving have relied on verbalizations during the presentation of hypothetical social problems to assess training effects. Demonstration that problem-solving intervention directly improves adolescents' social interactions outside the training setting remain uncommon in the literature; additional research on meaningful generalization is needed.

Representative Research on Self-management

From a self-management perspective, social avoidance is viewed as an example of immediate consequences taking precedence over long-term consequences. If the short-term consequence of meeting new people is aversive anxiety, this aversive immediate consequence can effectively control the adolescent's behavior and block the potential long-term positive consequences of being more outgoing (e.g., having more friends and enjoying social activities). Therefore, avoidant individuals may need a method of encouraging more outgoing behavior despite short-term feelings of anxiety, which will presumably lessen if they can interact with others more frequently.

In self-management training, the young person is taught to develop and implement behavioral contingencies intended to modify his or her own actions. The contingencies might include self-delivery of reinforcement for engaging in a desired but low-probability behavior, self-imposition of reinforcement loss for failing to engage in a desired behavior, and so on. Self-management assumes that the commitment response required to self-manage is more likely at certain times than others. For example, an adolescent wishing to make new friends is more likely to commit to talking to more people at school after a lonely weekend than when having fun.

Self-management has been used with a wide range of populations from young children to adults. The problem behaviors with which it has been employed include weight loss, modification of harmful habits, studying behavior, and problems involving gratification delay (see Karoly & Kanfer, 1982). Self-management procedures have also been used in the classroom with such behaviors as talking out, hitting other students, and leaving one's desk without permission (Johnson & Bolstad, 1972).

Behavioral self-management has only recently been applied to problems of interpersonal interaction. Brigham (1982) reported on a middle school student's efforts to control her social impatience through self-management. The adolescent in this self-management project was very impatient with friends. When her friends were late or dawdling when it was time to go, the adolescent paced, became irritable, and verbally pushed her friends along. This impatient social behavior had a deleterious effect on her peer relationships.

During a pretraining period of self-monitoring, the adolescent recorded instances when she became impatient and subsequently rude with friends. The antecedents of impatience identified by Brigham (1982) were situations in which the adolescent was forced to wait for others, such as waiting for friends after school, waiting for clerks while shopping, and waiting to use a phone.

The training intervention consisted of a series of individual sessions conducted by a school counselor. In training, the adolescent was taught to create a list of activities in which she could engage as substitutes for her impatient behavior. Whenever she found herself waiting and growing impatient, the adolescent practiced substituting an alternate behavior from her list, which included studying, reading, and watching TV. In addition to managing her own negative impatient behavior, she was taught to reinforce the on-time behaviors of others by complimenting and thanking them. Brigham (1982) notes that the teenager practiced making such reinforcing statements as "I'm so glad you're here early, now we have time to . . ." or "Thanks for coming on time, now we can get started on this sooner." During the post-training follow-up period, monitoring data indicated the adolescent was able to successfully self-manage her impatient behavior.

Brigham, Hopper, Hill, de Armas, and Newsom (1985) reported the results of a large-scale, 3-year project employing self-management with middle school students. One hundred and three sixth- to eighth-grade students participated in an 18-session, 6-week, after-school self-management training program. Students were selected based on their high rates of disruptive behavior and the high frequency with which they received after-school detentions. In addition, the students were reported to interact with peers and teachers in socially inappropriate ways. The investigators targeted self-management training to improve their peer social interaction skills and decrease rates of disruptive behavior.

Self-management was taught in a small group, classroom format. The program emphasized self-management concepts as well as specific behavioral skills, with students taught to analyze personal problem situations and to select appropriate self-management procedures for dealing with them. The first portion of the intervention consisted of an introduction to the analysis of social behavior. Additionally, the principles of self-reinforcement, punishment, extinction, and shaping were taught by role playing, modeling, and performance exercises. The second portion of the program consisted of reading written materials stressing the application of these procedures in dealing with self-management problems. Once basic knowledge of self-management was acquired, each student planned and implemented a self-management project on a self-selected maladaptive behavior. In addition to in-class procedures, students were encouraged and assisted by the self-management instructor to practice the skills outside of class. Most of the role-playing and modeling exercises were directed at school problems and interpersonal relations with peers and adults.

Several measures of program effectiveness were utilized by Brigham *et al.* (1985). They included frequency of student detentions, a teacher behavior-rating scale, and a self-management usage questionnaire. Pre- and post-training comparisons revealed student improvement on each of the dependent measures. As a group, the students significantly decreased their frequency of detentions, significantly improved their behavior ratings by teachers, and significantly increased the frequency with which they would respond with a self-management response in a problematic situation. The frequency of detentions continued to decrease during the next two years for most of the students. In addition, students reported themselves to be more satisfied with their peer social relationships.

EVALUATION AND CRITIQUE. Self-management training, long employed for problems of self-control and habit control, has only recently been utilized for relationship difficulties of adolescents. While it is reasonable to assume that some socially inactive or isolated teenagers can be assisted in developing plans to increase their social activity and participation frequency, empirical demonstrations of program effectiveness for such problems are still uncommon in the literature. Early, but primarily uncontrolled, studies on both an individual case (Brigham, 1982) and a large-scale intervention (Brigham *et al.*, 1985) basis appear promising; better controlled applications will be needed to examine the efficacy of self-management training to the social problems of adolescent.

Conclusions

Adolescence is a developmental period characterized by exposure to new social situations, requiring the acquisition of new social skills. While transitory feelings of social awkwardness, inhibition, and anxiety are common among teenagers, adolescents with more longstanding interaction difficulties may benefit from intervention to enhance social skills, to decrease anxiety, and to enable the young person to participate successfully in peer activities. Social skills training, practice or exposure interventions, social problem solving, and self-management training have each been reported as effective for remediating the interpersonal difficulties of adolescents. However, a number of key questions have not yet been substantially addressed in the literature.

Social skills training assumes that an individual lacks the behavioral repertoire to handle certain social interactions effectively, while problem-solving interventions postulate the existence of cognitive-planning deficits as antecedents of social ineffectiveness. Exposure-based models are based on an anxiety desensitization premise, while self-management defines social avoidance and inhibition as problems capable of control through self-regulation. While each approach may prove viable for certain adolescents, there has been virtually no research to address the question of what adolescents might benefit most from which intervention model.

One important dimension for matching adolescent problems with intervention programs probably involves the presence or absence of an effective social skills repertoire. Adolescents who have the behavioral competencies for handling social interactions—who can, for example, role-play interactions skillfully—but are inhibited or anxious may benefit from exposure, problem-solving, or self-management interventions. However, those adolescents who lack effective social skills may require more basic, direct training before being exposed or pushed into interactions requiring skills they do not yet have.

Although we have grouped the projects reviewed here by approach, some interventions have combined different training components. Christoff *et al.* (1985), for example, taught both conversational and social problem-solving skills to shy, avoidance adolescents. Since effective social functioning entails behavioral, cognitive, and physiological (anxiety-related) components (McFall, 1982), broadly based interventions utilizing multiple training elements merit further research attention.

Finally, the research surveyed in this chapter focused primarily on difficulties related to relationship skill and ease with adolescent peers. These are certainly not the only interpersonal demands faced by teenagers; adolescents are also expected to interact with parents and other adults and to become socialized into appropriate rather than delinquent, antisocial roles. Additional research that examines methods for enhancing these aspects of social relationship skill is also needed.

References

Arkowitz, H., Hinton, R., Perl, J., & Himadi, W. (1978). Treatment strategies for dating anxiety in college men based on real-life practice. *Counseling Psychologist, 7,* 41–46.

Bander, K. W., Steinke, G. V., Allen, G. J., & Mosher, D. L. (1975). Evaluation of three dating-specific treatment approaches for heterosexual dating anxiety. *Journal of Consulting and Clinical Psychology* **43,** 259–265.

Berler, E. S., Kelly, J. A., & Romanczyk, R. G. (1980). *The assessment of children's social skills.* Paper presented at the Association for Advancement of Behavior Therapy, New York.

Borkovec, T. D., Stone, N. M., O'Brien, G. T., & Kaloupek, D. G. (1974). Evaluation of a clinically relevant target behavior for analogue outcome research. *Behavior Therapy,* **5,** 503–511.

Brennan, T. (1982). Loneliness at adolescence. In L. Peplau & D. Perlman (Eds.), *Loneliness: A source book of current theory, research, and therapy.* New York: Wiley.

Brigham, T. A. (1978). Self-control, Part II. In A. C. Catania & T. A. Brigham (Eds.), *Handbook of applied behavior analysis: Social and instructional processes.* New York: Irvington.

Brigham, T. A. (1982). Self-management: A radical behavioral perspective. In P. Karoly & F. H. Kanfer (Eds.), *Self-management and behavior change: From theory to practice.* New York: Pergamon.

Brigham, T. A., Hopper, C., Hill, B., de Armas, A., & Newsom, P. (1985). Development and evaluation of a self-management program for disruptive adolescents. *Behavior Therapy* **16,** 99–115.

Bryant, B. M., & Trower, P. E. (1974). Social difficulty in a student sample. *British Journal of Educational Psychology, 44,* 13–21.

Chelune, G. J., Sultan, F. G., & Williams, C. L. (1980). Loneliness, self-disclosure, and interpersonal effectiveness. *Journal of Counseling Psychology, 27,* 462–468.

Christensen, A., & Arkowitz, H. (1974). Preliminary report on practice dating and feedback as treatment for college dating problems. *Journal of Counseling Psychology,* **21,** 92–95.

Christensen, A., Arkowitz, H., & Anderson, J. (1975). Practice dating as treatment for college dating inhibitions. *Behavior Research and Therapy*, **13**, 321–33.

Christoff, K. A., Scott, W. O. N., Kelley, M. L., Schlundt, D., Baer, G., & Kelly, J. A. (1985). Social skills and social problem-solving training for shy young adolescents. *Behavior Therapy*, **16**, 468–477.

Combs, M. L., & Slaby, D. A. (1978). Social skills training with children. In B. Lahey & A. E. Kazdin (Eds.), *Advances in child clinical psychology* (Vol. 1). New York: Plenum.

Cowen, E. L., Pederson, A., Babigan, H., Izzo, L. D., & Trost, N. (1973). Long-term followup of early detected vulnerable children. *Journal of Consulting and Clinical Psychology*, **41**, 438–446.

Curran, J. P. (1977). Skills training as an approach to the treatment of heterosexual social anxiety. *Psychological Bulletin*, **84**, 140–157.

Curran, J. P., & Gilbert, F. S. (1975). A test of the relative effectiveness of a systematic desensitization program and in interpersonal skills training program with date anxious subjects. *Behavior Therapy*, **6**, 510–521.

D'Zurilla, T. J., & Goldfried, M. R. (1971). Problem solving and behavior modification. *Journal of Abnormal Psychology*, **78**, 107–126.

Eisler, R. M., Miller, P. M., & Hersen, M. (1973). Components of assertive behavior. *Journal of Clinical Psychology*, **29**, 295–299.

Endler, N. S., Hunt, J. McV., & Rosenstein, A. J. (1961). An S-R inventory of anxiousness. *Psychological Monographs*, **76** (17, Whole No. 536).

Filipczak, J., Archer, M., & Friedman, R. M. (1980). In-school social skills training: Use with disruptive adolescents. *Behavior Modification*, **4**(2).

Foster, S. L., & Ritchey, W. L. (1979). Issues in the assessment of social competence in children. *Journal of Applied Behavior Analysis*, **12**, 625–638.

Franco, D. P., Christoff, K. A., Crimmins, D. B., & Kelly, J. A. (1983). Social skills training for an extremely shy young adolescent: An empirical case study. *Behavior Therapy*, **14**, 568–575.

Franzoi, S. L., & Davis, M. H. (1985). Adolescent self-disclosure and loneliness: Private self-consciousness and parental influences. *Journal of Personality and Social Psychology*, **48**, 768–780.

Gottman, J. M., Gonso, J., & Rasmussen, B. (1975). Social interaction, social competencies and friendship in children. *Child Development*, **46**, 709–718.

Grondlund, J., & Anderson, L. (1963). Personality characteristics of socially accepted, socially neglected, and socially rejected junior high school pupils. In J. Seidman (Ed.), *Educating for mental health*. New York: Crowell.

Haemmerlie, F. (1983). Heterosocial anxiety in college females. *Behavior Modification*, **7**, 611–623.

Hartup, W., Glazer, J., & Charlesworth, R. (1967). Peer reinforcement and sociometric status. *Child Development*, **38**, 1017–1024.

Heimberg, R. G., Madsen, C. H., Montgomery, D., & McNabb, C. E. (1980). Behavioral treatments for heterosocial problems: Effects on daily self-monitored and role played interactions. *Behavior Modification*, **4**, 147–172.

Hollandsworth, J. G., Jr., Glazeski, R. C., & Dressel, M. E. (1978). Use of social-skills training in the treatment of extreme anxiety and deficient verbal skills in the job-interview setting. *Journal of Applied Behavior Analysis*, **11**, 249–269.

Horowitz, L. M., French, R., & Anderson, C. A. (1982). The prototype of a lonely person. In L. A. Peplau & D. Perlman (Eds.), *Loneliness: A sourcebook of current theory, research, and therapy*. New York: Wiley (Interscience).

Johnson, O. D., & Bolstad, S. M. (1972). Self-regulation in modification of disruptive classroom behavior. *Journal of Applied Behavior Analysis, 5*, 443–454.

Jones, W. H. (1981). Loneliness and social contact, *Journal of Social Psychology,* **113**, 295–296.

Jones, W. H., Freeman, J. E., & Goswick, R. A. (1981). The persistence of loneliness: Self and other determinants. *Journal of Personality, 49*, 27–28.

Jones, W. H., Hobbs, S. A., & Hockenbury, D. (1982). Loneliness and social skill deficits. *Journal of Personality and Social Psychology, 42*, 682–689.

Kagan, J., & Moss, H. A. (1983). *Birth to maturity: A study in psychological development* (2nd ed.). New Haven, CT: Yale University Press.

Karoly, P., & Kanfer, F. H. (Eds.) (1982). *Self-management and behavior change: The theory to practice*. New York: Pergamon.

Kelly, J. A. (1982). *Social skills training: A practical guide for interventions*. New York: Springer.

Kupke, T. E., Hobbs, S. A., & Cheney, T. H. (1979). Selection of heterosocial skills. I. Criterion-related validity. *Behavior Therapy, 10*, 327–335.

McFall, R. M. (1982). A review and reformulation of the concept of social skills. *Behavioral Assessment, 4*, 1–33.

Marcoen, H., & Brumagne, M. (1985). Loneliness among children and young adolescents. *Developmental Psychology, 21*, 1025–1031.

Moore, N. V., Evertson, C. M., & Brophy, J. E. (1974). Solitary play: Some functional considerations. *Developmental Psychology, 10*, 830–834.

Platt, J. J., Spivack, G., Altman, W., Altman, D., & Peizer, S. B. (1974). Adolescent problem-solving thinking. *Journal of Consulting and Clinical Psychology, 43*, 787–793.

Plienis, A. J., Hansen, D. J., Ford, F., Smith, S., Stark, L. J., & Kelly, J. A. (1987). Behavioral small group training to improve the social skills of emotionally-disordered adolescents. *Behavior Therapy, 18*, 17–32.

Rachlin, H., & Green, L. (1972). Commitment, choice, and self-control. *Journal of the Experimental Analysis of Behavior, 17*, 15–22.

Rhodes, W. A., Redd, W. H., & Berggren, L. (1979). Social skills training for an unassertive adolescent. *Journal of Clinical Child Psychology, 8*, 18–21.

Roff, M. (1961). Childhood social interactions and young adult bad conduct. *Journal of Abnormal Social Psychology, 63*, 333–337.

Roff, M., Sells, B., & Golden, M. (1972). *Social adjustment and personality development in children*. Minneapolis: University of Minnesota Press.

Rosenberg, R. (1965). *Society and the adolescent self-image*. Princeton, NJ: Princeton University Press.

Royce, W. S., & Arkowitz, H. (1978). Multiple modal evaluation of practice interaction as treatment for social isolation. *Journal of Consulting and Clinical Psychology, 46*, 239–245.

Russell, D. W., Peplau, L. A., & Cutrona, C. E. (1980). The revised UCLA Loneliness Scale: Concurrent and discriminant validity evidence. *Journal of Personality and Social Psychology, 39*, 472–480.

Russell, D., Peplau, L. A., & Ferguson, M. L. (1978). Developing a measure of loneliness. *Journal of Personality Assessment, 42*, 290–294.

Sarason, I. G., & Sarason, B. R. (1981). Teaching cognitive and social skills to high school students. *Journal of Consulting and Clinical Psychology, 49*, 908–918.

Shure, M. B., & Spivack, G. (1972). Means–end thinking, adjustment, and social class among elementary school-aged children. *Journal of Consulting and Clinical Psychology, 38*, 348–353.

Solano, C. H., Batten, P. G., & Parish, E. A. (1982). Loneliness and patterns of self-disclosure. *Journal of Personality and Social Psychology*, **43**, 524–530.

Spivack, G., & Levine, M. (1963). *Self-regulation in acting-out and normal adolescents.* Report to National Institute of Health, M-4531, Washington, DC: United States Public Health Service.

Spivack, G., & Shure, M. B. (1974). *Social adjustment of young children: A cognitive approach to solving real-life problems.* San Francisco: Jossey-Bass.

Twentyman, C. R., & Zimering, R. T. (1979). Behavioral training of social skills: A critical review. In M. Hersen, R. M. Eisler, & P. M. Miller (Eds.), *Program in behavior modification* (Vol. 7). New York: Academic Press.

Twentyman, C. T., & McFall, R. M. (1975). Behavioral training of social skills in shy males. *Journal of Consulting and Clinical Psychology*, **43**, 348–395.

Van Hasselt, V. B., Hersen, M., Whitehall, M. B., & Bellack, A. S. (1979). Social skill assessment and training for children: An evaluation review. *Behaviour Research and Therapy*, **17**, 413–437.

Watson, D., & Friend, R. (1969). Measurement of social-evaluative anxiety. *Journal of Consulting and Clinical Psychology*, **33**, 448–457.

Zimbardo, P. G. (1977). *Shyness.* Reading, MA: Addison-Wesley.

Zimbardo, P. G., Pilkonis, P. & Norwood, R. (1975). The silent prison of shyness. *Psychology Today*, **8**, 69–72.

5

Moral and Social Education

Daniel K. Lapsley
Robert D. Enright
Ronald C. Serlin

An Overview

It is certainly no secret that Kohlberg's theory of moral development has generated intense professional interest in moral and social education. If one has any lingering doubts about the pervasiveness of Kohlberg's influence or the continuing vitality of his approach, one need only take notice of the very recent proliferation of books and articles on the techniques of program implementation (e.g., Scharf, McCoy, & Ross, 1979; Arbuthnot & Faust, 1981; Wilcox, 1979; Wilson, 1986; Leming, 1986; Hersh, Paolitto, & Reimer, 1979) and evaluation (e.g., Cline & Feldmesser, 1983; Kuhmerker, Mentkowski, & Erickson, 1980); on the philosophical justification of Kohlbergian moral interventions (e.g., Boyd, 1986; May, 1985; Reed & Hanna, 1982; Hamm, 1977; Pekarsky, 1983; Wonderly & Kupfersmid, 1980; Cochrane, Hamm, & Kazepides, 1979; Siegel, 1982, 1986; Hyland, 1979; Aron, 1977a,b) and of the moral theory proper (Modgil & Modgil, 1986; Kohlberg, Levine, & Hewer, 1983; Falikowski, 1982; Trainer, 1977; Flanagan, 1982; Rosen, 1980; Phillips & Nicolayev, 1978, 1984; Campbell, 1983). At least eight critical reviews of moral education literature have appeared in the last several years alone (Enright, Lapsley, & Levy, 1983a; Enright, Lapsley, Harris, & Shawver, 1983b; Lawrence, 1980; Leming, 1981; Lapsley & Quintana, 1985; Lockwood, 1978; Berkowitz, 1981). Kohlberg's theory has been featured in special issues of the journals *Social Education* (January, 1975) and *Ethics* (April, 1982), in every issue of the *Journal of Moral Education* and *Moral Education Forum,* in a recent AERA symposium on moral and social education (Nucci, Berkowitz, Power, & Smetana, 1984), and in the *Handbook of Child Psychology* (Rest, 1984). It has stirred the interest of political theorists (Damico, 1982), social psychologists (Vallacher & Solodky, 1979; Rholes, Bailey, & McMillan, 1982), curriculum experts (Galbraith & Jones, 1975), correctional personnel (Ventre, 1982), and business management specialists (Nichols & Day, 1982). It is most clear, then, that the influence of the Kohlbergian tradition has continued to increase over the years (Lapsley & Serlin, 1984), as it remains central to the thinking of educational planners and those concerned with adolescent development.

According to Kohlberg, how one reasons about moral dilemmas undergoes structural transformation with development, transformations that can be characterized in terms of a stage sequence. The sequence is held to be universal, invariant, and descriptive of qualitative changes in moral thought. Each successive stage is said to be more differentiated and articulated than previous stages, employing operations that are reversible and better equilibrated. Hence each stage advance yields psychologically more adequate modes of thought.

But not only are successive stages *psychologically* more adequate, they are also more adequate *morally* as well, according to Kohlberg (1985; Kohlberg *et al.*, 1983; Boyd, 1986; but see Reed & Hanna, 1982; Rosen, 1980). Each successive stage can be seen as an endorsement of an increasingly more adequate moral scheme for reciprocating benefits and obligations (Rest, 1984). Indeed, the attractiveness of Kohlberg's theory for educators is precisely its claim for the *moral* adequacy of the highest stages of development. When it can be shown that moral thoughts is related (somewhat) to moral behavior (Blasi, 1980; Rest, 1984), interest in Kohlberg's theory increases all the more. Thus, by our interventions, we intend not only to increase the psychological complexity of student reasoning about social dilemmas, but we intend most of all to increase the power of their *moral* reflection and to improve their moral conducts as well (Lapsley & Quintana, 1985).

The plus-one convention is the prototypic Kohlbergian intervention (Blatt & Kohlberg, 1975; Berkowitz, 1981; Turiel, 1966). The plus-one strategy assumes that development is motivated by cognitive conflict that results from exposure to reasoning that is one stage (+1) above the student's current level of reasoning. While the plus-one technique seems as popular as ever, the implementation of moral education programs are nonetheless becoming more diversified (Nucci, 1985a). For example, we are now seeing more attention devoted to communicative patterns in moral discussion (Berkowitz, 1985; Berkowitz & Gibbs, 1983; Berkowitz, Gibbs, & Broughton, 1980; Damon & Killen, 1982) and to the "moral atmosphere" of high schools (Kohlberg, 1985; Power, 1984; Higgins, Power, & Kohlberg, 1983). Many practitioners have become more eclectic in their use of intervention techniques (Boyd, 1981; Ventre, 1982; Arbuthnot, 1984; Galbraith & Jones, 1975; Wonderly & Kupfersmid, 1980). More concern is evidenced for educational interventions that are sensitive to more delimited domains of justice, such as children's understanding of fair distribution (Damon & Killen, 1982; Enright, Colby & McMullin, 1977) or punishment (Lapsley & Quintana, 1985; Lapsley & Madar, 1983) and to the distinction between moral and social conventional rules (Nucci, 1982; Smetana, 1983). Alternative assessments of moral thought are being developed (Gibbs, Widaman, & Colby, 1982), as well as alternative explanations for intervention effects (Rholes *et al.,* 1982).

The variety of recent approaches to moral education is obviously a healthy development in that it gives educators more flexibility in designing programs for adolescents. Adolescence is a particularly fertile period for intervention since much of a child's moral development can be expected to occur during this part of the lifespan. During adolescence a child will begin to engage in conventional levels of moral reasoning, and the goal of interventions is to motivate this development and to consolidate developmental gains. The purpose of this chapter is to critically examine these very recent developments in moral and social education, with the modest hope that the issues and problems that confront educators will become more clear. For the most part we will not be covering old ground. There are more comprehensive reviews available (e.g., Enright *et al.,* 1983a,b) that examine the plus-one convention, deliberate psychological education, didactic instruction and information-processing strategies, and just community research. Our intent will be to highlight those programs that have not been covered in previous reviews and to follow up on topics that have been previously reviewed. We will proceed by examining recent research on (1) the plus-one convention, (2) transactive discussion, and (3) moral atmosphere approaches to moral education.

The Plus-one Convention: Variations and Problems

Variations: The Plus-two Convention?

As noted above, the plus-one strategy assumes that development is motivated by exposure to arguments that are structured at the stage just above (+1) the student's current level of reasoning. Arguments structured at the stage just below (−1) the student's current stage of reasoning are rejected as inadequate, while arguments structured two stages (+2) above the student's level are not sufficiently comprehended. The actual implementation of the +1 convention may assume a variety of forms. For example, the +1 strategy may be structured or unstructured, adult directed or peer directed. Treatments may consist of discussion or role-play episodes, or a combination of discussion and role playing. The length of the interventions may vary from a single session to multiple sessions over the course of many weeks. In a review of 28 plus-one intervention studies, Enright *et al.* (1983a) found that all but four were successful in demonstrating significant moral development as assessed by Kohlberg's Moral Judgment Interview. The +1 literature suggests that educators should expect changes of one-third to one-half of a stage as a result of this intervention.

However, while the extant literature suggests that the +1 convention is a methodologically sound and proven intervention technique, recent research has called into question several key assumptions underlying the technique. Walker (1982), in a study designed to examine the sequentiality assumptions of Kohlberg's stages of moral development, attempted to experimentally induce regression and stage skipping. After initial assessments of cognitive, perspective-taking, and moral development, fifth-through seventh-grade children were exposed in a brief role-playing episode to one of the following treatment situations: (1) conflicting opinions supported by −1 reasoning, (2) conflicting opinions supported by +1 reasoning, (3) conflicting opinions supported by +2 reasoning, (4) consonant opinions supported by own-stage reasoning, or (5) no-treatment control condition. Walker (1982) found that the results clearly support the claim that the sequence of moral stages is invariant and that movement is always in the direction of the next higher stage. Thus there was no evidence of stage regression or stage skipping. The intervention produced robust development (about half a stage) that generalized to nontrained materials, the effect of which was still evident on a delayed posttest.

A most interesting finding, and one that is incongruous with Kohlberg's theory, is that exposure to +2 stage reasoning was found to be just as effective as exposure to +1 reasoning. As Walker (1982) points out, exposure to +2 reasoning did not induce +2 reasoning, only increases in +1 reasoning. Again, all development was in the direction of the next higher stage. Walker (1982) accounts for the effectiveness of +2 reasoning by suggesting that subjects did not *really* understand +2 argumentation. What they may have done was to distort +2 reasoning into +1 terms. Thus, "It is possible that +2 reasoning is disorted to the +1 stage, a stage that can be understood and assimilated. The subjects' reinterpretation of +2 reasoning may be due to the fact that they had attained cognitive and perspective-taking prerequisits only for the +1 stage, which limits their comprehension of higher stage reasoning'' (Walker, 1982, p. 1335).

This is an interesting conjecture, but one that presupposes the validity of the sequentiality assumptions. Since subjects are not *supposed* to be moved by +2 reasoning, what actually happens (it is argued) is that +2 reasoning is assimilated into +1 stage terms. Thus, according to this explanation, whenever one observes developmental effects due to a +2 treatment, one is actually observing the effect of a + treatment. One could also argue, however, that these results support the contention that individuals understand moral arguments across a range of moral stages (Rest, 1984), not just those arguments structured at +1. According to this view +2 treatments are effective for the very reason that +1 arguments are effective—they reveal inadequacies in one's current stage of reasoning. A more recent study, however, casts doubt on this latter interpretation. Walker, de Vries, and Bichard (1984) found that moral stages are indeed hierarchical in nature. While higher stage statements are preferred over lower stage statements, understanding of the moral stage statements is limited to one stage above the subject's own. Future research will need to clarify the mechanism by which any plus-stage treatment produces its effect. Fortunately for educators, they may not have to wait until these results are in, because the putative effectiveness of +2 treatments (whatever the mechanism) suggests that teachers need not be overly concerned with presenting +1 stage reasoning in moral education programs, a requirement that is inordinately difficult to carry out. According to Walker (1982, p. 1335), ''these findings indicate that such a close 'match' is unnecessary, and that +2 reasoning is also effective.'' It should perhaps be noted, however, that comprehension of +1 reasoning may be effective only for those subjects who already possess the cognitive and perspective-taking prerequisites for moral advancement.

One additional aspect of the Walker (1982) study deserves comment. He found that the effects of plus-stage treatments were stable after 7 weeks. The finding that experimentally induced effects are stable on a delayed posttest is usually an indication that a genuine structural change has taken place. If this interpretation is correct, then Walker (1982) was able to effect structural change by using a single 30-minute role-playing episode where adults modeled the different levels of reasoning as per condition.

The problem is that structural change is not supposed to be amenable to simple one-trial interventions, at least in theory. Thus, according to Berkowitz (1981), ''It is clear from the theoretical literature that one should not expect such a manipulation to have a developmental effect. Moral stage development is a slow process which includes both maturation of the individual and his/her experience in a dialectical integration (p. 21).

Yet the empirical literature is equivocal concerning the effectiveness of short-term interventions. Schlaefli *et al.* (1985), for example, in a meta-analysis of 55 intervention studies [most of which are unpublished dissertations, all of which assessed moral reasoning with the Defining Issues Test (DIT)], found that discussion programs of 0–3 weeks duration were generally ineffective in motivating moral development. On the other hand, there are numerous studies that find that brief (one-trial) interventions are also effective (e.g., Keasey, 1973; Arbuthnot, 1975; Walker, 1980, 1982; Walker & Richards, 1979). Thus after scores of intervention studies, we are still left with a serious conceptual conundrum. We intend with our interventions to effect structural change, but we often do so with intervention durations that cannot, in theory, be expected to produce such changes. If the theoretical literature, then, gives us no reason to believe that brief interventions can be effective, what are we to make of research that presumes to show exactly that?

Two options seem obvious. We can either decide that the findings from brief interventions are methodological artifacts, or we can presume that Kohlberg's theory of moral structure is incorrect (e.g., Flanagan, 1982). Neither alternative seems particularly attractive. While partisans of the Kohlbergian approach generally opt for the former alternative, it is also true that many of these studies (e.g., Walker, 1982; Walker & Richards, 1979) offer rather convincing support for other features of the Kohlbergian stage theory. To choose the latter option would seriously undermine the rationale for engaging in Kohlbergian moral education in the first place.

The current impasse over how to interpret evidence from brief interventions is perhaps symptomatic of the theoretical ambiguity surrounding the notion of "cognitive conflict," which is presumed to be elicited in plus-stage moral programming. What is needed is a clarification of this change mechanism. Haan (1985) argues that moral development "seems to rise out of the emotional, interactive experience of moral–social conflict and not from the cognitive experience of finding that one's reasoning [is] in disagreement with another's higher stage thinking" (p. 1005). In other words, advances in moral reasoning result not from (private, internal) *cognitive* disequilibrium, that is, from sensing that one's solutions are not as adequate as another's, but rather from *social* disequilibrium, that is, from the attempt to equalize (mutual, interactive) social relationships and experience. In support of this view, Haan (1985) found that playing moral games was more effective in advancing moral thought than was the discussion of hypothetical dilemmas. Further, while cognitive disequilibrium was pronounced, it had little effect on moral reasoning.

It is entirely possible that the effectiveness of plus-stage interventions lies not so much in the elicitation of cognitive conflict but in how conflict is managed or expressed in moral discourse; in how disparate moral opinions are manipulated in a "zone of proximal development" during an ongoing-dialogic interaction. Some support for this view is found in Crockenberg and Nicolayev (1979), who found that cognitive conflict may be only tenuously related to stage change. Similarly, Damon and Killen (1984) found that sociocognitive conflict tended to retard, and not promote, positive justice stage change. In this study, stage change was associated with a stage of peer interaction that was "characterized by a reciprocal quality of acceptance of transformation of one another's ideas" (Damon & Killen, 1982, p. 365). Hence an emphasis on communicative styles in peer interactions may permit us to specify with greater precision the conditions for change in moral discussion interventions, conditions that may have little to do with intervention duration. While this is an empirical question, of course, it is interesting to note that in the Damon and Killen (1982) study, children in the belief duration groups tended to change more than children in the long duration groups. This suggests that what may be more important than the duration of interventions is the quality of peer communicative interactions. Indeed, Haan argues that what develops in moral development is not moral understanding but rather the skills and resources that allow social conflict to be resolved. What is crucial "may be tolerance for conflict and the skills of conflict resolution that allow tension to be endured long enough for disputants to draw on their past experience, invent possibilities, and mutually determine the legitimacy of one another's self-interest to reach mutual resolution of their discord" (Haan, 1985, p. 1006). We will next consider a relatively new line of research within the Kohlbergian tradition that examines not only the quality of peer discourse and its relation to moral stage change but also with greater specificity the sufficient conditions for change in + convention.

Variations: Transactive Discussion and the Plus-one-third Convention (?)

In the Walker (1982) study it was found that the +1 convention may not be the optimal stage disparity for motivating moral development, inasmuch as +2 reasoning was found to be just as effective. In a new twist on the moral discussion paradigm, Marvin Berkowitz and his colleagues (Berkowitz, 1980, 1981, 1985; Berkowitz *et al.,* 1980; Berkowitz & Gibbs,

1983) found that the optimal stage disparity may actually be *one-third* of a stage, rather than +1 (or +2). In one study, Berkowitz *et al.* (1980) manipulated the stage disparity between dyad partners (college undergraduates) on the basis of pretest scores on the Moral Judgment Interview (MJI). By using the most recent MJI scoring procedures, the authors were able to stage-type dyadic partners into major and minor moral stages. Three levels of stage disparity were employed. The *no-stage disparity* condition included partners who were either *both* at Stage 3, or *both* at Stage 3 with a minor Stage 4 [i.e., 3(4)]. The *low-stage disparity* condition consisted of dyads where one partner was at Stage 3 while the other was State 3(4). The *high-stage disparity* condition consisted of one partner at Stage 3 while the other was Stage 4(3), or one partner at Stage 3 and the other at Stage 4 (full-stage disparity). What is unique about this study is not only the use of mixed stage types, but also the fact that it adopted an experimenter-free, leaderless peer interaction approach. After subjects were matched with a dyad partner as per condition, they were left alone to come to some agreement about the solution to a number of preselected moral dilemmas. As the authors point out, this procedure is similar to the one employed in the cognitive domain whereby conserving and nonconserving children (for example) are paired and asked to reach a consensus about the solution to a conservation task. Unlike the Walker (1982) study, the experimental sessions here were multiple and lengthy. The experimental treatments consisted of five 1-hour discussions that took place over the course of 2 months. The only posttest was administered 2 weeks following the completion of the discussion sessions. Again, evidence of developmental gains on a delayed posttest is presumed to reflect structural change.

Berkowitz *et al.* (1980) found that the degree of stage disparity among dyadic partners was indeed the most important factor promoting moral stage advance, and that the optimal disparity was one-third of a stage (Low Disparity condition). "No such pronounced effect was evidenced when the partners were more advanced by two-thirds to a full stage (High Disparity condition; cf. the '+1' condition frequently used in the literature, e.g., Turiel, 1966), when partners were at the same stage (No Disparity condition), or when subjects did not engage in any discussion (Control condition)" (Berkowitz *et al.*, 1980, p. 352).

When this important finding is compared to Walker's (1982) claim regarding the efficacy of +2 reasoning, educators may understandably feel that *any* plus-stage (+1, +2, +1/3) interventions technique, for any length of time, can be effective in promoting moral development. While this may be true, there are still difficult theoretical questions that need to be addressed. For example, Berkowitz *et al.* (1980) argue that in order for plus-stage manipulations to be effective there must be some overlap between the stage being moved *from* and the stage being moved *to*. That is, +1 interventions are effective only to the extent that the subject already uses +1 reasoning as a minor stage. But this would not explain the effectiveness of Walker's (1982) +2 condition, where there is obviously no overlap between adjacent stages. Fortunately, educators need not wait until the evidence is in our questions such as this one. The literature is clear that plus-stage interventions are effective, (Rest, Turiel & Kohlberg, 1969; Blatt & Kohlberg, 1975), though the precise reason for this effectiveness has yet to be determined.

One may well ask how a plus-1/3 strategy is to be implemented in a moral education program. While it is obviously possible to score (stage-type) responses into minor stages, we doubt whether teachers would be able to phrase responses at that level. This assumes, of course, that teachers should play the principle role in inducing cognitive conflict, but this is not the approach favored by Berkowitz (1981). He argues that teachers should facilitate student interaction and maintain a suitable atmosphere for the exchange of ideas. But they need not phrase arguments at any plus-stage. The interaction of peers in a sufficiently heterogeneous class should insure that a range of moral opinions will be represented in the discussion.

In a second study Berkowitz and Gibbs (1983) attempted to clarify the process by which moral discussions seem to effect moral development. The authors analyzed the discourse features of 30 dyads of young adults who discussed the solution to moral dilemmas (from the MJI). Of the 30 dyads, 16 showed stage change in moral development, while the remaining 14 dyads did not change. According to the authors, moral advance was associated with a style of "reasoning . . . that operates on the reasoning of another" (p. 402). Berkowitz and Gibbs (1983) termed such reasoning *transactive discussion*. They argue that

> moral stage development results from discussion in which each member engages in the reasoning of his/her discussion partners with his/her own reasoning. Rather than merely providing consecutive assertions, discussants 'operate' on each other's reasoning. In a very dialectical sense one's own reasoning confronts the other's antithetical reasoning in an ongoing dialogic dynamic. (Berkowitz & Gibbs, 1983, p. 402).

The authors identified 18 types of transactive behavior. Transactive behavior can be one of two types: It can *represent* another's reasoning (e.g., feedback request, paraphrase, justification request, dyad paraphrase, etc.) or it can *operate* upon the reasoning of the other (e.g., clarification, contradiction, competitive extension, common ground–integration, comparative critique, etc.). Operational transacts are assumed to be more sophisticated discussion patterns than are representational transacts. The authors found that transactive discussion, particularly operational transacts, are developmentally effective in motivating moral stage change. Indeed, they found that transactive discussion is the single best predictor of stage change, and it shares almost no variance with stage disparity between dyad partners, which was also a significant predictor of stage change.

To our knowledge this is the first study to apply a structural-process analysis to moral discussion. The evident importance of transactive features in moral discussions would seem to entail another set of recommendations for educators. In order to maximize the benefits of moral discussion one should attend to the communication (language and listening) skills of the student participants. Berkowitz (1984) suggests that interventions may be jeopardized because students often have substandard vocabularies, which contributes to their inability to engage in transactive communication. Indeed, in the Berkowitz and Gibbs (1983) study, operational transacts accounted for only 17.8% of all statements in the change dyads (as compared to 12.9% in the no-change dyads, a statistically significant difference). Given that both children and adolescents have difficulty conducting "good" discussions generally (F. Danner, personal communication, 1984), it would also seem worthwhile to instruct students in the use of operational transacts and in the conduct of group discussions, in order to enhance the effectiveness of moral discussion programs. This requirement would seem to be crucial particularly in light of Berkowitz' (1981; Berkowitz et al., 1980) promotion of leaderless discussion groups, where peer interactions provide the context for spurring moral development.

In sum, the research of Berkowitz and his colleagues suggests that the optimal stage disparity in moral discussions may be only one-third of a stage and that transactive discourse is a powerful predictor of moral stage advance. Further, peer-led discussions appear to be a viable moral education technique, with the important proviso that students must possess an optimal level of communication skills and that the class is sufficiently heterogeneous to insure that plus-stage reasoning is represented in the discussion.

Moral Atmosphere

A most important variation evident in the moral education literature concerns the "moral atmosphere" in which moral decisions are made (Kohlberg, 1985; Power, Kohlberg, & Higgins, 1989; Kohlberg, Scharf, &

Hickey, 1972; Kohlberg, Kauffman, Scharf, & Hickey, 1975). Moral atmosphere is said to be the educational bridge between moral judgment and moral action (Reimer & Power, 1980; Power & Reimer, 1978). According to this view an educational environment that provides the context for participatory democracy should give students a greater stake in resolving sociomoral dilemmas. Students should develop a greater sense of responsibility and a view of the school as a caring community. Further, "Students would develop shared or collective norms of helping, of trust, and of active participation on behalf of the group, norms supported by a sense of community or of a valued sense of group solidarity and cohesion" (Higgins *et al.,* 1983, p. 2). The moral atmosphere approach is greatly influenced by Durkheim's (1961) theory of moral education, which asserts that groups develop attachments (to the group) and that collective norms evolve from group activity itself. Thus, one could characterize the development of collective norms of sharing, trust, and responsibility in stage terms that are independent of the moral reasoning level of individuals.

A number of alternative schools, or "just communities," have been established as an intervention to examine the effects of moral atmosphere on moral reasoning and conduct. The task in just-community interventions is to cultivate a given level of normative collective responsibility so that it serves as a crucible around which individuals adapt, and as a motivator for advancing an individual's level of moral reasoning.

This approach assumes that the building of collective norms and ideas of community at advanced stages would promote morally better student action (Higgins *et al.,* 1983). Moral judgments are often made in group contexts, and the demand characteristics of groups often encourage or inhibit moral action. Hence, if we are interested in motivating the development of advanced levels of moral reasoning then there must be environmental support for such reasoning. A group decision-making context that emphasizes participatory democracy and a "just community" based on collective norms of caring and trust is the social support of a "moral atmosphere," an atmosphere that is considered crucial for developing judgments of responsibility and, in turn, serves as the bridge between moral thought and moral action (Higgins *et al.,* 1983; Kohlberg, 1985).

The moral atmosphere approach is certainly a welcome addition to the moral education literature. More than any other approach it emphasizes the social basis of moral reasoning and its critical impact on moral action, a matter of some concern to educators. As noted in a previous review (Enright *et al.,* 1983a), the just-community strategy is the most ambitious and most promising of all the moral education strategies, though its effectiveness is the least well documented. Much of the supportive evidence comes from attempts to implement just communities in prison settings (e.g., Kohlberg *et al.*, 1972), though there have been more recent attempts to evaluate its effectiveness in educational programs designed for adolescents.

In one study Maul (1981) attempted to determine how students evaluated the moral atmosphere of a high school devoted to intensive education (Gil/St. Bernard's in rural New Jersey), and whether this school environment had a beneficial effect upon the students' development of moral reasoning. Intensive education is a pedagogical technique whereby students take but a single course over an extended period of time, in contrast to the more traditional approach where students take a variety of courses in units of 50-minute periods. In an intensive education school, the day is restructured to allow longer periods both for work and for socializing. According to Maul (1981):

> Each class had complete flexibility in planning its own schedule. Thus a small independent community emerged, the class. . . . However, as with any circumstance where you put a number of students together for long periods of time, conflicts developed. These conflicts had to be solved by the class if it was to function. Such conflicts could not be solved by the teacher apart from the class. Thus, students were exposed to discussions of right and wrong, and fairness to the group, of the concept of individual freedom and responsibility which were inherent in their greater opportunities for independence and for group decision-making. (p. 11)

The intensive time schedule also led to a mixture of grade levels. This insured that class discussion would include a variety of stages of role taking as well as moral reasoning. Hence the intensive education program involves (1) opportunities for role taking, (2) a moderately discrepant environment, (3) the actual experienced of sociomoral conflict, (4) reciprocal relationships not based on status or authority, and (5) a sense of fellowship and community. Maul (1981) hypothesized that the positive effect of an intensive education program on moral reasoning and on the perception of moral atmosphere would vary as a function of the number of years that a student attended Gil/St. Bernard's. The longer a student attended, the more beneficial would be the effect of the program on moral reasoning and on the perceived atmosphere of the school. And, indeed, across two samples, Maul (1981) found that the number of years that an adolescent attended Gil/St. Bernard's was significantly correlated with moral reasoning (the DIT and MJI were both employed). In addition, the longer one was in attendance, the more one felt a strong sense of community and the more one felt that the role structure was fair.

These results must be viewed cautiously, however. Our reanalysis of the data (based on summary statistics) reveals that a quadratic relation existed between grade and years in attendance, a correlation that is of the same magnitude as the linear relation between these variables. This indicates that the amount of variance due to grade that remains after partialing grade is about as large as the amount of variance that is statistically removed. Thus the resulting significant correlation between moral reasoning and years-in-attendance may be spuriously high because of their common correlation with grade (age). Our calculations also show that if the intervention is at all effective, exposure to it must be at least of 2 years duration, with the important caveat that advances in moral reasoning were accompanied by declines in SAT verbal and math scores. Hence intensive education seems to have a deleterious effect on standard measures of achievement. We doubt whether educators will find this to be an acceptable trade-off. Finally, because the moral atmosphere findings were treated rather anecdotally, there is no indication of how perceptions of moral atmosphere related to moral reasoning. While the students' favorable perception of the moral atmosphere of the school is itself a favorable outcome of intensive education, no conclusion is possible concerning its impact on actual moral deliberation.

Jennings and Kohlberg (1983) attempted to determine the effects of a just-community program on the moral development of youth offenders and whether this program was superior to alternative treatment approaches. The just-community program consisted of 10 adolescents (aged 12–17) who lived in an unlocked residential home and attended a public day school. "The heart of the just community programme was the weekly community meeting. In its first weeks the community meeting was primarily used to make and change rules and [to] develop a 'constitution'. Later, meetings were used to discuss issues of rule enforcement, as well as interpersonal issues and conflicts" (Jennings & Kohlberg, 1983, p. 36). The alternative treatment programs included two behavior modification programs (an "open" versus a "secure" program) and a transactional analysis program. Moral atmosphere data were collected from residents in all four programs.

The authors found that after a 9-month treatment period the just-community residents had an average gain of 35 moral maturity points, which is about the magnitude of change one would expect from a "good" moral discussion group. The transactional analysis program ($n = 4$) motivated no change in moral maturity, while the behavior modification programs averaged a (statistically nonsignificant) mean change of 15 moral maturity points. An overall test of mean changes for the three programs demonstrated the superiority of the just-community approach over both the behavior modification and transactional analysis programs.

However, these findings did not survive an analysis of covariance. This analysis was required to determine if the just-community posttest scores were due to regression to the mean. The results showed that while the just community was still superior to transactional analysis (the small n in the transactional analysis group surely limited the power of the test), there was *no* significant difference between the just-community and the behavior modification programs ($p < .10$), the authors' claims notwithstanding.

This finding makes it difficult to evaluate the moral atmosphere data. While just-community residents rated the moral atmosphere of their treatment program in more positive terms than did the alternative treatment programs, one can argue that there is no necessary relation between moral atmosphere and moral reasoning. This is so given (1) there was no significant difference between just-community and behavior modification change scores on the MJI and (2) the relatively poor evaluation of the moral atmosphere of the behavior modification groups. Since the just community was not (statistically) superior to the behavior modification group on the MJI posttest, one cannot make any interesting claims regarding the effects of the superior moral atmosphere of the just-community group or the deleterious effect of the inferior atmosphere of the behavior modification program. Consequently, Jennings and Kohlberg (1983) offer no evidence for the benefits of moral atmosphere and none for the greater effectiveness of the just-community approach over behavior modifications.

Perhaps the most comprehensive, and most favorable, study on the effectiveness of moral atmosphere on moral thought and action is reported by Higgins *et al.* (1983; also, Power *et al.,* 1989; Kohlberg, 1985). This study represents a shift in focus in moral education research, a shift from depicting the context-free, general structures of development to the study of moral reasoning in the context of the school. Students in three regular high schools (Brookline, Cambridge, Scarsdale) and three democratic just communities (School-Within-A-School, Cluster School, Scarsdale just-community school) were asked to evaluate four practical moral dilemmas. Practical moral dilemmas are those that involve not only principles of justice and prescriptive judgments (as in "classical" moral dilemmas) but also further considerations that are more descriptive and factual in nature. The dilemmas were scored for judgments of responsibility, for stages of responsibility judgments, for the degree of collectiveness of norms and of community valuing, and for stages of collective normative values and the sense of community valuing. Higgins *et al.* (1983) found that students in the democratic schools were higher in the content of their school-dilemma choices (favoring prosocial responsibility) and in their mode of judgment (making more judgments of responsibility at higher stages of judgment) than regular high school controls. In general, students in democratic just communities were about one-half stage higher than controls both in practical school deontic judgments and in judgments of school responsibility. Students in alternative schools were superior to controls in the frequency of responsibility judgments, in the degree of collectiveness of norms, and in the degree of community valuing. When students were asked if they believed their peers felt that they should act prosocially, 80% of the democratic students agreed versus 40% of the students in the regular high schools. In predicting their peers' behavior, about 60% of the just-community students felt that their peers would act consistently with their prosocial choice versus about 40% of the regular high school controls. The authors "interpret these differences in practical moral judgment as due to the differential moral atmospheres of the democratic and comparison schools. The democratic schools have a high sense of collective prosocial norms and a strong sense of community" (Higgins *et al.*, 1983, p. 49).

It is interesting to note that the enriched moral atmospheres of the alternative schools did not necessarily lead to superior performance on classical moral dilemmas. For example, only 12 moral maturity points separated Brookline High School students from their counterparts in the democratic alternative School-Within-A-School, and only 18 moral maturity points separated Cluster School students from their counterparts in Cambridge High School. However, the authors do report that the yearly average change in Cambridge High School and the Scarsdale democratic alternative school was one-fourth of a stage, which is about the amount of change to be expected from a good moral discussion intervention. The average yearly advance for control subjects was not reported.

The Higgins *et al.* (1983) study represents an important advance in the moral education literature. It reorients educators to seek an understanding of how practical moral issues are resolved in school contexts and to seek outcome measures using indices other than the MJI. The success of interventions are to be sought instead in other types of stage developments, in stages of responsibility and practical deliberate judgment and in stages of collective normative values and the sense of community valuing (Kohlberg, 1985; Power *et al.*, 1989). These assessments are said to be more sensitive to the influence of the social context of the school than the MJI, which presents dilemmas that are devoid of complicating contextual factors.

There are, however, a number of issues that still need to be more fully explicated. For example in each of the studies reviewed here it was asserted that the effects of the intervention were equivalent to what one should expect from a good moral discussion program. The obvious question, then, is why not just conduct moral discussion programs? Educators would surely find the implementation of discussion programs to be less taxing than the formation of just communities and democratic alternative schools.

One response is to note that while the magnitude of stage change in just communities may be modest, it may also be more pervasive. In his dissertation Clark Power (1979) has shown, for example, that a just-community intervention developmentally advances a greater number of lower stage children than is the case for moral discussion programs. If this is the case, the just-community approach may prove to be the intervention with the greatest developmental impact in the sense that more students are positively affected by the program. It should again be emphasized that the just community also attempts to develop a sense of social responsibility, which is thought to translate moral judgment into action. Indeed, Kohlberg (1985; see also Gibbs, Clark, Joseph, Green, Goobrick, & Makowski, 1986) argues that moral advocacy against practical school problems such as cheating, stealing, school absence, and drug use is most compelling when it devolves from an appeal to the requirements of community and justice (cf. Niles, 1986). Hence, the success of the intervention must also be appraised in light of this standard as well.

This raises another issue. There is the impression that democratic moral education is most concerned with how adolescents resolve practical school dilemmas as a function of different types of school organizations or of a given collectivity of norms. It is not clear how this orientation helps individuals resolve real-life dilemmas in the absence of group norms and values beyond the organization of the school or even in the face of the pressure of group norms and values. According to Higgins *et al.* (1983), "Moral action usually takes place in a social or group context and that context usually has a profound influence on the moral decision-making of individuals. Individual moral decisions in real life are almost always made in the context of group norms or group decision-making processes" (p. 2). Yet one may argue that moral decisions are rarely made in *a* group context. Rather, individuals may belong and be committed to a plurality of groups in diverse contexts, where a variety of value alternatives may be evident. The adjudication of these claims may require principled levels of moral reasoning, though its difficult to know how the moral atmosphere approach, with its emphasis on the collective, can motivate development to this end. In addition, is it not possible to feel a sense of community valuing, a sense of caring, trust, and committment, in a group devoted to antisocial ends? If true, a moral atmosphere would thus seem capable of advancing equally the aims of both a just community and a street gang.

What may rescue this approach from "communal relativism" is the stage dimension, which developmentally orders group norms (e.g., caring, trust, degree of collectiveness) on the basis of stage criteria used to order individual moral judgments (C. Power, personal communication,

July 31, 1984). Presumably a just community would resonate toward "higher" stages of group caring, trust, sense of committment, and degree of collectiveness than would, say, a delinquent street gang. Further research will need to clarify not only the stage dimensions of collective stage development but also how the latter affects the acquisition of principled moral reasoning.

A final criticism is that the just-community approach blurs the distinction between moral prescriptions and social conventional thought (Nucci, 1984b). Social conventions are specific to the social context, alterable by consensus, relative to a group (Geiger & Turiel, 1983). Moral prescriptions are not validated by consensus, are not contextually defined, and are not relative to a given social group. Hence it is difficult to know how the emphasis on practical school issues bound by the context of a specific group (a just community) can be faithful to the training of distinctly moral decision making, which requires judgments to rise above context and consensus. In addition, Nucci (1982, 1984b, 1988) has argued that values education should focus on multiple acquisitions of social understanding and that social knowledge cannot be simply reduced to issues of morality. In addition to morality, social understanding includes knowledge of convention and a personal domain, each of which constitutes a distinct conceptual and development system (Nucci, 1981). According to Nucci (1984b), "the 'Just Community' approach, like other prevailing approaches to values education, is based on a theory of social growth which does not adequately account for the development of the student's concepts of morality, convention, or personal perogative" (p. 4). These domains tend to be conflated in discussions of practical school issues. As a remedy Nucci (1982) favors an approach that he calls "domain appropriate" values education. To this we now turn.

Social Education

One of the most important innovations in the domain of social cognitive development has been the emergence of social conventional reasoning (e.g., Turiel, 1977, 1978; Tisak & Turiel, 1984; Smetana, 1983, 1985; Nucci, 1982). Reasoning about social conventions is assumed to represent a domain distinct from moral reasoning proper, though the stage assumptions of conventional reasoning follow the strictures of structural developmentalism. Hence it is possible to subsume this domain under the broad theoretical umbrella of the cognitive–developmental approach (Enright, Lapsley, & Olson, 1986).

According to this approach, conventional rules involve behavioral regularities, they are established through convention to regulate the actions of others in a social system. In addition, conventional rules are arbitrary and involve no prescription. It is a conventional rule, for example, for individuals not to eat food with their fingers, for children not to address teachers by their first name, or to chew gum in class, or to talk without first raising their hands. Moral rules, on the other hand, are not arbitrary and do indeed involve prescription. They are not established through social consensus but rather are obligatory, universally applicable, and impersonal (Turiel, 1983). Rules that govern lying, stealing, and aggression, for example, are *moral* rules, since violation of these rules affronts ethical standards of conscience that exist apart from the pressure of consensus and convention. Hence, moral judgments are structured by conceptualizations of justice, while conventional judgments are structured by conceptualizations of social organization.

The bulk of the research on social conventional reasoning has been devoted to demonstrating the empirical independence of this domain from moral reasoning and to showing that even young children implicitly make the domain distinction. In two studies, for example (Nucci & Turiel, 1978; Nucci & Nucci, 1982), children were questioned about spontaneously occurring moral and conventional transgressions. The children were asked, "What if there was no rule in the school about (the observed event), would it be all right to do it then?" The results indicated that approximately 80% of the subjects at each grade felt that the social conventional act would be appropriate if no rule existed to prohibit it, while over 85% of the children at each grade stated that moral transgressions would not be right even if there were no rules to prohibit it. These results support the notion that moral and conventional domains are conceptually distinct. Actions are evaluated within the moral domain on the basis of their intrinsic features (e.g., justice, harm), while conventional acts are evaluated in terms of their status as regulations within a social context (Nucci, 1982). In general, then, actions within the conventional domain are judged as wrong only if a social rule or norm exists prohibiting the action, while moral transgressions are universally held to be wrong even in the absence of consensual norms. Further, children's understanding of conventional regulation is presumed to undergo stage development. In social conventional reasoning, each successive level progressively coordinates "increasingly broad aspects of the relationship between shared uniformities in social behavior and the organization of individuals' interactions within social systems or collectives" (Nucci, 1982, p. 106). That is, the development of social conventional concepts involves the progressive understanding that conventions involve shared knowledge of uniformities and that the uniformities serve to coordinate social interactions.

Nucci (1982, 1988) has recently addressed the implications that this domain has for values education. He argues (as noted earlier) that contemporary values education is limited in its failure to coordinate the teaching of social values with students' differentiated conceptions of morality and convention. It is domain inappropriate, for example, to generate moral discussion around the issue of dress codes, since the latter falls within the domain of social convention (Nucci, 1988). Similarly, one would not be well advised to advance knowledge of social conventions by consideration of moral dilemmas. It is often the case, however, that conceptions of morality are conflated in discussions of sociomoral dilemmas, with issues of great complexity usually being reduced to the morality component. Nucci (1982) urges that values instruction be coordinated with domain, since conceptions of justice and convention are constructed out of qualitatively distinct forms of interaction. Hence the aim of a social conventional intervention is

> to move students through the progression of stages in conceptions of convention toward a coordinated understanding of the importance of convention for the organization and coordination of social interactions within social systems. As a result students should be able to comprehend the function of these arbitrarily designated traditions and customs for the maintenance of cultural organization and cultural continuity, while appreciating the ways in which variations in convention serve to define differing cultural patterns both across and within systems as a function of the shifting consensual values over time. (Nucci, 1982, p. 107)

Again, this emphasis is required because the natural epistemology of the child is sensitive to the moral–conventional distinction, and therefore values education must necessarily follow suit (Nucci, in press).

While there is an increasing amount of research on the educational implications of this domain, we are aware of no published research on the effectiveness of a social convention program as a stage-advancing intervention. It is interesting to note that the early attempts at moral intervention were designed not so much to effect an educational program but to test the sequentiality assumptions of the Kohlbergian stage sequence (e.g., Turiel, 1966; Rest *et al.*, 1969). Similar "intervention tests" of the social conventional sequence do not seem to be available as yet. As a result we know relatively little about the empirical integrity of the sequence (Turiel, 1978; Geiger & Turiel, 1983), at least when compared to other social cognitive developmental sequences. There is some evidence that reasoning in the societal domain is unrelated to Piagetian logical development (Nucci, n.d.). This suggests that the traditional cognitive-development (Piagetian) approach to intervention may not be an appropriate model for stage-advancing interventions for conventional reasoning. Presumably educators are being urged to do more than just be sensitive to issues of conventionality in values education courses. The implicit recommendation is that students should (also) be moved to higher levels of social conventional understanding. Intervention tests would provide valuable information on the nature of transition mechanisms and provide guidelines for the design of appropriate stage-advancing educational programs.

We already have had occasion to mention some of the educational implications of the social conventional domain. Values education should be domain appropriate and coordinated with developmental level. Two recent studies provide evidence for another feature of the domain, the role that social conventional understanding plays in disruptive school behavior and in classroom management. Geiger and Turiel (1983) were interested in the relation between disruptive school behavior (e.g., violations of classroom regulations, defiance of school authorities) and levels of social conventional reasoning in early adolescence. The authors hypothesized that the disruptive behavior of junior high school students would be related to the transition *from* Level 3 (affirmation of the rule system) to Level 4 (negation of convention as part of the rule system) in the social conventional stage sequence, a stage where the validity of rules and authoritative demands is questioned. Similarly, the diminution of disruptive behavior in later adolescence should be associated with the acquisition of Level 5 reasoning (convention as mediated by social system). A sample of disruptive and nondisruptive students was administered the social convention interview (Turiel, 1978). A subset of the disruptive students was followed longitudinally (1 year later) to determine if shifts in stage reasoning are associated with behavioral change.

Geiger and Turiel (1983) found that virtually all of the nondisruptive students were at Level 5 (convention as mediated by social system), while 21 of the 28 disruptive students were at Level 4. Of the 20 disruptive students who were retested a year later, 13 were classified as nondisruptive and 7 as disruptive. Out of the 13 classified as nondisruptive of Time 2, 7 were entirely at Level 5, 5 showed acquisition of Stage 5 as a minor stage, and 1 showed no change. Of the 7 still classified as disruptive at Time 2, 4 showed no change, and 3 acquired Stage 5 as a minor stage. These results seem to indicate a relation between levels of social conventional reasoning and social behavior, although the correspondence is not a perfect one, as the authors point out. While Level 5 is firmly associated with nondisruptive behavior, Level 4 did not uniformly account for disruptive behavior. Seven disruptive students were not classified at Level 4 at Time 1, and 3 nondisruptive students still has vestiges of Level 4 thinking at Time 2. Geiger and Turiel (1983) suggest that behavioral change might precede the acquisition of Level 5, just as Level 5 reasoning may precede a behavioral change to nondisruption, and that the relation between thought and behavior in stimulating stage transition requires further study. We agree. The only plausible rationale for designing a social conventional program as an educational intervention would be if levels of reasoning reliably precedes social behavior, and not vice versa. While the author's caveat concerning behavior–thought reciprocity in stage transition is cautious and reasonable, we should not lose sight of the fact that synchrony between levels and level-appropriate behavior was more true than not. An acceptable *provisional* stratagem might be to consider cases of asynchrony as measurement error (e.g., Lapsley & Serlin, 1984). Future research should also address the significance of minor stage acquisition for the moderation of disruptive behavior and the conjecture that the "negation" stages (here Stage 4) are transitional and unstable, and hence more likely to show behavior—thought variability.

Nucci (1982, 1985c) suggests that one way the school contributes to social development is through the teacher's response to student social transgressions. Much of what students learn about social values comes not so much through symbolic interactions with sociomoral dilemmas but rather through direct interaction with peers and teachers. Teachers must become sensitive to the moral–conventional domain distinction when they react to student transgression because "teachers' attempts to moralize about acts students view as conventional issues or responses to the impropriety of moral transgressions in terms of social organization (e.g., school rules) would be domain inappropriate and therefore unlikely to stimulate development" (Nucci, 1982, p. 115). In addition students seem to evaluate teachers in terms of how well they respond to domain-specific transgressions. Nucci (1985c) asked third-, fifth-, seventh-, and ninth-grade subjects to evaluate not only teacher responses to moral and social conventional transgressions but also the teachers themselves. He found that students rate domain-appropriate responses higher than domain-inappropriate responses or command responses. Teachers who typically employ domain-appropriate responses to transgressions were rated higher than teachers who respond in a domain-inappropriate fashion. On the basis of these findings. Nucci (1985c) suggests that students evaluate the legitimacy of teachers as socialization agents on the basis of whether or not teachers differentiate their responses to moral and conventional transgressions in domain-appropriate ways.

Taken together the findings of Geiger and Turiel (1983) and Nucci (1985) suggest that educators should attend to the domain features of social knowledge. The conventional domain offers much promise for understanding the dynamics of adolescent misbehavior in school settings. It also suggests that the teacher's role as socialization agent can be legitimized to the extent that teachers coordinate the form of their responses with the moral or conventional nature of the transgression.

Summary and Conclusion

We have attempted in this review to highlight a number of issues in the fields of moral and social education. We have seen that recent research offers no consensus on what constitutes (1) optimal stage disparity in plus-stage interventions, (2) the optimal duration for effecting structural change, or (3) the form of the intervention. Indeed, virtually any plus-stage discussion format, for any length of time, seems to be effective in elevating moral reasoning scores (Lapsley & Quintana, 1985). There is evidence that the moral curricula will be particularly effective if educators attend to the developmental readiness of their students. That is, students must have competence in prerequisite levels of cognitive and role-taking development in order to support moral stage advance. In addition, the recent emphasis on transactive moral discussion suggests that communication skills may also be an important precondition for advancing moral thought in plus-stage interventions. Training in how to participate in discussions may also be required.

The moral atmosphere of the class is thought to provide contextual support for moral development. Two studies provide equivocal evidence at best on this point. A third (and the best) study does offer convincing evidence for the effect of moral atmosphere on practical moral judgments. It also highlights the important fact that giving students broad decision-making responsibilities within a democratic framework gives them a stake in the conduct of school affairs. While the level of investment in conducting just communities is high, the educational gains may be significant. Educators can expect maximum moral stage advance (equal to good discussion formats) that may be more pervasive than other interventions. In addition, students cultivate a sense of social responsibility, community valuing, trust, and caring. Anything that would transform the school into a (just) community of citizens rather than a teenage warehouse would certainly be desirable. In this respect a just-community structure may indeed be useful in providing the educational bridge between the moral gains of the discussion group and moral action.

The domain of social conventional reasoning is a promising development for values education. It recognizes that complex social issues involve not only morality components but also issues of social convention. The first phase of this research program was to demonstrate that even young children are sensitive to the moral–social convention domain distinction. The evidence is convincing on this point. Educators are thus urged to coordinate values instruction with domain, and with developmental level. The second phase, currently in progress, seeks to demonstrate additional educational implications for the social conventional domain. We have seen that the domain aids in our understanding of disruptive behavior in the school and of how teachers can legitimate their role as socialization agents. We might suggest that the educational benefits of this domain can be enhanced by a third phase of research that seeks intervention tests of the social conventional stage sequence. Such evidence will speak to the empirical integrity of the sequence, clarify transition mechanisms, and aid in the design of domain-appropriate educational programs. We would also like to see studies that explore the social cognitive developmental prerequisites of stage advancement in social conventional reasoning, and the empirical relationship of this stage sequence to moral development. It would also be of interest to know the educational benefits of combined domain (moral, conventional) interventions.

The research cited in this chapter reflects the widespread view that secondary education should involve much more than the transmission of knowledge and the inculcation of intellectual skills (Lapsley & Quintana, 1985). Adolescent education should also be concerned with values, ethics, and the moral dimensions of conduct. "The current clamor over prayer in the schools is perhaps symptomatic of the anxiety of those who perceive moral laxity in public education and the failure of public education to address its moral mission" (Lapsley & Quintana, 1985, p. 246). Of particular concern is the perception that many adolescents are ill prepared to confront issues like cheating, stealing, drug use, school absence, sexual promiscuity, vandalism, and the like in a morally responsible way. Educators look to academic research on moral and social education for helpful strategies on how to encourage better moral conduct.

The issue of how to promote moral *action* in adolescents has been addressed, perhaps obliquely, in a number of places throughout this chapter. We would like to conclude with a more forthright, if brief, consideration of this issue (see Blasi, 1983; Rest, 1984, for thoughtful discussions of moral thought and action).

It is certainly legitimate for educators to wonder just how moral education contributes to moral action. There are a number of reasons why an educator might be suspicious of Kohlbergian discussion techniques as a values intervention. One is that moral stages and justice reasoning seem to neglect the content of specific action choices. As Blasi (1980) notes, "many of Kohlberg's moral stages frequently do not seem to be related to any specific course of action, but in any one situation they may be compatible with contrasting alternatives" (p. 8). When this objection is combined with empirical evidence that stage advances in justice reasoning are not accompanied by improvements in moral conduct (e.g., Niles, 1986), one may be tempted to conclude that moral education is a luxury at best and irrelevant at worst, since, as everybody knows, *knowing* the right thing, and *doing* it, are very different matters.

Kohlberg (1985) has recently addressed the limitations of the dilemma discussion approach to moral education. He acknowledges that the nature of the relation between the moral reasoning advances obtained in educational programs and actual moral behavior is far from clear and that education for content is a legitimate concern. Certainly educators should be advocates of certain moral positions. However, Kohlberg (1985) insists that a distinction be respected between moral advocacy and indoctrination. The moral advocate introduces as *content* principles of justice. The *method* of advocacy should be by appeal to reason (versus, say, by appeal to authority). And students should be respected by the advocate as autonomous moral agents. For Kohlberg (1985),

> the thing that prevents teacher's advocacy from being indoctrination is the establishment of participatory democracy in the classroom. The teacher should advocate as an individual, the first among equals, speaking from a rational point of view and not from one of authority and power. . . . Effective teacher advocacy in what we have called a just community school rests on the use of appeals to reasons of fairness or community, usually at a relatively advanced stage, in a context of controversy about the rightness of a particular rate or policy. (p. 82)

The major point here is that the just-community intervention does not abandon the advocacy of moral content. What it does insist upon, however, is that the intervention not become a forum for indoctrination and the imposition of authority and power. What it insists upon is that the method and intention of the advocacy also be just, in addition to the content (Kohlberg, 1985). Such interventions have been shown to have beneficial effects on moral conduct (Higgins *et al.*, 1983).

This is not to say that the dilemma discussion approach must be abandoned in favor of just communities. The discussion of hypothetical moral dilemmas as a stage-advancing strategy still has an important role in moral education, particularly when it can be integrated within the general curriculum (Kohlberg, 1985). Certainly, moral cognition is some distance from moral action. Whether judgments of morality get translated into moral conduct may depend on a host of complicating motivational, affective, and contextual factors (Rest, 1984). Yet, whatever else moral action may require, what it minimally requires is a cognitive appraisal of the moral relevance of the situation. Issues like stealing and drug usage may or may not be *moral* issues, depending on the evaluation of the individual facing such choices (Blasi, 1980). Praiseworthy conduct (e.g., heroic action, not using drugs) may or may not constitute *moral* action unless it is so construed by the moral agent, that is, unless the action is motivated in light of moral considerations (Kohlberg *et al.*, 1983). The dilemma discussion approach may provide students with the necessary experience to adequately appraise the moral relevance of situations and action choices, that is, provide the cognitive motivation to act morally (Blasi, 1983).

The dilemma discussion approach may contribute to moral action in another way as well. Kohlberg (1984) has recently distinguished between A and B substages at each of the moral stages. These substages reflect types of moral decision making that correspond to Piaget's stage distinction between a heteronomous orientation to rules and authority (Type A) and an autonomous orientation to fairness, equality, and reciprocity (Type B). The B substage is said to better satisfy moral (e.g., prescriptivity, universalizability) and psychological (structural equilibration) criteria of adequacy. This suggests two things: First, the A and B distinction represents a developmental continuum. Whenever there is movement from substage to substage, it is from A to B. Second, the classification by substage is thus based partly on formal aspects of moral judgments, but it is also based on the content of particular moral action choices (Kohlberg *et al.*, 1983). That is, some features of moral reasoning lie between form and content, and the A–B distinction is a way to integrate this empirical reality into moral stage scoring. What this entails is that a relationship exists between moral thought and both the solution (content) of hypothetical dilemmas and moral action. Indeed Colby, Kohlberg, Gibbs, and Lieberman (1984) found that, for the most part, Stage 5 subjects tend to make the autonomous choice (e.g., stealing the drug) in resolving hypothetical dilemmas. That is, a relation exists between stage of reasoning and choice of moral action. Subjects below Stage 5 who display an autonomous orientation and who's reasoning satisfies formal criteria are classified at the B-substage, as opposed to subjects who's thinking betrays a heteronomous orientation to upholding existing social arrangements (Type A). According to Kohlberg *et al.* (1983), the A–B distinction should be helpful "in our attempts to relate moral judgement to moral action; that is, that subjects using B-substage reasoning would be more likely to engage in the moral action they believed to be just, than would be users of A-substage reasoning" (p. 44). This would be so because autonomous Type B reasoners would be more likely to make judgments of personal responsibility regarding themselves as moral agents (Blasi, 1983). Some support for this view is reported by Gibbs *et al.* (1986). They found that Type-B is related not only to situational "moral courage" but also to the tendency to appraise complex social situations in terms of moral significance. Given that the A–B continuum is assumed to be a developmental one, the dilemma discussion approach could be used to stimulate movement towards the autonomous orientation. This suggests that the success of such an approach need not be judged in terms of how well the next moral stage is acquired but in the acquisition of the B-substage.

We have tried to show that the Kohlbergian interventions are not neglectful of content and are not irrelevant to moral action. As a final note we would again urge educators to attend to the social conventional features of adolescent misbehavior. Not all troubling behavior is of a moral nature. As we have seen in this review, at least some student misconduct can be related to the developmental status of adolescents in their understanding of conventional rules. The bottom line is that developmental research still has much to contribute to the moral and social education of adolescents.

Acknowledgment

The authors are grateful for the criticism of Marvin Berkowitz, Larry Nucci, Clark Power, and the editors of this volume of an earlier version of this chapter. We retain, of course, all responsibility for its shortcomings. Our thanks also to Crescent Kringle, Edna Noble, Pauline Wright, and Linda Yuhas for their help with this manuscript. We dedicate this chapter to the memory of Lawrence Kohlberg.

References

Arbuthnot, J. (1975). Modification of moral judgment through the role playing. *Developmental Psychology*, **11**, 319–329.
Arbuthnot, J. (1984). A comparison of Kohlberg and AVER-based moral reasoning

development programs in a prison population. *Journal of Moral Education,* **13,** 112–123.

Arbuthnot, J., & Faust, D. (1981). *Teaching moral reasoning: Theory and practice.* New York: Harper.

Aron, I. (1977a). Moral philosophy and moral education: A critique of Kohlberg's theory. *School Review,* **85,** 197–217.

Aron, I. (1977b). Moral philosophy and moral education II. The formalist tradition and the Deweyan alternative. *School Review,* **85,** 513–534.

Berkowitz, M. (1980). The role of transactive discussion in moral development: The history of a six year program of research—Part II. Moral Education Forum, **5,** 15–27.

Berkowitz, M. (1981). A critical appraisal of the educational and psychological perspectives on moral discussion. *Journal of Educational Thought,* **15,** 20–33.

Berkowitz, M. (1984). *Process analysis and the future of moral education.* A symposium presentation at the annual meeting of the American Educational Research Association, New Orleans.

Berkowitz, M. (1985). Four perspectives on moral argumentation. In C. Harding (Ed.), *Moral dilemmas.* Chicago: Precedent.

Berkowitz, M. & Gibbs, J. (1983) Measuring the developmental features of moral discussion. *Merrill-Palmer Quarterly,* **29,** 399–410.

Berkowitz, M., Gibbs, J., & Broughton, J. (1980). The relation of moral judgment stage disparity to developmental effects of peer dialogues. *Merrill-Palmer Quarterly,* **26,** 341–357.

Blasi, A. (1980). Bridging moral cognition and moral action: A critical review of the literature. *Psychological Bulletin,* **88,** 1–45.

Blasi, A. (1983). Moral cognition and moral action: A theoretical perspective. *Developmental Review,* **3,** 178–210.

Blatt, M., & Kohlberg, L. (1975). The effects of classroom moral discussion upon children's level of moral judgment. *Journal of Moral Education,* **4,** 129–161.

Boyd, D. (1981). The condition of sophomorites and its educational cure. *Journal of Moral Education,* **10,** 24–39.

Boyd, D. (1986). The ought of is: Kohlberg at the interface between moral philosophy and developmental psychology. In S. Modgil & C. Modgil (Eds.), *Lawrence Kohlberg: Consensus and controversy.* London: Falmer.

Campbell, R. (1983). *Moral development theory: A critique of its Kantian presuppositions.* Unpublished manuscript. Available from the author, Department of Psychology, University of Texas, Austin, TX 78712.

Cline, H., & Feldmesser, R. (1983). *Program evaluation in moral education.* Princeton, NJ: Educational Testing Service.

Cochrane, D., Hamm, C., & Kazepides, A. (Eds.) (1979). *The domain of moral education.* Chicago: Paulist Press.

Colby, A., Kohlberg, L., Gibbs, J., & Lieberman, M. (1983). *A longitudinal study of moral judgment.* Monograph of the Society for Research in Child Development, Serial No. 300. Chicago: University of Chicago Press.

Crockenberg, S. B., & Nicolayev, J. (1979). Stage transition in moral reasoning as related to conflict experienced in naturalistic settings. *Merrill-Palmer Quarterly,* **25,** 185–192.

Damico, A. (1982). The sociology of justice: Kohlberg and Milgram. *Political Theory,* **10,** 409–434.

Damon, W., & Killen, M. (1982). Peer interaction and the process of change in children's moral reasoning. *Merrill-Palmer Quarterly,* **82,** 347–367.

Durkheim, E. (1961). *Moral education: A study in the theory and application in the sociology of education.* New York: Free Press.

Enright, R., Colby, S., & McMullin, D. (1977). A social cognitive developmental intervention with sixth- and first-graders. *Counseling Psychologist,* **4,** 10–12.

Enright, R., Lapsley, D., Harris, D., & Shawver, D. (1983b). Moral development interventions in early adolescence. *Theory in Practice,* **22,** 134–144.

Enright, R., Lapsley, D., & Levy, V. (1983a). Moral education strategies. In M. Pressley & J. Levin (Eds.), *Cognitive strategy research: Educational applications.* New York: Springer-Verlag.

Enright, R., Lapsley, D., & Olson, L. (1986). Moral judgment and the social cognitive developmental research program. In S. Modgil & C. Modgil (Eds.), *Lawrence Kohlberg: Consensus and controversy.* London: Falmer.

Falikowski, A. (1982). Kohlberg's moral development program: Its limitations and ethical exclusiveness. *Alberta Journal of Educational Research,* **28,** 77–89.

Flanagan, O. (1982). Moral structures? *Philosophy of Social Science,* **12,** 25–277.

Galbraith, R., & Jones, T. (1975). Teaching strategies for moral dilemmas. *Social Education,* **39,** 16–22.

Geiger, K., & Turiel, E. (1983). Disruptive school behavior and concepts of social convention in early adolescence. *Journal of Educational Psychology,* **75,** 677–685.

Gibbs, J., Clark, P., Joseph, J., Goodrick, T., & Makowski, D. (1986). Relations between moral judgment, moral courage, and field independence. *Child Development,* **57,** 185–193.

Gibbs, J., Widaman, K., & Colby, A. (1982). Construction and validation of a simplified, group-administered equivalent to the Moral Judgment Interview. *Child Development,* **53,** 895–910.

Haan, N. (1985). Processes of moral development: Cognitive or social disequilibrium? *Developmental Psychology,* **21,** 996–1006.

Hamm, D. (1977). The content of moral education, or in defense of the 'bag of virtues.' *School Review,* **85,** 218–227.

Hersh, R., Paolitto, D., & Reimer, J. (1979). *Promoting moral growth: From Piaget to Kohlberg.* New York: Longmans.

Higgins, A., Power, C., & Kohlberg, L. (1983). *Moral atmosphere and moral judgment: The influence of the school on moral reasoning and action.* Paper presented at the meeting of the Society for Research in Child Development, Detroit.

Hyland, E. (1979). Towards a radical critique of morality and moral education. *Journal of Moral Education,* **8,** 156–167.

Jennings, W., & Kohlberg, L. (1983). Effects of a just community programme on the moral development of youthful offenders. *Journal of Moral Education,* **12,** 33–50.

Keasey, C. (1973). Experimentally induced changes in moral opinions and reasoning. *Journal of Personality and Social Psychology,* **26,** 30–38.

Kohlberg, L. (1973). The claim to moral adequacy of a highest stage of moral judgment. *Journal of Philosophy,* **70,** 630–646.

Kohlberg, L. (1984). *The psychology of moral development: Essays on moral development.* (Vol. 2). San Francisco: Harper.

Kohlberg, L. (1985). Resolving moral conflicts with the just community. In C. Harding (Ed.), *Moral dilemmas.* Chicago: Precedent.

Kohlberg, L., Kauffman, K., Scharf, P., & Hickey, J. (1975). The just community approach to corrections: A theory. *Journal of Moral Education,* **4,** 243–260.

Kohlberg, L., Levine, C., & Hewer, A. (Eds.) (1983). *Moral stages.* New York: Karger.

Kohlberg, L., Scharf, P., & Hickey, J. (1972). The justice structure of the prison: A theory and intervention. *Prison Journal,* **51,** 3–14.

Kuhmerker, L., Mentkowski, M., & Erickson, L. (Eds.) (1980). *Evaluating moral develop-*

ment and evaluating educational programs that have a value dimension. Chicago: Character Research Press.

Lapsley, D., & Madar, M. (1983). *Retributive justice reasoning in children.* Paper presented at the biennial meeting of the Society for Research in Child Development. Detroit.

Lapsley, D., & Quintana, S. (1985). Recent approaches in children's elementary moral and social education. *Elementary School Guidance and Counseling, 19*, 246–259.

Lapsley, D., & Serlin, R. (1984). On the alleged degeneration of the Kohlbergian research program. *Educational Theory, 34*, 157–170.

Lawrence, J. (1980). Moral judgment intervention studies using the 'Defining Issues Test.'' *Journal of Moral Education, 9*, 178–191.

Leming, J. (1981). Curricular effectiveness in moral/values education: A review of research. *Journal of Moral Education, 10*, 147–164.

Leming, J. (1986). Kohlbergian programs in moral education: A practical review and assessment. In S. Modgil & C. Modgil (Eds.), *Lawrence Kohlberg: Consensus and controversy.* London: Falmer.

Levine, C., Kohlberg, L., & Hewer, A. (1985). The current formulation of Kohlberg's theory and a response to critics. *Human Development, 28*, 94–110.

Lickona, T. (1978). Moral development and moral education. In J. Gallagher & J. Easley (Eds.), *Knowledge and development* (Vol. 2). New York: Plenum.

Lockwood, A. (1978). The effects of values clarification and moral development curricula on school-age subjects. A critical review of recent research. *Review of Educational Research, 48*, 325–364.

Maul, J. (1981). A high school with intensive education: Moral atmosphere and moral reasoning. *Journal of Moral Education, 10*, 9–17.

May, L. (1985). The moral adequacy of Kohlberg's theory. In C. Harding (Ed.), *Moral dilemmas.* Chicago: Precedent.

Modgil, S. & Modgil, C. (Eds.). (1986). *Lawrence Kohlberg: Consensus and controversy.* London: Falmer.

Nichols, M. & Day, V. (1982). A comparison of moral reasoning of groups and individuals on the 'Defining Issues Test.' *Academy of Management Journal, 25*, 201–208.

Niles, W. (1986). Effects of a moral development discussion group on delinquent and predelinquent boys. *Journal of Counseling Psychology, 13*, 45–51.

Nucci, L. (1981). Conceptions of personal issues: A domain distinct from moral or societal concepts. *Child Development, 52*, 114–121.

Nucci, L. (1982). Conceptual development in the moral and conventional domains: Implications for values education. *Review of Educational Research, 52*, 93–122.

Nucci, L. (1984a). Evaluating teachers as social agents: Students' ratings of domain appropriate and domain inappropriate teacher responses to transgressions. *American Educational Research Journal, 21*, 364–378.

Nucci, L. (1984b). *Piagetian stage and development in the societal domain.* Unpublished manuscript. Available from the author, College of Education, Box 4348, University of Illinois at Chicago, Chicago, IL 60680.

Nucci, L. (1984c). Values education: A domain analysis. Paper presented as part of the symposium: *Moral and social education for 1984 and beyond* at the annual meeting of the American Educational Research Association, New Orleans.

Nucci, L. (1985a). Future directions in research on children's moral reasoning and moral education. *Elementary School Guidance and Counseling, 19*, 272–282.

Nucci, L. (1985b). Children's conceptions of morality, societal convention, and religious prescription. In C. Harding (Ed.), *Moral dilemmas.* Chicago: Precedent.

Nucci, L. (1985c). Teaching children right from wrong: Education and the development of children's moral and conventional concepts. *Teacher Education Quarterly.*

Nucci, L., Berkowitz, M., Power, C., & Smetana, J. (1984). *Moral and social education for 1984 and beyond.* Symposium presented at the annual meeting of the American Educational Research Association, New Orleans.

Nucci, L., & Nucci, M. (1982). Children's responses to moral and social conventional transgressions in free-play settings. *Child Development, 53,* 1337–1342.

Nucci, L., & Turiel, E. (1978). Social interactions and the development of social concepts in preschool children. *Child Development, 49,* 400–407.

Pekarsky, D. (1983). Moral choice and education. *Journal of Moral Education, 12,* 3–13.

Phillips, D. C., & Nicolayev, J. (1978). Kohlbergian moral development: A progressing or degenerating research program? *Educational Theory, 28,* 286–301.

Phillips, D. C., & Nicolayev, J. (1984). In its final stages? A reply to Lapsley and Serlin, *Educational Theory, 34,* 171–175.

Power, C. (1984). Moral atmosphere. Paper presented at the symposium *Moral and social education for 1984 and beyond* at the annual meeting of the American Educational Research Association, New Orleans.

Power, C., Kohlberg, L., & Higgins, A. (1989). *Moral education, community, and justice: A study of three democratic high schools.* New York: Columbia University Press.

Power, F. C., & Reimer, J. (1978). Moral atmosphere: An educational bridge between moral judgment and action. In W. Damon (Ed.), *Moral development. New Directions for child development* (No. 2, pp. 105–116). San Francisco: Jossey-Bass.

Reed, T., & Hanna, P. (1982). Developmental theory and moral education: Review essay. *Teaching Philosophy, 5,* 43–55.

Reimer, J., & Power, F. C. (1980). Education for democratic community: Some unresolved dilemmas. In R. Mosher (Ed.), *Moral education: First generation of research* (pp. 303–320). New York: Praeger.

Rest, J. (1974). Developmental psychology as a guide to values education: A review of Kohlbergian programs. *Review of Educational Research, 49,* 241–259.

Rest, J. (1979). *Revised manual for the Defining Issues Test.* Minneapolis: Minneapolis Moral Research Projects.

Rest, J. (1984). Morality, In P. Mussen (Ed.), *Handbook of child psychology* (4th ed., Vol. 3). New York: Wiley.

Rest, J., Turiel, E., & Kohlberg, L. (1969). Level of moral development as a determinant of preference and comprehension of moral judgments made by others. *Journal of PErsonality, 37,* 225–252.

Rholes, W., Bailey, S., & McMillan, L. (1982). Experiences that motivate moral development: The role of cognitive dissonance. *Journal of Experimental Social Psychology, 18,* 524–536.

Rosen, B. (1980). Kohlberg and the supposed mutual support of an ethical and psychological theory. *Journal for the Theory of Social Behavior, 10,* 195–210.

Scharf, P., McCoy, W., & Ross, D. (1979). *Growing up moral: Dilemmas for the intermediate grades.* Boston: Winston.

Siegel, H. (1981). Kohlberg, moral adequacy, and the justification of educational interventions. *Educational Theory, 31,* 275–284.

Siegel, H. (1986). On using psychology to justify judgments of moral adequacy. In S. Modgil & C. Modgil (Eds.), *Lawrence Kohlberg: Consensus and controversy.* London: Falmer.

Smetana, J. (1983). Social-cognitive development: Domain distinctions and coordinations. *Developmental Review, 3,* 131–147.

Smetana, J. (1985). Preschool children's conceptions of transgressions: Effects of varying moral and conventional domain attributes. *Developmental Psychology, 21,* 18–29.

Tisak, M., & Turiel, E. (1984). Children's conceptions of moral and prudential rules. *Child Development, 55,* 1030–1039.

Trainer, F. E. (1977). A critical analysis of Kohlberg's contributions to the study of moral thought. *Journal of the Theory of Social Behavior, 7,* 41–63.

Turiel, E. (1966). An experimental test of the sequentiality of developmental stages in the child's moral judgments. *Journal of Personality and Social Psychology, 3,* 611–618.

Turiel, E. (1977). Distinct conceptual and developmental domains: Social convention and morality. *Nebraska symposium on motivation* (Vol. 25). Lincoln, NE: University of Nebraska Press.

Turiel, E. (1978). Social regulations and domains of social concepts. In W. Damon (Ed.), *New directions for child development Vol. 1: Social cognition.* San Francisco: Jossey-Bass.

Turiel, E. (1983). Domains and categories in social-cognitive development. In W. Overton (Ed.), *The relationship between social and cognition development* (pp. 53–90). Hillsdale, NJ: Erlbaum.

Vallacher, R., & Solodky, M. (1979). Objective self-awareness, standards of evaluation, and moral behavior. *Journal of Experimental Social Psychology, 15,* 254–262.

Ventre, R. (1982). Cognitive moral development in the prison classroom. *Journal of Correctional Education, 33,* 18–26.

Walker, L. (1980). Cognitive and perspective-taking prerequisites for moral development. *Child Development, 51,* 131–139.

Walker, L. (1982). The sequentiality of Kohlberg's stages of moral development. *Child Development, 53,* 1330–1336.

Walker, L., de Vries, B., & Bichard, S. (1984). The hierarchical nature of stages of moral development. *Developmental Psychology, 20,* 960–966.

Walker, L., & Richards, B. (1979). Stimulating transitions in moral reasoning as a function of stage of cognitive development. *Developmental Psychology, 15,* 95–103.

Wilcox, M. (1979). *Developmental journal: A guide to the development of logical and moral reasoning and social perspective.* Abington.

Wilson, J. (1986). First steps in moral education: Understanding and using reasons. In S. Modgil & C. Modgil (Eds.), *Lawrence Kohlberg: Consensus and controversy.* London: Falmer.

Wonderly, D., & Kupfersmid, J. (1980). Promoting postconventional morality: The adequacy of Kohlberg's aim. *Adolescence, 25,* 609–631.

6

Self-awareness and Self-identity in Adolescence

Jerry Suls

Adolescence is commonly considered a period of "storm and stress," a view promulgated by G. S. Hall (1904) and by literature such as Goethe's Young Werther and more recently Salinger's Holden Caulfield. The storm and stress account of adolescence places much of the responsibility for the supposed turmoil on the "self" the adolescent is in the process of developing. The present chapter reviews relevant psychological evidence on adolescent self-identity and self-awareness to assess popular notions of this developmental period. Actually, contemporary research does not find adolescence to be quite so stormy as, for example, Hall described it. Nonetheless, adolescents do undergo a number of important psychological changes, which will be reviewed here.

The emphasis of the chapter is on the adolescent's changing sense of self and identity. Four topics are given extensive coverage: (1) self-concept; (2) self-esteem; (3) identity formation; and (4) adolescent egocentrism. These topics were chosen because they have received extensive empirical and conceptual attention and each of the four provides an important aspect of how adolescents construct a view of themselves and their place in the world. *Self-concept* refers to the attributes the individual believes characterize him- or herself. *Self-esteem* refers to the evaluative notions one has about oneself—global self-worth and evaluative judgments of specific aspects of the self. In simple terms, self-concept refers to "Who am I?"; self-esteem refers to "How do I feel about myself?" *Identity formation* concerns how the individual develops a clear and consistent view of the self and its commitments to others, and plans for the future. Finally, *adolescent egocentrism* is a developmental phenomenon in which there is a failure to differentiate the process of one's own thinking from that of others. This appears to be a normal phenomenon connected with cognitive changes occurring in adolescence.

By considering self-esteem, self-concept, identity formation, and adolescent egocentrism together, a more complete picture of how the adolescent negotiates and constructs a self in the social world should be gained. Since educational settings are one of the primary social settings for adolescents, the emphasis on a social development perspective is most appropriate for the present volume.

In addition to these four major topics, I will also devote some discussion to recent social psychological work on such topics as self-consciousness, self-monitoring, and social comparison. Although this research has not been applied to an adolescent development context, it may be fruitful to do so. Finally, since this volume is aimed primarily at educators, the educational implications of the work will be emphasized throughout the chapter.

Changes in the Self-concept

Many external and internal physiological changes occur during the adolescent period (ages 12 to 18 or 21). Also, as constituted in Western society, adolescence involves a set of roles and transitions from middle childhood to adulthood. During this phase of the life cycle, individuals must begin to make important decisions about what they will do with their lives. Such decisions necessitate a sense of "who one is." Of course, earlier in life the individual has a sense of self, but the urgency and importance of decision planning for adulthood during adolescence places the spotlight on the self in a way that is different from earlier periods.

Also, there are significant cognitive changes that may influence thinking about the self. Piagetian theory and research have shown that beginning in middle childhood and proceeding through adolescence, the individual becomes increasingly adept at formal operations and hypothetical thinking (Inhelder & Piaget, 1958). This cognitive shift is strongly related to changes in thinking about one's self. Just as the adolescent begins to think in abstractions, notions about the self shift from an emphasis on the social exterior to psychological elements (Rosenberg, 1986). For example, Secord and Peever (1974) questioned children and adolescents about "who they are" in a free-response format. During childhood the respondents described themselves in terms of specific acts and qualities, especially behavioral "observables." At the start of adolescence, the self was described in terms of general abstractions and general evaluations. By the middle of adolescence, the self was seen as an active monitor of one's experience. Also, middle adolescents recognize discrepant aspects of the self—differences between conscious and unconscious motivations and conflicting feelings (see Broughton, 1978, 1980). But according to Bernstein (1980), who asked adolescents how they explained acting and thinking differently depending on the situation, these discrepancies were not resolved until the end of adolescence. Older adolescents (ages 18–20) form integrating principles that recognize diversity but maintain the coherence of the self-system.

To be more specific about these changes, consider a study by Montemeyer and Eisen (1977), who asked a sample of children and youth in grades 4, 6, 8, 10, and 12 to answer "Who am I?" in 20 words or phrases. The younger subjects identified themselves in three major categories: (1) possessions–resources, (2) physical self–body image, and (3) territoriality–citizenship. Livesley and Bromley (1973), Rosenberg and Simmons (1972), among others, find similar results suggesting an exterior-specific orientation on the part of young children. In contrast, midadolescents (ages 16–18) were more likely to describe themselves in terms of internal beliefs and internal standards, as well as in terms of stable personality traits that generalize across behavior.

How are we to account for these data? Are they merely a function of vocabulary changes with age? This would still itself require an explanation. Rosenberg (1979, 1986) argues that vocabulary probably does not explain the difference between adolescents and younger children. Even adolescents do not use trait words very frequently, but they do use their own words to formulate generalizations about themselves. The self-shifts are most likely associated with the cognitive changes in abstraction and generalization also occurring in adolescence.

One of the more interesting findings that nicely incapsulates the exterior–interior shift concerns children's and adolescents' responses to the question "Who knows the self best?" Rosenberg (1979) asked his respondents, "Who knows best what you really feel and think deep down inside?", a question about interior social knowledge. Fifty-two percent of the 8 to 11-year-olds identified a parent, but only 24% of the age 15-or-older subjects gave that response. Rosenberg also asked, "Who knows best how good-looking you are?", a question about external social knowledge. Again, there was a similar shift from exterior sources of knowledge—from parents or peers to the self. As Rosenberg (1986) observed, with increasing age, the child becomes less a Skinnerian or demographer, more of a Freudian or clinician.

Although research suggests that the adolescent undergoes some significant self-concept changes, they are gradual. This is best illustrated by Dusek and Flaherty's (1981) 3-year longitudinal study conducted with students in grades 5–12. The initial sample was retested each year and a new sample of subjects was added in each grade level each year. The self-concept scale was made up of 21 items in which each concept was rated as characteristic of self. Factor analyses of the cross-sectional and longitudinal samples revealed four factors: adjustment, achievement–leadership, congeniality–sociability, and masculinity–femininity. Inspection of the longitudinal data showed that the same four factors emerged at each time point and grade level. In addition, stability correlations and analysis of mean responses to the various items exhibited more continuity than discontinuity, especially in consecutive years. Such findings suggest there is considerable continuity in self-concept during the adolescent years, which is contrary to the storm and stress view of this period. What changes in self-conception that were observed tended to be gradual.

The discussion has emphasized differences in self-orientation between childhood and adolescence, but another tendency worth mentioning appears not to be age-related. McGuire and his associates (McGuire & Padawer-Singer, 1976; McGuire & McGuire, 1982) have asked children, adolescents, and adults to tell "Who I am", leaving the guidelines and dimensions up to the respondents (this is similar to the open-ended method used by Montemeyer and Eisen, 1977; Livesley and Bromley, 1973; Mullener and Laird, 1971; Gordon, 1968). Across age, the spontaneous self-concept has features that reflect aspects of identity that make people distinct from those around them. For example, for children of average height, only 17% had spontaneously described themselves in terms of their height, whereas 27% of the tall and short children had spontaneously mentioned their height. Similar findings have been reported for weight, gender, left- or right-handedness, and ethnicity. Thus, as a trait becomes more unique in a social setting, it comes to play a more prominent role in one's self-definition. It should be mentioned that peculiarities are used more in a relative sense; McGuire also finds a high use of commonplace traits.

The evidence for a distinctiveness principle in self-definition may have some significant implications for educational policy. People may be more likely to think about themselves in terms of ethnicity to the extent that racial integration of their social environment makes their ethnicity more distinctive. As McGuire and McGuire (1982) observed:

> If one wishes to have an integrated society in school and elsewhere, but also wishes to have a society where people do not think of themselves or one another in terms of ethnicity, then these findings suggest that one has a conflict of values, because increasing integration will tend to enhance racial salience in self and others. (pp. 78–79)

Before concluding this section, some limitations and concerns about the self-conception work should be discussed. First, most of the data discussed above are from studies that were cross-sectional in design. Given problems of sampling error and comparability, it would be desirable to have more longitudinal studies of changes in the nature of self-conception. A second problem concerns the possibility of a self-presentation bias. Are respondents telling us how they think about themselves or what they think we, as psychologists or educators, want to hear. Although responses are made anonymously in some studies, it is not entirely clear that impression management or demand cues can be ruled out entirely (Orne, 1959), Thorough debriefing and interviewing after responses are given may provide information about the extent that self-presentation is a problem in previous work.

Despite these limitations, there is sufficient evidence indicating a general trend with age toward a more internalized, abstract self-conception among adolescents. However, educators should recognize that these changes are gradual rather than abrupt, unlike some of the physical changes that occur in adolescence. Focusing on physical changes may lead parents and teachers to overestimate the level of abstraction and psychological changes of adolescents. Also, given that self-conception changes in a number of subtle ways in the middle and late phases of adolescence, educators should be careful about lumping all adolescents together into one category.

Self-esteem of Adolescents

In this section, I review the major findings concerning self-esteem in adolescence. As noted above, self-concept refers to attributes that define or describe the person, but self-esteem is concerned with the affect or feelings the individual has about his or her overall worth or specific attributes. The distinction between self-concept and self-esteem is important because one can readily conceive of two adolescents who provide the same attributes as self-descriptive but who differ greatly in their evaluations of these attributes. On the other hand, one can conceive of two adolescents with similar levels of global self-esteem who have very different self-concepts.

The emphasis here will be on global self-esteem, the *overall* evaluation of one's self either in positive or negative terms. However, some attention will be given to self-esteem related to specific domains—notably academic self-esteem. Reviewing the literature on self-esteem is no mean task; it is estimated there are over 6 thousand articles published on self-esteem. Moreover, there are numerous measures of self-esteem and much controversy about whether self-esteem should be treated as a global concept—a summary evaluation across dimensions. Or whether people only make judgments of their worth or ability relevant to specific domains, such as school, social, athletic, and so on (see Harter, 1983; Shavelson & Bolus, 1982; Fleming & Courtney, 1984, for discussions of the benefits and liabilities associated with global versus multidimensional approaches). My view, which concurs with Harter (1983, 1986), is that self-esteem should be measured in terms of multidimensional domain-specific judgments, as well as in terms of global self-worth. As a result, I will devote discussion to both kinds of measures with special attention to those most frequently used in recent empirical research.

The Rosenberg (1965) Self-esteem Scale was specifically designed for adolescents and adults and consists of ten items (although some subsequent researchers have used only a subset of the items) concerning the degree to which one is satisfied with, for example, the "kind of person one is," "feels useful," thinks they are "not much good at anything." Usually these items are answered in a 5-point Likert format (strongly agree to strongly disagree). These measures are summarized to yield a total global self-esteem index. The Coopersmith Self-esteem Scale draws its items from four domains (e.g., school, peers, parents, and general references to the self) but calculates a total score. Subsequent factor analysis by Kokenes (1974) found that treating the Coopersmith scale as unidimensional is unwarranted; the Coopersmith is multidimensional. A third, widely used measure, especially in educational settings, is the Piers-Harris (1969) Self-concept Scale, which originally was intended to be unidimensional, but factor analysis revealed six factors: behavior, intellectual status, physical appearance, anxiety, popularity, and happiness and satisfaction (Piers, 1977).

Another approach, proposed by Shavelson, posits that global self-esteem represents a superordinate category under which other categories or domains are organized. These subdomains include emotional, social, physical, and academic areas. In addition to Shavelson and Bolus (1982), Marsh and his associates (see, for example, Marsh, Barnes, & Hocevar, 1985; Marsh, 1986) have developed an instrument building directly on Shavelson's hierarchical model. Finally, Harter (1983) has developed the Perceived Competence Scale, which assesses specific domains (cognitive, physical, social competence) and also contains a separate set of items, similar to Rosenberg's, that tap general self-worth. This method contrasts with Shavelson's in which commonalities among the specific components of the self are extracted as an index of general self-esteem.

This summary only skims the surface; as noted earlier, there are many other instruments that have been developed to assess self-esteem. Questions about the validity of unidimensional versus multidimensional models of self-esteem assessment, and independent versus hierarchical models, cannot be considered in detail here. The reader is referred to Harter (1983), Shavelson, Hubner, and Stanton (1976), and Marsh (1986) for discussion of these issues.

Although there is controversy about issues of operationalization and conceptualization, I will consider whether there are systematic changes in self-esteem over time, and, if so, what accounts for them. Surprisingly, despite interest in the adolescent period, there are few comprehensive hypotheses or theories about self-esteem change from early to late adolescence. An exception is Erikson (1968), who proposed that the identity crisis may produce a disturbance in self-image that may be reflected in lowered self-esteem. However, we will see later that there is considerable variation in the occurrence of the identity crisis. Zigler, Balla, and Watson (1972) also suggest self-esteem will be lowered in adolescence as a result of the rapid development of ideals that should create a gap between the real and the ideal. Other perspectives suggest, however, that self-esteem will increase with age. For example, Kaplan (1975) argues that individuals are motivated to experience positive self-attributes and to avoid the experience of negative self-attitudes. As a result, people act in ways that accomplish their goals and manifest a decrease in self-rejecting attitudes over time.

In her review of the self literature, Wylie (1979) summarized studies on self-esteem and concluded, "the bulk of the studies . . . show no association of age and self-regard scores" (p. 21). However, McCarthy and Hoge (1979) observe that of the "seven studies that showed increases in self-esteem with age, six were longitudinal in nature. Of the studies showing no relationship between self-esteem and age, 21 out of 22 were cross-sectional in design" (p. 373). McCarthy and Hoge argue that the longitudinal studies provide stronger data because they do not suffer from as many problems of sampling variability and error as the cross-sectional work. By piecing together the results of several strong studies, a fairly clear picture emerges.

Although it is cross-sectional, Rosenberg's study of a large sample of Baltimore children in grades 3 to 12 was well conducted in other respects. Using his Self-esteem Scale, Rosenberg (1979) reported that between the ages of 8 and 11, the children had relatively stable levels of self-esteem, but between the ages 12 and 14, self-esteem was lowered. Then, in the years 15 to 18, there was a rise in self-esteem. The decrease in self-esteem in the 12 to 14-year age range has been subsequently replicated in another sample by Simmons, Blyth, Van Cleave, and Bush (1979), and also by Harter and Connell (1984). Longitudinal studies of large national samples by Bachman and O'Malley (1977) find that there are steady increases in global self-esteem from ages 16 to 23. The rise in self-esteem during middle and late adolescence is also found in McCarthy and Hoge's sample of high school students who were assessed longitudinally for 1 year with a variation of the Rosenberg instrument. The McCarthy-Hoge study is particularly interesting because it tested for the effects of subject attrition, retesting, and carelessness on the part of the subjects. Taking cross-sectional and longitudinal data sets together (Bachman, O'Malley, & Johnston, 1978; Kaplan, 1975; Simmons, Rosenberg, & Rosenberg, 1973; Simmons *et al.*, 1979), it appears that entry into early adolescence brings a lowering of self-esteem, but, thereafter, global self-worth rises and continues to rise (according to O'Malley and Bachman, 1983) during the 5 years after high school.

This data pattern is consistent with Kaplan's (1975) notions. If people have a desire or need to maintain positive self-regard, high self-esteem people will work to maintain it while low self-esteem people will work to improve it, leading to an overall gain over time. McCarthy and Hoge (1979) suggest that increasing ability in role taking may also be responsible: "a person with improved role-taking ability may be able to behave socially in ways that actually enhance evaluation of the self by others. Also, adolescent gains in person autonomy and freedom of action . . . may allow them to manage their personal interactions in ways more effective in bolstering self-esteem" (pp. 378–379). These are interesting and plausible explanations for the rise in self-esteem found from middle to late adolescence. Unfortunately, there are no empirical studies available that permit these alternative explanations to be tested.

A question that remains is why global self-esteem should decrease in early adolescence with the largest change at age 12. Simmons *et al.* (1973) suggested that the disturbance may be the result of recently entering junior high school. The investigators were persuaded by their finding that 12-year-olds in seventh grade (hence junior high) were more likely to show negative self-images than were 12-year-olds in sixth grade (elementary school). Additional study of children in middle-level schools (K–8) where the shift from sixth to seventh grade does not involve a change in schools showed no decrease in self-esteem (Simmons *et al.*, 1979). The latter study also found that the girls entering junior high school are most likely to exhibit negative self-esteem, particularly those who are pubertal and dating. Simmons *et al.* (1979) suggest that girls may be most vulnerable because adolescence entails an increased emphasis on physical appearance and popularity, which assume more importance earlier for girls than for boys. This notion is bolstered by supplementary data on rankings of popularity, competence, appearance, and independence by boys and girls.

This evidence suggests that girls are more uncertain about their standing with regard to attractiveness and popularity in a new school. Presumably, with time, the adolescent "sorts out" her position, focuses on her strengths, and consequently gains in self-esteem. This explanation is not a complete one, however. For example, when boys' values change, should they not be subject to the same ambiguities? Evidence for self-esteem lowering in adolescent boys is not clear-cut. Also, why is there no parallel effect on self-esteem during the transition from junior high school to high school? Simmons *et al.* suggest that the difference between junior high school and elementary school may be experienced as much greater than the difference between junior and senior high school. More systematic research on changes in self-esteem across age and school setting would be helpful in answering these questions.

Another basic question is the relationship between self-esteem and gender. The general conclusion of Maccoby and Jacklin's (1974) review on sex differences was that there are no overall gender differences in self-esteem, but Wylie (1979) concluded that the studies were diverse and inconclusive. More recent work on adolescents in the Youth and Transition and Monitoring the Future Projects—longitudinal studies of large national samples—show that, if there are differences, the females have slightly lower scores, but it is on the order of .10 of a standard deviation or less (O'Malley & Bachman, 1979). There is also evidence that determinants of global self-esteem might be different across gender. Walker and Greene (1986) found that popularity was more strongly related to global self-esteem in girls but school performance was more important in boys. These results do not contradict the work of Simmons *et al.* since the national study samples deal with middle and late adolescents (ages 16–22).

Self-esteem and Educational Achievement

The relationship between self-esteem and academic performance has clear implications for the school setting. A meta-analysis of studies in the area (Hansford & Hattie, 1982) found that measures of ability correlated about .2 with general self-esteem, but correlated .4 with self-esteem relevant to ability. Such results emphasize the need to take into account the multidimensional nature of self-esteem. Hansford and Hattie (1982) also found that previously noted pattern applied across grade level; that is, there were no differences in the relationships between self-esteem and performance across early, middle, and late adolescence. Recently, however, Bachman and O'Malley (1977, 1984) found that educational accomplishments (i.e., grades) had greater importance or centrality for self-esteem during the high school years than during the 5 years beyond high school. Since Bachman and O'Malley based their conclusions on two large national samples studied longitudinally, while Hansford and Hattie (1982) had to rely on many smaller cross-sectional studies, we place more confidence in Bachman and O'Malley's results.

The general consensus of researchers is that there is a positive relationship between self-esteem and academic achievement (Faunce, 1984), but the direction of causality is controversial. Does self-esteem cause academic achievement or does achievement cause self-esteem? Or is the relationship reciprocal? If self-esteem enhances academic achievement, then perhaps efforts should be taken to increase self-esteem. On the other hand, if the causal relationship is actually reversed, then it may be more profitable to restructure the curriculum, for example, compensatory education. A number of empirical studies have examined these possibilities.

Calsyn and Kenny (1977) performed a secondary analysis of a longitudinal study of 556 adolescents from 8th to 12th grade. The measure of self-esteem was the Brookover Self-concept of Ability Scale, a measure oriented to academic self-esteem, and the achievement variable was grade point average. Using cross-panel correlation analysis, Calsyn and Kenny found that academic achievement was causally predominant over self-concept of ability. In a study of males from grade 10 to 5 years after high school graduation, Bachman and O'Malley (1977) examined the causal relationships between global self-esteem and academic (grade point average) and occupational achievement with panel-model analysis. Their results showed that academic achievement had a positive effect on self-esteem, but self-esteem had no effect on academic or occupational achievement. Harter and Connell (1984) found achievement was causally predominant over perceived cognitive competence in a cross-sectional study of 3rd to 9th graders. Maruyama, Rubin, and Kingsfield (1981) studied a group of children from ages 9 to 15 using the Coopersmith total score as an index of self-esteem and grades as an index of academic performance. Achievement measures and self-esteem measures were temporally separated to assess causal direction. Maruyama *et al.* reported that academic performance influenced academic self-esteem, but there was no effect of self-esteem on achievement. Taking the results of these studies together, it appears that compensatory models of skill development may be more beneficial than models emphasizing self-esteem enhancement. It should be noted, however, that two of the three longitudinal data sets employed a general measure of self-esteem rather than a measure of academic self-esteem. (Recall the earlier discussion that academic self-esteem relates more strongly to achievement than does general self-worth.)

The picture is further complicated by Shavelson and Bolus' (1982) longitudinal study of 99 junior high school students, which found that specific subject matter esteem (in mathematics, science, and English) was causally predominant over achievement as indicated by causal-modeling statistics. Although it has a smaller sample size than other studies and employed a shorter time interval, in its favor it employed specific self-esteem measures. Whether methodological differences account for the discrepancy in results across the studies is unclear.

From the preceding review it is difficult to draw any strong conclusions although, overall, the achievement–esteem link has found more support than the esteem–achievement link (cf. Bohrnstedt & Felson, 1983). Thus, programs developed along skill-development lines would appear to provide a better payoff. There is a need for large-sample longitudinal studies assessing global and specific domains of academic self-esteem, as well as multiple measures of academic performance and achievement.

Self-esteem and Socioeconomic Status

One common assumption is that socioeconomic status (SES) is positively linked to self-esteem, and particularly that disadvantaged youth are likely to think poorly of themselves. Wylie's (1979) review concluded that the "alleged positive association of SES level and overall regard is not supported by available investigations involving the better-known tests" (p. 93). There were positive trends, however, indicated for academic self-esteem and SES. In addition, there is evidence that the relationship between self-esteem and SES increases with age. Demo and Savin-Williams (1983) found that the correlation between social class and self-esteem (indexed by the Coopersmith measure and a more academic self-esteem measure) was nearly null among fifth graders, but moderate ($\gamma = .37$) among eighth graders (who were the oldest subjects in their sample). These results are consistent with Rosenberg and Pearlin's (1978) notion that young children live in a relatively homogeneous world in terms of SES and therefore view themselves as equals. With entry into secondary school, heterogeneous social class comparisons are more frequent and likely to influence self-esteem.

The literature is further complicated by a few studies finding that SES is negatively correlated with self-esteem; that is, higher self-esteem with lower class status (Soares & Soares, 1969; Trowbridge, 1972). In an intriguing paper, Marsh and Parker (1984) observed that previous studies finding a negative relationship between self-esteem and SES are based on school average SES; studies reporting a positive relationship are based on family SES. Marsh and Parker then suggest that the relationship between SES and self-esteem may be clarified by adopting a "frame of reference" or social comparison approach (see also Suls & Miller, 1977; Rosenberg & Pearlin, 1978). According to this view, children compare their own ability with the abilities of other students in their school and these impressions are the basis of their academic self-concept. This means that attending a low SES–ability school should induce higher academic self-esteem than attending a high SES–ability school that is more competitive. In contrast, when one controls for school average SES, family SES, because of the greater educational opportunities that higher family SES provides, is positively related to academic self-esteem.

Consistent with these arguments, Marsh and Parker (1984) found with a sample of sixth graders that "within a given level of school SES, the higher the family SES, the higher is the academic self-concept, but at a given level of family SES, the higher the school SES is, the lower is the academic self-concept" (p. 227). These results suggest that family SES and school SES have opposing effects and that school social comparisons need to be considered if we are to understand how children and adolescents construe their general and domain-specific self-esteem. Marsh and Parker note that the "frame of reference" approach works well for young children whose comparisons are limited to observation of a homogeneous group of classmates. What will happen if these children from exclusively high- and low-SES primary schools later come together in the same secondary school? Recent data reported by Bachman and O'Malley (1986) suggest that high school ability contexts have weaker effects: "By the time a student reaches high school, she or he has been exposed to such a sufficiently wide range of ability in schoolmates that mean differences from one school to another are not large enough to matter much" (p. 44). More study is needed to determine when and in what educational contexts "frame of reference" effects on self-esteem are most pronounced.

Problems and Prospectives

In this section, some additional questions about self-esteem are considered. One such question concerns self-esteem differences between blacks and whites as well as other ethnic groups. Research findings are even more conflicting than the work on self-esteem and SES. Many studies are characterized by null findings (Wylie, 1979), but those reporting differences tend to show blacks have higher self-esteem than whites (e.g., Rosenberg & Simmons, 1972; Bachman, 1970; Hoelter, 1983). A number of explanations have been offered for the latter pattern: situational–environmental conditions that restrict social comparisons between blacks and whites, thus restricting invidious comparisons with more advantaged whites; or methodological factors such that blacks and whites may apply different meanings to the self-esteem scales. Whether the black–white difference is a real one is not settled. It is worth noting, however, that Bachman and O'Malley (1984) have recently found that black respondents tend to use the extreme categories (of the self-esteem scales) more than do whites. As a result, they score higher in self-esteem if one uses the full-scale scores, but if one brackets or collapses the scale, the racial difference disappears.

A more basic question is whether self-esteem is a relatively stable entity or situationally specific. Longitudinal data suggest self-esteem is relatively stable (correlating between .70 and .92) from one year to the next, at least in the years subsequent to high school (O'Malley & Bachman, 1983), but self-esteem appears to change gradually over time. In contrast, self-theorists such as Gergen (1971, 1982) propose that there is more variability than stability in self-conception and esteem. However, variability is more commonly observed in laboratory studies (Morse & Gergen, 1970) than in survey studies (but see Swann, 1983). Thus differences in methodology may account for the apparent discrepancy. On the other hand, perhaps the self should be thought of as both stable *and* unstable. William James (1890) observed that there are rapid shifts and fluctuations of self-attribution from moment to moment, but there is also a sense of self-stability that serves as a baseline. The important empirical and conceptual questions, which remain unresolved, concern the kinds of situational and/or developmental processes that make a rapid shift or fluctuation into a permanent part of the self.

Methodological problems still remain in self-esteem research. One correctable problem is that many studies rely on a single measure of self-esteem. Some contradictory findings in the literature may be due more to different instruments than to differences in the underlying phenomena (Savin-Williams & Demo, 1983). A more serious problem is that respondents may report a more positive self-image than they privately experience. Greenwald and Pratkinis (1984) note that this is a routine problem in personality measurement: "However it takes a special twist in the case of self-esteem measurement because the wish to present a desirable image to others is, itself, an aspect of self-esteem" (p. 16).

In a recent secondary analysis of Rosenberg and Simmons' Baltimore sample data, Elliot (1982) found that the lower the respondent's self-esteem, the greater the extent of fabrication (as indexed by a separate scale). There were also differences depending on age and gender. For preadolescent boys (ages 8–11), the lower the self-esteem, the greater the tendency to cover one's feelings with a false front, but in middle (ages 12–14) and later adolescence (ages 15–19), there was no effect of self-esteem. For girls, low self-esteem was related to more self-fabrication in preadolescence and in the years 12–14; in the later phase, the relationship between self-esteem and fabrication disappeared. These data, which need replication, suggest that a self-presentation bias is more likely to contaminate the data from adolescent girls than from adolescent boys. In discussing his results, Elliott (1982) suggests that girls with low self-esteem may fabricate because their socialization puts more pressure on girls than boys to present a socially acceptable impression and maintain pleasant relationships (F. Rosenberg & Simmons, 1975). In contrast, boys may be more oriented to success and less concerned about hiding unpleasant feelings (or only when their success goals require this deception). These results alert us to possible self-presentation biases that interact with gender. Needless to say, then, there is a need to temper any strong conclusions about gender differences in self-esteem.

Finally, there have been calls from several quarters that self-esteem measurement needs to be complemented by means other than surveys. Savin-Williams (Savin-Williams & Demo, 1983; Savin-Williams & Jaquish, 1981) has conducted studies in which the Rosenberg scale is used in conjunction with behavioral observations suggestive of high or low self-esteem (e.g., maintains eye contact versus hesitates when speaks), and self-reports made repeatedly when signaled by a paging beeper. Multimethod approaches are likely to yield significant new information about self-stability and self-presentation.

Identity Formation

Previous sections concentrated on cognitive and evaluative aspects of the self in adolescence. In this section, identity, a topic that falls somewhere between the cognitive and evaluative self, is discussed. According to Erikson (1968), identity in adolescence involves the search for a consistent image of who one is and to what one is committed. Identity, then, is cognitive, evaluative, and also instrumentally or action oriented.

To understand Erikson's arguments, one must recognize that his notions about identity formation are only a part of his larger life-span developmental theory. Erikson proposes that individuals experience a series of major psychological crises as they go through the life cycle. At each stage, there is a confrontation between the self that the individual has achieved thus far and the new demands posed by the social setting. Erikson described eight such conflicts, but we will discuss only the ones leading up to adolescence, the adolescent "crisis" and the crisis that presumably follows. Between age 6 and puberty, the crisis is between *competence versus inferiority*. During this stage, the individual must attain a sense of making things well. Otherwise, the person will suffer from a sense of inferiority of being unable to cope with the inanimate or the social world.

During adolescence (ages 12 to 18 or 21), the crisis is *identity versus role confusion*. Of course, prior to this time the individual has a sense of self as an independent entity, but Erikson (1968) thinks the individual lacks a sense of wholeness: "a progressive continuity between that which he has come to be and that which he promises to become in the anticipated future" (p. 87). There is also an active social element in a well-developed identity in the sense that others should recognize the conception one has of one's self. The sense of wholeness also includes commitment to occupation and a world view (political, religious, or both). A successful resolution of the crisis, in which one figures out who one is, what one holds to be important, and what one will do in the future, permits the individual to better resolve the next crisis, that of *intimacy* (bonds of love and friendship) *versus isolation*. However, if the person does not develop a sense of identity, a feeling of role confusion will be dominant and only make it more difficult to establish intimate bonds later.

One problem with Erikson's theory is that his terms elude easy empirical operationalization, but, in his defense, he introduced these ideas for the purposes of clinical analysis and most of his ideas come from actual clinical practice. Nonetheless, his theory has inspired considerable research. James Marcia (1967) was one of the first to develop measurement procedures for assessing identity and for extending Erikson's ideas conceptually. Marcia (1967) constructed a semistructured interview to assess both the clarify of personal identity and the process by which it develops. The 15–30 minute interview includes a series of questions the answers to which are taped and rated by trained judges. A representative question is, "How willing do you think you'd be to give up going into _____ if something better came along." Answers are coded into four categories that correspond to Marcia's differentiations of ego identity status: identity achievement, moratorium, foreclosure, and identity diffusion.

An *identity achiever* is someone who has gone through a period of crisis and has developed firm commitments. A representative response to the question above is: "Well, I might, but I doubt it. I can't see what 'something better' would be for me." Individuals would be classified in the *moratorium* phase if they were currently in a state of crisis and were actively seeking among alternatives in an attempt to arrive at a choice. These are persons who are having an "identity crisis" at the time. An example of their response to the question would be: "I guess if I knew for sure I could answer that better. It would have to be something in the general area—something related." A person is classified as in *foreclosure* if he or she has never experienced a crisis but is nevertheless committed to particular goals, values, or beliefs. The commitments that foreclosures make generally reflect the wishes of parents or other authority figures. A foreclosure response to the question is: "Not very willing. It's what I have always wanted to do. The folks are happy with it and so am I." The *identity diffusion* category includes individuals who do not have firm commitments and are not actively trying to form them. They may never have been in a crisis or they may have been but were unable to resolve it, subsequently emerging without having made a decision. A person in this category might answer: "Oh sure. If something better came along, I'd change just like that."

Other measures of identity stage include self-report questionnaires such as Dignan's (1965), Rasmussen's (1964), and Constantinople's (1969), but these have been used less extensively than Marcia's. Despite the ease of their use, Bourne (1978) observes that self-report measures are more susceptible to social desirability response sets, which may have contributed to their receiving less empirical attention. The Marcia instruments also permit the four-category classification rather than a simple identity-achiever versus role-confusion classification.

There has been much research testing the construct validity of Erikson's and Marcia's notions. For example, persons in the moratorium stage should be highest in anxiety because they are in the midst of an identity crisis. This appears to be the case as indexed by responses to established anxiety questionnaires (Marcia, 1967; Oshman & Manosevitz, 1974). Respondents in foreclosure are lowest in anxiety, which is consistent with the idea that they are avoiding the issues of identity altogether (Podd, Marcia, & Rubin, 1970). Marcia (1966) also provided evidence that foreclosure subjects report more authoritarian values than do identity achievers. In a conformity experiment (Toder & Marcia, 1973), identity achievers conformed less than those with presumably unstable statuses (moratorium and diffusion); the foreclosure subjects also conformed less than the unstable groups. The latter result may seem surprising since foreclosures seem to conform to adult or parent pressure; but in the Toder and Marcia study the conformity pressure came from peers, so the results are not inconsistent.

In terms of self-esteem, identity achievers score the highest followed by moratorium subjects. The lowest scores were exhibited by those in foreclosure and identity diffusion (Breuer, 1973; Bunt, 1968). Marcia (1967) also found that male identity achievers and moratorium adolescents were less vulnerable to attempts to manipulate their self-esteem than were foreclosed or diffused male adolescents. A study of women (Marcia & Friedman, 1970) found that identity achievers scored lower than the other categories in self-esteem, while foreclosures scored the highest. The authors suggest that foreclosure status may be particularly adaptive for women in a male-dominated society. The picture is blurred, however, by Orlofsky's (1977) finding of no differences among the identity statuses for males and females. The Marcia instrument only taps occupational, political, and religious commitments, but some observers have suggested that identity for females may also include intimacy commitments. Hence, the Marcia interview may be inappropriate for females.

Despite some mixed findings, Damon's (1983) assessment of the ego identity area is a fair summary:

> Persons who have prematurely established a pseudo-identity (those in foreclosure) are temporally non-anxious, but are negative and unstable in their opinions of themselves. Those who are wrestling with the task of identity formation (classified as in moratorium) are anxious, but self-valuing. Those who have achieved identity are stable and positive in their self-esteem, and they experience anxiety to a normal and moderate degree. (p. 32)

Before leaving the subject of the construct validity of the identity concept, some findings are of special relevance to educators. One interesting question is whether the development of cognitive processes is related to the likelihood or solution of the identity crisis. Berzonsky, Weiner, and Raphael (1975) and Cauble (1976) tested the hypothesis that the acquisition of formal-operational thought would be related to the occurrence and resolution of identity formation; however, the results were negative—there was little or no relationship. These were cross-sectional studies that may be too insensitive to detect associations between the two domains. Also, it seems clear that intellectual level is necessary but not sufficient to produce identity formation.

A substantial body of literature suggests that basic scholastic aptitude is unrelated to identity status (Bourne, 1978). However, when scholastic aptitude (e.g., SAT scores) is controlled, identity formation and grade point average are highly correlated (Cross & Allen, 1970). This finding suggests that academic performance is associated with identity achievement, but findings also indicate that achiever and foreclosure subjects chose more difficult majors than the other statuses (Marcia & Friedman, 1970). A recent study by Berzonsky (1985) showed that neither high school nor college students classified as diffusions in Marcia's (1967) scheme showed a significant tendency to underachieve. Based on this summary, one must conclude that there are few, if any basic differences in ability between those who have progressed in terms of identity formation and those in foreclosure or diffusion. Thus, educators should not assume that the students who perform the best academically have resolved their commitments or identities.

Longitudinal Development of Identity

What is the empirical status of Erikson's hypothesis that the transition from adolescence involves a progressive strengthening in the sense of identity? Waterman (1982) observed that progressive shifts could be represented by three possibilities: from identity diffusion into either foreclosure or moratorium status, from foreclosure into moratorium status, or from moratorium into identity-achievement status. In contrast, a change into the identity-diffusion status from any of the others can be viewed as developmentally regressive at least from Erikson's perspective.

Cross-sectional studies (Meilman, 1979), with college-bound and younger males (ages 12, 14, and 18), using the Marcia interview found that the youngest subjects were in foreclosure or diffusion status. The oldest high school students showed more evidence of identity achievement. Waterman (1982) points out that the greatest gains occur in the college years. For example, using her questionnaire instrument, Constantinople (1969) found consistent increases in successful resolution of identity from freshman to senior year. A 10-year follow-up of Constantinople's sample with the addition of a new cohort also found increases in identity achievement, but there were sex differences: college women had lower scores than college men in 1966 whereas college women in 1976 had higher scores than college men. The implication is that the cohort effect for females may be the result of the changing climate with respect to sex-role definition in the last decade or so. Whitbourne and Waterman (1979) found that the greatest increases occurred for industry versus inferiority (rather than identity formation versus role confusion). This result is surprising and somewhat disconcerting for Erikson's theory as the former crisis is supposed to occur much earlier (before puberty).

Longitudinal research with the Marcia instrument provides a more consistent picture. Waterman and Waterman (1971) studied a group of male college adolescents through the course of their freshman year. There was a significant increase in the number of moratorium subjects with respect to occupation commitment and a decrease in the number of identity-diffusion subjects. However, men who had identity-achiever status at the beginning of their freshman year were just as likely to change as those who initially had the less "progressive" statuses. Lerner and Spanier (1980) noted that this puzzling result may be the result of the demands of the first year of college producing instability in identity. With time, however, identity should be achieved.

Empirical results are consistent with this expectation. Waterman, Geary, and Waterman (1974) followed up a group of male college seniors who had been part of the Waterman and Waterman (1971) freshman study. They found significant increases in the number of men who fell into the identity-achievement group, and a substantial portion remained at that status (see also Schiedel & Marcia, 1985). Marcia (1976) followed up 30 men who had initially been interviewed 6 years earlier while in college and found results similar to Waterman *et al.* (1974). Although there were trends indicating progressive development, the longitudinal data indicated that

> where individuals had firm commitments at the start of the study, approximately one-third to one-half were no longer in the same identity status by the time of the follow-up (four years later). . . . This finding for the identity achievement status makes it clear that the successful resolution of an identity crisis does not give a permanence to the commitment formed. (Waterman, 1982, p. 349)

However, consistent with Erikson's theory, identity achievement was more stable than the other statuses.

Most of the research reviewed above has involved college student samples in the late stage of adolescence. In fact, the vast majority of work with the Marcia instrument has been with college students. Fortunately, there is a body of research with younger subjects. Meilman's (1979) cross-sectional study included 12 to 24-year-olds and found the greatest shifts in the 18 to 21-year age range. LaVoie (1976), using a paper-and-pencil measure, and Raphael (1979), using an interview, also found little evidence of achiever status in early or middle adolescents. In a study of high school adolescents with the Marcia interview, Archer (1981) reported that diffusion and premature foreclosure were the principal identity statuses expressed among early adolescents (87% of the 8th and 10th graders, and 81% of the 12th graders). There was a trend for identity achievement to increase with age, especially in the vocational and religious belief areas, a point to be discussed later. Finally, a study by Adams and Jones (1983), using a questionnaire measure with females, found that middle adolescence (10th to 12th grades) was a period of gradual change, with the onset of foreclosure status most typical.

In general, it appears that only limited changes occur prior to and during the high school years at least with respect to identity formation. In contrast, much appears to happen during the years following high school, but it is so gradual that words like "turmoil" and "storm and stress" are probably inappropriate descriptors. Thus, available data contradict Erikson's notion of an identity "crisis" occurring during the teenage years. The discrepancy may be the result of Erikson's reliance on data from clinical experience with troubled adolescents who sought therapy. Most youths tend to go through the identity-formation process at a gradual rate and later in adolescence than Erikson's analysis proposes. The available data also suggest that identity achievement is not irreversible, for example, some individuals may retrogress from identity achievement to moratorium. As in many areas of development, there is considerable plasticity.

The identity-formation research literature has problems that should be noted (Cote & Levine, 1983). First, we lack large-scale longitudinal studies of adolescents from pre- to postadolescence. As noted in the discussion of self-esteem, cross-sectional studies are more subject to sampling error, cohort effects, and so on. There have also been some concerns raised about possible interviewer influence on subjects' responses to the Marcia instrument, excessive reliance on verbal skills (Bourne, 1978, p. 381), and overemphasis of occupational and ideological commitments in relation to other kinds of commitments. Some questionnaire measures, notably the OM-EIS devised by Adams, Shea, and Fitch (1979), have attempted to correct these deficits and have met validity criteria, although more study is needed (cf. Craig-Bray & Adams, 1986). Full-scale comparisons of the Marcia interview with recent questionnaire measures should be a high priority item for researchers in this area. Another weakness is that there has been little research with noncollege samples of equivalent age to determine the relative contribution of ontogenetic and situational variables to identity change. It is interesting to note that a comparison of a college sample with a working sample of equivalent age found the latter to be more likely in identity-achievement status. Munro and Adams (1977) suggest that full-time employment might stimulate rapid movement toward identity formation. More study of same-age groups in different situations is needed.

Also, Adams *et al.* (1979) note that there is a need to move from the typology perspective taken by Erikson and Marcia to one of developmental processes. "Instead of asking what stage a subject is in, the question should be to what extent and under what conditions does a subject's thinking exhibit various stages of thinking" (Rest, 1975, pp. 739–740). The Adams *et al.* instrument is suited to such an approach but more research is needed.

The reader can discern that the body of research on identity formation is neither as consistent or as methodologically elegant as work on self-concept and suffers from some of the same problems as work on self-esteem. Nonetheless, certain conclusions do emerge that may be of assistance to the educator. Although adolescence is frequently thought of as a period of storm and stress,'' the weight of the empirical evidence suggests that the sorting out of values, commitments, and sense of one's self occurs during the years following high school. During middle adolescence, most young people appear to be in foreclosure. This conclusion is consistent with the work of Douven and Adelson (1966), Kandel and Lesser (1972), and Offer (1969) who find that middle adolescence is not a particularly troublesome period in terms of relationships between adolescents and their parents.

There are some data suggesting that when identity-achievement gains are made in high school, they are most frequently in the vocational and religious belief areas. This may be the result of the school's emphasis on curricular tracks, college majors, and employment (Archer, 1982). Also, the study of evolution may prompt conflicts with religious teaching. Archer also notes that when identity diffusion is present among high schoolers, it tends to be in the political area. Perhaps diffusion occurs because middle adolescents learn much about government and political orientation but lack opportunities for meaningful political activity.

A comment by Archer (1982) is worth quoting as this section is concluded:

> Psychologists, educators, religious leaders and parents who have made the assumption that early and middle adolescents are actively considering alternatives and developing firm, personal commitments with regard to life-goal decisions may need to re-examine the appropriateness and timing of their demands . . . Premature foreclosure commitments may prove inappropriate as they may be more expressive of the psychologist or parent advocating them than of the adolescent. (p. 1556)

Egocentrism in Adolescence

Some writers and laypeople treat the next phenomenon under discussion, *adolescent egocentrism,* as part of identity formation; however, they are best treated separately. An aspect of the Piagetian theory of intellectual development, egocentrism refers to a lack of differentiation in some area of subject–object interaction. The best known form of egocentrism occurs during the concrete-operational phase, when children confuse mental representations with perceptual givens. With the growth of formal-operational thought in the teenage years, another form of egocentrism—adolescent egocentrism—is observed (Elkind, 1967). Adolescents not only conceptualize their own thoughts but also have the capacity to take into account other people's thoughts. This new capacity leads the adolescent to fail to differentiate between those objects toward which the thoughts of others are directed and those that are the focus of one's own attention. As a result, adolescents tend to believe that others are as concerned with the adolescent's thoughts, feelings, and behavior as they themselves. This leads to heightened self-consciousness, a sense of being evaluated by others, or playing to an "imaginary audience." Another feature of this kind of thought is the construction of a *personal fable*—a complex of beliefs in the uniqueness of one's own feelings and immortality—a story that individuals tell themselves, which they believe is true.

Although adolescent egocentrism may seem related to identity formation, the former seems to be independent of the later process. This is suggested by the fact that egocentrism peaks and diminishes before identity moratorium or identity achievement is found in most adolescents. Possibly, adolescent egocentrism is more a function of cognitive development while identity formation involves a complex mix of cognitive, emotional, and social factors.

According to Elkind (1967), the imaginary audience and the personal fable should appear during the beginning of adolescence (or rise of formal-operational thought) and only diminish by the age of 15 or 16. Presumably, the imaginary audience recedes because it is progressively modified in the direction of the reactions of the real audience. Used as a kind of test against reality, the imaginary audience gradually comes closer to the actual preoccupations and interests of others. Elkind thinks the personal fable recedes when the individual has established intimacy with others, which allows the individual to understand that others have similar feelings to one's own.

Although these ideas are interesting, they have not generated much empirical research. Simmons *et al.* (1973) observed that 12-year-olds report the highest levels of self-consciousness, that is, reluctance to perform before an audience. Elkind and Bowen (1979) developed an Imaginary Audience Scale that evaluates self-consciousness about the abiding self—long-lived characteristics—and the transient self—momentary appearances and behaviors. This scale presents a series of stories, for example: "You notice a grease spot on your trousers on the way to a party. Do you go home or go to the party?'' Or, ''If you went to a party where you didn't know anyone, would you wonder about what they think about you?'' Elkind and Bowen (1979) administered the scale to a sample of 4th, 6th, 8th, and 12th graders. Their results showed that 8th graders (ages 13–14) were less willing than older or younger subjects to reveal their transient or abiding selves; also, girls tended to be more reluctant than boys.

Enright, Shukla, and Lapsley (1980) have also devised an instrument, consisting of Likert-type items, to assess beliefs in the imaginary audience and the personal fable. But they found that these beliefs declined from 6th grade to college. The reason for the discrepancy between Elkind and Enright's results is unclear; Enright *et al.* find these features of adolescent egocentrism occur earlier and decline sooner than reported by Elkind, who finds a curvilinear function with the peak at age 14.

A more recent study (Gray & Hudson, 1984), using the Elkind-Bowen scale, replicated the curvilinear pattern but found, contrary to Elkind's thinking, that imaginary-audience scores were not the highest among those subjects whose formal-operational thought was just beginning to be established. Gray and Hudson (1984) propose that concrete operations may be necessary and sufficient to produce the subjectivity that characterizes adolescent egocentrism. These authors mention Blasi and Hoeffel's (1974) suggestion that the adolescent's personal, social, and civic life may produce an understanding of subjective possibility, quite apart from the systematic formal thought usually considered necessary for subjectivity.

Although there is only a small body of literature to rely on, the belief in the imaginary audience and personal fable appear and peak either in early or middle adolescence. Unfortunately there has been no work to examine the relationship between adolescent egocentrism and identity formation. Taking the two literatures together, I suggest that the imaginary audience and personal fable should precede the moratorium and identity-achievement phase.

Although little studied, adolescent egocentrism may have some important educational implications. Egocentrism may cause the adolescent to retreat for a time from adults and peers. Rather than considering this a problem, it is probably best to view such behavior as a necessary retreat. Instead of reacting against it and trying to draw the teenager out of his or her shell, parents and teachers would best acknowledge this phase and let it take its course. One expects that teenagers' communication with others will be problematic and school work may suffer for a period. Perhaps the most significant contribution to be made by the schools would be to acknowledge this phenomenon and treat it as normal.

Social Psychological Approaches

In this section, I will briefly review some topics from social psychology that have implications for adolescent self-development. Most of this work has not taken a developmental direction, although it may be fruitful if it does so in the near future.

In the early 1970s, Robert Wicklund and his associates (Duval & Wicklund, 1972; Wicklund, 1975) proposed a theory of self-awareness to describe when people focus attention on themselves and what happens when they do. Focusing of attention on specific aspects of the self is considered a state of *objective self-awareness*. This state can be created in the laboratory by placing a mirror in front of the subject, by playing back a tape recording of the subject's voice, or by placing the person in an unstructured or unfamiliar setting. According to Wicklund, the state of awareness induces a process of self-evaluation; a consideration of how the person's behavior matches with some internal rule or standard. If a negative discrepancy is detected, then the person will experience negative feelings and try to avoid further self-reflection, or the person will try to do something to correct the discrepancy.

Extending Wicklund's analysis, Scheier and Carver (1987) have proposed a cybernetic model that assumes that self-attention is best represented as a continual adjustment process between present behavior and standards. (A good analogy is a thermostat that continually tests the present temperature with the temperature standard.) Carver and Scheier (1981) and Buss (1980) also distinguish between different kinds of self-focused attention. *Public self-consciousness* refers to the tendency to be concerned with how one is seen as a social object. *Private self-consciousness* involves a focus on more private aspects of the self-bodily sensations, moods, and feelings. Situational factors can increase public or private self-consciousness. For example, looking at one's reflection in a mirror or listening to a tape recording of one's voice are thought to increase private self-consciousness, but speaking before an audience or being filmed by a videotape camera increase public self-consciousness (Scheier & Carver, 1983). These two different forms of self-consciousness also have dispositional manifestations. Fenigstein, Scheier, and Buss (1975) have developed an inventory to assess the chronic disposition to be publicly and privately self-conscious. (These dimensions are considered independent; a person can be high or low on one and high or low on the other.)

Whether a person is in a state of public or private self-consciousness has significant behavioral effects. For example, high private self-consciousness, either dispositional or situationally induced, makes people more aware of internal sensations (Scheier, Carver, & Gibbons, 1979). Also, persons high in private self-consciousness are less likely to change their attitudes in accord with their behavior (Scheier & Carver, 1980) and are less suggestible (Gibbons, Carver, Scheier, & Hormuth, 1979). In contrast, high public self-consciousness, either dispositional or situationally induced, is associated with more variability in behavior (presumably because there is an increased need to fit one's behavior to different social situations), and with more fear of being rejected by others (Fenigstein, 1979).

The empirical data summarized above come from studies that examine each form of self-consciousness separately. More compelling data are found in experiments where both kinds of self-focus should influence behavior, but in opposing ways. For example, Froming and Carver (1981) hypothesized that high levels of private self-consciousness, because associated with awareness and responsiveness to one's own feelings and opinions, should prompt individuals to rely on their own opinions and to disregard the misleading opinions of other group members. In contrast, because high levels of public self-consciousness should make people more sensitive to how they appear to others, it was expected that high public self-conscious individuals should comply with the group even if it is wrong. These hypotheses were tested in an Asch-type conformity experiment where subjects were induced to make incorrect responses on a perceptual task by means of simulated group pressure. Froming and Carver's results showed that private self-consciousness was inversely related to compliance; public self-consciousness was positively associated with compliance. Studies of attitudinal expression, distributive justice, and reactance also indicate that public and private self-focus have opposing effects on behavior (see Scheier & Carver, 1983, 1987).

Research to date has typically employed college students as research subjects. The assumption is made that findings with this group generalize to other samples, hence to individuals in early and middle adolescence. Unfortunately, there has been little cross-sectional study and no longitudinal research in this area. What data are available are tentative. Enright *et al.* (1980) administered the Fenigstein *et al.* inventory to students in the 6th, 8th, 10th, and 12th grades and college. Private self-consciousness was correlated with age ($r = .24$) with college students exhibiting more than the younger groups. There were no significant age differences for the public aspect of self-consciousness. Since the Enright *et al.* study involved relatively small samples, there is a need for more study. If these findings are replicated, then concern about the social aspects of self-presentation would appear not to change greatly over the various phases of adolescence. (Note that public self-consciousness in this approach entails a focus of attention on social aspects of identity that is distinct from the anxious concern about revealing one's self before other people. The anxious form of self-consciousness may peak in midadolescence, according to Elkind & Bowen, 1979.) Enright *et al.* (1980) show that concern about the private aspects of the self increases from early to late adolescence, a result consistent with our review of the ego identity literature indicating the identity crisis was more likely to occur in the college years.

Research on self-awareness may be helpful in understanding adolescent development. First, as indicated above, previous authors have written about the self-preoccupation of the adolescence, but it is important to distinguish between different forms of self-awareness. As some research indicates, focusing on discrepancies between one's performance and privately held standards may have different consequences than focusing on discrepancies with public standards. The schools have a significant role in making certain standards salient for the adolescent. Thus, for example, teachers may encourage students to improve on the basis of their past performance, an internal private standard, or, alternately, encourage students to perform competitively according to an external social standard. If students are becoming increasingly more privately self-conscious, then self-improvement may be more motivating than competitive advantage. In addition, criterion-referenced rather than normative-referenced testing may be preferred if adolescents as a whole increase in private self-consciousness. In a more general way, the appreciation that there are two sides of the self, the private and public, which frequently pull in different directions, may help to understand some of the dilemmas of adolescents. After all, this is the first period in which the individual is forging both a unique private and public identity.

Self-monitoring

Another example of a social psychological concept that needs developmental study is the individual difference of self-monitoring (Snyder, 1979, 1987). According to Snyder (1987), people differ in the extent to which they can and do exercise control over their verbal and nonverbal self-presentation. High self-monitoring persons are "sensitive to the expression and self-presentation of relevant others in social situations and use these cues as guidelines for monitoring their own verbal and nonverbal self-presentation" (p. 89). In contrast, the low self-monitoring person is not "vigilant to social information about situationally appropriate self-presentation" (p. 89). Snyder (1979) developed an inventory to assess the individual's position on the self-monitoring continuum (see also Snyder & Gangested, 1986). For example, someone high in self-monitoring is likely to subscribe to the item, "In different situations and with different people, I often act like very different persons," while persons low in self-monitoring are not likely to.[1]

A considerable amount of evidence has accumulated that supports Snyder's notions about this individual difference. For example, Snyder and Monson (1975) have demonstrated that when group norms call for conformity, high self-monitors conform, but when group norms call for autonomy, high self-monitors act independently. In contrast, low-self-monitors are unaffected by differences in group norms; they exhibit their own personal attitudes and dispositions regardless of what is situationally appropriate. Other studies (Snyder, 1987) show that attitudes are a better predictor of future behavior among low than among high self-monitors. Also, high self-monitors have more heterogeneous friends and their social worlds are more segmented than the friendships and social worlds of low self-monitors. High self-monitors also like to enter into social situations that provide clear expectations of the type of character one ought to be in the situation. Low self-monitors are as willing to enter situations of clearly defined as of vaguely defined character. In either case, low self-monitors act in accord with their personal dispositions. Additional construct validation for the self-monitoring dimension can be found in Snyder (1987; Snyder & Gangestad (1986).

Although self-monitoring should have developmental antecedents, they have not been studied. In general, one would expect that young children would not be high in self-monitoring; in fact, cognitive egocentrism would preclude such behavior. Even after egocentrism has passed in middle childhood, the individual is unlikely to have acquired the tools of self-presentation or a knowledge of how to construe social situations. It is likely that such knowledge and skill develop in the adolescent years as the teenager's acquaintanceship network expands. Some of the awkwardness of adolescents when they are around adults might be seen as early attempts at self-monitoring, trying to exhibit the appropriate behaviors for the situation. Unfortunately, social and developmental psychologists have not studied factors that might lead to dispositional or age-related

---

[1] There are obvious similarities between the concepts of self-monitoring and public self-consciousness. Although the two dimensions are related, high public self-conscious persons may not be high self-monitors. Public self-consciousness refers to the awareness of the impression one is making, but the individual may not act on that information. In contrast, self-monitors use this information to guide their presentations so as to gain social approval.

changes in self-monitoring. Some potential factors leading to high levels of self-monitoring are parental modeling and exposure to diverse situations that demand pragmatic behavior.

It is possible that there is an overall increase in self-monitoring with entry into adolescence. For one thing, teenagers' social world expands so that the sources of social reward diversify. Also, the search for opposite-sex companionship should highlight the need to behave in ways that are socially appropriate. Both factors may encourage teenagers to focus on the social world and their own verbal and nonverbal self-presentations. Upon entry into adulthood and with the development of intimate ties, self-monitoring may wane as one becomes one's own person.

Although speculative, research on self-monitoring has some implications for education. For example, Snyder and Campbell (1982) note that an individual's choice of occupation and hence educational preparation may reflect their level of self-monitoring. High self-monitoring individuals may choose professions that permit or even demand the portrayal of a range of roles, such as in theatre, public relations, or law. Persons low in self-monitoring may aim for professions that require and support the enactment of behaviors that express their true dispositions. Thus, this individual difference may influence the choice of curriculum in high school and in higher education. There may also be significant differences in the diversity of social worlds and experiences between high and low self-monitors. Such differences could have important consequences for the individual's subsequent decision making. Hopefully, these speculations can be replaced by empirical data in the near future as social and developmental psychologists examine self-monitoring in the adolescent context.

Self as an Information-processing System

Recently the self has been conceptualized as an information-processing system, particularly as a memory system (Greenwald, 1981). Empirical work has demonstrated, for example, that material that is encoded with reference to the self is more easily retrieved than is material passively encountered; judgments are better remembered when they are made relevant to the self versus relevant to others. Greenwald (1980) also summarized evidence concerning the pervasiveness of three biases in self-knowledge: (1) egocentricity or the tendency for judgment and memory to be focused on the self, (2) benefectance or the tendency for the self to be perceived as effective in achieving desired ends while avoiding undesired ones, and (3) cognitive conservatism or the tendency to resist cognitive change. It is argued that these biases function to preserve the ego's organization of knowledge.

One implication of Greenwald's analysis is that it should take considerable effort to change a person's basic conception of the self. Hence, sporadic feedback from educators, parents, and so on is unlikely to produce major changes in self-esteem or self-conception. Of course, much (although not all) of the empirical evidence for these biases comes from studies with college students. Whether these "totalitarian" (Greenwald's descriptor) ego biases apply to earlier phases of adolescence remains an empirical question. Since the ego identity literature (Waterman, 1982) indicates that the greatest changes occur in the college years, perhaps these biases are actually defensive maneuvers employed at a time when self-definition is shifting. Developmental study is needed to evaluate this possibility.

Other social psychological work has focused on the determinants of self-concept and self-esteem. Three primary bases of self-information are mentioned in most discussions of this topic: (1) reflected appraisals (Mead, 1934; Hoelter, 1984) or the perceptions about how one appears to others, (2) social comparison with others (Festinger, 1954), and (3) self-perceptions or the self-evaluations of one's own achievements or attributes (Bem, 1972).

Reflected appraisal and self-perception are acknowledged as sources of information used during all phases of the life cycle. In contrast, social comparison information may only be utilized during certain periods. Suls (1986) proposed that children do not actively compare their performances with others and evaluate their capabilities until the age of 5 or 6. And even when similarities of disparities in performance with others are noted, children rarely draw inferences about self-capacity. The lack of interest in social comparison is thought to result from the young child's egocentrism and inadequate appreciation of abstract concepts such as ability. When children enter into formal schooling, their interest in social comparison increases, but their comparisons are initially indiscriminate, that is, with both similar and dissimilar others. The lack of selectivity reflects the children's lack of appreciation that peers who share comparable experiences are the most appropriate others with which to gauge one's performance. During middle childhood, children begin to focus on similar others, a tendency continuing through adolescence (e.g., Rosenberg, 1979; Suls, Gastorf, & Lawhon, 1978).

The increasing reliance on similar others in the teenage years may be partially responsible for the heavy peer pressure that is commonly observed. There is evidence that one's position in the world influences adolescent self-esteem (Brown & Lohr, 1987). However, parents and other adults still remain important sources of standards and feedback (Douvan & Adelson, 1966; Kandel & Lesser, 1972). Thus, adolescents probably use multiple sources of feedback to evaluate how well they are doing, with peers probably exerting somewhat more influence.

Unfortunately, there has been little systematic study of the additive or interactive effects of social comparison, reflected appraisal and self-perception, especially in the adolescent years. Thus, it is unclear whether social comparison, reflected appraisal, and self-perception are equally influential or whether some kinds of information are more important than others during the early, middle, or late phases of adolescence. Data on these issues might be very useful to educators in understanding why some students have a high opinion of their academic abilities while others have a low opinion. A better understanding of how different forms of information are used by the adolescent to make self-appraisals may aid in the development of more successful educational interventions.

Conclusions

This chapter has covered a lot of ground both in the developmental and the social psychological areas. Despite some empirical weaknesses in the research literature, several conclusions stand out. First, with age adolescents acquire an increasingly internal sense of their attributes. As Rosenberg (1986) observes, the self proceeds from exterior to interior, from overt behavior to internal traits. Second, self-esteem tends to decrease, particularly for girls, upon entry to junior high school but then rises and continues to rise through high school and in the 5 years that follow high school. The initial dip in self-esteem appears to be best explained by entry into a new and less homogeneous school environment. Third, with respect to identity formation, the majority of evidence suggests that shifts involving questioning and decision making, and subsequent identity achievement, occur most often during the college years and not during high school. If the high schooler has begun to tackle the identity versus role-confusion dilemma, he or she tends to make a premature foreclosure. In the college years, there is a progressive identity achievement, but new situations and problems may engender new crises. Hence, identity is in no sense permanent or irreversible. Fourth, concern about performance before others and development of the imaginary audience and the personal fable begin in early adolescence and peak in midadolescence, followed by a decline.

There has also been much work devoted to different aspects of self-awareness—the public and private self and self-monitoring—but this has not yet been examined with a developmental perspective. Similarly, study of ego biases and sources of self-evaluative information during adolescence have thus far received little attention. Research in developmental and social psychology has been separated for too long, suggesting that a certain egocentrism may plague social scientists as well as adolescents.

In general, the present essay makes a simple, but nevertheless, significant point. The phenomena that are thought to be part of adolescence—self-consciousness, introspection, confusion—are not necessarily simultaneous. Instead, they are manifested and worked out at different times during the period from 12 to 18 or 21 years of age. The self-development of the adolescent is similar to what has been observed in cognitive development—gradual within-stage changes and less unity, consistency, and developmental interdependence within each stage than Piagetian theory assumed (Flavell, 1977).

During the behaviorist heyday, the "self" was not a respectable area of psychological research. That situation has changed although many questions remain. It may be appropriate to conclude this chapter with a quote from Kevin Lynch (1984), who was speaking about an altogether different topic but whose words are relevant to the psychological study of the self: "Of course, it may only be the tip of the iceberg, whose base is hidden far below, but the tip is the tip of a real iceberg, nonetheless' (p. 162).

References

Adams, G. R., & Jones, R. M. (1983). Female adolescents' identity development: Age comparisons and perceived child-rearing experience. *Developmental Psychology,* **19,** 245–256.

Adams, G. R., Shea, J., & Fitch, S. A. (1979). Toward the development of an objective assessment of ego-identity status. *Journal of Youth and Adolescence,* **8,** 223–237.

Albert, S. (1977). Temporal comparison theory. *Psychological Review,* **84,** 485–503.

Archer, S. L. (1982). The lower age boundaries of identity development. *Child Development,* **53,** 1551–1556.

Bachman, J. G. (1970). *Youth in transition* (Vol. 2). Ann Arbor, MI: Institute for Social Research.

Bachman, J. G., & O'Malley, P. (1977). Self-esteem in young men: A longitudinal analysis of the impact of educational and occupational attainment. *Journal of Personality and Social Psychology,* **35,** 365–380.

Bachman, J. G., & O'Malley, P. M. (1984). Black-white differences in self-esteem: Are they affected by response styles? *American Journal of Sociology,* **90,** 624–639.

Bachman, J. G., & O'Malley, P. M. (1986). Self-concepts, self-esteem, and educational experiences: The Frog Pond revisited (Again). *Journal of Personality and Social Psychology,* **50,** 35–46.

Bachman, J. G., O'Malley, P. M., & Johnston, J. (1978). *Youth in transition* (Vol. 6). Ann Arbor, MI: Institute for Social Research.

Bem, D. J. (1972). Self-perception theory. In L. Berkowitz (Ed.), *Advances in experimental social psychology* (Vol. 6, pp. 1–62). New York: Academic Press.

Bernstein, R. M. (1980). The development of the self-system in adolescence. *Journal of Genetic Psychology, 136,* 231–245.

Berzonsky, M. D. (1985). Diffusion within Marcia's identity-status paradigm: Does it foreshadow academic problems. *Journal of Youth and Adolescence, 14,* 527–538.

Berzonsky, W. M., Weiner, A. S., & Raphael, D. (1975). Interdependence of formal reasoning. *Developmental Psychology, 11,* 258.

Blasi, A., & Hoeffel, E. (1974). Adolescence and formal operations. *Human Development, 17,* 344–363.

Bohrnstedt, G. W., & Felson, R. B. (1983). Explaining the relations among children's actual and perceived performances and self-esteem. A comparison of several causal models. *Journal of Personality and Social Psychology, 45,* 43–56.

Bourne, E. (1978). The state of research on ego identity: A review and appraisal. Part 1. *Journal of Youth and Adolescence, 7,* 223–251.

Breuer, H. (1973). *Ego identity status in late-adolescent college males, as measured by a group-administered incomplete sentences blank and related to inferred stance toward authority.* Unpublished doctoral dissertation, New York University.

Broughton, J. (1978). Development of concepts of self, mind, reality and knowledge. *New Directions for Child Development, 1,* 75–100.

Broughton, J. (1980). The divided self in adolescence. *Human Development, 24,* 13–32.

Brown, B. B., & Lohr, M. J. (1987). Peer-group affiliation and adolescent self-esteem: An integration of ego-identity and symbolic interaction theory. *Journal of Personality and Social Psychology, 52,* 47–55.

Bunt, M. (1968). Ego identity: Its relationship to the discrepancy between how an adolescent views himself and how he perceives that others view him. *Psychology, 5,* 14–25.

Buss, A. (1980). *Self-consciousness and social anxiety.* San Francisco: Freeman.

Calcyn, R. J., & Kenny, D. (1977). Self-concept of ability and perceived evaluation of others: Cause or effect of academic achievement? *Journal of Educational Psychology, 69,* 136–145.

Carver, C. S., & Scheier, M. F. (1981). *Attention and self-regulation: A control-theory approach to human behavior.* New York: Springer-Verlag.

Cauble, M. A. (1976). Formal operations, ego identity, and principled morality: Are they related? *Developmental Psychology, 12,* 363–364.

Constantinople, A. (1969). An Eriksonian measure of personality development in college students. *Developmental Psychology, 1,* 357–372.

Coopersmith, S. (1967). *The antecedents of self-esteem.* San Francisco: Freeman.

Cote, J. E., & Levine, C. (1983). Marcia and Erickson: The relationship among ego identity status, neuroticism, dogmatism, and purpose in life. *Journal of Youth and Adolescence, 12,* 43–53.

Craig-Bray, L., & Adams, G. R. (1986). Different methodologies in the assessment of identity; Congruence between self-report and interview techniques. *Journal of Youth and Adolescence, 15,* 191–204.

Cross, H., & Allen, J. (1970). Ego identity status, adjustment and academic achievement. *Journal of Consulting and Clinical Psychology, 34,* 288.

Damon, W. (1983). *Social and personality developoment.* New York: Norton.

Demo, D. H., & Savin-Williams, R. C. (1983). Early adolescent self-esteem as a function of social class: Rosenberg and Pearlin revisited. *American Journal of Sociology,* **88,** 763–774.

Dignan, M. H. (1965). Ego identity and maternal identification. *Journal of Personality and Social Psychology,* **1,** 476–483.

Douven, E., & Adelson, J. (1966). *The adolescent experience.* New York: Wiley.

Dusek, J. B., & Flaherty, J. R. (1981). The development of the self-concept during the adolescent years. *Monographs of the Society for Research in Child Development,* **46,** (4, Serial No. 191).

Duval, S., & Wicklund, R. A. (1972). *A theory of objective self-awareness.* New York: Academic Pres.

Elkind, D. (1967). Egocentrism in adolescence. *Child Development,* **38,** 1025–1034.

Elkind, D., & Bowen, R. (1979). Imaginary audience behaior in children and adolescents. *Developmental Psychology,* **15,** 38–44.

Elliott, G. C. (1982). Self-esteem and self-presentation among the young as a function of age and gender. *Journal of Youth and Adolescence,* **11,** 135–153.

Enright, R. D., Shulka, D., & Lapsley, D. (1980). Adolescent egocentrism-sociocentrism and self-consciousness. *Journal of Youth and Adolescence,* **9,** 101–116.

Erikson, E. (1968). *Identity, youth and crisis.* New York: Norton.

Faunce, W. A. (1984). School achievement, social status and self-esteem. *Social Psychology Quarterly,* **47,** 3–14.

Fenigstein, A. (1979). Self-consciousness, self-attention, and social interaction. *Journal of Personality and Social Psychology,* **37,** 75–86.

Fenigstein, A., Scheier, M. F., & Buss, A. H. (1975). Public and private self-consciousness: Assessment and theory. *Journal of Consulting and Clinical Psychology,* **43,** 522–527.

Festinger, L. (1954). A theory of social comparison processes. *Human Relations,* **7,** 117–140.

Flavell, J. H. (1977). *Cognitive development.* Englewood Cliffs, NJ: Prentice-Hall.

Fleming, J. S., & Courtney, B. E. (1984). The dimensionality of self-esteem: II. Hierarchical facet model for revising measurement scales. *Journal of Personality and Social Psychology,* **46,** 404–421.

Froming, W. J., & Carver, C. S. (1981). Divergent influences of private and public self-consciousness in a compliance paradigm. *Journal of Research in Personality,* **15,** 159–171.

Gergen, K. J. (1971). *The concept of self.* New York: Holt.

Gergen, K. (1982). From self to science: What is there to know? In J. Suls (Ed.), *Psychological perspectives on the self* (Vol. 1, pp. 129–149), Hillsdale, NJ: Erlbaum.

Gibbons, F. X., Carver, C. S., Scheier, M. F., & Hormuth, S. E. (1979). Self-focused attention and the placebo effect: Fooling some of the people some of the time. *Journal of Experimental Social Psychology,* **15,** 263–274.

Gordon, C. (1968). Self-conceptions: Configurations of content. In C. Gordon & K. J. Gergen (Eds.), *The self in social interaction* (Vol. 1, pp. 115–137) New York: Wiley.

Gray, W. M., & Hudson, L. M. (1984). Formal operations and the imaginary audience. *Developmental Psychology,* **20,** 619–627.

Greenwald, A. G. (1980). The totalitarian ego: Fabricationa nd revision of personal history. *American Psychologist,* **35,** 603–618.

Greenwald, A. G. (1981). Self and memory. In G. H. Bower (Ed.), *The psychology of learning and motivation* (Vol. 15, pp. 202–236). New York: Academic Press.

Greenwald, A. G., & Pratkinis, A. R. (1984). The self. In R. S. Wyer & T. K. Srull (Eds.), *Handbook of social cognition.* Hillsdale, NJ: Erlbaum.

Hall, G. S. (1904). *Adolescence* (2 vols.). New York: Appleton.

Hansford, B. C., & Hattie, J. A. (1982). The relationship between self and achievement/ performance measures. *Review of Educational Research, 52,* 123–142.

Harter, S. (1983). The development of the self system. In M. Hetherington (Ed.), *Carmichael's manual of child psychology: Social and personality development.* New York: Wiley.

Harter, S. (1986). Processes underlying self-concept formation in children. In J. Suls & A. G. Greenwald (Eds.), *Psychological perspectives on the self* (Vol. 3, pp. 136–182). Hillsdale, NJ: Erlbaum.

Harter, S., & Connell, J. P. (1984). A comparison of alternative models between academic achievement and children's perceptions of competence, control, and motivational orientation. In J. Nicholls (Ed.), *The development of achievement-related cognitions and behaviors* (pp. 214–250). Greenwich, CT: J.A.I. Press.

Hoelter, J. W. (1983). Factorial invariance and self-esteem: Reassessing race and sex differences. *Social Forces,* 834–845.

Hoelter, J. W. (1984). Relative effects of significant others on self-evaluation. *Social Psychology Quarterly, 47,* 255–262.

Inhelder, B., & Piaget, J. (1958). *The growth of logical thinking for childhood to adolescence.* New York: Basic Books.

James, W. (1890). *Principles of psychology.* New York: Holt.

Kandel, D. B., & Lesser, G. S. (1972). Parental and peer influences on educational plans of adolescents. *American Sociological Review, 34,* 213–223.

Kaplan, H. B. (1975). The self-esteem motive and change in self-attitudes. *Journal of Nervous and Mental Disease, 161,* 265–275.

Kokenes, B. (1974). Grade level differences in factors of self-esteem. *Developmental Psychology, 10,* 954–958.

LaVoie, J. C. (1976). Ego identity in middle adolescence. *Journal of Youth and Adolescence, 5,* 371–385.

Lerner, R. M., & Knapp, J. R. (1975). Actual and perceived intrafamilial attitudes of late adolescents and their parents. *Journal of Youth and Adolescence, 4,* 17–36.

Lerner, R. M., & Spanier, G. (1980). *Adolescent development.* New York: McGraw-Hill.

Lerner, R. M., & Shea, J. A. (1982). Social behavior in adolescence. In B. Wolman (Ed.), *Handbook of developmental psychology* (pp. 503–527). Englewood Cliffs, NJ: Prentice-Hall.

Livesley, W. J., & Bromley, D. B. (1973). *Person perception in childhood and adolescence.* London: Wiley.

Lynch, K. (1984). Reconsidering the image of the city. In L. Rodwin & R. M. Hollister (Eds.), *Cities of the mind* (pp. 151–162). New York: Plenum.

Maccoby, E. E., & Jacklin, C. N. (1974). *The psychology of sex differences.* Stanford, CA: Stanford University Press.

Marcia, J. E. (1966). Development and validation of ego-identity status. *Journal of Personality and Social Psychology, 3,* 551–558.

Marcia, J. E. (1967). Ego identity status: Relationship to change in self-esteem, "general maladjustment," and authoritarianism. *Journal of Personality, 1,* 118–133.

Marcia, J. E. (1976). Identity six years after: A follow-up study. *Journal of Youth and Adolescence, 5,* 145–160.

Marcia, J. E., & Friedman, M. L. (1970). Ego identity status in college women. *Journal of Personality, 5,* 145–160.

Marsh, H. W. (1986). Global self-esteem: Its relation to specific facets of self-concept and their importance. *Journal of Personality and Social Psychology, 51,* 1224–1236.

Marsh, H. W., Barnes, J., & Hocevar, D. (1985). Self-other agreement on multidimensional self-concept ratings: Factor analysis and multitrait-multimethod analysis. *Journal of Personality and Social Psychology, 49,* 1360–1377.

Marsh, H., & Parker, J. (1984). Determinants of student self-concept: Is it better to be a relatively large fish in a small pond even if you don't learn to swim as well? *Journal of Personality and Social Psychology, 47,* 213–231.

Maruyama, G., Rubin, R. A., & Kingsfield, G. G. (1981). Self-esteem and educational achievement: Independent constructs with a common cause? *Journal of Personality and Social Psychology, 40,* 962–975.

McCarthy, J. D., & Hoge, D. R. (1982). Analysis of age effects in longitudinal studies of adolescent self-esteem. *Developmental Psychology, 18,* 372–379.

McGuire, W. J., & McGuire, C. (1982). Significant others in self-space: Sex differences and developmental trends in the social self. In J. Suls (Ed.), *Psychological perspectives on the self* (Vol. 1, pp. 71–96). Hillsdale, NJ: Erlbaum.

McGuire, W. J., & Padawer-Singer, A. (1976). Trait salience in the spontaneous self-concept. *Journal of Personality and Social Psychology, 33,* 743–754.

Mead, G. H. (1934). In C. Morris (Ed.), *Mind, self, and society.* Chicago: University of Chicago Press.

Meilman, P. W. (1979). Cross-sectional age changes in ego identity status during adolescence. *Developmental Psychology, 15,* 230–231.

Montemeyer, R., & Eisen, M. (1977). The development of self-conceptions from childhood to adolescence. *Developmental Psychology, 13,* 314–319.

Morse, S. J., & Gergen, K. J. (1970). Social comparison, self-consistency and the presentation of self. *Journal of Personality and Social Psychology, 16,* 148–159.

Mullener, N., & Laird, J. (1971). Some developmental changes in the organization of self-evaluations. *Developmental Psychology, 5,* 233–236.

Munro, G., & Adams, G. R. (1977). Ego identity in college students and working youth. *Developmental Psychology, 13,* 523–524.

Offer, D. (1969). *The psychological world of the teenager.* New York: Basic Books.

O'Malley, P. M., & Bachman, J. G. (1979). Self-esteem and education: Sex and cohort comparisons among high school seniors. *Journal of Personality and Social Psychology, 37,* 1153–1159.

O'Malley, P. M., & Bachman, J. G. (1983). Self-esteem: Change and stability between 13 and 23. *Developmental Psychology, 19,* 257–268.

Orlofsky, J. L. (1977). *Identity formation, achievement and fear of success in college men and women.* Unpublished manuscript.

Orne, M. (1962). On the social psychology of the psychological experiment: With particular reference to demand characteristics and their implications. *American Psychologist, 17,* 776–783.

Oshman, H. P., & Manosevitz, M. (1974). The impact of the identity crisis on the adjustment of late adolescent males. *Journal of Youth and Adolescence, 3,* 207–216.

Piers, E. (1977). *The Piers-Harris children's self-concept scale.* Research Monograph. Nashville, TN: Counselor Recordings and Tests.

Piers, E., & Harris, D. (1969). *The Piers-Harris children's self-concept scale.* Nashville, TN: Counselor Recordings and Tests.

Podd, M. H., Marcia, J. E., & Rubin, B. M. (1970). The effects of ego identity and partner perception on a prisoner's dilemma game. *Journal of Social Psychology, 82,* 117–126.

Raphael, D. (1979). Identity status in high school females. *Adolescence, 14,* 73–79.

Rasmussen, J. E. (1964). The relationship of ego identity to psychosocial effectiveness. *Psychological Reports, 15,* 815–825.

Rest, J. R. (1975). Longitudinal study of the defining issues test of moral judgment:

A strategy for analyzing developmental change. *Developmental Psychology,* **11,** 738–748.

Rosenberg, F. R., & Simmons, R. G. (1975). Sex differences in the self-concept at adolescence. *Sex Roles,* **1,** 147–159.

Rosenberg, M. (1965). *Society and the adolescent self-image.* Princeton, NJ: Princeton University Press.

Rosenberg, M. (1979). *Conceiving the self.* New York: Basic Books.

Rosenberg, M. (1986). Self-concept from middle childhood through adolescence. In J. Suls & A. G. Greenwald (Eds.), *Psychological perspectives on the self* (Vol. 3, pp. 107–135). Hillsdale, NJ: Erlbaum.

Rosenberg, M., & Pearlin, L. (1978). Social class and self-esteem among children and adults. *American Journal of Sociology,* **84,** 53–77.

Rosenberg, M., & Simmons, R. (1972). *Black and white self-esteem: The urban school child.* Washington, D.C.: The American Sociological Association.

Savin-Williams, R. C., & Demo, D. H. (1983). Conceiving or misconceiving the self: Issues in adolescent self-esteem. *Journal of Early Adolescence,* **3,** 121–140.

Savin-Williams, R. C., & Jaquish, G. A. (1981). The assessment of adolescent self-esteem: A comparison of methods. *Journal of Personality,* **49,** 324–336.

Scheier, M. F., & Carver, C. S. (1980). Private and public self-attention, resistance to change, and dissonance reduction. *Journal of Personality and Social Psychology,* **39,** 390–405.

Scheier, M. F., & Carver, C. S. (1983). Two sides of the self: One for you and one for me. In J. Suls & A. G. Greenwald (Eds.), *Psychological perspectives on the self* (Vol. 2, pp. 123–157). Hillsdale, NJ: Erlbaum.

Scheier, M. F., & Carver, C. S. (1987). A model of behavior self regulation: Translating intention into action. In L. Berkowitz (Ed.), *Advances in experimental social psychology* (Vol. 20, pp. 303–346). Orlando, FL: Academic Press.

Scheier, M. F., Carver, C. S., & Gibbons, F. X. (1979). Self-directed attention, awareness or bodily states, and suggestibility. *Journal of Personality and Social Psychology,* **37,** 1576–1588.

Schiedel, D. G., & Marcia, J. E. (1985). Ego identity, intimacy, sex role orientation and gender. *Developmental Psychology,* **21,** 149–160.

Secord, P., & Peever, B. (1974). The development and attribution of person concepts.In T. Mischel (Ed.), *Understanding other persons* (pp. 117–142). Totowa, NJ: Rowman & Littlefield.

Shavelson, R. J., & Bolus, R. (1982). Self-concept: The interplay of theory and methods. *Journal of Educational Psychology,* 3–17.

Shavelson, R. J., Hubner, J. J., & Stanton, G. C. (1976). Self-concept: Validation of construct interpretation. *Review of Educational Research,* **46,** 407–441.

Shrauger, J. S., & Schoeneman, T. J. (1979). Symbolic interactionist view of self-concept: Through the looking glass darkly. *Psychological Bulletin,* **86,** 549–573.

Simmons, R., Blyth, D. A., Van Cleave,, E. F., & Bush, D. M. (1979). Entry into early adolescence: The impact of school structure, puberty, and early dating on self-esteem. *American Sociological Review,* **44,** 948–967.

Simmons, R., Rosenberg, F., & Rosenberg, M. (1973). Disturbance in the self-image at adolescence. American Sociological Review, **38,** 553–568.

Snyder, M. (1979). Self-monitoring processes. In L. Berkowitz (Ed.), *Advances in experimental social psychology* (Vol. 12, pp. 86–131). New York: Academic Press.

Snyder, M. (1987). *Public appearances/private realities: The psychology of self-monitoring.* New York: Freeman.

Snyder, M., & Monson, T. C. (1975). Persons, situations, and the control of social behavior. *Journal of Personality and Social Psychology, 32,* 637–644.

Snyder, M., & Campbell, B. (1982). Self-monitoring the self in action. In J. Suls (Ed.), *Psychological perspectives on the self* (Vol. 1, pp. 185–208). Hillsdale, NJ: Erlbaum.

Snyder, M. & Gangestad, S. (1986). On the nature of self-monitoring: Matters of assessment, matters of validity. *Journal of Personality and Social Psychology, 51,* 125–139.

Soares, A. T., & Soares, L. M. (1969). Self-perceptions of culturally disadvantaged children. *American Educational Research Journal, 6,* 31–45.

Suls, J. (1986). Comparisons processes in relative deprivation: A life-span analysis. In J. M. Olson, C. P. Herman, & M. P. Zanna (Eds.), *Relative deprivation and social comparison: The Ontario Symposium* (Vol. 4, pp. 95–116). Hillsdale, NJ: Erlbaum.

Suls, J., Gastorf, J., & Lawhon, J. (1978). Social comparison choices for evaluating a sex- and age-related ability. *Personality and Social Psychology Bulletin, 4,* 102–105.

Suls, J., & Miller, R. L. (Eds.) (1977). *Social comparison processes: Theoretical and empirical perspectives.* Washington, D.C.: Hemisphere.

Swann, W. B., Jr. (1983). Self-verification: Bringing social reality into harmony with the self. In J. Suls & A. G. Greenwald (Eds.), *Psychological perspectives on the self* (Vol. 2, pp. 33–66). Hillsdale, NJ: Erlbaum.

Toder, N. L., & Marcia, J. E. (1973). Ego identity status and response to conformity pressure in college women. *Journal of Personality and Social Psychology, 26,* 287–294.

Trowbridge, N. (1972). Self-concept and socioeconomic status in elementary school children. *American Educational Research Journal, 9,* 525–537.

Walker, L. S., & Greene, J. W. (1986). The social context of adolescent self-esteem. *Journal of Youth and Adolescence, 15,* 315–322.

Waterman, A. (1982). Identity development from adolescence to adulthood: An extension of theory and a review of research. *Developmental Psychology, 18,* 341–358.

Waterman, A., & Waterman, C. (1971). A longitudinal study of changes in ego identity status during the freshman year at college. *Developmental Psychology, 5,* 167–173.

Waterman, A., Geary, P., & Waterman, C. (1974). Longitudinal study of changes in ego identity from the freshman to the senior year of college. *Developmental Psychology, 2,* 121–133.

Whitbourne, S. K., & Waterman, A. (1979). Psychosocial development during the adult years: Age and cohort comparisons. *Developmental Psychology, 15,* 373–378.

Wicklund, R. A. (1975). Objective self-awareness. In L. Berkowitz (Ed.), *Advances in experimental social psychology* (Vol. 8, pp. 233–277). New York: Academic Press.

Wylie, R. (1979). *The self-concept: A review of methodological considerations and measuring instruments* (rev. ed., Vol. 1). Lincoln, NE: University of Nebraska Press.

Zigler, E., Balla, D., & Watson, N. (1972). Developmental and experimental determinants of self-image disparity in institutionalized and noninstitutionalized retarded and normal children. *Journal of Personality and Social Psychology, 23,* 81–87.

7

Adolescent Motivation and Achievement

Russell Ames and Carole Ames

Introduction

This chapter examines adolescent motivation in the context of school achievement. It takes a qualitative rather than a quantitative view of adolescent motivation. As a quantitative variable, motivation is equated with concepts such as activity, energy, and persistence and, as such, is often inferred from achievement levels or from changing levels of achievement. We have argued elsewhere (C. Ames & R. Ames, 1984) that motivation can also be conceptualized as a qualitative variable that represents different value or goal orientations, different ways of processing or attending to information, and different cognitions about one's performance. In this work the study of motivation has involved how students think about what they are doing, including their goals, perceptions, interpretations, and patterns of self-regulation. These cognitions have been shown to influence how students approach a task, how they attend to salient features of the situation, and how they interpret their performance.

This chapter will apply the qualitative view of motivation to the special problems of adolescence and school achievement. Within this framework, adolescents are seen as processing information from the school environment in terms of salient goals or values. Their specific goals and values affect their perceptions, attributions, self-evaluations, and beliefs about strategies of action. Adolescence, however, is a period in which students are coming to grips with the problems of becoming an adult. Specifically, this means that they are formulating and reformulating values and goals as they move from the immaturity of childhood to the maturity of adulthood. It is these goals and values that set the direction for adolescent attention

The Adolescent as Decision-maker

and activity, and they serve as the central organizing theme for the cognitive activities of the adolescent student engaged to a greater or lesser degree in achievement activities in school. According to Csikszentmihalyi and Larson (1984) school is a major socializing institution preparing teenagers to assume a multitude of adult roles. The school is a work environment that can help the teenage student focus on productive activities related to learning and the assumption of adult roles and skills, or it can fail to serve the important socializing function of helping adolescents focus on learning how to be productive members of society.

Most of our motivational concerns are not that students are doing nothing but that they are not doing what others, for example, the school, parents, or teachers, desire them to do (Maehr, 1984). The school is a work place and increasingly it is a work place reflecting the "real world" of work in terms of information transmission, problem solving, task orientation, and complex high technology (Csikszentmihalyi & Larson, 1984). The goal of schooling in junior high and high school, then, focuses on motivating adolescents to prepare effectively for this kind of adult role. At the same time that schools are attempting to help adolescents prepare for these productive adult roles, adolescents are struggling to achieve a sense of identity and independence. The task, then, is a complex one in which goal setting and value clarification must be tempered by an understanding of the developmental processes of adolescence.

A view of motivation that focuses on specific cognitive-based processes helps us understand the difference between effective and ineffective adolescent motivation. We will attempt to characterize specific classroom and school experiences that serve to enhance, debilitate, or undermine effective student motivation. To do so, we are guided by certain a priori assumptions:

1. Motivation when studied as a continuing process is an important outcome of education in its own right, independent of achievement.

2. Motivation is viewed more as a state than a trait, depending on the environmental experiences in the classroom and the school.

3. Students experience success and failure in the context of certain goals, cultural values, and evaluation systems (e.g., competitive), and it is these contextual factors that serve to shape the student's motivation and opportunities to become significantly involved in learning.

4. Achievement is not the only, nor necessarily the best, way of evaluating what students gain from school experiences. We are interested in the kind of commitment adolescents make to learning, to assuming productive adult roles, and to making significant contributions to society.

Although schools want to have high-achieving students, they also wish their students to pursue certain types of goals (e.g., discovering new knowledge versus making money), to focus on certain kinds of information and feedback (e.g., possible strategies for improving versus evidence for high ability), to construct for themselves certain strategies for approaching a task, and to develop a certain set of attitudes related to assuming a productive adult role. At times, we may have high achievement on the part of a student as reflected in a specific test score and not have many of these specific motivational outcomes occurring. For example, a student may get straight *A*s in math but have no desire to pursue a career involving the use of mathematics.

In summary, the purpose of the chapter is to present a theoretical framework for understanding the motivational conditions underlying adolescent development in student roles in school organizations. The chapter begins by reviewing various cognitive approaches to motivation. An integrated theory of student motivation is then described based on the qualitative view, and supporting data are reported. The adolescent period has often been described as one in which the teenager must sort through a myriad of competing demands on time and attention, including adult expectations for achievement and behavioral maturity, social goals and peer pressure, and the student's own developing sense of identity (Csikszentmihalyi & Larson, 1984). In attempting to explain how adolescents sort through these competing demands, the qualitative view is concerned about what leads to a particular frame and focus of attention. This view helps us understand why the adolescent pursues particular goals, the inferences students draw about the meaning of their efforts in particular achievement settings, and their use of particular achievement strategies. In the last section of the chapter, we present the implications of this qualitative view of adolescent motivation for the design of the high school curriculum, the redesign of the classroom and high school learning environment, and motivation training. We turn now to a description of the general cognitive view of motivation taken in this chapter.

General Cognitive View

The cognitive view of student motivation presented in this chapter begins with an examination of students' explanations for performance in a school setting. After completing an assignment, test, or project, students receive feedback about the effectiveness of their achievement strategies in the form of formal and informal evaluations from the teacher, peers, and sometimes parents. In accordance with Weiner (1979), the search for understanding is considered a basic "spring of action" that underlies a student's explanation for his or her performance and the subsequent selection and use of a strategy to strive toward and achieve a particular goal. This search, for example, leads the teenage student to ask, "Why did I get a *C* on my English term paper?" or, "Why did the science committee select my project as winner of the Science Fair?" Two motivational questions thus arise: (1) when the information is negative, what motivates the student to try to improve performance, persist with a difficult assignment or course and bring about a positive outcome? and (2) when the information is positive, what motivates the student to continue striving and to try to accomplish new and even more challenging goals? The answers to the above questions are sought here by examining the student's thought patterns, in particular, causal attributions for effective and ineffective performance and value beliefs related to the importance of various outcomes. Before examining this attribution analysis of student motivation in depth, we will turn to a brief examination of two lines of research and theory that serve as the basis for the theoretical paradigm to be employed here: attribution theory (Heider, 1958; Kelley, 1972; Weiner, 1979, 1984) and self-worth theory (Covington, 1984; Covington & Beery, 1976; Covington & Omelich, 1979a).

Attribution Theory

Weiner's attribution theory of motivation suggests that persons do a careful analysis of the causes of their performance in an effort to develop achievement strategies that address those causes. According to Weiner's (1979, 1984) formulations of the theory, persons search for causes along four basic dimensions: Locus of causality, stability, controlability, and globality. Achievement outcomes are attributed to specific attributional factors such as ability, effort, task difficulty, and luck. Weiner (1979) has reviewed numerous studies that have found these attributions to be related to specific achievement behaviors. For example, a person who believes that he or she failed because of low ability is likely to feel less confident about the probability of future success than a person who attributes failure to low effort. Further, a person who attributes failure to a lack of effort may try harder in the future by engaging in a variety of instrumental acts to achieve, such as organizing his or her study time more effectively.

Self-worth Theory

The self-worth formulation suggests that individuals process information and make attributions to maintain a positive sense of self-worth. The self-worth theory of achievement behavior (Covington & Beery, 1976; Covington & Omelich, 1979a; Covington, 1984; Nicholls, 1979, 1984) is based on the assumption that ability is universally valued among persons in achievement situations and that persons attribute their success and failure in ways to maintain a positive self-concept of ability. Nicholls (1975) has noted that when a task is thought to measure skills important to the self-image, there may be a greater desire to protect one's sense of esteem than when the task is thought relatively unimportant.

Covington and Omelich (1979a) have shown that persons can and do avoid negative low-ability inferences by ascribing their failures to low effort or by using a variety of excuses for why effort did not or would not pay off. Excuses can be used to defend against the belief that one lacks ability, control, or influence by explaining why one did not try or why external factors were of sufficient force to render ability as insufficient cause even in the presence of effort (see Kelley, 1972). While these excuses may serve to protect one's sense of ability, they may be nonfunctional in the pursuit of future achievement. External attributions to such factors as "unfair grading practices" or "tricky test items" suggest there is little one can do to obtain future success. And these excuses probably serve to limit future achievement-oriented strivings while at the same time protecting a sense of self-worth. Thus, actions associated with being an effective student may be related to a complex pattern of ability and effort attributions that often involve various excuses for failure.

However, failing when one has tried is a strong indicator of low ability (Covington & Omelich, 1979b). Individuals, then, may not take achievement-oriented action in order to avoid such a low-ability inference; to have failed once is probably seen as a minor blow to esteem compared to the loss of esteem associated with a second failure after having tried hard. Persons who have failed are apparently faced with a real dilemma: striving to achieve may be necessary for improving his or her chances of success in the future, resulting in enhanced self-worth, but at the same time it may risk loss of esteem from having tried and failed again.

Relationship among Self-worth, Attribution, and Achievement-oriented Action Beliefs

On the basis of this self-worth analysis of attributions (R. Ames, 1983, 1986), two attributional patterns have been derived, both of which serve to maintain a self-concept of student ability, but one is relevant to student actions associated with striving towards learning and achievement and the other is not. It was reasoned that a pattern relevant to student achievement-oriented action involves the following attributional beliefs (Ames, 1983, p. 170):

1. a global attribution that one's general ability is adequate;
2. a more specific ability attribution that one did not grasp certain key concepts or skills;
3. an attribution that effort was necessary but that one had not tried, worked, or studied hard enough; and
4. a rejection of various excuses and external factors as the causes of a poor performance.

In contrast, an attribution pattern that does not logically entail achievement-oriented action focuses on excuses such as "I didn't have enough time," "I'm enrolled in many hard courses", or "the teacher doesn't like me." In this way, the student avoids the inference of a low-global ability attribution by linking the specific lack of apparent ability in the situation to external, uncontrollable factors. In essence, an attribution pattern relevant to the student's taking achievement-oriented actions to either prevent or correct failure says: "I am a capable student, but I did not try hard enough. I should have put forth more effort and possibly tried alternative study strategies." Whereas, an attribution pattern that is irrelevant to student achievement-oriented action and does not logically entail such action says: "You cannot infer that I am incapable because external factors over which I have no control prevented me from doing my best."

The action-relevant and irrelevant attributional patterns are designed either to maintain a self-concept of high student ability or to avoid a concept of low student ability, respectively. Twenty exemplary student achievement, action-relevant, and irrelevant attributions have been classified in Tables 7.1 and 7.2 along the controllability, globality, locus, and stability dimensions (see Weiner, 1979). Both patterns are similar in that they entail a positive global ability attribution, but the action-relevant pattern entails a belief in higher ability than the action-irrelevant one. Further, both patterns involve a specific low-ability attribution. However, the specific low-ability attribution within the action-relevant pattern is considered a relatively unstable skill deficiency that could be overcome with enhanced effort and/or learning because the belief that one can improve a specific ability is enhanced by a strong belief in one's global ability. In contrast, the specific low-ability inference within the action-irrelevant pattern is relatively stable, and this stability belief is supported not only by low-effort and external task attributions but also by the weaker, positive, global sense of ability within the action-irrelevant pattern.

Table 7.1 Exemplary Achievement: Action-relevant and Action-irrelevant Attributions (Uncontrollable Factors)

	Ability	Task	Luck
Action-relevant			
Global:	I have high ability and successful performance requires ability.	Moderate-to-hard tasks can be overcome and do not in and of themselves inhibit success.	Performance is not a function of luck.
Specific:	I did not know the specific concepts or skills required for achievement (relatively unstable).	The task was not overly difficult.	Good or bad luck did not affect my performance.
Action-irrelevant			
Global:	I have some ability and successful performance in achievement settings requires ability.	Irrelevant features of the task can make the task overly difficult and therefore inhibit success.	Successful performance is often a matter of luck.
Specific:	I did not know specific concepts or skills required for achievement (relatively stable).	The task was difficult because it was "tricky," "unfair."	I had bad luck.

Table 7.2 Exemplary Achievement: Action-relevant and Action-irrelevant Attributions (Controllable Factors)

	Effort	Bias and/or unusual help from others
Action-relevant		
Global:	Performance is a function of effort and I usually try.	Sources of aid are usually available that increase the chances of success; I often take advantage of them (usual and unusual help from others).
Specific:	I did not try hard enough this time.	I did not take advantage of the usual as well as specially arranged sources of help.
Action-irrelevant		
Global:	Effort was not related to achievement; or I was not interested in achieving this goal anyway.	Success is less likely because my teacher never recognizes my accomplishments.
Specific:	I did not try hard, but I would have done better if I had tried; I was bored.	My advisor did not give me proper guidance.

Turning now to differences between the patterns, examination of Tables 7.1 and 7.2 shows that action-relevant attributions focus on internal and external factors within the student's control (Table 7.2) and the action-irrelevant ones focus on external factors beyond the students control (Table 7.1). The most important difference between students making action-relevant achievement attributions versus action-irrelevant achievement attributions is the former's belief in effort as a key factor in achieving success versus the latter's belief that external, uncontrollable factors prevent success. Some interesting features of the action-irrelevant pattern relate to task, effort, and bias attributions. As shown in Table 7.1, in order to avoid an inference of low ability, the student cannot make task-difficulty attributions that imply that a student with more ability could have overcome the difficulty level of the task; hence, the student must imply that the task was difficult in an unfair way and thus insurmountable even by someone with more ability. As shown in table 7.2, students invoking action-irrelevant patterns also infer that powerful others, for example, a teacher, are biased against their achievement. Low-effort attributions are thus consistent with these task and bias assessments in that the attributor asserts that effort would not have made any difference even if he or she had tried.

Close examination of these attribution patterns suggests they are consistent with the general achievement-oriented and non-achievement oriented attribution patterns outlined by Weiner in his attributional analysis of the achievement motive (Weiner, 1979; Weiner and Kukla, 1970). That is, achievement-motivated individuals tend to focus more on internal, unstable, and controllable factors as the causes of success or failure (Table 7.2); whereas non-achievement motivated individuals tend to focus more an external, uncontrollable factors that help them fend off a belief that they are not capable (Table 7.1; see also Nicholls, 1984).

The theoretical analysis presented so far assumes that achievement orientation is coordinated to the enhancement or protection of a global self-concept of ability. The action-relevant attribution pattern appears to support a goal of demonstrating high student ability while the action-irrelevant pattern appears to support a goal of protecting against a perception of low ability. Both attribution patterns appear quite rational when viewed from the perspective of the goals they support. Low-effort attributions allow the person the option of trying harder to perform better in the future and confirm his or her high concept of ability. External attributions or excuse factors suggest that it would have been impossible and perhaps unimportant for someone even with high ability to have succeeded.

In summary, the cognitive view of adolescent motivation focuses heavily on the different kinds of attributions teenage students make for their academic performance. These attributions are classified according to Weiner's eightfold category system (see Tables 7.1 and 7.2). More importantly, however, these attributions are coordinated to maintaining a sense of self-worth. In school achievement settings the sense of worth is closely tied to the student's academic self-concept. A study by Zarb (1984) demonstrates the importance of academic self-concept in differentiating high and low achievers. Ninety-six 9th and 10th-grade adolescents were asked to complete a battery of self-perception instruments including academic self-concept, self-report of efficiency of their study habits, relationship with peers, and educational aspirations. Only academic self-concept differentiated remedial and failure groups from a control group of "successful" students; the remedial and failure students scored lower than "control" students on the academic self-concept measure, but the groups did not differ on the other measures.

According to the cognitive view of adolescent motivation presented here, students work to preserve a high self-concept of academic ability or avoid a low self-concept of academic ability. Students who utilize an achievement action-relevant attribution pattern do not question their global academic self-concept but rather look to improving a specific ability through effort. In contrast, students who wish to avoid a low self-concept of ability focus on an achievement action-irrelevant pattern and employ a variety of excuses that help them avoid taking responsibility for their performance. We turn now to a consideration of various classroom and school environmental factors that tend to focus students on one or the other of these attribution patterns.

The Theory of Qualitative Motivation

Adolescents are viewed as processing information about their behavior and performance in the context of a value orientation that assigns a level of importance to various goals related to achievement in school and the development of an emerging adult identity. These values and sense of identity are closely tied to the adolescent's developing sense of self-worth (Covington & Beery, 1976). According to this "value-belief" framework (R. Ames, 1983), adolescents are thought to select and pursue a goal because the attainment of the particular goals implies something desirable about themselves, such as that they are competent in academics or sports, popular, or friendly and helpful. Adolescents then process information about their performance in school through a belief system centrally organized around certain values (Rokeach, 1973). Attributions and other cognitive and emotional reactions are made in response to these overriding values that serve as reasons or purposes for behavior (Buss, 1978; Kruglanski, 1975, 1980).

Ames and Ames (1984) outlined three systems of motivation corresponding to three different systems of goals–values that are elicited by specific educational or classroom learning structures, namely, competitive, individualistic, and cooperative. These systems of motivation, associated cognitive factors, and specific examples are outlined in Table 7.3. The cognitive factors relevant to the study of the qualitative view include the goals, salient information, attributions, and specific self-evaluations of students. The systems of motivation are classified as ability evaluative, task mastery, and moral responsibility.

The Ability Evaluative System

In the *ability evaluative system,* the student's attention is focused on self-enhancement as the overriding goal. The meaning of the adolescents' efforts is interpreted in terms of whether specific activities will lead to greater or lesser enhancement of their sense of high ability. Information is processed in terms of its meaning for their self-perception of ability. Success and failure are explained either in terms of high ability or in terms of factors that help oneself and others avoid the conclusion that one is not able. One's self-worth is linked to whether or not one perceives oneself as able, and specific action strategies are related either to the demonstration of high ability or to the avoidance of demonstrating low ability. For example, a student may avoid trying hard in order to protect against the impression that he or she is unable (see Table 7.3). Nicholls (1984) has shown that when ability assessments are based on a comparison to the accomplishments of others, individuals tend to focus more on themselves and become more self-aware and concerned with whether or not they are able; hence he refers to students in this frame of mind as ego-involved.

According to Ames and Ames (1984), the ability evaluative system is most commonly evoked by a competitive goal structure where rewards are restricted so that only the few who are the best or highest performers are acknowledged as being successful or rewarded in some way. Competition is evident in various school and classroom practices such as ability tracking, grading on "the curve", and publicly calling attention to exemplary behavior. The competitive structure is an external dimension of an achievement situation that commands students to pay attention to the relative performance of their peers even when they did not have any

Table 7.3 Systems of Student Motivation

| | Systems | | |
Cognitive factors	Ability evaluative	Task mastery	Moral responsibility
Goal	Self-enhancement/protection (competitive)	Task accomplishment (individualistic)	Welfare of a group (cooperative)
Salient information	Self–Other comparison	Self–Self comparison	Self–Group comparison
Attributional focus	Ability-related	Effort-related	Effort and cooperativeness
Self-evaluational and strategy focus	"Am I smart enough?" "Can I do this?"	"Am I trying hard enough?" "How can I do this?"	"Are we trying hard enough?" "How can we do this?"

prior interest in such information (see, for example, Pepitone, 1972, 1980; Veroff, 1969). Numerous studies (C. Ames, 1978, 1981; Ames, Ames, & Felker, 1977; Ames & Felker, 1979; Covington & Omelich, 1979a,b; Nicholls, 1979, 1984) have shown that the social comparison information elicited by competitive structures focuses students on evaluating their ability. As a consequence, responses to questions such as "Was I smart?" and "How smart am I?" are central in students' thoughts, and subsequent achievement behaviors are dependent upon these responses. In competition, self-perceptions of ability are closely linked to perceptions of winning and losing, and subsequent achievement behaviors are dependent on these ability inferences.

Task Mastery Motivational System

In the individualistic or task mastery system, the student is focused on task accomplishment. Task accomplishment takes on meaning not because it reflects on one's high ability, but because it reflects a sense of effort and commitment of having done something well that one intended to do. The meaning of the student's efforts is interpreted in terms of whether specific activities will lead to accomplishment of an important goal, for example, setting a new personal record in a track meet, writing an essay on "the appropriate role of government in society," or completing a science project. The student pays attention to information that will help accomplish the goal. Such information may reference past performance, sources of assistance or advice from others, and a careful analysis of ineffective strategies (see Table 7.3).

According to Ames and Ames (1984) the task mastery system is associated with an individualistic goal structure, which means that whether or not a goal or reward is attained by a particular student is not dependent on another's achieving the goal. This structure involves the presence of self-referenced goals based on one's past performance or self-generated and determined pursuits. Others have referred to such structures as success-oriented (Covington & Beery, 1976), mastery-based (Block, 1977; Deci, 1975), and origin-like (deCharms, 1976). Individualistic structures are noncompetitive where students are (1) encouraged to try and effort expenditure is rewarded (Ames, 1981, 1986), (2) provided with multiple opportunities for improvement (Covington & Omelich, 1979a), (3) asked to monitor or evaluate their own progress (Salili, Maehr, Sorensen, & Fyans, 1976; Wang, 1976), or (4) asked to establish goals that exceed their past performance (e.g., Slavin, 1980). An individualistic structure elicits a strong sense of "task engagement" (Corno & Mandinach, 1983), "task involvement" (Nicholls, 1984), or perhaps even "flow" (Csikszentmihalyi, 1985). Students focus on the instrumentality of their behaviors for accomplishing the task with a corresponding absence of concern or worry about whether or not they are able to do the task. When students encounter a problem or difficulty, they take it as challenge—something to be figured out—not as a negative evaluation of their ability. Their underlying belief is, "I can if I try."

The Moral Responsibility System

In the moral responsibility or cooperative system, goals are focused on the welfare of others and on one's social commitments. Task accomplishment takes on meaning only in that it reflects one's sense of responsibility to others or to a group norm. The meaning of the student's efforts is interpreted in terms of whether specific activities will lead to the enhancement of the group goal and the welfare of others. Part of the meaning of one's efforts in this system is established from the negative perspective of avoiding low peer evaluations because one did not put forth a fair share of work towards accomplishing the goal. Goals here, as in the the other systems, can vary, for example, from completing a group project in science class to mustering group effort to fight the authority of the school administration.

According to Ames and Ames (1984), in a cooperative goal structure, a common objective is shared by a set of individuals. The actions of the individuals are interdependent in that their efforts converge toward a common goal. In this structure, group performance itself is important and impacts a student's self-evaluations in similar fashion to past performance information in the individualistic structure and social comparison information in the competitive structure. Here, students are imparted with a sense of pride or shame from the group performance. Cooperative norms impart a sense of responsibility for helping and fear of negative sanctions for failing to do one's part. Research on cooperative learning (Aronson, 1978; Johnson & Johnson, 1975; Slavin, 1983) suggests that such a moral norm for helping is quickly established. Such norms lead students to focus on the importance of doing one's fair share of work, that is, the importance of effort, in order to fulfill one's responsibility to the group. Ames and Ames (1984) have argued that such effort does not have the same motivational meaning under cooperative versus individualistic conditions. The value of effort under cooperation is related to the strong sense of social responsibility directed toward accomplishing a common group goal. Effort is not as intrinsic to the task as it is in the individualistic goal structure but rather is intrinsic to the group norm. Thus, students compare their effort relative to group expectations, evaluate themselves on the basis of whether they are doing their fair share, and focus on strategies related to improving group performance (see Table 7.3).

Summary

In summary, a qualitative view involves an analysis of various systems of motivation involving specific goals, information foci, attributions, and specific thoughts about strategies of action. The basic premise of the qualitative view is that specific classroom or school learning environments can serve to focus students on particular goals. Competition leads to an ability evaluative motivational system and the salient goal is one of maintaining a self-perception of high ability or avoiding a perception of low ability. An individualistic goal structure evokes a task mastery motivational system and the salient goal is one of completing an important task at a self-referenced standard of excellence. A cooperative goal structure evokes a moral responsibility motivational system making salient the importance of the common group goal. We turn now to an examination of the extent to which the typical junior high and high school learning environments evokes one or more of these motivational systems.

The Learning Environment of Junior and Senior High School: The Changing Environment

We turn now to a description of the classroom and school environment that adolescents face as they move into junior high and on through high school. Eccles, Midgley, and Adler (1984) describe the school environment as becoming increasingly more negative for students as they enter junior high school. In fact, their studies show that a negative orientation toward achievement increases with age. One of the single largest declines in attitude towards school occurs in the transition from elementary to junior high school. These changes in adolescents' attitudes toward school and achievement are most pronounced for children experiencing failure.

Eccles et al. (1984) suggest that these negative attitudes are related to a common and pervasive set of instructional practices. In elementary school, the classroom is more personal in that the student is with the same teacher and group of students for the better part of the day. In junior high and high school, however, students see from five to seven teachers in a given day, and each class may involve a new mix of students. Classroom discipline practices become more formal; students are expected to sit in their seats for longer periods of time. Grades, too, become more important. Grade point averages are used from grades 9–12 for admission to college and professional training schools, for example. Classroom teaching practices tend to utilize whole class instruction rather than individualized or small group instruction, and students are exposed to ability tracking for the first time. Instructional practices are competitive, characterized by public drill, frequent testing, grading on a curve, and an emphasis on being right.

In the junior high and high school students are faced with an impersonal, formal, competitive, and evaluative environment. Eccles *et al.* suggest that these instructional practices lead students to focus on whether or not they are able rather than on processes associated with learning and mastering the material. Thus, it appears that the common instructional practices evoke an ability evaluative motivational system leading to a focus on social comparison information, ability attributions, and concern over negative self-evaluation, particularly if one is failing.

Even within the academic achievement domain, however, the decline in students' attitudes and motivation varies across subject area (Eccles *et al.*, 1984). This decline is particularly characteristic of beliefs regarding mathematics and not of beliefs regarding English (Eccles *et al.*, 1984). Students see math instruction that is increasingly more formal (i.e., greater emphasis on getting the "right" answer, more frequent testing, competition, and grading on the curve) as they progress through school (see Brush, 1980; Dawson & Hill, 1986). In contrast, students see English as becoming more informal in the upper grades. Group discussion and the exploration of meaning become the norm, and students are encouraged to give their opinions without regard to a unitary criterion of correctness. Foreign languages are usually introduced in 8th, 9th, or 10th grade. National statistics indicate that only 25% of the nation's students complete even 2 years of a foreign language, and a mere 15% make it through 4 years. In fact, the first 2 years of foreign language instruction necessarily emphasize rote learning, public drill and practice, and single right answers in vocabulary and grammar drills. It is only when students enter the 3rd and 4th years of the language that the subject becomes more open-ended as they study literature and culture in more depth.

Unfortunately, this increase in the formality of instruction comes right at a time when, developmentally, adolescents are ready for the in-depth exploration of open-ended questions often involving value or moral dilemmas (see Eccles *et al.*, 1984). As adolescents search for an adult identity, the open-ended value questions allow them to make a close emotional identification with the subject matter, hence increasing its motivational relevance for them.

In part, we see parallels between motivation shifts and key cognitive-developmental changes in children. As children get older, they process and integrate achievement-related information in a more logical fashion (see also Nicholls, 1984). Just when environmental characteristics focus adolescents on the question, "How smart am I?", they also begin to regard smartness as capacity; meaning the smarter they are, the less effort they put forth, and vice versa (see Nicholls, 1984). Intelligence is no longer seen as incremental, something one can improve on with practice and learning. When the "capacity" view is held, it is easy to see how adolescents can logically draw the conclusion that there are limits to achievement as a function of capacity. If adolescents continue to hold an incremental view, then they could logically draw the conclusion that capacity could be increased through diligence. Nicholls clearly shows that adolescents move away from this incremental view as they get older. The juxtaposition of the capacity view of intelligence with the ability evaluative learning environment makes the adolescent student extremely vulnerable to a number of motivational problems associated with an excessive focus on demonstrating high ability or avoiding the demonstration of low ability.

Student Priorities

In an extensive study of how adolescents divide their time between school and leisure activities, Csikszentmihalyi and Larson (1984) asked a sample of high school subjects to wear page beepers. The students were paged at random times during the day and were asked to record on a questionnaire where they were, what activity they were doing, what they were thinking and feeling, who they were with, and whether or not they would rather be somewhere else. They concluded from their work that productive activities take up little of the teenagers' time. Schooling, classwork, or studying occupy only 25% of the waking hours of the adolescent and only for 9 months. They also concluded that adult socialization is relatively rare in the classroom in that of 20 hours per week spent in the classroom, only 4 are spent listening to teachers. Five hours per week are spent listening to other students. Thirteen percent of the teenagers' total waking time is spent in individual study. And, thus, opportunities for adult socialization are relatively rare. In general, American students spend fewer hours in school than students in other technologically advanced societies, for example, Japan and Russia.

   Their study is largely descriptive and is intermixed with a heavy dose of psychological and sociological theory and some philosophy. First, the basic statistics. Adolescents spend approximately 32% of their time in school, 20% of which is in the classroom. Forty-one percent of the adolescents time is spent at home, and the other 27% is spent in public settings. Of the time spent in school, one-third unfolds in the various fringe areas outside the classroom, for example, halls, playground, student center, and cafeteria. Forty percent of the teenagers time is spent in leisure activities while the remaining 60% is divided evenly between maintenance activities (e.g., eating, caring for one's appearance) and academically productive activities (e.g., schoolwork and studying).

After describing how adolescents divided their time between home, school, and public domains, these authors described the intrinsic motivation of the teenagers in these various settings. They found that intrinsic motivation in environments structured by adults, for example, classrooms, jobs, and church, was significantly lower than in peer-dominated environments. When in an adult-oriented environment, teenagers consistently reported that they would rather be somewhere else. The lowest intrinsic motivation occurs in those places most structured by adult society (class, school halls, and library), and the highest motivation occurs where teenagers are furthest from adult control (student center and lunchroom). In fact, the general pattern suggests that teenage students are least motivated when doing things they have to do. Since Csikszentmihalyi and Larson place such heavy emphasis on the role of adult socialization in effective adolescent growth and development, they find this low intrinsic-motivation finding quite disturbing. They surmise that adult-oriented goals conflict with the goals of teenagers, and that if adolescence is a preparation for adulthood and adolescents waste time in unproductive activities, teenagers are likely to grow into nonproductive adults.

What constitutes intrinsic motivation for Csikszentmihalyi and Larson? They characterize intrinsic motivation as a "flow" or autotelic state, meaning the goal is endogenous to or is the activity itself. The characteristics of a "flow" state involve an ordered processing of information and an equal balance between the challenge of a task and one's perceived skill level. When the challenge of a situation is greater than one's perceived skill level then one experiences anxiety and worry. When one's skill level is perceived to be greater than the challenge of the situation then boredom occurs. Persons in a state of flow have given the following accounts of their mental activities:

1. "My mind isn't wandering; I am not thinking of something else . . . I'm less aware of myself and my problems."
2. "I am so involved in what I am doing . . . I don't see myself in what I am doing."

According to the descriptive data of their study, adolescents are so uninvolved in what they are doing when under adult supervision that they wish they were doing something else most of the time. And, according to Eccles *et al.*'s description of the school environment, adult supervision in school is rife with a heavy emphasis on ability evaluation, on activities that lead students to constantly question their self-worth, and away from activities that allow students to explore a subject for a deeper understanding. More often than not, the focus tends to be on rote learning under very formal learning conditions.

General Summary and Theoretical Integration

The chapter has attempted to present a qualitative view of adolescent motivation derived from attribution and self-worth theory perspectives. The model derived here stresses the role of the adolescent's value priorities related to accomplishing various goals (Ames, 1975, 1983; Maehr and Nicholls, 1980; Parsons *et al.,* 1985; Rokeach, 1973) as important determinants of subsequent achievement-related thoughts and behaviors.

The value–belief attribution model depicted in Fig. 7.1 shows that any achievement situation can be viewed as more or less uncertain and ambiguous with respect to goals and actions. Even though there may be some broad goal of achieving success (e.g., get all *A*s, be popular), such a goal is vague and general and open to a variety of interpretations. We know, for example, that good grades can be obtained by cheating, increasing study efficiency, taking easy courses, and so on. Thus, the particular goal, subgoals, and methods of achievement a student chooses are largely up to the student to construct from an ambiguous and uncertain setting. The qualitative view stresses the role of value, attribution, and achievement-action beliefs.

Fig. 7.1 shows that both personal and situational factors (e.g., competitive versus cooperative goal structure) contribute to determining what values are relevant to a specific achievement setting. In a probable temporal sequence, the elicited value has a subsequent effect on the student's attribution for his or her own achievement actions or performance. The final decision to use a particular achievement strategy from a number of available instrumental actions is preceded by cognitive and affective evaluations related to perceived esteem risks and the importance of the particular goal. Thus, the cognitive construction involves a set of related beliefs about goals and causes of behavior or outcomes, in addition to the cognitions related to expectancies, emotions, behavioral intentions, and self-instructions.

Figure 7.1   Value–belief attribution model.

Recently, Nicholls completed a study that shows the interrelationship of adolescents' educational values, their personal goals, and specific attributions. Nicholls, Patashnick, & Nolen (1985) found that high school students' beliefs about the purposes of education, their personal goals in school, and their perceptions of the causes of success in school were found to be related to one another in a logically consistent manner. They asked high school students to rate the importance of various purposes of education, namely: (1) to obtain wealth and status, (2) to acquire a sense of commitment to society, (3) to understand the world and how nature works, and (4) to develop a sense of achievement motivation. Three kinds of personal goals were assessed: (1) avoidance of work ("I get out of work"), (2) ego and social orientation ("I show people I'm smart"), and (3) task orientation ("Something I learned really makes sense"). Nicholls *et al.* found that high school students who endorsed wealth and status as the most important aim of school also highly endorsed the personal goal of "avoidance of work." In contrast, students who endorsed a personal goal of learning and understanding on the "task orientation" scale believed that the most important goals of school were to foster understanding, social commitment, and achievement motivation.

The three categories of personal goals also showed distinctive patterns associated with attributions for academic success. Adolescents whose personal goal was to avoid work linked success to external attribution factors of luck and to one's ability to bias the teacher in their favor. Ego and social orientation was associated with a combination of external, teacher-pleasing, and internal effort factors. In contrast, task orientation goals were strongly linked to success attributions of effort and to trying to understand rather than just memorize. Views about the broad goals of education were also linked to specific attributions. The wealth and status purpose was linked to a view that success is obtained by besting others in competition and through the teacher's faith in one's ability. Individual and cooperative effort attributions were closely associated with the view that education should foster responsibility, understanding, and achievement motivation.

While this study by Nicholls does not indicate why students adopt a particular broad educational value, it shows that their values, personal goals, and attributions are closely linked in a belief system. Our work on qualitative motivation (Ames & Ames, 1984) has also shown this interrelationship of values, goals, and attributions but has gone one step further to include beliefs about action strategies or instrumental beliefs in this cognitive network. Thus, students who have a personal goal of winning and a broad ego and social orientation value will not only focus on ability attributions but also are more likely to focus on strategies that protect that high-ability image, such as "not trying" and "making sure the teacher favors them." In contrast, students holding a more task-oriented value are likely to believe in the utility of strategies that they believe will lead to deeper understanding or mastery of a problem. And, they are more likely to pursue such strategies even in the face of failure or setbacks, which only serve as information to help refine their task-oriented strategies.

Recommendations for Enhancing Adolescent Motivation

In the final section of this chapter, we turn to making some specific suggestions for how the motivation of adolescents in school can be enhanced.

1. Avoid an ability attribution focus. A number of common organizational and instructional practices focus the adolescent unnecessarily on the question, "How smart am I?" These practices include grading on the curve, regular reporting of class rank, tracking, and evaluative practices that leave students with little hope that they will be able to improve in the future. When students are concerned about the ability question, they are unable to focus on the challenge of the task, and effort and striving may indicate a lack of ability rather than a desire to concentrate on an important task.

2. Increase the perceived value of task orientation and task involvement. When a sense of task involvement is high, students are more likely to experience a state of flow. They are concentrating on the task and its various dimensions and are not distracted by a concern for how able they are. Teachers can increase the task-orientation value and subsequent task involvement in a number of ways. First, they should remove most of the instructional factors that are likely to focus students on the ability question. They should justify the study of a particular subject not because it is likely to lead to wealth and status but because it will lead to a deeper understanding of the world around them. Teachers should directly state to students that effort is necessary to succeed, and they should help students set specific goals and subgoals in accomplishing various course tasks.

3. Little attention is paid to the transition from elementary school to junior high and from junior high to high school. Further, these transitions

occur at times when adolescents are undergoing some major cognitive and socioemotional developmental changes. The transitions generally have the impact of making school more formal, impersonal, and competitive. These restrictive instructional practices come at a time when students are cognitively mature enough to explore open-ended questions in a discipline in-depth. In the classroom, teachers should strive to create more informal, personal, and noncompetitive environments. Students should be encouraged to use critical thinking to explore the open-ended nature of subject matter rather than be rotely focused on the "right answer."

4. Adults need to become significant role models and socialization agents in the classroom and the school. According to Cszikszentmihalyi and Larson (1984) adults are leaving too much of the socialization of students up to the peer group. Adults must take charge of the socialization process by setting clear expectations and standards for student behavior and achievement. These standards and expectations must be high. Adults must work to establish positive affective relationships with students so that students will see the adult as someone they desire to emulate. Finally, teachers must strive in every way possible to help the students achieve these high expectations and goals.

5. Teachers need to understand the importance of students' motivational thoughts. We have stressed that the most important aspects of motivation are not external indicators of concentration, energy, or achievement but internal thought patterns of the students. It is these thoughts that relate to the meaning of the students' effort and the relationship of effort to self-worth. Thus, teachers need to look for more nontraditional indicators of motivation—how students are thinking about themselves, whether trying in a particular course is perceived to indicate a lack of ability, and what broad educational and personal goals the students are pursuing.

References

Ames, C. (1978). Children's achievement attributions and self-reinforcement: Effects of self-concept and competitive reward structure. *Journal of Educational Psychology,* **70,** 345–355.

Ames, C. (1981). Competition versus cooperative reward structures: The influence of individual and group performance factors in achievement attributions and affect. *American Educational Research Journal,* **18,** 273–387.

Ames, C. (1986). Effective motivation: The contribution of the learning environment. In R. S. Feldman (Ed.), *Social psychology applied to education.* London and New York: Cambridge University Press.

Ames, C., & Ames, R. (1984). Systems of student and teacher motivation: Toward a qualitative definition. *Journal of Educational Psychology,* **76,** 535–556.

Ames, C., Ames, R., & Felker, D. (1977). Effects of competitive reward structure and valence of outcome on children's achievement attributions. *Journal of Educational Psychology,* **69,** 1–8.

Ames, C., & Felker, D. (1979). An examination of children's attributions and achievement-related evaluations in competitive, cooperative, and individualistic reward structures. *Journal of Educational Psychology,* **71,** 413–420.

Ames, R. (1975). Teachers' attributions of responsibility: Some unexpected nondefensive effects. *Journal of Educational Psychology,* **67,** 688–696.

Ames, R. (1983). Teachers' attributions for their own teaching. In J. Levine & M. Wang (Eds.), *Teacher and student perceptions* (pp. 105–124). Hillsdale, NJ: Erlbaum.

Ames, R. (1986). Adult motivation in the leadership role: An attributional-value analysis. In M. Maehr (Ed.), *Advances in motivation and achievement* (pp. 333–369). Greenwich, CT: JAI Press.

Aronson, E. (1978). *The jigsaw classroom.* Beverly Hills, CA: Sage.

Block, J. (1977). Motivation, evaluation, and mastery learning. *UCLA Educator,* **12,** 31–37.

Brush, L. (1980). *Encouraging girls in mathematics: The problem and the solution.* Cambridge, MA: Abt Books.

Buss, A. (1978). Causes and reasons in attribution theory: A conceptual critique. *Journal of Personality and Social Psychology,* **36,** 1311–1321.

Corno, L., & Mandinach, E. (1983). The role of cognitive engagement in classroom learning and motivation. *Educational Psychologist,* **18,** 88–108.

Covington, M. (1984). The motive for self-worth. In R. Ames & C. Ames (Eds.), *Research on motivation in education: Student motivation* (pp. 17–113). New York: Academic Press.

Covington, M., & Beery, R. (1976). *Self-worth and school learning.* New York: Holt.

Covington, M., & Omelich, C. (1979a). Effort: The double edged sword in school achievement. *Journal of Educational Psychology,* **71,** 169–182.

Covington, M., & Omelich, C. (1979b). It's best to be able and virtuous too: Student and teacher evaluative responses to successful effort. *Journal of Educational Psychology,* **71,** 688–700.

Csikszentmihalyi, M. (1985). Emergent motivation and the evolution of the self. In D. A. Kleiber & M. L. Maehr (Eds.), *Advances in motivation and achievement* (Vol. 4, pp. 93–119). Greenwich, CT: JAI Press.

Csikszentmihalyi, M., & Larson, R. (1984). *Being adolescent.* New York: Basic Books.

Dawson, S., & Hill, K. T. (1986). *Math anxiety and doing one's best in school.* Paper presented at the Annual Meeting of the National Association of Laboratory Schools, Chicago, April.

deCharms, R. (1976). *Enhancing motivation: Change in the classroom.* New York: Irvington.

Deci, E. L. (1975). *Intrinsic motivation.* New York: Plenum.

Eccles (Parsons), J., Midgley, C., & Adler, T. F. (1984). Grade-related changes in the school environment: Effects on achievement motivation. In M. L. Maehr (Ed.), *Advances in motivation and achievement* (Vol. 3, pp. 283–331). Greenwich, CT: JAI Press.

Feldman, N., & Ruble, D. (1977). Awareness of social comparison interest and motivations: A developmental study. *Journal of Educational Psychology,* **69,** 579–585.

Heider, F. (1958). *The psychology of interpersonal relations.* New York: Wiley.

Johnson, D. W., & Johnson, R. T. (1975). *Learning together and alone: Cooperation, competition, and individualization.* Englewood Cliffs, NJ: Prentice Hall.

Kelley, H. H. (1972). *Causal schema and the attribution process.* New York: General Learning.

Kruglanski, A. (1975). The endogenous-exogenous partition in attribution theory. *Psychological Review*, **82**, 387–406.

Kruglanski, A. (1980). Lay epistemo-logic-process and contents: Another look at attribution theory. *Psychological Review*, **87**, 70–87.

Maehr, M. (1984). Meaning and motivation: Toward a theory of personal investment. In R. Ames & C. Ames (Eds.), *Research on motivation in education: Student motivation* (pp. 115–144). New York: Academic Press.

Maehr, M., & Nicholls, J. (1980). Culture and achievement motivation: A second look. In N. Warren (Ed.), *Studies in cross-cultural psychology* (Vol. 3, pp. 221–267). New York: Academic Press.

Nicholls, J. G. (1975). Causal attributions and other achievement-related cognitions: Effects of task outcome, attainment value, and sex. *Journal of Personality and Social Psychology*, **31**, 379–389.

Nicholls, J. G. (1979). Quality and equality in intellectual development: The role of motivation in education. *American Psychologist*, **34**, 1071–1084.

Nicholls, J. G. (1980). The development of the concept of difficulty. *Merrill-Palmer Quarterly*, **26**, 271–281.

Nicholls, J. G. (1984). Conceptions of ability and achievement motivation. In R. Ames & C. Ames (Eds.), *Research on motivation in education: Student motivation* (pp. 39–73). New York: Academic Press.

Nicholls, J. G., Patashnick, M., & Nolen, S. B. (1985). Adolescents' Theories of education. *Journal of Educational Psychology*, **77**, 683–692.

Parsons, J., & Goff, S. B. (1980). Achievement and motivation and values: An alternative perspective. In J. Fyans (Ed.), *Achievement motivation: Recent trends in theory and research* (pp. 349–373). New York: Plenum.

Parsons, J., *et al.* (1985). Expectancies, values, and academic behavior. In J. Spence (Ed.), *Perspectives on achievement and achievement motivation* (pp. 75–146). San Francisco: Freeman.

Pepitone, E. (1972). Comparison behavior in elementary school children. *American Educational Research Journal*, **9**, 45–63.

Pepitone, E. (1980). *Children in cooperation and competition: Toward a developmental social psychology*. Lexington, MA: Heath.

Rokeach, C. F. (1973). *The nature of human values*. New York: Free Press.

Salili, F., Maehr, M., Sorensen, R., & Fyans, L. (1976). A further consideration of the effects of evaluation on motivation. *American Educational Research Journal*, **13**, 85–102.

Slavin, R. (1980). Effects of individual learning expectations on student achievement. *Journal of Educational Psychology*, **72**, 520–524.

Slavin, R. (1983). *Cooperative learning*. New York: Longman.

Veroff, J. (1969). Social comparison and the development of achievement motivation. In C. P. Smith (Ed.), *Achievement-related motives in children* (pp. 46–101). New York: Sage.

Wang, M. C. (1976). *The self-schedule system for instruction-learning management and adaptive school learning environments*. Pittsburgh: Learning Research and Development Center, University of Pittsburgh.

Weiner, B. (1979). A theory of motivation for some classroom experiences. *Journal of Educational Psychology*, **71**, 3–25.

Weiner, B. (1984). Principles for a theory of student motivation and their application within an attributional framework. In R. Ames & C. Ames (Eds.), *Research on motivation in education: Student motivation* (Vol. 1, pp. 15–38). New York: Academic Press.

Weiner, B., & Kukla, A. (1970). An attributional analysis of achievement motivation. *Journal of Personality and Social Psychology,* **15,** 1–20.

Zarb, J. (1984). A comparison of remedial, failure and successful secondary school students across self-perception and past and present school performance variables. *Adolescence,* **19,** 335–348.

III

Transitions to Adulthood

Overview

The journey through adolescence takes the developing individual across the personal, social, and cognitive domains that provide the contexts for effective decision making. As adolescents struggle with the universal issues of autonomy and connection, the requirements of living in a world that offers multiple options for freedom and self-gratification demand attention. The decision-making skills developed earlier are challenged to engage in novel arenas of life experience, in which new sources of stimulation and new demands are encountered. Every individual who completes the adolescent journey must confront unavoidable decisions regarding how to deal with one's sexuality, one's place in the world as a woman or a man, and one's legal status as a responsible adult. The chapters in Part III address these issues of freedom and responsibility in approaching maturity and highlight the central concerns of entry into adulthood. Each of these chapters examines some core questions that arise in the experience of every adolescent, the answers to which may determine important future life directions.

Concern with one's sexuality begins in early adolescence and probably continues in some form until senescence. For the young person, coping with a changing body image, responding to new hormonal stimulation, and reconsidering relationships with the other half of the adolescent population provide challenge enough. In Chapter 8, the authors point out that sexuality involves biological, psychological, and social dimensions, emphasizing the complexity of sexual development. Although certain physical changes are an inevitable part of the pubertal process, the individual and the family–school–peer culture may respond in very different ways. The personal and social outcomes of puberty for each individual depend on a set of increasingly difficult decisions on the part of the adolescent, as well as attitudes and behaviors of the adult community that facilitate effective choices. Boxer, Levinson, and Petersen consider in detail the multiple changes that transpire in adolescent puberty, the decisions that confront the individual coping with emerging sexuality, and the possibilities for adult assistance and effective intervention.

Moving from sexuality to conceptions of what it means to be a woman or a man in contemporary society involves the examination of sex-role development. Chapter 9 reviews theory and research on adolescent beliefs and behaviors concerning appropriate and desirable roles for women and men. Critical issues involve whether adolescent decisions about desirable gender roles change across the adolescent years, and whether the adolescent of today is making decisions about future roles that diverge from past generations. How influential is the revolution in women's societal roles, and how do these societal changes affect the perceptions of life options for today's adolescent? Does the adolescent of today perceive that life roles are expanding and becoming less gender-stereotyped, thereby increasing the opportunities for individual choice? The answers to these questions suggest that adolescents are choosing both to retain some traditional aspects of gender-related role behavior as well as to move in the direction of new patterns and plans for becoming contemporary men and women.

The transition to adulthood would not be complete without a thoughtful consideration of the implications, limitations, and outcomes of adolescent decision-making behaviors. In Chapter 10, Melton points out that, under the law, adolescents are treated legally as no different than toddlers but become "magically" transformed into adults at the time of their 18th birthday. Melton contends that adolescents do not differ from adults in terms of their judgment and decision-making capabilities, their understanding of alternatives, and the "reasonableness of their choices." Legal constraints on adolescents in terms of freedom, entitlement, and responsibility therefore place them in deep conflict between their knowledge of their own competence and the social message that they are incapable of assuming moral and legal responsibility for their lives. The chapter discusses a range of social, ethical, and legal issues that are indeed fascinating for the educator to consider and imperative for everyone who deals with adolescents to understand. For example, what are the rights of the students versus the schools in determining privacy of person and property, freedom from random search, responsibility for making educational decisions, expression of political ideas, and access to controversial literature? Clearly, these are not easy conflicts to solve, but they highlight the inherent contradictions between our encouragement of individual responsibility and contemporary educational policy.

8

Adolescent Sexuality

Andrew Boxer
Ruth Andrea Levinson
Anne C. Petersen

Adolescent Sexuality in the Life Span: An Introduction

Adolescence is frequently identified with the emergence of adult forms of sexual behavior. Owing to the contributions of Freud (1905/1953) and other pioneers in the study of sexuality, such as Richard von Krafft-Ebing (1886/1965) and Havelock Ellis (1936), one may view sexuality as a lifelong process emerging in different forms through phases of the life cycle. The important distinction between sexual interest or motivation and sexual expression is particularly relevant as both motivation or interest and sexual expression take different normative forms over the life span.[1] The life-course perspective (Elder, 1975) provides an explicit and useful framework for adolescent sexuality that relates it to both earlier and later phases of development and considers historical time as well as the important social structures, particularly families and schools, for adolescent development.

Social scientists who study the life span have increasingly focused their attention on differentiating those behaviors that are age related (and in this sense developmental) and those that may result from the impact of sociocultural and historical events (Schaie, 1965; Schaie & Hertzog, 1982). Phenomena such as the so-called sexual revolution and increased teenage pregnancy may be termed sociohistorical events in that they have

---

[1] The distinction has been made between sexual interest or motivation and sexual expression (Laws, 1980). To infer one from the other may confound efforts to understand these dimensions of sexuality; at the same time direct measurement of sexual interest presents several problems. If sexual interest or motivation is inferred from self-reports of sexual activity, it is important to consider the context and social constraints within which sexual activity took place.

emerged during particular historical times. The concept of cohort is central to understanding how members of a generation respond to sociohistorical circumstances (Cain, 1964; Riley, 1976; Ryder, 1965). However, the parameters of a cohort and the particular sociohistorical events that are significant to a given generation of individuals are as yet little understood.

The division of the life cycle itself into particular stages or periods is a culturally based phenomenon and is strongly affected by cultural systems (Neugarten & Hagestad, 1976). Although the biological aspects of human sexuality may be viewed as universal, along with the emergence of secondary sex characteristics during puberty, cultural meanings are ascribed to various phases of biological development (see, for example, Ford & Beach, 1951; Herdt, 1981). These cultural meanings are often based on socially shared age-based definitions and structure an individual's behavior with regard to privileges, obligations, rights, and accompanying role expectations. Thus, adolescent sexuality is regulated by sociocultural phenomena that help give shape to the sexual experiences of adolescents and may result in altered patterns of sexual development across different historical periods (e.g., Downey, 1980) and diverse cultures. For example, what one culture may prohibit as forbidden another may prescribe.

It was Sigmund Freud (1905/1953) who first brought attention to the sexual nature of infants and small children. His examination of the development of erotogenic zones, such as the oral sucking of an infant or the anal preoccupations of a toddler, led to his theory of psychosexual stages of development. Freud's discussions of children's sexual knowledge and their sexual fantasies suggested that sexual interests and behaviors begin to develop in the earliest stages of life. Recently, investigators of adulthood and aging have pointed to the sexual needs and behaviors of middle-aged and older adults (Pfeiffer, Verwoerdt, & Davis, 1972). In our society, adolescence is typically identified as the time during which adult forms of sexuality fully emerge.

Puberty is often considered to be the biological event that marks the beginning of adolescence (Petersen & Taylor, 1980). With the onset of puberty, a child's body changes into an adult one. Secondary sex characteristics (body hair, breast development for girls, facial hair for boys, mature genitalia in both sexes) emerge, culminating in the attainment of adult reproductive and sexual capacity. The sexual potential of adolescents is readily apparent to others, signaled by increasingly mature physical stature. Thus, adolescent sexuality has become an important issue to parents, teachers, and others who are involved in the lives of adolescents.

The development of sexual behavior differs in some important respects from other aspects of development at adolescence. It is essential to our species that at least some members of the society are reproducing. Therefore, there is some expectation that individuals will learn behaviors that facilitate reproduction. However, sexuality is not simply the result of social biological factors. We employ the term biopsychosocial development (e.g., Petersen, 1979) to underscore the fact that biological, psychological, and social aspects of development become interwoven in a way that is usually synergistic.

Biological aspects of sexuality include reproductive capacity, sex drive, and secondary sex characteristic development. By the term "sex drive" we mean motivation to reproduce or engage in sexual behavior rather than an uncontrollable urge to achieve orgasm. Similarly, secondary sex characteristics may facilitate, though are in no way essential for, many forms of sexual expression. Psychological aspects of sexuality include motivation for sexual involvement, self-esteem, body image, as well as more personal meanings that sexuality may hold for the individual. Social dimensions include sociocultural mores and values in general, as well as parental constraints and the norms of peers in particular. Social comparison is an important influence in adolescent development. Not only do adolescents compare themselves with their peers in regard to their physical development (Frank & Cohen, 1979) and its timing (Tobin-Richards, Boxer, & Petersen, 1983), but they come to share various conceptions of age-appropriate behavior despite differing levels of biological maturity (Dornbush, Carlsmith, Gross, Martin, Jennings, Rosenberg, & Duke, 1981). An adolescent male and female who experience bodily sensations may label them as desire for sex or some type of sexual behavior, or they may totally ignore these sensations or attempt to suppress them, depending upon their values and attitudes as well as those of their parents and peers. Whether a sexual encounter ensues and the manner in which it is experienced will depend on many psychological and social factors. Further motivation for sex is thereby affected and the cycle continues, involving many transactions and reciprocal effects among the biological, psychological, and social domains of functioning (Petersen & Boxer, 1982).

In this chapter we shall examine the biological, social, and psychological dimensions with regard to current knowledge and, where available, historical changes that have occurred in adolescent heterosexual development.[2] There is perhaps no other aspect of adolescent development that

---

[2] In order to adequately cover the topic of heterosexual development in this chapter, we shall not include discussion of homosexual behavior in general, and recent studies of self-identified gay and lesbian youth in particular (for recent work in this area see, for example, Herdt, 1989; Boxer & Cohler, 1989; Remafedi, 1987a,b; Roesler & Deisher, 1972; Savin-Williams, 1989).

has changed so much over the past decade as sexual behavior. What has changed dramatically over this span is sexual behavior, particularly that of adolescent girls. In addition, some behavioral differences between boys and girls have diminished (see Chilman, 1978/1980).

In order to understand the phenomenon of adolescent sexuality as well as answering the questions of whether and how it has changed over historical periods, we must rely on research conducted by diverse investigators with diverse methods of study. There are also social factors that have shaped the research process itself. For example, in order to understand adolescent sexuality it is necessary to interview or question adolescents themselves. Many parents and educators may not necessarily want their children interviewed about their sexuality, due to the belief that discussion of sexuality may actually cause adolescents to become sexual. Because the issue of sexuality may be a charged one for many adults, it is often difficult for investigators to gain access to samples of adolescents in order to study sexuality. In addition, it may be difficult for an adolescent to describe or discuss sexual feelings and behaviors. At least for young adolescents, bodily changes bring new sexual feelings, increased strength, and a widening array of intellectual and emotional capacities. Therefore, they may be unable as yet to find a set of concepts or language by which to label the experience of their bodies. Finally, owing to the difficult nature of studying sexuality in adolescence, many investigators have made use of convenience samples composed of college-age youth. Their experiences of sexuality may be quite different than those of younger groups of youth. Extrapolating from college youth to younger adolescents may be both misleading and inaccurate. One must be cautious in interpreting the results of various studies of "adolescent sexuality."

The biopsychosocial framework will be imposed upon several dimensions of adolescent sexuality. We first turn our attention to puberty and its impact on sexual development and then to adolescents' experiences of their sexuality and the various forms of sexual expression that emerge during this phase of life. We also consider the consequences of adolescent sexual expression as well as social responses to adolescent sexuality. Finally, we discuss interventions with adolescents.

The Role of Puberty in Adolescent Sexuality

Designated by a set of physical changes, puberty is actually a culminating phase in a lengthy and complex maturational process that begins before birth (see Petersen & Taylor, 1980). The rate of growth and development occurring during puberty is more rapid than any other phase of life with the exception of infancy. In general, the developmental changes of puberty emerge over 4 years and begin and end approximately 2 years earlier for girls than for boys.

During puberty the levels of particular hormones increase sharply, setting into motion the growth of secondary sex characteristics and the increases in body size. Although these physically apparent changes are dramatic, the underlying hormonal process itself is very gradual and lasts much longer, starting as early as 7 years of age. In essence, puberty is a time when a system established prenatally becomes activated.

Levels of major androgens (dihydrotestosterone and testosterone) and estrogens (estrone and estradiol) as well as other hormones increase during puberty. Estrogens are primarily responsible for breast development, while androgens influence the growth of pubic hair and the genitals. The hormonal increments differ by sex with higher levels of estrogens present in girls and higher levels of androgens found in boys.

The visible manifestations of puberty, that is, the physical changes, have been most discussed in the literature by the pediatrician Jerome Tanner (1962, 1974). The major changes of puberty include a dramatic growth in height and weight, the growth of pubic and axillary (underarm) hair, facial hair on boys, breasts on girls, and genital development in both boys and girls, Growth in height coincides also with growth in muscle, both of limbs and heart, caused by the same hormones (Tanner, 1971). Other changes during puberty include voice deepening, acne and other skin eruptions, and the development of sebaceous (oily) and apocrine (sweat) glands, the latter producing a body odor not present before puberty. Skin changes result, in part, from the activity of androgen and can occur in both males and females. However, acne is more common in boys because of the higher level of androgens (Tanner, 1971).

Certain physical sex differences emerge and others are enhanced during puberty. After the growth in height and weight, boys are taller and heavier than girls, an outcome due primarily to the earlier onset of puberty in girls, as well as the development of a greater muscle-to-fat ratio in boys. The earlier onset of puberty in girls means that the prepubertal, or childhood, growth period is curtailed sooner than it is in boys. This results in shorter stature for girls by the conclusion of the growth spurt. At the conclusion of puberty, boys generally have greater strength and musculature. Body shape also changes during puberty, with girls developing broader hips and boys broader shoulders (Faust, 1977; Petersen, 1979).

As noted above, specific changes occur during puberty and each change follows an invariant sequence. In contrast, the timing of these specific changes, relative to each other, can vary, although normative patterns emerge for boys and girls. For girls, growth spurt is one of the first signs of puberty with the onset of menstruation (menarche) occurring later in the pubertal sequence. Two of the earlier visible changes are the appearance of body hair and the beginning of breast development; further development of both of these characteristics continues across the pubertal phase. For boys, pubic hair growth and penis growth frequently initiate the visible pubertal changes, while voice change and facial hair generally appear somewhat later.

For both boys and girls, the relations among the developmental sequences of each physical characteristic also can vary considerably from individual to individual. It is not unusual for body hair, for example, to be developing at the same time and rate as breasts in one girl, while, in another, body hair may be developing at a much faster pace than breasts and be almost completed while breast development continues for an additional year or 2.

Not only does the timing of the individual pubertal changes vary, but the timing of the whole pubertal process varies considerably from person to person. How fast a child goes through puberty does not seem to be related to whether puberty is occurring early or late (Tanner, 1971). Although girls begin and end puberty about 2 years before boys, there is much variation in the timing of pubertal onset and completion. The normal range of pubertal onset and completion for girls extends from 8 to 18 years of age. For boys the range for the beginning and completion of puberty extends from 9 to 19 years.

Many have noted a trend for puberty to begin earlier and earlier since at least the last century, a trend affecting both boys and girls (Tanner, 1971). Although the processes involved are somewhat controversial, it is generally believed that the underlying factor is that nutrition and health conditions have improved, causing people to grow taller and heavier, probably approaching their optimal genetic potentials. This generally better fitness may be the main cause of the earlier pubertal onset. Nutrition and health status for most in America today is adequate; therefore, both final height attained and the timing of pubertal onset appear to have plateaued.

A major outcome of puberty is the biological ability to reproduce. This reproductive capacity for girls means cyclical ovulation, which is marked by a menstrual period. For boys, the capacity to reproduce is defined by the ability to produce sperm and ejaculate seminal fluid. Like other aspects of pubertal change, reproductive capacity also develops gradually rather than being a single event. For example, although menarch happens only once, the underlying hormonal and anatomical changes occur over a few years (Petersen, 1979). This more gradual change is initially reflected in the sometimes irregular menstrual cycles that are generally, though not always, anovulatory (i.e., no egg is released). A few girls, however, are fertile (ovulatory) with their very first menstrual cycle (Zabin, Kantner, & Zelnik, 1979). The onset of the reproductive capacity in boys is also probably gradual, although research evidence is not definitive (e.g., Whiting, 1986).

It has often been assumed that biology and psychology interact in a unidirectional manner, with biological systems influencing psychological domains in the individual. More recently, however, research has indicated that the direction of influence is actually reciprocal, with psychological and social factors also exerting influence on biological systems. That the young adolescent is conscious of and can attribute meaning to pubertal change contributes to the potential for influencing biological development. Thus, not only does a child respond psychologically to biological change, but a child's psychological state may, in turn, influence the biological systems. Both the timing and the final outcome of the pubertal process can be affected by a number of social and psychological events. By influencing the onset of puberty, the length of the prepubertal or childhood period is influenced and consequently the time available for height growth is affected. It has been found, for example, that the onset of menarche can be delayed by maintaining a low fat-to-muscle ratio. Achieved through strenuous exercise and restricted diet, this routine has been maintained by some serious dancers and runners (Frisch, 1980; Frisch, Wyshak, & Vincent, 1980). As another example of the psychological influences on biology, under conditions of extreme stress, the menstrual cycle may be interrupted or cease completely for a time. This is frequently the case in anorexia nervosa, a weight-loss disorder that has been found to mainly affect middle and upper middle-class white females. If anorexia nervosa continues for long enough during important periods of growth, it can permanently stunt an individual's height growth. Therefore, the biological cannot be delineated neatly from the psychological or the social. These biopsychosocial phenomena illustrate the complex interplay among biological, social, and psychological domains of development.

Adolescent Feelings and Ideas About Pubertal Change

There is an increasing corpus of research that suggests that during early adolescence, one's sense of self or self-concept and self-image is more negative and less stable than in later adolescence (e.g., Abramowitz, Petersen, & Schulenberg, 1984), with one study also finding that it is more negative than earlier in childhood (Simmons, Rosenberg, & Rosenberg, 1973). In other words, young adolescents appear to feel somewhat less happy about themselves relative to older adolescents. In particular, girls tend to suffer from a somewhat disturbed self-image that includes lower self-esteem, heightened self-consciousness, and greater instability of self-image (Simons *et al.*, 1973). A review of the sex-differences research in general reveals that during early adolescence boys start to report higher self-esteem than girls and this continues into adulthood (Petersen, 1981).

Similarly, feelings about the body or body image differ for young adolescent boys and girls, with girls seeming to feel less satisfied with their bodies at this stage of life (Petersen, 1981). Feeling attractive may become overly important to girls in the traditional female role, with perceptions that an attractive body may enhance dating opportunities. Weight has been found to become a particularly important component of how a girl feels about her body. A strong cultural pressure to be tall and slim may contribute to the finding that the heavier a girl is, or the heavier she thinks she is, the more dissatisfied she is with both her weight and figure (Faust, 1983; Simmons, Blyth, & McKinney, 1983; Tobin-Richards *et al.*, 1983). Greater weight appears to be an important aspect of the negative feelings that early maturing girls experience about their bodies.

Previous research in this area has been conducted largely on the timing of physical changes and the links between timing and social psychological factors (cf. Petersen & Taylor, 1980). Of particular interest in past research were those children who were late or early in their physical maturation, relative to the maturation of their peers. Two patterns, differentiated by sex, have emerged from both past and current research (e.g., Tobin-Richards *et al.*, 1983). For boys, being an early maturer, both in terms of objective evaluations as well as self-perceptions, is associated with a more positive set of self-perceptions and more positive evaluations by others. Being late in physical maturation is associated with a poorer evaluation by adolescent males as well as by others. The "on-time" or mid-developers fall somewhere in between these two extreme groups in their feelings about themselves and the attitudes others have toward them. Therefore, maturing early for a boy is a clear psychological and social advantage, at least during this period of life. Once beyond adolescence, when physical maturation has been completed, the social advantages and psychological differences appear to dissipate (Clausen, 1975).

When we look at the different physical changes occurring for boys, the growth of facial hair appears to be one of the most important visible pubertal changes to a young male adolescent's feelings about his physical self (Tobin-Richards *et al.*, 1983). It has been thought that increased physical size with the accompanying heightened physical prowess might constitute the most important element to the positive feelings and attitudes connected with early male puberty. The appearance of facial hair is a visually apparent change with powerful symbolic meaning for adult physical status. Thus, the reactions from adults and peers to this physical change may stimulate a change in self-image. The overall positive associations found to occur with early physical maturation for boys may be caused by the favorable social response given to those who have attained adult male physical status. A mature male body brings with it the physical advantage of greater respect from adults, more attention from girls, and leadership roles among peers (Clausen, 1975).

For girls the picture is quite different. Being in the middle of puberty is related to more positive perceptions of self and more positive evaluations by others (Tobin-Richards *et al.*, 1983). Being early or late, that is "off time," is associated with more negative feelings and attitudes. Those girls who perceive themselves as late in their pubertal maturation feel better about themselves than those who are early. These findings may reflect a mixed social response to the physical maturation of girls. Becoming an adult in this society may not bring with it the same social advantages for a female as it does for a male. Traditionally devoid of several of the social advantages experienced by a similarly maturing boy, such as athletic prowess, leadership roles, and expectations of occupational success, physical maturation for a girl may carry more explicitly sexualized meanings and generate concomitant social responses. This sexualized response, perhaps an unconscious one, may be enacted with restrictions on the pubertal girl's freedoms, with parents becoming concerned with protecting their daughters. Lacking other ways of evaluating girls, evaluation may rest more on appearance and weight. A girl who is further along in puberty and perceives herself as so also tends to perceive herself as heavier and be less satisfied with her weight, thereby affecting her self-esteem (Tobin-Richards *et al.*, 1983).

There appear to be two extreme physical ideals for women in this culture. The first ideal, discussed above, is that of a prepubertal look, one of a svelte body, flat chest, and long legs (e.g., Faust, 1983). In contrast to that, the second ideal is that of the full-bodied large-breasted sexual look representative of the figures displayed in both popular and pornographic media. Here a more mature body is emphasized with particular focus on large breasts. Findings from our own research indicate that the meaning of breast development differs from the other pubertal changes in that the greater the development, the more positive are girls' self-perceptions.

Thus, a girl with breast development tends to feel more positive about her physical self than a girl who is more flat chested (Tobin-Richards *et al.,* 1983).

The experience of menarche, or first menstruation, appears to arouse ambivalent feelings in girls. Many of these mixed feelings may be culturally determined (Brooks-Gunn & Ruble, 1983). The greater physical maturity signified by menarche may have a positive personal impact, but the positive feelings may be reduced or diffused by a negative interpersonal significance as girls become increasingly self-conscious, embarrassed, and secretive. One example of the confused cultural messages are those presented through booklets distributed by sanitary products companies. Menstruation is portrayed both as a normal noninterruptive aspect of life and because of sanitation concerns, as something to be constantly attended and carefully concealed. We have found that most of the girls in our research investigation were both happy and frightened by menstruation (Petersen, 1983). However, for a very small percentage of girls—all of them early maturers—menarche was an especially troublesome event that was at least initially denied in their self-reports of pubertal change.

Several sets of researchers have been studying the experience of menarche (e.g., Brooks-Gunn & Ruble, 1983; Petersen, 1983; Rierdan & Koff, 1985). Some of the results from these ongoing projects indicate that earlier maturers felt far more negative about the event than later maturers and that this was related to preparedness for menarche. The better prepared the woman felt she was as a girl, the more positive her memory of the experience of menarche and the less likely she was to experience menstrual distress as an adult. Girls' beliefs about their mothers menstrual distress are also significant in this regard. Girls who believe that their mothers experience menstrual distress are more likely to anticipate or report being affected by menstrual distress (Brooks-Gunn & Ruble, 1983). Ambivalence seems best to describe the feelings girls hold about menarche (e.g., Petersen, 1983; Brooks-Gunn & Ruble, 1983).

The first ejaculation of seminal fluid frequently is proposed of as a male analogue to menarche (e.g., Gaddis & Brooks-Gunn, 1985). This generally occurs about a year after the beginning of accelerated penis growth, although there is great variation in the timing of his event. Penis growth is accompanied by the development of seminal vesicles, the prostate, and bulbourethal glands. Ejaculation during sleep, so-called wet dreams or nocturnal emisisons, also occurs during this time. In addition, because of increasing and fluctuating levels of hormones, the occurrence of spontaneous erections may become more frequent. Preadolescent erections often occur in response to a whole array of physical and emotional situations, both sexual and nonsexual in nature. During puberty, males begin to respond to physical or psychological stimulation that is culturally defined as sexual. The physiological capacity for erections takes on sexual meanings through both biological changes and experience or learning (Gagnon & Simon, 1973).

First ejaculation is a normative event, but it is one of those events that are hidden (Brim & Ryff, 1980) and most often only discussed among boys in general terms, if at all. Although considerable research has been conducted on the event of menarche, little research has investigated the feelings and experiences of the pubertal male's first ejaculation. Although first ejaculation may be considered a comparable event to menarche in its implications for reproductive potential, its link to sexual pleasure and functioning is more direct than menarche (Gaddis & Brooks-Gunn, 1985). Research on topics of puberty and related issues are often equated with sexuality by adults. Researchers may be reluctant to investigate this topic as well, particularly since it is viewed as such a personal event. Thus, while first ejaculation is a normative event, the sexual meaning associated with it may make investigators reluctant to examine this topic.

The timing of first ejaculation may be quite important to boys, as this event appears to signify an important marker of one's status as a male. For most boys, first ejaculation is associated with some level of orgasmic pleasure, although it is possible to have an ejaculation without orgasm. Although many boys may be prepared through health or sex education courses for the event to occur, the actual experience may stir numerous feelings and fantasies. While boys talk among themselves about the development of their bodies or their sexual fantasies, they may actually share little information about the personal significance of first ejaculation or the feelings and thoughts that may result from it (Gaddis & Brooks-Gunn, 1985). From our study of young adolescents we have found that, for girls, one of the most valued aspects of their bodies is facial features (including skin and hair) (Tobin-Richards *et al.*, 1983). For boys, athletic-related strengths and abilities are most frequently endorsed. The growth spurt appears to be a more psychologically important aspect of puberty for boys than for girls. For girls, menarche appears to be a more salient pubertal event than the growth spurt.

We have also found that earlier maturers are more likely to be advanced in heterosocial behavior (Crockett & Petersen, 1987; Dorn, Crockett, & Peterson, 1988). Among both boys and girls, more advanced pubertal status is related to calling the other sex on the telephone and dating. This is similar to findings that link earlier maturation to heterosocial and sexual behaviors, as seen in several other recent studies (Simmons & Blyth, 1988; Udry, Talbert, & Morris, 1988).

Cultural definitions of what is desirable and expectable play an important part in mediating the psychological experience of puberty (see Petersen & Taylor, 1980). The social constraints on behavior presumably serve broad social and economic functions for a given society. While, for example, increased interest in sexuality may be a constant feature of adolescence across cultures, what is variable is the social control of sexual initiation and behavior (Petersen & Boxer, 1982).

In our society, adolescence has been characterized as a time of turbulence and inner turmoil. Recent research has demonstrated such conceptions to be uncharacteristic of most adolescents (Petersen, 1985). The role of puberty in adolescent development has been attributed a more powerful influence than appears to be justified. It is quite clear, however, that puberty culminates in a dramatic and visually apparent set of changes. The sociocultural meanings of these changes are an important social psychological component to understanding the significance of puberty for adolescents and their behavior, particularly sexuality.

Adolescents' Feelings and Attitudes About Sexual Behaviors

Much has been written since the 1960s on teenagers' increased permissiveness in their feelings about and attitudes toward sexual behaviors. The samples and the methodologies of the few studies that deal with adolescents' attitudes are quite different and, in some cases, present different results. There appeared to be a trend, however, toward greater similarity in the way both boys and girls think and feel about sexual behavior for members of their own sex, the opposite sex, and themselves. This single standard was described by Reiss (1966) as "permissiveness with affection" and "the acceptance of a variety of sexual practices without judgment or discrimination by sex, if both partners are consenting and willing" (p. 135).

Although most studies confirm that the majority of American teenagers are increasingly accepting in their attitudes toward dating, petting, premarital sexual intercourse, homosexuality, masturbation, and oral sex, some significant gender differences of opinion still exist even though the size of the differences has narrowed. In Haas' (1979) questionnaire study of 625 teenagers aged 15–18, 90% of whom resided in Southern California, he found that premarital sexual intercourse was differentially endorsed depending on the respondents' sex and age. Eighty-three percent of the boys (with no differences between younger and older boys) responded affirmatively to the statement "I believe it is okay for a boy (girl) my age to have sexual intercourse with a girl (boy)." Fifty-four percent of the girls aged 15–16, and 64% of the girls aged 17–18, likewise affirmed that statement. Thus, something of a double standard remains.

More girls than boys would also qualify the conditions under which they would have initial, premarital sexual intercourse, Most girls still feel that a romantic involvement is a necessary component of sexual activity while only a minority of boys would agree with a romantic requirement for sexual relations (Haas, 1979; Scales, 1977; Sorensen, 1973). When Haas' sample of adolescents was asked, "Do you feel you have to be romantically involved with a girl (boy) before you have sexual contact with her (him)?", 68% of the girls and only 41% of the boys said yes (Conger & Petersen, 1984). In an earlier study (Schofield, 1965), 46% of the sexually experienced males responded to an open-ended question that their first intercourse experience occurred because of sexual "appetite" or desire, while only 16% of females responded that way. Only 10% of males said their first experience occurred because they were in love, while 42% of the females gave that response. Similarly, the reasons that males and females give for avoiding premarital coitus also demonstrate sex differences. In a national random sample of 1177 college youth in the late 1960s, it was found that a majority of females cited fear of the reactions of significant others: fear of parental disapproval (60%) and fear of damaging personal reputation (55%). In contrast, 55% of the males said that the unwillingness of a partner was the major reason that they did not have premarital coitus (Miller & Simon, 1980).

Traditionally, the attitudes of American boys have been more liberal than those of girls in regard to petting, masturbation, and oral sex (Kinsey, Pomeroy, Martin, & Gabhard, 1948, 1953; Schofield, 1965). One of the more recent studies on adolescent sexual attitudes (Haas, 1979) supports the tendency of this attitudinal direction while the other available study on teenagers' attitudes indicates that females may be just as accepting of a variety of sexual behaviors as males, although females are still less likely than boys to be "sexual adventurers" themselves (Sorensen, 1973).

The changes in adolescents attitudes are most probably related to actual changes in behavior and to changes in the cultural milieu; both boys and girls tend to become more liberal about sexual behavior as they get older and particularly as their sexual experience increases (Haas, 1979; Scales, 1979; Sorensen, 1973). In addition, boys may have been more permissive about sexual acts in the past because it was more socially acceptable for males rather than for females to be aroused by specifically sexual stimuli (e.g., when the parts of sexual anatomy are viewed as "sex objects," when the erotica in film, art, or literature are appreciated as such, or when physical manipulations are made for the purposes of stimulation) (Conger & Petersen, 1984; Miller & Simon, 1980). There is growing evidence both from measures of physiological response and from cross-cultural comparisons that girls can and do experience as much if not more sexual excitement and pleasure than boys when inhibiting psychological factors are controlled (Conger & Petersen, 1984; Miller & Simon, 1980).

Attitudes About Contraception

The pattern of increased liberality in sexual attitudes on the part of teenagers is interrupted in several areas. Both males and females have tended to retain more traditional and conservative attitudes toward sexual behavior when the content deals with anticipating or dealing with the consequences of sexual involvement. A recent study (Clark, Zabin, & Hardy, 1984) of 660 black inner-city adolescent males of junior and senior high school age revealed that nearly 9 in 10 respondents recognize that the boys share responsibility for preventing pregnancy when they have sex, but more than half were willing to tolerate unprotected intercourse (54%). Furthermore, nearly half of the boys (43%) reported that they would be too embarrassed to buy contraceptives in a store and nearly one-third of the respondents said that it is hard for them to talk to their girlfriends about using birth control.

In spite of the fact that most sexually active teenagers do not want to become pregnant (or to cause a pregnancy), first intercourse is generally an unplanned and unprotected event (Alan Guttmacher Institute, 1981; Miller, 1976; Shah, Zelnik, & Kantner, 1975; Zelnik & Kantner, 1980; Zelnik & Shah, 1983). In a recent survey, Zelnik and Shah (1983) found that only 17% of young women and 25% of the men had planned their first act of intercourse. Of the teenage girls who did plan their first intercourse, three-quarters were protected by contraception. However, very few of these women used a contraceptive themselves; more than two-thirds of them depended on their partner to use either a condom or withdrawal. Thus, both teenage girls and boys appear to be generally passive in their attitudes toward assuming responsibility for contraceptive use. The reasons that teenagers typically give for not using contraceptives have been related to the disbelief in the possibility of pregnancy. In Sorensen's sample, 29% of all boys currently having intercourse are "often" and 60% "sometimes" worried about their sex partners becoming pregnant, compared to 35% of the girls currently having intercourse who are "often" and 36% who are "sometimes" worried about becoming pregnant. In a sample of all inner-city black males (Zelnik & Shah, 1983), only 34% say that they would be "very upset," 41% would be "a little upset," 13% would not be upset, and 12% would be happy about a pregnancy. Half of the sample of 258 adolescent females attending a family-planning clinic stated that they would be "very worried" about getting pregnant, while just under half the group said that they would be "somewhat worried" (Levinson, 1981). If a pregnancy did occur, somewhat more boys than girls tend to endorse the option of an abortion; but the predominant choice for both girls and boys is for the girl to have the baby and raise it, either married or unmarried (Sorensen, 1973).

Sexual Behavior

The continuing changes in sexual attitudes and values among contemporary adolescents are reflected in sexual behavior, but with variations depending on *what* behaviors one is referring to, among *which* adolescents, and *how recently*.

Masturbation

Available information indicates that among boys the number who have engaged in masturbation by age 19 has remained fairly stable since their parents' generation at around 85–90% (Arafat & Cotton, 1974; Chilman, 1983; Haas, 1979; Kinsey *et al.*, 1948). But is also appears that the number involved at younger ages is increasing significantly. In Kinsey's original sample (Kinsey *et al.*, 1948), only 45% of males reported masturbating by age 13; in contrast, in recent surveys (Haas, 1979) that number had increased to between 52 and 65%. Among girls, recent data indicate that there has been an increase in masturbation at all age levels, with incidences doubling to around 33% by age 13 and about 60% by age 20 (compared to percentages around 15% and 30% for their mothers at ages 13 and 20, respectively (Haas, 1979; Kinsey *et al.*, 1953; Sorensen, 1973).

Even with recent changes, however, girls as a whole appear to engage in masturbation during adolescence only about half as often as boys. Furthermore, among those with masturbation experience, girls masturbate less frequently, on the average, though with wider variability (Kinsey *et al.*, 1953; Sorenson, 1973). Masturbation among contemporary adolescents occurs about three times as frequently among those engaged in sexual intercourse or petting to orgasm as among the sexually inexperienced (Sorenson, 1973).

Petting

Petting does appear to have increased somewhat in the past few decades, and it tends to occur slightly earlier (Chilman, 1983; Haas, 1979; Vener & Stewart, 1974). The major change, however, has probably been in frequency of petting, degree of intimacy of techniques involved, the frequency with which petting leads to erotic arousal or orgasm, and, certainly, frankness about this activity (Chilman, 1980; Haas, 1979; Sorenson, 1973; Vener & Stewart, 1974).

Light petting (i.e., touching above the waist), increases chronologically for teenagers. According to two studies conducted in the early 1970s, approximately 50–60% of 14- and 15-year-old boys and girls have engaged in light petting and by ages 16 and 17 these figures increase to about 70% (Miller & Simon, 1974; Vener & Stewart, 1974). Heavy petting is less common for younger teens, and the average percentages for boys and girls are about 45% and 32% respectively; by 16 and 17 these figures increase to about 55% and 47% (Wagner, 1980).

Sexual Intercourse

A national survey of adolescents aged 13 to 19 (Sorensen, 1973) found that 44% of boys and 30% of girls had sexual intercourse prior to age 16. These figures increased to 72% of boys and 57% of girls by age 19 (Sorensen, 1973). More recently, Zelnik and Kantner (1980) found that 38% of unmarried 16-year-old girls in metropolitan areas in the United States had engaged in premarital intercourse, compared to 21% in a similar survey in 1971 and 29% in 1976. Among unmarried 19-year-olds in 1979, 69% had engaged in intercourse (up from 46% in 1971 and 59% in 1976). In 1979, 50% of all 15 to 19-year-old females reported having engaged in premarital intercourse, compared to 30% in 1971 and 43% in 1976. The average age at which young women had their first intercourse experience was 16.2 years.

Among males aged 17 to 21 in 1979, these investigators found that 70% had engaged in premarital intercourse. Of these, 56% had intercourse by age 17, and 77% by age 19. Comparable results have been obtained recently in another large, but somewhat less systematically controlled, national sample of adolescents, aged 13 to 18. Among 13 to 15-year-olds, 41% of boys and 21% of girls reported having sexual intercourse; among those aged 16 to 18, 70% of boys and 46% of girls had done so (Norman & Harris, 1981).

Rates of sexual intercourse vary according to sex and age and are affected by race, socioeconomic, cultural, religious, and geographical variables. Blacks generally experience first coitus at younger ages than whites (Kantner & Zelnik, 1972, 1973; Zelnik & Kantner, 1977, 1980). In 1979, 75% of black men were sexually active compared with 70% of white males aged 17 to 21 (Zelnik & Shah, 1983). There was no change between 1976 and 1979 in the proportion of black teenage women who were sexually active, whereas there was an increase among young white women from 38% to 47% during that period. As a result, black women were 74% more likely than whites to be sexually active in 1976 but only 40% more likely to be so in 1979 (Zelnik & Shah, 1983). Politically conservative and religiously oriented youth are more conservative in their sexual behavior than liberal or religiously inactive young people (Chilman, 1978, 1983; Conger, 1980; Jessor & Jessor, 1977; Herold & Goodwin, 1981; Kantner & Zelnik, 1972; Reiss & Miller, 1979). In general, economically privileged, more highly educated adolescents and youth are less conservative in their sexual attitudes than their less economically favored peers but these attitudinal differences are reversed in terms of behavior (Chilman, 1978; Katchadourian & Lunde, 1975; Miller & Simon, 1980). Poor, inner-city youth with low educational aspirations are more likely to engage in sexual intercourse at younger ages and with more partners than are their privileged peers (Dreyer, 1982; Kantner & Zelnik, 1972; Vener & Stewart, 1974). It also is apparent that rates of sexual intercourse vary with culture and region (e.g., Conger & Petersen, 1984).

Sex differences appear to influence the nature of the first intercourse experience (Eastman, 1972; Schofield, 1973; Sorensen, 1973; Weis, 1983; Zelnik & Shah, 1983). In Zelnik and Shah's (1983) report, young women tended to have their first intercourse experience with a partner nearly 3 years older than themselves, whereas men had their first intercourse with a partner less than 1 year older. Young women's first coitus generally occurred with someone toward whom they felt a commitment; more than 6 in 10 young women said that they had been going steady with or were engaged to their first sexual partner. In contrast, fewer than 4 in 10 young men said that they had been engaged to or going steady with their first partner, and more than 1 in 3 of the males said that they and their first partner had been friends.

Schofield (1973), Sorensen (1973), and others have found that young men are more likely than young women to enjoy their first intercourse. Young men commonly report feelings of excitement, satisfaction, happiness, and joy. In contrast, girls commonly report feelings of fear, guilt, anxiety, pain, and embarrassment. It has been speculated that some of the painful feelings for females are related to the feelings of anxiety in combination with the state of her physical arousal and the condition of her hymen (Katchadourian & Lunde, 1975).

Contraceptive Behavior

Despite the significant progress in the last decade in making access to and information about contraceptives more available to teenagers, less than half of adolescents or their partners use any contraceptive method at first intercourse (Zelnik & Kantner, 1980; Zelnik & Shah, 1983). Compared to younger adolescents (age 15), older adolescents (age 19) are twice as likely to have used contraception in their last intercourse (Alan Guttmacher Institute, 1981; Kantner & Zelnik, 1973; Zelnik & Kantner, 1977, 1978; Zelnik & Shah, 1983). Among those using some form of contraception, the most popular methods used initially are, in order of frequency, the male-controlled methods of condoms and withdrawal (each about 35% of total use), followed by the pill. Intrauterine devices (IUDs) and other methods accounted for only a relatively small percentage of the total. However, the pill is likely to be the method most recently used (Zelnik & Kantner, 1980; Zelnik & Shah, 1983). Probably largely as a result of health-related concerns, use of the pill and IUD declined 16% in only a 3-year period from 1973 to 1976; the biggest relative gains were for the diaphragm, rhythm, and withdrawal, in that order.

Among young women who use a method at first intercourse, blacks were more likely to use a prescription method than whites (41% versus 15%). Differences between black and white men in contraceptive use were small; the major variation is that white men whose first intercourse was unplanned were somewhat more likely than comparable black men to have used a method themselves (Zelnik & Shah, 1983).

The Outcomes of Adolescent Sexual Activity

Many adults are concerned about adolescent sexual activity because they fear that early initiation into sexual relationships will have deleterious short- and long-term consequences for the adolescent. The research literature on the consequences of adolescent pregnancy (e.g., Klerman & Jekel, 1973) and the incidence of sexually transmitted diseases among adolescents may give a factual basis for fears about the outcomes of adolescent sexual activity.

Reports from a national survey (Zelnik & Kantner, 1978) indicate that a quarter of the women, both married and unmarried, in the United States became pregnant before their 19th birthday and that 4 out of every 10 sexually active teenage women between the ages of 15 and 19 became pregnant every year (Zelnik & Kantner, 1978). More recent comparisons between 1971, 1976, and 1979 survey data show that the level of out-of-wedlock pregnancy among metro-area teens almost doubled between 1971 (9%) and 1979 (16%) and grew by one quarter between 1976 (13%) and 1979 (16%) (Koenig & Zelnik, 1982). This study and others have found that the increases in teenage pregnancies are largely attributed to teenagers who become sexually active before the age of 15 (Alan Guttmacher Institute, 1981).

Of the 1.1 million teenage girls under 20 years old who became pregnant in 1978, 38% chose to terminate the pregnancy by induced abortion (Alan Guttmacher Institute, 1981). Earlier research on abortion rates among New York City teens (Pakter, Nelson, & Svigir, 1975) revealed that the rates of abortion varied by ethnic group; for white girls under age 19, there were 543 abortions per 1000 live births compared to 828 and 1130 for Puerto Rican and black girls, respectively. Seventeen percent of the teenage pregnancies in 1978 were to married girls; 22% resulted in out-of-wedlock births; 10% resulted in marital births that were conceived premaritally; and 13% resulted in miscarriages (Alan Guttmacher Institute, 1981). Thus, 49% of the teenagers who became pregnant in 1978 carried the pregnancy to term. Of the unmarried teenagers who gave birth, 96% kept their children with them (although in many cases grandparents or other relatives helped take care of the baby).

It is reported that few teenagers want to become pregnant or have babies, especially if they are unmarried. Eight in 10 out-of-wedlock teenage pregnancies and two-thirds of out-of-wedlock teenage births are unintended. The social, emotional, financial, and physical consequences of unwanted pregnancies have been well documented to have negative associations for the child, the mother, a young couple, and the society (Card, 1977). Teenage mothers often become welfare mothers, dependent on public support and assistance due to their inability to earn sufficient income (Hofferth & Moore, 1979; Trussel, 1977). School dropout is a major factor thought to be important for a variety of the problems related to adolescent pregnancy (e.g., Card & Wise, 1978); a recent long-term follow-up study suggests, however, that almost all women who become parents as adolescents complete at least their secondary education (Furstenberg & Brooks-Gunn, 1987). Teenage parents are more prone than older parents to experience marital problems, divorce, and a stressful cycle of poverty and unemployment (Lorenzi, Klerman, & Jekel, 1977). Furthermore, unwed mothers are more likely than other women of their age to have a second unwanted pregnancy, thereby increasing a cycle of financial and social deprivation with added physical, emotional, and psychological stresses (Dytrych, Matejick, Schuller, David, & Friedman, 1975; Furstenberg, 1976; Koenig & Zelnik, 1982). Children of teenage parents are more likely than other children to be the

victims of child abuse (Schwartz, 1969). Children of unwanted pregnancies have been found to be less socially well adjusted within the school
environment than other groups of children (Baldwin & Cain, 1980;
Dytrych et al., 1975). Finally, children of teenage mothers show heightened risks of infant mortality, prematurity, and congenital neurological
impairments (Hunt, 1976).

In considering the statistics on the incidence of teenage pregnancy and
the outcomes of adolescent pregnancies carried to term, one must adjust
the figures that represent overall trends to reflect differences among
teenagers. Factors such as age, socioeconomic status, educational level,
race, religion, and geographical area appear to be related to teenagers'
sexual activity and even pregnancy outcomes. Demographic studies have
shown that factors associated with a higher risk of teenage pregnancy are
beginning sexual intercourse under age 15, having low educational
aspirations, belonging to a low socioeconomic group, living in an urban
area, residing with a single parent, being Black or Latin-American, and
maintaining no strong religious affiliations (Vener & Stewart, 1974; Zelnik
& Kantner, 1975, 1977, 1978, 1980; Zelnick, Kantner, & Ford, 1981).
Similarly, the risks of physical and mental health problems for babies or
for teenagers vary with environmental conditions and social-class status.
The risks of infant mortality, neurological defects, and childhood illnesses
are increased when there is inadequate prenatal and postnatal care and a
poor nutritional diet for the young mother and her child (Baldwin & Cain,
1980; Conger & Petersen, 1984).

Another problematic outcome associated with sexual intercourse
among teenagers is the spread of sexually transmitted diseases (STDs).
The rapid increase of gonorrhea in recent years has alarmed public health
officials. In 1971, there were 620,000 reported cases of gonorrhea in the
United States (Allgeier, 1983), and this figure increased to 1,013,436
reported cases in 1978. According to Katchadourian and Lunde (1975),
the preponderance of cases occur in the 15 to 19-year-old age group; it is
currently estimated that 50% of American young people will contract
syphillis or gonorrhea by age 25. It is not an overstatement to describe the
present situation in the United States as an epidemic. Of all the conta-
gious diseases, STDs are second in prevalence only to the common cold.
(Other STDs common among teenagers include trichomonasis, nongono-
coccal urethritis, nonspecific vaginitis, herpes, genital warts, pubic lice,
and scabies.)

The research literature on pregnancy and the prevalence of STDs
among the teenage population suggest quite strongly that the consequences of early teenage initiation into sexual intercourse are undesirable. Yet, one must ask if there are any conditions under which early

teenage sexual activity may be beneficial or at least not harmful. Social psychological and developmental theorists have viewed experimentation with sexual relationships as an integral part of the process of adolescent development (Elkind, 1975; Erikson, 1968). According to these perspectives, sexual experimentation is an important component in establishing a personal identity and in developing mature relationships. Therefore, one could speculate that teenage sexual activity and even sexual intercourse would enhance social psychological growth if physical protections were guaranteed. Most would argue that young adolescents (under the age of 15) are not ready emotionally or cognitively to integrate the experience of sexual intercourse (e.g., Petersen & Crockett, 1988). It is also important to make distinctions between experimentation with (noncoital) sexual activity and engaging in sexual intercourse. The early adolescent years may not be developmentally appropriate years for sexual intercourse experiences to occur (at least for girls in this society), but they may be very appropriate times for noncoital sexual experimentation. Experiences with sexual intercourse may be more appropriately postponed until the later adolescent years.

Thus far, although there is evidence that the average age at first intercourse is decreasing for women, there is no body of empirical research that can be consulted to determine whether early initiation into sexual intercourse has deleterious or beneficial effects on the social psychological or sexual development of adolescents in this culture. Researchers have only recently begun to investigate the relationship between social psychological outcomes, age at first intercourse, sexual activity and attitude measures, and gender (Schofield, 1973; Sorensen, 1973; Weis, 1983). Preliminary findings indicate that boys may have more positive experiences with first sexual intercourse than girls; one important factor here may be the relatively high incidence of forced sex or rape as a first sexual experience for girls (Russell, 1983; Wyatt, 1985). Reactions may be affected not only by the age at first intercourse but also by the expectations about and the context within which the first intercourse experience occurs (Haas, 1979; Bell, 1980; Sorensen, 1973; Weis, 1983).

Parental and Social Response

It is widely accepted that teenagers' attitudes about and experiences with sexual activity are shaped by parental, peer, and societal influences. Most parents, regardless of their lifestyles, tend to hold more conservative views about adolescent premarital sexual relationships than those of their children (Jessor & Jessor, 1977; Reiss, 1980; Shah & Zelnik, 1981). One of the reasons that parents are more conservative than their children may stem from their feeling that they are responsible for protecting their children from harm and for preparing them for the future. Some parents only react to the potential hazards involved with sexuality when children become sexually active. Some adults seem to believe that the way to regulate adolescent sexual behavior and to prevent problematic outcomes is to restrict services to adolescents: to ban sex education in the schools, to censor materials that teenagers can read or see in the movies, to enforce dress codes and dating limitations, to make unavailable contraceptive methods and abortion services, and to disapprove of or avoid discussions about sexuality.

It appears, however, that negative parental and societal sanctions may not produce the desired effects. Sexually active girls who have either experienced trouble using contraceptives or have become pregnant often report that they did not use contraceptives because they were afraid of what their parents would do if they found out about their daughter's sexual activity or because they felt guilty about having premarital sexual intercourse (Levinson, 1981; Miller, 1976; Youth Values Project, 1979; Shah, Zelnik, & Kantner, 1975). Studies have shown that teenagers who perceive their sexual feelings and activities to be in conflict with parental or religious values experience guilt (Herold & McNamee, 1982; Mosher & Cross, 1971; Rains, 1971). Feelings of guilt may actually inhibit one's ability to responsibly regulate sexual activity, as sex guilt has been found to be highly associated with poor contraceptive use and high frequency of episodes of unprotected intercourse (DeLamater & MacCorquodale, 1979; Herold & McNamee, 1982; Lindeman, 1974; Mosher & Cross, 1971; Rains, 1971). Therefore, attempts at control appear to fail to prevent sexual behavior and may increase its likelihood.

Curtailing information and access to contraceptives and abortion services may also prove to be ineffective strategies for restraining teenagers' sexual activity. "Family planning clinics report an average lag of a year or more between the time a young woman first has intercourse and the time she comes to a clinic for services" (Zabin et al., 1979, p. 222). Sexually active teenagers who were not initially motivated to use contraceptives have said that they did not use contraceptives because of misinformation, inadequate information, or embarrassment (Clark et al., 1984; Shah et al., 1975; Youth Values Project, 1979; Zelnik & Shah, 1983). Thus, many teenagers commonly experience psychological, informational, and logistical barriers to contraceptive use; these problems do not inhibit sexual activity as much as they inhibit the use of contraceptives.

Most researchers who study the antecedents to teenage pregnancy recommend a different strategy for affecting teenagers' responsible sexual behavior. They recommend that sexuality education, contraceptive information, and family-planning services be extended to teenagers in school, home, community, and medical settings (Alan Guttmacher Institute, 1981; Kirby, 1983; Levinson, 1983; Lincoln, 1984; Zabin *et al.*, 1979; Zelnik, Koenig, & Kim, 1984; Zelnik & Shah, 1983). Although a national evaluation of sex education programs revealed little support for effects in most aspects of sexual behavior, studies of specific factors suggest that some forms of sex education may delay teenagers' initiation into sexual intercourse, increase their effective use of contraceptives, and improve the quality of their sexual experiences and relationships (Edwards, Steinman, Arnold, & Hakanson, 1980; Fox & Inazu, 1980; Lewis, 1973; Weis, 1983).

Several studies indicate that parents may potentially be the most effective sex educators of their children. It has been found that young women whose mothers acted as the primary source of sexual information were more likely to delay initiation into sexual activity, to use contraceptives effectively, and to express more positive feelings about their sexual relationships than their counterparts for whom the primary source of sexual information was either peers, siblings, books, media, or magazines (Fox & Inazu, 1980; Kallen, Stephenson, & Doughty, 1983; Lewis, 1973; Spanier, 1977). Therefore, it is unfortunate that parents currently play a minor role as the formal sex educators of their children (Fox, 1981).

Teenagers and young adults in small sample studies and large survey studies have consistently revealed that they received most of their sex education as adolescents from sources other than their parents (Fox, 1981; Haas, 1979; Kallen *et al.*, 1983; Sorensen, 1973). Moreover, it has been suggested that currently parents may be poor sex educators of their children because they experience conflict in role relationships and are not well informed themselves about issues related to sexuality (Gagnon & Simon, 1973).

The ambivalence and discomfort that most parents feel in actually providing their children with sex education is made apparent when we discover that their general attitudes toward sex education are supportive. A poll conducted in 1981 by the National Broadcasting Company established that 75% of American adults favor sex education courses in school and 80% of parents support sex education in general (Orr, 1982). An earlier survey conducted by Yankelovich, Skelly, and White in 1979 showed that 97% of parents with teenage children believed that teenagers should be taught about birth control and sexuality (Orr, 1982).

Paradoxically, Haas (1979) and others have found that parents may appear "unapproachable" to their adolescents on matters concerning sexuality. When white, middle-class adolescents in Southern California were asked if they had ever tried to talk openly with either of their parents about sex, 44% of the boys and 54% of the girls reported that they had at one time or another. When asked how the parents responded, a minority were found to have responded favorably (Conger & Petersen, 1984). It must be remembered, however, that these are adolescents' reports; it is possible that they feel some conflict about discussing sex with parents.

It seems that of the majority of American adults who favor sex education many may actually prefer that sex education be provided in school. Data on the status of sex education in the schools and student participation indicate that parents may be making a serious mistake if they rely solely on the schools to educate their children about sexuality and contraception. About 60% of U.S. high school seniors polled in 1978 said that they had had sex education in school but fewer than 50% reported that they had studied birth control (Bachman, Johnston, & O'Malley, 1978). The nationwide evaluations of school sex education programs conducted by Kirby and his associates in 1979 and followed up in 1983 confirm the perception that the quality of sex education courses varies greatly from school to school and from district to district. The report produced by the Alan Guttmacher Institute in 1981 emphasizes the fact that, even when states mandate sex education courses in the high school (only three states and the District of Columbia do), there is still no guarantee that all students will take the special sex education course that is offered. A national survey conducted in 1982 of 198 large, city school districts found that 80% of the districts offered sex education to their students at some point but that only 14% provided comprehensive sex education. The criteria used in defining comprehensive sex education included assessments of topic coverage, percentage enrollment, class time devoted to any of 24 selected topics, and the grade level at which topics were introduced (Sonenstein & Pittman, 1984).

Implications for Interventions

In this chapter, we have discussed the role that pubertal development and sexuality play in adolescent development. We have also presented some information about adolescents' sexual feelings and behavior. There are still, however, many questions to be explored in the understanding of adolescent sexuality and its role in development over the life cycle. One such topic that continues to be hotly debated by public policy makers, family-planning service providers, educators, and parents is whether sex education programs should be supported, whether they can affect teen-agers' sexual behavior, and, if so, in what directions?

Currently, there is little conclusive evidence to show that sex education improves adolescents' responsible sexual behavior (e.g., using contraceptives effectively when sexually active or abstaining from sexual intercourse when contraceptively unprotected, decision making about sexual intercourse, etc.). The national evaluation of sex education programs conducted by Kirby and his associates (Kirby, Alter, & Scales, 1979; Kirby, 1983, 1984) indicates that most nonclinic sex education courses increase knowledge; however, they generally have no statistically significant impact on participants': (1) attitudes toward many sexually related topics, (2) patterns of communication with partners or parents about sex or birth control, (3) frequency of sexual intercourse, and (4) utilization of different methods of birth control. The only programs that had a clear impact on behavior were those that provided a directly relevant experiential component. Thus, a parent–child workshop that actually initiated communication between parents and their children about sexuality produced improved communication at posttest. Likewise, when a health clinic was included within a high school's educational intervention program, the use of birth control increased and births to teens were reduced (Kirby, 1984).

In summarizing his research for educators, Kirby recommends that if educators want programs to affect behavior, they may need to focus on a particular goal and design both the structure and content of the program to achieve that goal. Therefore, sex education courses must concern themselves with more than the recitation and discussion of facts and must work on changing behavioral patterns using role-play situations and real-life experiences.

Other researchers who have investigated teenagers' contraceptive behavior have found that individuals who feel either guilty or negative about their sexuality are less likely both to seek and retain contraceptive information or to use contraceptives when sexually active than those who do not feel anxious and express positive feelings about sex (Fisher, 1980; Fisher, Byrne, Edmunds, Miller, Kelley, & White, 1979; Schwartz, 1973). Byrne and Fisher (1983) suggest that negative emotional responses to sexuality are learned directly and indirectly through many childhood experiences. If children learn that sex is dirty, shameful, or disgusting and if as developing adolescents they feel ashamed of their sexual impulses, then it is likely that they will deal with their sexuality in a manner that can best be described as an approach–avoidance style.

Fisher (1978) found that those males who are erotophobic (who responded to sex with mostly negative emotions) were less likely than their erotophilic (responding positively) counterparts to have accurately anticipated having sexual intercourse during the next month. These data imply that erotophobic men and women would also be more likely to be at risk of pregnancy because they would be more apt to engage in unprotected intercourse. Researchers in this area have all recommended that we teach teenagers about sexuality with an emphasis on communication and affective education to help adolescents to accept and integrate their sexuality in a more positive manner. Further support for emphasizing the acceptance of sexuality in educational programs comes from the research literature on young women's contraceptive behavior (Goldsmith, Gabrielson, Gabrielson, Matthews, & Potts, 1972; Levinson, 1983, 1986; Lindeman, 1974; Luker, 1975; Miller, 1976). These researchers have all found that the acceptance of one's own sexuality was a more important predictor of successful contraceptive use than either sexual knowledge or sexual experience.

In sex education programs with adolescents, it is important to discuss the fact that sex is pleasurable and exciting, because many teenagers experience sex in this manner (Levinson, 1983, 1986). Students would be unlikely to relate to a model (teacher) who treats sexual decision making as only an informational, biological, social, moral, or cognitive process because such approaches do not coincide with their own experience. Levinson (1984, 1986) argues that our most effective intervention strategy for many teenagers who have experienced strong sexual arousal may be to help them recognize, accept, and plan for these feelings. Teenagers may be able to gain mastery of their sexual feelings by correctly attributing their highly aroused physical and emotional states to sexual arousal rather than to mysterious external forces (e.g., the powers of love, passion, drugs, persuasive partners, etc.). Researchers working within the attributional paradigm have attempted to change avoidance behavior by directly manipulating the cognitive labeling of emotional arousal (Valens & Nisbett, 1971).

Another important component of successful sex education programs may be the sex educators themselves. Whether or not an adolescent accepts and acts on sexual information found in a sex education program may be as strongly affected by who or what that source is (the individual or the institution) as by what they say and how they say it. Social psychologists have long recognized that a person will most likely be able to influence others' behavior if she or he is a salient model to the audience: credible, similar to the audience, attractive, and trustworthy.

As we discussed earlier, peers, are generally the most relied upon source of adolescent sexual information, but in some cases parents or adult role models may be extremely effective (and affective) sex educators for adolescents. Today, many sex educators realize that adolescent sexual behavior is determined through complex processes. Furthermore, they do not believe that an adolescent's sexual behavior can be affected by participation in school classes or clinic-counseling sessions unless the teenager's social support system or network also supports the educational message delivered. Thus, innovative programs throughout the country are trying to engage the media, teen role models, peer group leaders, parents, and social and religious institutions in a unified effort to educate boys and girls for responsible sexual behavior. Jaccard and Davidson's (1972) research on family-planning behaviors indicates that young women's actions are largely determined by a set of normative beliefs and expectations about the consequences they associated with that act. The normative beliefs and expectations are largely derived from partners, parents, peers, and the religious or cultural environment. The model and data imply that we have to develop normative beliefs and expectations that encourage teenagers to be sexually responsible in order to motivate them to act accordingly.

Sometimes it is difficult for teachers and clinicians to talk nontechnically and personally in their interactions with adolescents about sex. They may have been taught that discussing personal issues or challenging expressed values is intrusive, directive, or unprofessional. Parents may also believe that it is unwise to speak openly with their children about sexual decision making, feelings, and situations. There is reason to believe, however, that frank, open, and directive approaches may be more important motivationally to teenagers than a reserved stance. We know that often teenage girls become involved sexually at an early age because they are seeking someone to care for them; likewise, many girls say that they would not mind becoming pregnant because then they would have someone to care for and to love them in return. It seems clear that under such conditions girls may be very welcoming and appreciative of some adult interference and guidance as they may have been deprived in these areas. McCormack (1984) studied what kinds of adults were most influential to teenagers from the teenagers' perspectives. She found that high school students most often cited as role models people who had a sense of humor and enjoyed what they were doing; people who were comfortable with themselves. One can extrapolate from these findings that educators who wish to influence teenagers should feel comfortable talking about their subject and probably should talk about it directly with confidence, even addressing those areas where they feel that there are uncertainties and no easy answers. One student who participated in an experientially oriented intervention (Levinson, 1984) led by a man and woman who were very clear about their feelings concerning what constituted responsible sexuality for teenagers described her feelings about the course in this way:

> I have already been in a sex education class before, so I didn't learn anything but it refreshed my mind. Some things I'd forgotten. The class was better than the one that I went to. You two gave your information clearly to us. If we didn't understand you would tell us. I felt more comfortable in this class because it was smaller. The other one was a lot larger so there wasn't so many questions asked. I really enjoy you two. I think you should teach this more to other youths. I felt that you two were good with adolescents. You were sure of yourselves you had everything together. I really like you two. Hope to see you in the future.

POSTSCRIPT

As this manuscript goes to press the advent of acquired immune deficiency syndrome (AIDS), both as a life threatening illness and as an historical context, makes adolescent sexuality today unlike any other time in recent history. While there are few existing data on human immunodeficiency virus (HIV) seroprevalence rates among adolescents, the number of reported AIDS cases among adolescent populations, although epidemiologically low, is doubling each year (1% of all reported AIDS cases, which is 705 adolescents between the ages of 13 to 21 as of May 1988) (Brooks-Gunn, Boyer, & Hein, 1988). Heterosexual transmission of HIV accounted for 46% of U.S. adolescent female cases. For males, homosexuality, bisexuality, and IV drug use were the leading risk behavior categories. Additionally, when compared to the adult population, a greater proportion of adolescent cases were female minority group members and were due to heterosexual transmission (Brooks-Gunn, Boyer, & Hein, 1988; Hein, 1987). Therefore, understanding patterns of adolescent sexual behavior is paramount for understanding AIDS risk factors. In addition, little knowledge is currently available on the specific sexual behaviors of adolescents outside of genital intercourse. The AIDS crisis has heightened awareness of the need for additional research on demographic and cultural trends in sexual behavior, pubertal development, and the relations of these behaviors to other forms of risk-taking, such as substance use (see, for example, Zabin, Hardy, Smith, & Hirsch, 1986), in order to form carefully designed AIDS education and risk reduction interventions to prevent HIV infection in adolescents (see also Baldwin & Baldwin, 1988; Fine, 1988; Flora & Thoresen, 1988; Irwin & Millstein, 1986; Nelkin, 1987).

References

Abramowitz, R. H., Petersen, A. C., & Schulenberg, J. E. (1984). Changes in self-image during adolescence. In D. Offer, E. Ostrov, & K. I. Howard (Eds.), *Patterns of adolescent self-image* (pp. 19–28). San Francisco: Jossey-Bass.

Alan Guttmacher Institute (1981). *Teenage pregnancy: The problem that hasn't gone away.* New York.

Allgeier, A. R. (1983). Informational barriers to contraception. In D. Byrne & W. A. Fisher (Eds.), *Adolescents, sex, and contraception* (pp. 27–63). Hillsdale, NJ: Erlbaum.

Arafat, I., & Cotton, W. (1974). Masturbation practices of males and females. *Journal of Sex Research, 9,* 293–307.

Bachman, J., Johnston, L., & O'Malley, P. (1978). *Monitoring the future: Questionnaire responses from the nation's high school seniors.* Ann Arbor, MI: Survey Research Center, University of Michigan.

Baird, D. T. (1972). Reproductive hormones. In C. R. Austin & R. V. Short (Eds.), *Reproduction in mammals, Book 3: Hormones in reproduction.* London and New York: Cambridge University Press.

Baldwin, J. D., & Baldwin, J. I. (1988). Factors affecting AIDS-related sexual risk-taking behavior among college students. *Journal of Sex Research, 25,* 181–196.

Baldwin, W., & Cain, V. (1980). The children of teenage parents. *Family Planning Perspectives, 12,* 34–43.

Bell, R. (1980). *Changing bodies, changing lives: A look for teens on sex and relationships.* New York: Random House.

Bock, R. D., Wainer, H., Petersen, A. C., Thissen, D., Murray, J., & Roche, A. F. (1973). A parameterization for individual human growth curves. *Human Biology, 45,* 63–80.

Boxer, A. M., & Cohler, B. J. (1989). The life course of gay and lesbian youth: An immodest proposal for the study of lives. *Journal of Homosexuality, 17*(1/2), 313–353.

Brim, O. G., Jr., & Ryff, C. (1980). On the properties of life events. In P. B. Baltes & O. G. Brim, Jr. (Eds.), *Life-span development and behavior* (Vol. 3, pp. 368–388). New York: Academic Press.

Brooks-Gunn, J., & Ruble, D. (1983). The experience of menarche from a developmental perspective. In J. Brooks-Gunn & A. C. Petersen (Eds.), *Girls at puberty: Biological and psychosocial perspectives* (pp. 155–177). New York: Plenum.

Brooks-Gunn, J., Boyer, C., & Hein, K. (1988). Preventing HIV infection and AIDS in children and adolescents. *American Psychologist, 43,* 958–964.

Buchbinder, G. (1976). *Man and woman in the New Guinea highlands.* Washington, DC: American Anthropological Association.

Byrne, D. (1972). Social psychology and the study of sexual behavior. *Personality and Social Psychology Bulletin, 3,* 3–30.

Byrne, D., & Fisher, W. A., Eds. (1983). *Adolescents, sex, and contraception.* Hillsdale, NJ: Erlbaum.

Cain, L. (1964). Life course and social structure. In R. E. L. Farris (Ed.), *Handbook of modern sociology* (pp. 272–309). Washington, DC: Rand McNally.

Card, J. J. (1977). *Consequences of adolescent childbearing for the young parent's future personal and professional life.* Palo Alto, Ca: American Institute for Research.

Card, J. J., & Wise, L. L. (1978). Teenage mothers and teenage fathers: The impact of early childbearing on the parents' personal and professional lives. *Family Planning Perspectives, 10,* 199–205.

Chilman, C. S. (1978). *Adolescent sexuality in a changing American society: Social and psychological perspectives.* Washington, DC: U.S. Government Printing Office (reprinted in 1980).

Chilman, C. S. (1983). *Adolescent sexuality in a changing American society: social and psychological perspectives for the human services professions* (2nd ed.). New York: Wiley.

Christenson, H. T., & Carpenter, G. R. (1962). Value behavior discrepancies regarding premarital coitus in three Western cultures. *American Sociological Review,* **27,** 66–74.

Clark, S., Zabin, L., & Hardy, J. (1984). Sex, contraception and parenthood: Experience and attitudes among urban black young men. *Family Planning Perspectives,* **16,** 77–82.

Clausen, J. A. (1985). The social meaning of differential physical and sexual maturation. In S. E. Dragastin & G. H. Elder, Jr. (Eds.), *Adolescence in the life cycle: Psychological change and social context.* New York: Wiley.

Conger, J. J. (1975). Sexual attitudes and behavior of contemporary adolescents. In J. J. Conger (Ed.), *Contemporary issues in adolescent development* (pp. 221–230). New York: Harper.

Conger, J. J. (1980). A new morality: Sexual attitudes and behavior of contemporary adolescents. In P. H. Mussen, J. J. Conger, & J. Kagan (Eds.), *Readings in child and adolescent psychology: Contemporary perspectives.* New York: Harper.

Conger, J. J., & Petersen, A. C. (1984). *Adolescence and youth: Psychological development in a changing world* (3rd ed.). New York: Harper.

Crockett, L. J., & Petersen, A. C. (1987). Pubertal status and psychosocial development: Findings from the Early Adolescence Study. In R. M. Lerner & T. T. Foch (Eds.), *Biological–psychosocial interactions in early adolescence: a life-span perspective* (pp. 173–188). Hillsdale, NJ: Erlbaum.

DeLamater, J., & MacCorquodale, P. (1979). *Premarital sexuality: Attitudes, relationships, and behavior.* Madison, WI: University of Wisconsin Press.

Dorn, L. D., Crockett, L. J., & Petersen, A. C. (1988). The relations of pubertal status to intrapersonal changes in young adolescents. *The Journal of Early Adolescence,* **8,** 405–419.

Dornbusch, S., Carlsmith, M., Gross, R., Martin, J.A., Jennings, D., Rosenberg, A., & Duke, P. (1981). Sexual development, age, and dating: A comparison of biological and social influences upon one set of behaviors. *Child Development,* **52,** 179–185.

Downey, L. (1980). Intergenerational change in sex behavior: A belated look at Kinsey's males. *Archives of Sexual Behavior,* **9,** 267–317.

Dreyer, P. H. (1975). Sex, sex roles, and marriage among youth in the 1970's. In R. J. Havighurst & P. H. Dreyer (Eds.), *Youth: 74th Yearbook of the National Society for the Study of Education* (Part 1). Chicago: University of Chicago Press.

Dreyer, P. H. (1982). Sexuality during adolescence. In B. B. Wolman & G. Stricker (Eds.), *Handbook of developmental psychology* (pp. 559–601). Englewood Cliffs, NJ: Prentice-Hall.

Dytrych, Z., Matejick, Z., Schuller, V., David, H., & Friedman, H. (1975). Children born to women denied abortion. *Family Planning Perspectives,* **7,** 165–171.

Eastman, W. F. (1972). First intercourse. *Sexual Behavior,* **2,** 22–27.

Edwards, L. E., Steinman, M. E., Arnold, K. A., & Hakanson, E. Y. (1980). Adolescent pregnancy prevention services in high school clinics. *Family Planning Perspectives,* **12,** 6–14.

Elder, G. H., Jr. (1975). Age differentiation and the life course. *Annual Review of Sociology,* **1,** 165–190.

Elkind, D. (1967). Egocentrism in adolescence. *Child Development, 38,* 1025–1034.

Elkind, D. (1975). *Children and adolescents: Interpretive essays on Jean Piaget.* New York: Oxford University Press.

Ellis, H. (1936). *Studies in the psychology of sex.* New York: Random House.

Erikson, E. (1968). *Identity: Youth and crisis.* New York: Norton.

Faust, M. S. (1977). Somatic development of adolescent girls. *Monographs of the Society for Research in Child Development, 31,* 1 (Serial No. 169).

Faust, M. S. (1983). Alternative constructions of adolescent growth. In J. Brooks-Gunn & A. C. Petersen (Eds.), *Girls at puberty: Biological and psychosocial perspectives* (pp. 105–125). New York: Plenum.

Fine, M. (1988). Sexuality, schooling, and adolescent females: The missing discourse of desire. *Harvard Educational Review, 58,* 29–53.

Fisher, W. A. (1978). *Affective, attitudinal, and normative determinants of contraceptive behavior among university men.* Unpublished doctoral dissertation, Purdue University.

Fisher, W. A. (1980). *Erotophobia–erotophilia and performance in a human sexuality course.* Unpublished manuscript, University of Western Ontario.

Fisher, W. A., Byrne, D., Edmunds, M., Miller, C. T., Kelley, K., & White, L. A. (1979). Psychological and situation-specific correlates of contraceptive behavior among university women. *Journal of Sex Research, 15,* 38–55.

Flora, J. A., & Thoresen, C. E. (1988). Reducing the risk of AIDS in adolescents. *American Psychologist, 43,* 965–970.

Ford, C., & Beach, F. (1951). *Patterns of sexual behavior.* New York: Harper.

Fox, G. L. (1981). The family's role in adolescent behavior. In T. Onms (Ed.), *Teenage pregnancy in the family context* (pp. 89–120). Philadelphia: Temple University Press.

Fox, G. L., & Inazu, J. K. (1980). Patterns and outcomes of mother-daughter communication about sexuality. *Journal of Social Issues, 86,* 7–29.

Frank, R. A., & Cohen, D. J. (1979). Psychosocial concomitants of biological maturation in preadolescence. *American Journal of Psychiatry, 136,* 1518–1524.

Freud, S. (1905/1953). Three essays on the theory of sexuality. *Standard Edition* (Vol. 7). London: Hogarth Press.

Frisch, R. E. (1980). Fatness, puberty, and fertility. *Natural History, 89,* 16.

Frisch, R. E., Wyshak, G., & Vincent, L. (1980). Delayed menarche and amenorrhea in ballet dancers. *New England Journal of Medicine, 303,* 17–19.

Furstenberg, F. (1976). The social consequences of teenage parenthood. *Family Planning Perspectives, 8,* 148–164.

Furstenberg, F. F., Brooks-Gunn, J., & Morgan, S.P. (1987). *Adolescent mothers in later life.* New York: Cambridge University Press.

Gaddis, M., & Brooks-Gunn, J. (1985). The male experience of pubertal change. *Journal of Youth and Adolescence, 14,* 61–69.

Gagnon, J., & Simon, W. (1973). *Sexual conduct: The social sources of human sexuality.* Chicago: Aldine.

Goldsmith, S., Gabrielson, M., Gabrielson, I., Matthews, V., & Potts, L. (1972). Teenagers, sex, and contraception. *Family Planning Perspectives, 4,* 32–38.

Haas, A. (1979). *Teenage sexuality: A survey of teenage sexual behavior.* New York: Macmillan.

Hein, K. (1987). Acquired immune deficiency in adolescence. *New York State Journal of Medicine, 87,* 290–295.

Herdt, G. H. (1981). *Guardians of the flutes: Idioms of masculinity.* New York: McGraw Hill.

Herdt, G. H. (1989). Gay and lesbian youth: Emergent identities and cultural scenes at home and abroad. *Journal of Homosexuality,* **17**(1/2), 1–29.

Herold, E., & Goodwin, M. S. (1981). Adamant virgins, potential nonvirgins, and nonvirgins. *The Journal of Sex Research,* **17**, 97–113.

Herold, E., & McNamee, J. (1982). An explanatory model of contraceptive use among young single women. *The Journal of Sex Research,* **18**, 20–35.

Hofferth, S. L., & Moore, K. A. (1979). Early childbearing and later economic well-being. *American Sociological Review,* **44**, 784–815.

Hunt, W. (1976). Adolescent fertility: Risks and consequences. *Population Report, Series* **J**(10), 157–171.

Irwin, C. E., & Millstein, S. G. (1986). Biopsychosocial correlates of risk-taking behaviors during adolescence. *Journal of Adolescent Health Care,* **7**, 82S–92S.

Jaccard, J. J., & Davidson, A. R. (1972). Toward an understanding of family planning behaviors. *Journal of Applied Social Psychology,* **2**, 228–235.

Jesor, R., & Jessor, S. L. (1977). *Problem behavior and psychological development.* New York: Academic Press.

Kallen, D. J., Stephenson, J. J., & Doughty, A. (1983). The need to know: Recalled adolescent sources of sexual and contraceptive information and sexual behavior. *The Journal of Sex Research,* **19**, 137–159.

Kantner, J. F., & Zelnik, M. (1972). Sexual experiences of young unmarried women in the U.S. *Family Planning Perspectives,* **4**, 9–17.

Kantner, J. F., & Zelnik, M. (1973). Contraception and pregnancy: Experience of young unmarried women in the United States. *Family Planning Perspectives,* **5**, 21–35.

Katchadourian, H., & Lunde, D. (1975). *Fundamentals of human sexuality* (2nd ed.). New York: Holt.

Kinsey, A. C., Pomeroy, W. B., Martin, C. E., & Gebhard, P. H. (1948). *Sexual behavior in the human male.* Philadelphia: Saunders.

Kinsey, A. C., Pomeroy, W. B., Martin, C. E., & Gebhard, P. H. (1953). *Sexual behavior in the human female.* Philadelphia: Saunders.

Kirby, D. (1983). The Mathtech research on adolescent sexuality education programs. *SIECUS Report,* **12**, 11–22.

Kirby, D. (1984). A summary of the national study of selected sexuality programs. *Family Life Educator,* **2**, 24–26.

Kirby, D., Alter, J., & Scales, P. (1979). *An analysis of U.S. sex education programs and evaluation methods.* Bethesda, MD: Mathtech.

Klerman, L. V., & Jekel, J. F. (1973). *School-age mothers: Problems, programs, and policy.* Hamden, CT: Linnet Books.

Koenig, M. A., & Zelnik, M. (1982). Repeat pregnancies among metropolitan-area teenagers: 1971–1979. *Family Planning Perspectives,* **14**, 341–344.

Laws, J. L. (1980). Female sexuality through the life span. In P. B. Baltes & O. G. Brim, Jr. (Eds.), *Life-span development and behavior,* (Vol. 3, pp. 207–252). New York: Academic Press.

Levinson, R. A. (1981). *Teenage women and contraceptive behavior: Self-efficacy in sexual and contraceptive situations.* Unpublished doctoral dissertation, Stanford University, Stanford, CA.

Levinson, R. A. (1983). *The development of young women's contraceptive behavior: Contraceptive self-efficacy.* Paper presented at the 26th annual meeting of the Society for the Scientific Study of Sex, Chicago.

Levinson, R. A. (1986). Contraceptive self-efficacy: A perspective on teenage girls contraceptive behavior. *Journal of Sex Research,* **22**, 347–369.

Levinson, R. A. (1984). Contraceptive self-efficacy: Primary prevention. *Journal of Social Work and Human Sexuality*, **3**, 1–15.

Lewis, R. A. (1973). Parents and peers: Socialization agents in the coital behavior of young adults. *The Journal of Sex Research*, **9**, 156–170.

Lincoln, R. (1984). Too many teen pregnancies. *Family Planning Perspectives*, **16**, 132–137.

Lindeman, C. (1974). *Birth control and unmarried women*. New York: Springer.

Linner, B. (1967). *Sex and society in Sweden*. New York: Pantheon.

Lorenzi, E., Klerman, L., & Jekel, J. (1977). School-age parents: How permanent a relationship? *Adolescence*, **12**, 13–22.

Luker, K. (1975). *Taking chances: Abortion and the decision not to contracept*. Berkeley, CA: University of California Press.

Malatesta, V. J., Pollack, R. H., Crotty, T. D., & Peacock, L. J. (1982). Acute alcohol intoxication and female orgasmic response. *The Journal of Sex Research*, **18**, 1–17.

McCormack, J. B. (1984). *Interpersonal influences and the channeling of goals in adolescence*. Unpublished doctoral dissertation, University of Chicago.

Miller, P., & Simon, W. (1974). Adolescent behavior: Context and change. *Social Problems*, **22**, 58–76.

Miller, P., & Simon, W. (1980). The development of sexuality in adolescents. In J. Adelson (Ed.), *Handbook of adolescent psychology* (pp. 383–407). New York: Wiley.

Miller, W. (1976). Sexual and contraceptive behavior in young unmarried women. *Primary Care*, **3**, 427–453.

Mosher, D. L., & Cross, H. J. (1971). Sex guilt and premarital sexual experiences of college students. *Journal of Consulting and Clinical Psychology*, **36**, 22–32.

Myers, D. R., Kilman, P. R., Wanloss, R. L., & Stout, A. (1983). Dimensions of female sexuality: A factor analysis. *Archives of Sexual Behavior*, **12**, 159–166.

Nelkin, D. (1987). AIDS and the social sciences: Review of useful knowledge and research needs. *Review of Infectious Diseases*, **9**, 980–986.

Neugarten, B. L., & Hagestad, G. O. (1976). Age and the life course. In R. Binstock & E. Shanas (Eds.), *Handbook of aging and the social sciences* (pp. 35–55). New York: Van Nostrand Reinhold.

Norman, J., & Harris, M. (1981). *The private life of the American teenager*. New York: Rawson, Wade.

Orr, M. T. (1982). Sex education and contraceptive education in U. S. public high schools. *Family Planning Perspectives*, **14**, 304–313.

Packard, V. (1968). *The sexual wilderness*. New York: McKay.

Pakter, J., Nelson, F., & Svigir, M. (1975). Legal abortion: A half decade of experience. *Family Planning Perspectives*, **7**, 248–255.

Petersen, A. C. (1979). Female pubertal development. In M. Sugar (Ed.), *Female adolescent development* (pp. 23–46). New York: Brunner/Mazel.

Petersen, A. C. (1980). Puberty and its psychosocial significance in girls. In A. J. Dan, E. A. Graham, & C. P. Beecher (Eds.), *The menstrual cycle* (pp. 45–55). New York: Springer.

Petersen, A. C. (1981). The development of self-concept in adolescence. In M. D. Lynch, A. Norem-Heibeisen, & K. Gergen (eds.), *The self concept* (pp. 191–202). New York: Balinger.

Petersen, A. C. (1983). Menarche: Meaning of measures and measuring meaning. In S. Golub (Ed.), *Menarche: An interdisciplinary view* (pp. 63–76). New York: Heath.

Petersen, A. C. (1985). Pubertal development as a cause of disturbance: Myths, realities, and unanswered questions. *Genetic, Social, and General Psychology Monographs*, **111**, 205–232.

Petersen, A., & Boxer, A. (1982). Adolescent sexuality. In T. J. Coates, A. C. Petersen, & C. Perry (Eds.), *Promoting adolescent health: A dialog on research and practice* (pp. 237–253). New York: Academic Press.

Petersen, A. C., & Taylor, B. (1980). The biological approach to adolescence. In J. Adelson (Ed.), *Handbook of adolescent psychology* (pp. 117–155). New York: Wiley.

Pfeiffer, E., Verwoerdt, A., & Davis, G. C. (1972). Sexual behavior in middle life. *American Journal of Psychiatry*, **128**, 82–87.

Piaget, J. (1972). Intellectual evaluation from adolescence to adulthood. *Human Development*, **15**, 1–12.

Rains, P. (1971). *Becoming an unwed mother*. Chicago: Aldine.

Reiss, I. L. (1966). The sexual renaissance: A summary and analysis. *Journal of Social Issues*, **2**, 123–137.

Reiss, I. L. (1980). *Family systems in America* (3rd ed.). New York: Holt.

Reiss, I. L., & Miller, B. C. (1979). Heterosexual permissiveness: A theoretical analysis. In W. R. Burr, R. Hill, F. J. Nye, & I. L. Reiss (Eds.), *Contemporary theories about the family* (Vol. 1). New York: Free Press.

Remefedi, G. (1987a). Male homosexuality: The adolescent's perspective. *Pediatrics*, **79**, 326–330.

Remefedi, G. (1987b). Adolescent homosexuality: Psychosocial and medical implications. *Pediatrics*, **79**, 331–337.

Rierdan, J., & Koff, E. (1985). Timing of menarche and initial menstrual experience. *Journal of Youth and Adolescence*, **14**, 237–244.

Riley, M. (1976). Age strata in social systems. In R. Binstock & E. Shanas (Eds.), *Handbook of aging and the social sciences* (pp. 186–217). New York: Van Nostrand Reinhold.

Roesler, T., & Deisher, R. W. (1972). Youthful male homosexuality. *JAMA*, **219**(8), 1018–1023.

Ruble, D. (1977). Premenstrual symptoms: A reinterpretation. *Science*, **197**, 291–292.

Russell, D. E. H. (1983). The incidence and prevalence of intrafamilial and extrafamilial sexual abuse of female children. *Child Abuse & Neglect*, **7**, 133–146.

Ryder, N. (1965). The cohort as a concept in the study of social change. *American Sociological Review*, **30**, 843–861.

Savin-Williams, R. (1989). Parental influences on the self-esteem of gay and lesbian youth: A reflected appraisals model. *Journal of Homosexuality*, **17**(1/2), 93–109.

Scales, P. (1977). Males and morals: Teenage contraceptive behavior amid the double standard. *The Family Coordinator*, **26**, 211–220.

Schaie, K. W. (1965). A general model for the study of developmental problems. *Psychological Bulletin*, **64**, 94–107.

Schaie, K. W., & Hertzog, C. (1982). Longitudinal methods. In B. Wolman, G. Stricker, S. Ellman, P. Keith-Spiegel, & D. S. Palermo (Eds.), *Handbook of developmental psychology* (pp. 91–115). Englewood Cliffs, NJ: Prentice-Hall.

Schofield, M. (1965). *The sexual behavior of young people*. Boston: Little, Brown.

Schofield, M. (1973). *The sexual behavior of young adults*. Boston: Little, Brown.

Schwartz, R. A. (1969). The role of family planning in the primary prevention of mental illness. *American Journal of Psychiatry*, **125**, 125–132.

Schwartz, S. (1973). Effects of sex guilt and sexual arousal on the retention of birth control information. *Journal of Consulting and Clinical Psychology*, **44**, 61–64.

Shah, F., & Zelnik, M. (1981). Parent and peer influence on sexual behavior, contraceptive use, and pregnancy experience of young women. *Journal of Marriage and the Family*, **43**, 339–398.

Shah, F., Zelnik, M., & Kantner, J. F. (1975). Unprotected intercourse among unwed teenagers. *Family Planning Perspectives, 7,* 39–44.

Simmons, R. G., & Blyth, D. A. (1987). *Moving into adolescence: The impact of pubertal change and school context.* Hawthorne, NY: Aldine.

Simmons, R. G., Blyth, D. A., & McKinney, K. L. (1983). The social and psychological effects of puberty on white females. In J. Brooks-Gunn & A. C. Petersen (Eds.), *Girls at puberty: Biological and psychosocial perspectives* (pp. 229–272). New York: Plenum.

Simmons, R. B., Rosenberg, M. F., & Rosenberg, M. C. (1973). Disturbance in the self-image at adolescence. *American Sociological Review, 38,* 553–568.

Smith, E., Udry, J. R., & Morris, N. (1985). Pubertal development and friends: A biosocial explanation of adolescent sexual behavior. *Journal of Health and Social Behavior, 26,* 183–192.

Sonenstein, F. L., & Pittman, K. J. (1984). The availability of sex education in large city school districts. *Family Planning Perspectives, 16,* 18–25.

Sorensen, R. C. (1973). *Adolescent sexuality in America: Personal values and sexual behavior ages 13–19.* New York: Abrams.

Spanier, G. B. (1977). Sources of sex information and premarital sexual behavior. *The Journal of Sex Research, 13,* 73–88.

Tanner, J. M. (1962). *Growth at adolescence.* Springfield, IL: Thomas.

Tanner, J. M. (1971). Sequence, tempo, and individual variation in the growth and development of boys and girls aged twelve to sixteen. *Daedalus, 100,* 907–930.

Tanner, J. M. (1974). Sequence and tempo in the somatic changes in puberty. In M. M. Grumbach, G. D. Grave, & F. E. Mayer (Eds.), *Control of the onset of puberty* (pp. 448–470). New York: Wiley.

Tobin-Richards, M., Boxer, A. M., & Petersen, A. C. (1983). The psychological significance of pubertal change: Sex differences in perceptions of self during early adolescence. In J. Brooks-Gunn & A. C. Petersen (Eds.), *Girls at puberty: Biological and psychosocial perspectives* (pp. 127–154). New York: Plenum.

Trussel, T. (1977). Economic consequences of teenage childbearing. *Family Planning Perspectives, 8,* 184–190.

Udry, J. R., Billy, J. O. G., Morris, N. M., Groff, T. R., & Raj, M. H. (1985). Serum androgenic hormones motivate sexual behavior in adolescent boys. *Fertility and Sterility, 43,* 90–94.

Valens, S., & Nisbett, R. E. (1971). *Attributional processes in the development and treatment of emotional disorders.* Morristown, NJ: General Learning Press.

Vener, A. M., & Stewart, C. S. (1974). Adolescent sexual behavior in middle America revisited: 1970–1973. *Journal of Marriage and the Family, 36,* 728–735.

Von Krafft-Ebing, R. (1886/1965). *Psychopathia sexualis* (1886, first unexpurgated edition in English, original in Latin). New York: Putnam.

Wagner, C. A. (1980). Sexuality of American adolescents. *Adolescence, 15,* 567–579.

Weinberg, M. S., & Williams, C. J. (1980). Sexual embourgeoisement? Social class and sexual activity: 1938–1970. *American Sociological Review, 45,* 33–48.

Weis, D. L. (1983). Affective reactions of women to their initial experience of coitus. *The Journal of Sex Research, 19,* 209–237.

Whiting, J. (1986). In J. Lancaster & B. Hamburg (Eds.), *School-age pregnancy and parenthood: Biosocial dimensions.* Chicago: Aldine.

Wyatt, G. E. (1985). The sexual abuse of Afro-American and white-American women in childhood. *Child Abuse & Neglect, 9,* 507–519.

Youth Values Project (1979). Washington, DC: The Population Institute.

Zabin, L., Kantner, J., & Zelnik, M. (1979). The risks of adolescent pregnancy in the first months of intercourse. *Family Planning Perspectives,* **11,** 215–222.

Zabin, L. S., Hardy, J. B., Smith, E. A., & Hirsch, M. B. (1986). Substance use and its relation to sexual activity among inner-city adolescents. *Journal of Adolescent Health Care,* **7,** 320–331.

Zelnick, M., & Kantner, J. F. (1975). Attitudes of American teenagers towards abortion. *Family Planning Perspectives,* **7,** 89–91.

Zelnik, M., & Kantner, J. F. (1977). Sexual and contraceptive experience of young unmarried women in the United States, 1976 and 1971. *Family Planning Perspectives,* **9,** 55–71.

Zelnik, M., & Kantner, J. F. (1978). Contraceptive patterns and premarital pregnancy among women aged 15–19 in 1976. *Family Planning Perspectives,* **10,** 135–142.

Zelnik, M., & Kantner, J. F. (1980). Sexual activity, contraceptive use, and pregnancy among metropolitan-area teenagers: 1971–1979. *Family Planning Perspectives,* **12,** 230–237.

Zelnik, M., & Kim, Y. (1982). Sex education and its association with teenage sexual activity, pregnancy, and contraceptive use. *Family Planning Perspectives,* **14,** 117–126.

Zelnik, M., Kim, Y. J., & Kantner, J. F. (1979). Probabilities of intercourse and conception among U.S. teenage women, 1971 and 1976. *Family Planning Perspectives,* **9,** 35–71.

Zelnick, M., Kantner, J. F., & Ford, K. (1981). *Sex, pregnancy and adolescence.* Beverly Hills, CA: Sage.

Zelnik, M., Koenig, M., & Kim, Y. (1984). Source of prescription contraceptives and subsequent pregnancy among young women. *Family Planning Perspectives,* **16,** 6–13.

Zelnik, M., & Shah, F. (1983). First intercourse among young Americans. *Family Planning Perspectives,* **15,** 64–70.

9

Sex Roles in Transition

Judith Worell

Conceptions of what it means to be a girl or boy, woman or man, take a nonlinear path of development across the life span. In early and middle childhood, both boys and girls tend to view appropriate roles for the two sexes as relatively divergent. Children categorize gender-related characteristics and activities according to physical appearance, personality traits, interpersonal transactions, role behaviors, and occupational–family expectations. During adolescence, however, each individual must come to some personal decisions about how to fit into the fabric of the larger society as a woman or man. As a result, stereotyped sex-role conceptions may be submitted to the same kinds of critical appraisal as are other aspects of the adolescent's life space.

Pressures toward consideration of personal sex-role orientation come from both internal and external sources. Internal demands include biological and physical changes that signal a newly emergent "self," expectations about evolving relationships with cross-sex peers, and anticipations about future career and family decisions. External sources of pressure toward sex-role decisions are multiple: sociocultural messages about appropriate roles for women and men; parental and teacher expectations for new forms of current and future behavior; and peer groups that both model and reinforce gender-typed behavior. In addition, entry into junior high and high school settings confronts the adolescent with situational factors that require new adjustments. With the move to a different school situation, the adolescent is faced with loss of previous social support structures, expectations for new forms of interaction with cross-sex peers, integration into larger and more diverse social units, and requirements for increased curricular and life–career decision making. These multiple expectations encourage reconsideration of the woman–

man self and impel the adolescent to raise questions about appropriate self-presentation strategies in gender-related activities. As a result of changing influences, sex-role conceptions and behaviors should become more flexible in some areas of functioning and more traditional in other areas during the adolescent years.

How the adolescent views the woman–man self will influence many aspects of personal development. In this chapter, adolescent sex-role development will be considered within three areas of contemporary research: (1) stability and change in sex-role orientation during the adolescent years; (2) sex typing in relation to psychological well-being; and (3) future plans for vocational, marital, and family functioning. The introductory section will discuss some current issues in developmental research as they relate to alternative conceptions of sex, gender, and sex roles. A final section of the chapter will suggest some applications to educational practice. An interesting question is raised concerning the ethical implications of planned intervention in areas that touch on individual value systems. The professional community is not without dissent on the issues surrounding the relative advantages of traditional or nontraditional sex-role orientations. These ethical issues will be considered and conclusions drawn that reflect the professional and personal convictions of the author.

The research to be covered is restricted to the early and middle adolescent periods, covering the age range from 12 through 18. College populations are considered here mainly for comparison purposes. Although some developmentalists view the 18 to 21-year-old age period as "late adolescence" and provide empirical evidence of continuing development in "identity" (Lerner, Sorell, & Brackney, 1981; Marcia & Friedman, 1970), developmental comparisons are confounded here by basic population differences. Sex-role ideology and belief systems have been shown to relate both to socioeconomic classification (Angrist, Mickelson, & Penna, 1976, 1977; Emmerich, 1979) and to level of education (Mason, Czjaka, & Arber, 1976; Scanzoni, 1975; Spence & Helmreich, 1978). Evidence across many studies supports the conclusion that less traditional sex-role ideation and behavioral enactment is associated with higher socioeconomic status (SES) and educational levels. Therefore, college populations, although a legitimate source of investigation, do not provide an appropriate comparison with high school samples for testing developmental hypotheses.

Conceptions of Sex and Gender

A survey of researchers in the field of sex-role development reveals considerable variation in the use of major constructs such as sex, gender, and sex role. A similar disarray exists in the attempt to define the domain of behaviors encompassed by gender-related development, such as preferences, attitudes, identity, typologies, beliefs, stereotypes, and so on (see more extensive discussions of these definitional issues by Ashmore & Del Boca, 1984; Deaux, 1984; Sherif, 1982; Unger, 1979; Worell, 1981, 1982). For purposes of this chapter, definitions will follow the format provided by Huston (1983).

Sex and Gender

The developmental literature has traditionally used the concept of *sex differences* to describe modal group measurements of boys and girls. More recently, researchers have argued that "true" sex differences are confounded by socialization effects and social stereotyping and have proposed the concept of *gender* to encompass the cultural component of sex differences. Since *sex* implies reproductive capabilities and sexuality (*Webster's New World Dictionary*, 1978), *gender* is a more functional term when only the social aspect of male and female categorization is implied.

GENDER AS A SUBJECT VARIABLE. Within research models, gender has been used in two ways: as a *subject* variable and as a *stimulus* variable (Deaux, 1984; Worell, 1981; Unger, 1979). Using gender as a subject variable, studies have reported differences between adolescent girls and boys on self-concept, self-esteem, parental and peer relationships, sexual beliefs, educational aspirations, and family–career plans. Simple tabulation of the psychological and behavioral differences between groups of males and females has been criticized on both theoretical and methodological grounds. At the broadest level, reported gender differences describe only modal patterns and mean levels of response between males and females, thus ignoring the wide variability within each group on almost all variables assessed (Block, 1983; Tittle, 1981).

Among the specific variables that confound the gender-difference research are (1) moderating variables such as SES and ethnic background (Block, 1983), (2) method of obtaining data such as self-report or behavioral observations (Eisenberg & Lennon, 1983), (3) gender of experimenter (Eagley & Carli, 1981), and (4) situational expectations and constraints (Deaux, 1984; Eagley, 1978). Taken together, these considerations impose a cautionary posture when drawing conclusions about true population differences between females and males.

GENDER AS A STIMULUS VARIABLE. Gender also functions as a stimulus variable that invokes previously learned stereotypes about how males and females *should* think, feel, or act. Gender now becomes a social category that provides a set of cues for judging self and others or for taking personal action (Deaux, 1984; Deaux & Major, 1987). Individuals use gender categories to attribute traits, desirable roles, and expectations to both self and others. The correspondence between gender-related attributions to self and others, however, is not isomorphic. Children and adolescents use more stereotypes when describing others than when describing the self, thus believing the self to be less culturally bound by the dictates of gender than others are believed to be (Etaugh, Levine, & Manella, 1984; Guttentag & Longfellow, 1977; Spence & Helmreich, 1978; Spence, Helmreich, & Stapp, 1975). In a similar manner, boys and girls from second grade through middle adolescence assign more positive traits to their own than to the other gender group (Etaugh *et al.,* 1984), implying that responses on gender-related measures may reflect the effects of conscious self-presentation strategies (Deaux, 1984).

The stimulus function of gender, then, may provide an important source of sex-role orientation for adolescents as they strive to present an acceptable male or female image to the assumed "social audience" (Elkind, 1967) of their parents and peers. Some of the adherence to stereotypic gender-related behavior in early and middle adolescence may be explained by assuming a calculated self-presentation deployment as well as by invoking the more popular global concept of "gender identity." Recent research on self-presentation and impression management suggests that what people say and do in social situations is frequently an attempt to create desired impressions on other people (Schlenker, 1980; Tetlock & Manstead, 1985). The salience of gender categorization during adolescence (Hill & Lynch, 1983) may thus influence both self-evaluation processes and social display, as well as expectations for judgment by others about one's effectiveness in achieving the man–woman person one is striving to become.

Sex Roles

As an alternate way of conceptualizing the differences between males and females, researchers have focused attention on sociocultural *sex roles.* Research on sex roles generally takes the position that observed gender differences in behavior are mediated by the individual's culturally determined conceptions of appropriate and desirable behaviors for females and males (Bem, 1974; Katz, 1979; Spence & Helmreich, 1978). In the attempt to integrate sex-role conceptions into the process of psychological development, four models of sex-role orientation have been proposed: congruence, androgyny, masculinity, and gender-free. Each of these models will be examined briefly in terms of their major assumptions and implications for male and female development.

THE CONGRUENCE MODEL. Prior to the onset of the women's movement, both the lay public and the professional community viewed the convergence of gender and sex-role adoption as a healthy and appropriate developmental task. Thus, boys were to be raised as "masculine" and girls as "feminine," and their personality adjustment was assessed accordingly (Mussen, 1969). Indeed, major theories of development encouraged a bipolar view of male and female behavior, implying that the two strands of development are mutually exclusive. Furthermore, failure to adopt the role-assigned behaviors and attitudes of one's gender was assumed to place the individual at developmental risk (Erickson, 1963; Kagan, 1964; Kohlberg, 1969). Whitely (1983) refers to this traditional stance as the "congruence" model of the relationship between sex-role orientation and psychological well-being.

THE ANDROGYNY MODEL. In contrast to the bipolar congruence model, recent approaches to sex-role development have viewed masculinity and femininity as reflecting orthogonal dimensions that can be measured separately and independently, thus paving the way for the possibility of both sets of qualities residing in the same individual. The androgyny model of psychological well-being (Bem, 1974; Block, 1973; Gilbert, 1981; Kaplan, 1976; Whitely, 1983; Worell, 1978) takes the position that the masculine and feminine components of personality and behavior are complementary rather than incompatible. From an androgyny viewpoint, both males and females benefit from adopting the traits and role behaviors of both genders because they will have greater behavioral flexibility and can adapt to a wider variety of social situations (Bem, 1974, 1979). New assessment strategies to evaluate the androgyny model have been developed in such a way that the masculine and feminine components can be measured separately, supporting the hypothesis that these reflect two relatively independent dimensions of personal functioning (Bem, 1974; Spence *et al.,* 1975). Subsequent research suggests that scores for masculinity and femininity on these scales may better be described as "instrumental" and "expressive" personality traits.

THE MASCULINITY MODEL. Recent research to evaluate the androgyny model of well-being has suggested a third approach to psychological adjustment with respect to sex roles, the masculinity model (Kelly & Worell, 1977; Whitely, 1983). As a result of obtained correlations between measures of self-esteem and masculinity, it was proposed that the instrumental, dominant, and assertive characteristics assessed by scales of masculinity are more functional and highly valued in American society than are the interpersonal and expressive traits represented in femininity scales. High levels of masculine-typed traits, then, should be associated with higher self-esteem. Bem (1977), for example, found higher self-esteem in masculine-typed college students, supporting the relationship between instrumental traits and self-esteem. Whitely's (1983) meta-analysis of 35 studies on a total of 12,116 adolescents and adults supports the conclusion that, in comparison to other sex-role attributes, masculinity is the most robust contributor to self-esteem.

THE GENDER-FREE MODEL.   More recently, a gender schema approach to sex-role stereotyping has been offered by Bem (1981) and by Martin and Halverson (1981). Both approaches propose that sex-role stereotyping is an example of normal information processing in which social information is categorized into discrete and simple units. Gender cues serve as an organizing schema that focuses the individual's attention and recall of information about females and males. Martin and Halverson proposed a two-step process in which children first define the in-group and out-group by gender and then apply the schema in an anticipatory manner to their own behavioral routines and plans. Bem emphasized the salience of gender schemata in the evaluative processes of sex-typed persons and suggested that androgynous persons are relatively gender-free in their judgments of self and others. Although the gender schema approach to sex roles has interesting implications for the development of sex-role stereotyping of self and others, it has not been applied to developmental changes over the life span. The concept of a gender-free perceptual base, however, is compatible with the androgyny model and should lead to similar predictions concerning well-being in adolescence.

Sex Roles and Psychological Well-being

The androgyny model of psychological development has captured the imagination of the research community and has received considerable attention in the adolescent sex-role literature. The applications of the androgyny or gender-free models are particularly intriguing for the adolescent population, since this is the age period during which conscious choices are made regarding future life roles.

The major developmental questions concerning androgyny are these: (1) Are advances in age and cognitive development accompanied by a trend toward increasing psychological androgyny; and (2) do androgynous adolescents demonstrate increased psychological well-being? Some of the research to be reviewed here will respond to these questions. The importance of the androgyny concept for today's educational strategist lies in its promise for a well-balanced individual who may be better prepared to function in contemporary society than the traditional sex-typed individual. Can the concept of androgyny bear all this weight?

Conceptualizing Sex-role Development

One methodological barrier to drawing conclusions regarding the utility of sex-role models in adolescence is the unsystematic approach to conceptualization and measurement of sex-role development. The concept of sex roles is used here in the broadest sense, to encompass cognitive, evaluative, and behavioral components of gender-related characteristics. When we consider the range of conceptualizations, values, attitudes, beliefs, preferences, and enactments that are gender-related in American society, it becomes meaningless to view sex roles as other than a complex set of variables, many of which do not interrelate (Katz, 1979; Spence & Sawin, 1985).

Huston (1983) provides a convenient format for organizing the research literature on sex-role development that recognizes the complexity and multideterminism of gender-related development. Huston's format for sex typing contains two orthogonal vectors, one for the gender-related content area to be observed and measured and the other for the constructs under consideration.

The first vector occupies the horizontal axis, and includes five major content areas: biological gender (male–female), activities and interests (work–play), personal–social attributes (traits–social behavior), relationships (parental–peer), and stylistics (gender-related attributes such as language or nonverbal behaviors). The second vector in Huston's model lies on the vertical axis and includes four construct categories represented in the sex-typing literature: cognition (concepts–beliefs), affect (preferences, attitudes, values), self-description (identity–self-perception), and behavior (observable enactment). The resulting matrix can be used to test developmental hypothesis in varying formats.

The importance of this multivariate conceptualization of sex roles is threefold: First, it provides a format for organizing the diverse methods and findings of separate research studies. Second, it cautions us to resist the temptation to oversimplify the course of sex-role development in the adolescent years. That is, findings from one content or construct domain should not be used a priori to generalize to all of adolescent sex-role issues in order to support or refute a theoretical position. In particular, those theories that predict broad increments or decrements in sex-role traditionality or flexibility during adolescence tend to adopt a unitary view of sex-role "identity" that is assumed to cut across all components of behavior. Finally, a multivariate approach to the assessment of sex roles reminds us of the importance of looking at both gender and sex-role variables in the measurement and evaluation of adolescent development.

Theories of Stability and Change

Since the adolescent period is viewed as a time of instability in both internal and external events, to what extent are sex-role conceptions and behaviors affected by these changing events? The question of the developmental course of gender-related behavior is raised in almost all research on adolescent sex roles. As the individual moves from middle childhood through the high school years, does the adolescent's sex-role orientation remain stable, become more flexible and less stereotyped, or is there an intensification of gender-related characteristics leading to more stereotyped trends?

There is general consensus that gender-differentiated behavior in adolescence is a complex function of physiological, physical, cognitive, social–historical, and socialization factors (Block, 1976, 1983; Peterson, 1980; Peterson & Taylor, 1980). Nevertheless, conflicting predictions have been proposed for developmental changes in stereotyping of self and others, depending on the theoretical position of the researcher. Three theories have received the most research attention in the literature: the cognitive developmental view, the gender-intensification view, and the life-span social learning view. Each of these theoretical positions is associated with broad predictions about the course of sex-role development across the adolescent years.

The Cognitive Developmental View

First, the cognitive developmental view of sex typing, based on Kohlberg's (1966, 1969) theorizing, predicts a gradual decrease in gender stereotyping from middle childhood through adulthood. Thus, gender stereotyping should be highest at the point that children attain gender constancy, at about age 8, and then should relax gradually as (1) concrete-operational thinking enables children to conceptualize and tolerate cross-gender behavior in themselves and others, and (2) formal-operational thinking enables them to consider multiple options and possibilities for females and males in general.

The Gender-intensification View

Secondly, the gender-intensification approach focuses on entrance into puberty as a gender marker that changes internal stimulation, modifies personal appearance toward increased gender identification, and mobilizes the reactions of both the adolescent and the parent–peer environment to new forms of gender typing (Erickson, 1966; Feldman, Nash, & Cutrona, 1977; Hill & Lynch, 1983; Petersen & Taylor, 1980; Plumb & Cowan, 1984; Simmons, Blyth, & McKinney, 1983; Tobin-Richards, Boxer, & Peterson, 1983). At the biological–physical level, entrance into puberty provides internal stimulation for interest in the other gender and a concomitant reevaluation of the self as an attractive male or female. Body changes add to the configuration of biological factors, encouraging the pubertal child to focus attention on reevaluation and self-presentation of gender-related attributes. Thus, increased sex typing is expected to occur as children move into the pubertal period. At the social interaction level, for example, new forms of contact with cross-gender peers should produce increased ambiguity about interpersonal behavior and appropriate norms, setting the stage for the young adolescent to revert to earlier levels of secure stereotyped behavior with clear rules for each gender.

The Life-span View

The life-span view places adolescent development within a broad social–historical perspective. Life-span theorists suggest that relevant life events become markers for reconsideration of gender-related behavior (Emmerich, 1973; Katz, 1979; Nash & Feldman, 1981). These life events may be specific to each individual, present in the social environment of a particular group, or experienced as part of the larger sociocultural context of a cohort. From the life-span view, adolescents are facing new cultural requirements and trying out new social roles, incorporating the behaviors and attributes of these role expectations into their self-definitions and behavioral display. Accordingly, role prescriptions and expectations may change with modifications in a variety of important life events, making sex-role development a lifelong process.

Although life-span approaches target early and midadolescence for increased stereotyping in some behaviors, gender differences are expected to emerge only when the social role demands diverge for females and males. In particular, cognitive expectancy factors exert a powerful influence as individuals move into new social situations with role demands that differ from previous experiences (Ahammer, 1973). Life-span theorists are also cognizant of changes in cultural values and expectations and predict that there will be cohort differences in sex-role behavior and ideation between adolescents maturing before and after the rise of the women's movement. In particular, later cohorts are expected to show less traditional sex-role attitudes as a function of changes in visible social role models. Finally, since sociocultural change comes about gradually and differentially across varying segments of the social scene, some attitudes and behaviors are expected to remain more stereotyped and traditional than others.

Life-span theory is compatible with a general social learning theory approach to development, which emphasizes visible social role behaviors and the processes of vicarious reinforcement as important contributors to sex-role expectations and behavior (Bandura, 1977). Considering these conflicting views of development, it seems clear that some divergent pathways are predicted for the course of sex-role development in adolescence. The following section will consider research evidence for each of these theoretical views.

Research on Stability and Change

Are adolescents as a group less stereotyped than elementary school children as a group? Do sex-role stereotypes become more flexible with increasing maturity? Three sources of research variation make these questions difficult to answer. With a few exceptions, most studies do not report either (1) pubertal status, (2) level of formal-operational or conceptual thinking, or (3) school placement information, presence of dating behavior, and so on. Thus, differences attributed to cognitive development are usually identified with age progression, ignoring other internal and external changes that may be taking place. Furthermore, the answer to these questions is clouded by cross-sectional designs that fail to account for changes in social–historical time. Cross-sectional designs also tend to inflate the transitory effects of between-group differences (Livson & Peskin, 1980; Schaie, 1965). I was unable to find any studies that reported overall group differences between elementary school and adolescent subjects across content and construct domains. Studies generally found that some measures showed decreased stereotyping, some showed increased trends, and others found no developmental trends at all in sex-typed assessments. The following research examples evaluated groups of children across at least two age or grade levels for evidence of developmental change.

Evidence for the Cognitive Developmental View

If cognitive developmental changes are the major precursor to changes in gender-related conceptualization, we should expect a decreasing degree of sex typing from late childhood or early pubescence to middle and later adolescence. Since the theory does not discriminate clearly among gender-related domains and between males' and females' development, change should occur evenly across gender and content domains.

Stericker and Kurdick (1982) reported data on 238 middle-class white children from third through eighth grades, using two measures of sex typing: a modified version of the Bem Sex-Role Inventory (BSRI: Bem, 1974, 1977), and the Occupational Sex Stereotyping Scale (Schau & Kahn, 1978; as cited in Stericker & Kurdick, 1982). No cross-grade or age differences were found either for factored masculinity or femininity scores or for percentage of children in each of the four sex-role categories of masculine, feminine, androgynous, or undifferentiated. Correlations of sex-role group membership with age were not significant for any of the four sex-role groups, indicating no developmental trends across these six grade-levels. Thus, entry into adolescence was not marked by a significant change in self-assessment of instrumental or expressive traits. Turning to occupational stereotyping, children were asked to state for each of seven masculine, feminine, or neutral occupations (classified by U.S. census data on percentage of men and women in each field) whether adult men or women, or both, could do these jobs. Children in Grades 3 and 4 were more likely than the others to stereotype masculine occupations, but no other age–grade trends were found for occupational gender classification. In contrast, all three categories of occupations were stereotyped more across grade levels by boys than by girls, with boys seeing neutral as well as masculine occupations as more appropriate for men. Thus, there was minimal support for occupational stereotyping becoming more relaxed as children enter adolescence, and boys maintained a more rigid classification of occupations across grade levels than did girls, a consistent finding to be discussed in a later section.

In a cross-sectional study using children from grades 4, 6, 8, and 10 and a group of college adults, Plumb and Cowan (1984) asked subjects to rate the appropriateness of each of 24 activities for a typical 11-year-old boy or girl. No significant differences in sex typing were found across Grades 4 through 8, but a significant increase in stereotyping for both male and female activities was found for the 10th-grade group. The authors attributed this finding to Erickson's (1966) hypothesis that midadolescence is a period of strong sex typing due to the need to establish "identity." The hypothesis of increased sex typing in 10th grade does not match formulations by other Ericksonian researchers, who find that midadolescence is a time of incomplete and modulating identity development (see Archer, 1985; Della Selva & Dusek, 1984; Marcia, 1966; Marcia & Friedman, 1970). Again, this study found sex-typing differences between male and female respondents, with males showing more stereotyping of masculine activities. Subjects were also divided according to whether the females described themselves as having been a "tomboy" or "not a tomboy," and all children were asked about their own preferences for activities. Boys at all grade levels preferred male-typed activities. Female "non-tom boys" preferred female-typed activities, and girls who described themselves as "tomboys" showed no differences in sex typing of activity preferences, except at Grade 4, where all the girls preferred girls' activities. These data do not support a general relaxation of either self or other stereotyping on sex-typed activities, suggesting rather that both gender and sex-role preference have stronger effects than age or cognitive development.

Taking a look at the adolescent period in relation to older populations, several studies have assessed sex-role traits cross-sectionally over wider age ranges. These studies found no effects of age grouping per se on self-described traits (Hyde & Phillis, 1979; Urberg & Labouvie-Vief, 1976; Urberg, 1979). If sex-role stereotypes are relaxing as students approach adulthood, the adolescent groups should report less traditional self-concepts than younger groups. In relation to the ideal person of the same and other gender, however, Urberg (1979) found that 12th graders were more stereotyped than 7th graders, with males desiring a more submissive and dependent female than did the females themselves. As adolescents approach the mate-selection process, it may be that stereotyped idealization of cross-gender traits enables the mate seeker to narrow the search. Since these ideal types do not match real self-descriptions, the search may be frequently difficult or disappointing.

It seems important to unravel the confounding effects of cross-sectional designs on the evaluation of change during adolescence. Dusek and Flaherty (1981) designed a 3-year longitudinal study that included students from grades 5 through 12 (ages 11–18). Each sample was retested annually, and new samples were added to each grade level every year, so that both cross-section and longitudinal data were obtained. The design was a sophisticated attempt to separate the *continuity* of individual self-definitions across time, the *stability* of individual self-concept from one testing period to another, and cohort effects. The semantic differential measure of self-concept contained three factors that were clearly gender-relevant: masculinity, expressivity (congeniality–sociability), and instrumentality (achievement–leadership). Significant gender differences in the expected sex-typed directions were found on all three factors, but no significant changes appeared in factor scores across the 3 years or across grade levels. Also, there were no effects of cohort or time-of testing on adolescent sex-role self-concepts. Dusek and Flaherty (1981) concluded that "the person who enters adolescence is basically the same as that who exits it" (p. 39). Although some support was found for individual inconsistency from one testing period to another (instability), the high coefficients of congruence (.93–.95) indicated a stable developmental function (continuity). It does seem unfortunate that well-developed designs such as this one limit their generalizability by failing to use more than one type of assessment. However, the robust findings lend no support to the view that the adolescent years are characterized by a gradual movement toward androgynous orientations. Rather, the findings suggest that the instability that does occur in adolescent self-conceptions is probably a function of situational and individual factors.

Using multiple assessments and a wider range of student age levels, Guttentag and Bray (1976) reported an intervention study that looked at gender stereotyping in kindergarten, 5th-grade, and 9th-grade students. A total of 409 students from 19 classrooms participated. Assessments included occupational roles, personality trait attributions, self-descriptors of typical day activities as an adult, and a sex-role activity preference questionnaire. Of the three age groups, the 5th graders were the least stereotyped across measures, with relatively high degrees of sex typing appearing both at the kindergarten and 9th-grade levels prior to intervention. However, within each age group, unsystematic differences appeared for boys and girls on specific measures. Occupations and daily activities were stereotyped more than were self-attributed traits. In terms of the linear developmental hypothesis, it is interesting to note that following a destereotyping intervention, 9th-grade boys remained the most resistant to considering equalization or overlap of interpersonal and occupational roles for men and women. This finding seems inconsistent with a cognitive developmental view, especially in light of the authors' report that change following intervention was highly dependent upon situational cues of classroom structure and teacher behavior (Guttentag & Longfellow, 1977).

An alternative view of the 9th grade boys' persistent stereotyping

(Guttentag & Bray, 1976) might be extrapolated from Elkind's (1967) hypotheses about egocentrism in adolescence. Elkind proposed that, as a function of formal-operational thinking, the early to midadolescent is playing to an imaginary "social audience," rendering the young person more self-conscious about self-presentation. This focus on the self might motivate the adolescent to increase attention to gender presentation, thus increasing efforts to present a public image of the traditional male or female self. In a test of this hypothesis, however, Enright and his associates (Enright, Lapsley, & Shukla, 1979; Enright, Shukla, & Lapsley, 1980) found an increase in self-focus only at Grade 6 and at college level, and less self-focus in Grades 8, 10, and 12. Thus, while Elkind's hypothesis is an intriguing one, it fails to account for the 9th-grade peak in gender stereotyping. Finally, it is important to restate that the effect was found only in boys and thus does not support a broad cognitive developmental interpretation.

The cognitive developmental hypothesis has also been tested by comparing sex-role prescriptions and stages of moral development. Leahy and Eiter (1980) tested three groups, 8th graders, 11–12th graders, and college students, on the Rest Defining Issues Test as a measure of principled or postconventional morality, and on the Bem Sex-Role Inventory (Bem, 1974), scored for both real and ideal self. No significant age by sex-typing effect was found for "real" self, indicating that self-defined androgyny did not increase with age for this group of students. On the "ideal" sex-role measure, the 8th graders preferred masculine characteristics more than did the other two groups, suggesting a move toward androgyny for 8th-grade females. However, the real–ideal disparity analysis showed that across age and gender, *all* subjects wanted to increase their masculinity scores, a finding that throws a shadow on the significance of the 8th-grade results. Support for the cognitive developmental hypothesis for either androgyny or moral judgment scores was not forthcoming. However, preference for masculine–instrumental characteristics once more shows up as a robust finding.

Finally, data comparing large samples (ranging from $N = 963–1769$) of midadolescent high school students and late adolescent college students on the Personality Attributes Questionnaire (PAQ) revealed a relaxation across age levels of sex-typed traits in males but not in females (Spence & Helmreich, 1978). High school females were significantly higher on self-reported androgyny scores than both high school males and college women, but college males were found to be more androgynous than high school males. The explanation of these findings requires more space than is possible here, but, again, it is not consonant with a cognitive developmental hypothesis for both females and males.

In summarizing the attempts to relate cognitive development to modifications in adolescent sex-role orientation, it must be concluded that the evidence is not impressive. Although several of the studies reviewed above did imply support for developmental trends in their conclusions, a careful look at the data for each study indicated more inconsistencies than consistency across childhood and adolescent groups. Studies either found no trends for an age-correlated decrease in sex-typed self-concepts and occupational stereotyping or reported results that contradict the theory. These studies inform us that as adolescents become older, they do not necessarily become less stereotyped in their attitudes and behavior. If we as teachers and adults wish to see a modification in adolescent sex-typed views, it will be necessary to do something other than to wait for the passage of time. It seems more fruitful, then, to look closely at the specific events that mark the adolescent period and to consider data that correlate sex-typed behaviors with these events.

Evidence for Gender-intensification Effects

In the studies reviewed earlier, gender differences in sex-typed behavior and attitudes stand out more firmly than do differences correlated with age. In adolescence, as well as across earlier age groups, males are found to be more traditionally stereotyped in most areas of gender-related functioning. A number of theorists have proposed that adolescence presents a somewhat different set of tasks for boys and girls, with particular emphasis for girls on increased stress in heterosexual situations, more gender-related socialization by parents, teachers, and peers, and stereotyped self- and other expectations (Bardwick, 1971; Douvan & Adelson, 1966; Hill & Lynch, 1983; Huston-Stein & Higgens-Trent, 1978; Katz, 1979; Konapka, 1976; Marini, 1978; Simmons *et al.,* 1983).

The gender-intensification hypothesis suggests that differences between boys and girls on certain measures will increase in adolescence, either as compared to earlier age levels or across adolescent development (Feldman & Nash, 1979; Hill & Lynch, 1983). These differences arise from increased gender salience as puberty, dating patterns, and career–family planning become current realities. In addition, it is proposed that parental and cultural messages augment pressures on boys and girls to attend closely to their respective sex roles in order to conform to societal expectations for future behavior (Block, 1978; Hill & Lynch, 1983).

The problems in careful evaluation of these expectations for increased gender-differentiated behavior are similar to those discussed earlier for evaluating developmental change. Few studies have compared gender-related behavior across wide age periods to evaluate a gender-intensification effect. An extensive review by Hill and Lynch (1983) summarized six areas of personal functioning in which gender differences might support the hypothesis: anxiety, achievement-related behaviors, self-esteem, social relationships, activity level, and aggression. In all areas, consistent differences on selected variables appeared between boys and girls in the expected sex-typed directions. Since many of these differences appeared at earlier ages as well, the authors emphasized that only in studies in which two or more age levels are compared can the hypothesis be confirmed. They concluded that gender-intensification finds some limited support, especially for certain achievement behaviors, self-esteem, and some components of social relationships. However, there was considerable inconsistency across studies, so that gender salience alone seems insufficient to explain the variance in sex-role orientations across tasks and grades for boys and girls. The gender-salience hypothesis is particularly problematic for me in attempting to understand the greater stereotyping by boys than by girls, in view of the evidence presented by these authors that parents increase their sex-typed demands more on girls than on boys in adolescence.

Hill and Lynch (1983) attribute some of the inconsistencies in confirming the gender salience hypothesis to the failure of most studies to report or control for time of entry into puberty as an important mediating variable in gender-related assessments. The effect of early and late entrance into puberty is treated more in depth in Chapter 8 but has some relevance here to the appearance and persistence of sex-typed characteristics. In particular, early entry into puberty may have differing gender-typing effects for boys and girls, both immediately and in the follow-up data on adult personality status. In evaluating the contributions of pubertal timing to the consolidation of sex-typed behaviors, it is imperative to consider the interactions of cognitive development, self-evaluative processes, and the responses of the social environment. We may also want to have a continuing evaluation of these pubertal status relationships as changes in the sociocultural milieu provide a differing psychological environment for each succeeding generation of adolescents.

Evidence for a Life-span Hypothesis

The life-span theory of sex-role development suggests that the social–historical time will be reflected in changing cultural and personal expectations. Certainly, boys and girls growing into adulthood in the past 10 years have been exposed, as never before, to changing mores about appropriate roles and behaviors for men and women. These evolving societal expectations for gender-related behavior suggest that the gap between women and men is closing, especially in the following areas: (1) adoption of some cross-gender behavior, with women being encouraged to show more assertion and leadership qualities, and men being encouraged to release their softer propensities and to show more warmth and affection; (2) assumption of work and family roles previously regarded as the domain of only one gender, so that over half of all married women are currently in the work force and more men are shouldering home and child-care responsibilities (Hoffman, 1977; Worell, 1979); and (3) the opening up of occupational opportunities for women in domains previously reserved for men, so that occupational stereotyping should be undergoing a relaxation in the direction of greater overlap in male and female job selection. Although none of these changes has resulted in the gender-free society prescribed by Bem (1981), they do herald a different world to the coming generation and provide new role models both in parental behavior and in the public media. As role models and messages change, there should be a gradual move toward reduced stereotyping on the part of contemporary youth.

To what extent are these societal changes reflected in adolescent sex-role behaviors? Only a few studies have looked at selected aspects of changing sex-role orientations across sufficient time spans to test the life-span view. These cross-cohort studies are difficult to evaluate because earlier methods of assessing sex-role preferences and behaviors relied on a bipolar theory of sex typing, resulting in two measurement problems: (1) the assumption that masculinity and femininity were negatively correlated, so that a high score on one dimension denoted a low score on the other, and (2) the forced-choice format between masculine or feminine activities and preferences, with no opportunity to select an egalitarian choice of "both males and females." A number of researchers have shown that, in comparison to an egalitarian choice, requiring children to choose between dichotomized male or female preferences results in inflated stereotyping effects (Brush, Gold, & Sprotzer, 1979; Garrett, Ein, & Tremaine, 1977).

In the following list, the major findings are summarized from data across five studies that used large samples, several grade levels, and at least two cohorts, assessing the impact of social–historical changes on sex-role conceptions. Bush, Simmons, Hutchison, and Blyth (1978) compared 6th and 7th graders on data collected in 1968 and 1975. Etaugh *et al.* (1984) looked at sex-role biases on personality traits across grades 2 through 10, comparing children over a time span of 45 years. Lueptow (1984) looked at graduating seniors in 17 high schools in 1964 and 1975 in a survey of achievement, goals, and values. Herzog and Bachman (1982) compared a national survey of high school seniors on career and family plans in 1976 and again in 1980. Helmreich, Spence, and Gibson (1982) compared sex-role attitudes on the Attitudes Toward Women Scale for college samples in 1972, 1976, and 1980. As found in many previous studies, cohort effects depend upon content area of sex-role assessment, gender and age of cohort group, and time periods under consideration. What do these studies tell us about changes in adolescent sex-role attitudes over time?

1. For all cohort measures, differences in attitudes between boys and girls were larger than differences between cohorts.

2. In every study, girls remained less traditional than boys. Girls were more willing to consider cross-gender behavior for self and others and were more open to sex-role change for both personality traits and situational role behaviors.

3. Girls may be becoming more ambivalent toward their own gender role. Although girls currently assign more positive traits to girls than they did in 1939 (Etaugh *et al.*, 1984), they also became more negative about the desirability of being female (Bush *et al.*, 1978) and had a greater discrepancy than did boys between their ideal and expected future occupations (Lueptow, 1984).

4. Both boys and girls showed some attitudinal shifts over cohorts in the direction of less stereotyping on personality traits (Etaugh *et al.*, 1984; Helmreich *et al.*, 1982), less occupational segregation of adult females (but not males), and more preference for role sharing by husbands and wives (Herzog & Bachman, 1982; Lueptow, 1984).

5. Both boys and girls remain steadfastly traditional in many areas, however, and are less committed to an option of egalitarianism than might be suggested by the ethic of the women's movement. In fact, Helmreich *et al.* (1982) reported a tendency in college students toward a leveling or stabilizing of attitudes toward women's and men's roles from 1976–1980 as compared to the decreased stereotyping of roles found in the 1972–1976 comparison. Since the Helmreich *et al.* studies were of college populations with restricted socioeconomic backgrounds, they may reflect recent effects of a business–economic focus in current college students and consequent conservatism in many areas.

In summarizing the findings of these cohort studies for the life-span hypothesis, it seems clear that historical events, such as the women's movement, do indeed play a significant role in the attitudes and aspirations of boys and girls during adolescence. However, the persistence of many traditional attitudes toward interpersonal behavior and occupational and family roles suggests as well that other factors continue to exert an influence. Social learning theorists would point to the persistence of traditional role models at all levels of society, so that children and youth are still presented with greater *frequencies* of males and females in typical home, occupational, and political–public roles (see Bussey & Perry, 1976; and Perry & Bussey, 1979, for a discussion of sex-role modeling effects). Nevertheless, young persons are being exposed, through the culture at large, to new possibilities and reconsideration of what it means to be a woman or man, and these idealized conceptions are having an effect on their values and aspirations for both current and future behavior.

Sex Roles and Psychological Well-being

In view of the current trend toward each gender becoming more open to flexible role adoptions and less stereotyped interpersonal behavior, researchers have questioned the adjustment value of traditional sex typing in contrast to the possible advantages of an androgynous life-style. Previous research on both earlier and later age groups suggests that a mixture of both instrumental and expressive traits may be more advantageous to females than to males, and that masculine instrumental traits contribute more to self-esteem than do feminine expressive traits (see reviews by Feather, 1984; Maffeo, 1982; Schaffer, 1980; Sobol & Russo, 1981; Whitely, 1983; and Worell, 1978, for extended discussions of sex roles and personal well-being). The question remains as to whether an androgynous personality orientation is advantageous to the adolescent, who is still engaged in the quest for a personal life-style and is forming family and occupational plans that may influence important life choices.

Functional answers to questions about psychological well-being in adolescence are limited by at least three factors: (1) the lack of comparison data on baselines for general well-being in this population, (2) the paucity of research on sex roles and well-being in adolescence, and (3) the diversity of approaches to the conceptualization and measurement of well-being. In particular, it should be recalled that Bem's earlier (1976) argument for the advantages of androgyny included two conceptually distinct outcomes: (1) Androgynous individuals should be more flexible across a variety of gender-related situations than sex-typed individuals and, as a consequence, (2) androgynous persons are expected to be more adaptive and to exhibit greater psychological or emotional adjustment. These two outcomes have not been sufficiently developed in the literature on adolescent androgyny to evaluate the separate components of the theory. In this section, comparisons between girls and boys on the broad concept of well-being will be followed by a summary of the relationships reported between gender-typed personality traits and measures of adjustment, self-esteem, and life satisfaction.

Gender and Well-being

Baseline data on adolescent well-being is mixed. Several studies report no gender differences on either a measure of self-esteem (Texas Social Behavior Inventory) or a bipolar rating on personal feelings of adjustment (Spence & Helmreich, 1978; Dusek & Flaherty, 1981, respectively). The Spence and Helmreich data were collected from large samples of high school and college students. The Dusek and Flaherty study used longitudinal cohorts from grades 5 through 12. These data revealed that socioeconomic status played a greater role in self-esteem scores than did gender or age.

In contrast, other studies find differences in self-esteem, self-consciousness, and general life satisfaction associated with race, gender, and age. Early adolescence appears to be a time of particular vulnerability for girls, especially those who are undergoing multiple changes in pubertal status, school placement, and dating behavior (Bush *et al.*, 1978; Hanes, Prawat, & Grissom, 1979; Simmons, Berth, van Cleave, & Bush, 1979; Simmons & Rosenberg, 1975). Simmons and Rosenberg (1975) reported further that the early disadvantage of girls in both self-esteem and self-consciousness increased over time for white girls and decreased for black girls. By late adolescence, white boys and girls continued to differ on these measures, but black boys and girls did not.

At a more general level, a measure of happiness and life satisfaction for a large, stratified sample of black and white 9th–12th graders revealed differences in the perceived quality of life associated with race, gender, and age (Torgoff, Torgoff, & Ponder, 1979). Although mean life satisfaction appeared fairly high (rated 76.6 out of a possible 100), 42% of the respondents saw themselves as worse off than the average adolescent and, as a group, had higher self–other satisfaction discrepancies than did older adult samples. Of particular interest were the gender and race effects. White females reported the lowest overall life satisfaction, which is consistent with young adult data reported by Shichman and Cooper (1984). Black females were second lowest in life satisfaction and most frequently reported being "not too happy," with only 7% seeing themselves as "very happy."

Thus, there is mixed evidence for gender differences in perceived personal well-being in adolescence. Where differences have been found, they favor higher personal adjustment and satisfaction for both black and white males than for females. There were no reported studies in which females' well-being exceeded that of the males. Interestingly enough, these gender differences are reflected in person perception; both boys and girls from grades 7 through 12 agree that boys have higher self-esteem than girls (Hanes *et al.*, 1979).

Sex Typing and Well-being

Of greater relevance to psychological models of well-being in adolescence are the studies relating sex-role orientation to indices of adjustment. In general, the findings on adolescent noncollege populations replicate the adult studies on androgyny and are summarized here:

1. Masculine or instrumental traits comprise the largest contributor to measures of adjustment and self-esteem across gender and index of measurement. Adolescents who describe themselves as assertive, autonomous, and dominant tend to report higher self-esteem, better coping and problem-solving skills, fewer indices of maladjustment, and, for males only, higher peer status (Cate & Sugarawa, 1986; Lamke, 1982a; Massad, 1981; Spence & Helmreich, 1978; Wells, 1980).

2. Androgynous adolescents score equally or almost as high as masculine-typed persons on many of the same adjustment measures, and higher than masculine-typed on other measures. These findings suggest that the combination of instrumental and expressive traits may be advantageous to both boys and girls (Lamke, 1982b; Hurtig & Peterson, 1982; Paul & Fischer, 1980; Small, Teagno, & Selz, 1980). Androgynous girls, interestingly enough, show higher peer acceptance and social relationships than sex-typed girls, which certainly runs counter to some stereotypic conceptions of female adolescent friendships (Massad, 1981; Wells, 1980).

3. Traditional sex typing is advantageous to males in certain situations (peer acceptance, feelings of mastery) and bears a negligible or negative relationship for adolescent girls to most measures of personal well-being. Although femininity alone in girls predicts both self-esteem and good social relationships, androgynous girls score higher on both indices than do sex-typed girls (Massad, 1981; Small *et al.*, 1980; Wells, 1980).

4. The findings on cross-gender behavior and traits are mixed and contradictory. High femininity or nurturance in boys has been found to be associated with low peer acceptance and high anxiety (Massad, 1981; Richmond, 1984) but also with self-reports of good social relationships and high self-esteem (Lamke, 1982a; Richmond, 1984; Wells, 1980). Only one study reported negative effects for masculine-typed girls, with

self-reported dominance being associated with higher anxiety for both 12-
and 16-year-old girls (Richmond, 1984).

5. The measurement category of "undifferentiated" has been applied
to those individuals who score below the median on measures of both
instrumental and expressive traits. Although the relationship of this
category to sex-role orientation is currently unclear, these individuals
tend to score the lowest on all measures of peer acceptance, self-esteem,
coping skills, and personal well-being. These low-scoring adolescents
may be the ones who are having the most difficulty in establishing a sense
of self in the areas of both social relationships and personal autonomy,
suggesting that their concepts and feelings of male and female self are
similarly disturbed or underdeveloped. The undifferentiated group may
indeed be the "identity-diffused" adolescents described by Erikson
(1966).

In summarizing the literature on sex typing and well-being, it is
important to consider that relevant research is sparse and not well
replicated. Nevertheless, the balance of findings weighs heavily on the
side of androgyny in self-reported characteristics as a psychological
advantage in personal well-being and adjustment over traditional sex-
typed orientations for both boys and girls. That is, adolescents who view
themselves as independent and capable of making decisions, as well as
sociable, warm, and sensitive with others, stand to gain the most rewards
in terms of overall psychological well-being and peer acceptance.

There is some evidence that traditional sex typing is more advantageous to boys than it is to girls, a finding that makes sense in the light of
current attitudes and values associated with male-typed behaviors. More
importantly, cross-gender-typed boys, who use very few of these mastery
and competency behaviors, may suffer more in the realm of social
acceptance than boys who demonstrate traditional male dominance and
assertiveness. However, adolescents who are competent in both instrumental and expressive spheres appear to be more effective across a
variety of domains than boys and girls who are sex-typed. These
conclusions run counter to some current literature (e.g., Massad, 1981)
suggesting that boys will experience more negative feedback for violations of traditional sex typing than will girls. Only in the area of
cross-gender adjustments, in which boys showed more feminine than
masculine-typed characteristics, did some negative effects appear. The
importance for both boys and girls of appropriate displays of both
assertiveness and nurturance also contradicts traditional developmental
theory regarding healthy sex typing. More importantly, these conclusions, if supported in further research, contrast strongly with current

socialization practices of parents (Block, 1983; Emihovitch, Gaier, & Cronin, 1984; Hill & Lynch, 1983; Lueptow, 1984; Peterson, Rollins, Thomas, & Heaps, 1982) and school environments (Guttentag & Bray, 1976), both of which remain staunchly traditional.

Sex Roles and Life–Career Planning

The consideration of gender and sex-role orientations in the lives of today's adolescents extends beyond questions of developmental theory. The period between 10th and 12th grades is a critical one for important choices relating to career and family planning. Both gender and sex-role conceptions have been shown to be important moderators of adolescent life plans related to educational and occupational aspirations, marital and family plans, and preferences for division of labor within family structures (Aneshensel & Rosen, 1980; Eccles & Hoffman, 1984; Herzog & Bachman, 1982; Marini, 1978; Tittle, 1981). Although a review of adolescent life-career development is beyond the scope of this chapter, several aspects of current social organization mentioned earlier are relevant to adolescent sex-role development. These social variables include increased entry of women into the work force, the prevalence of working mothers in the salaried occupational arena, and expanded opportunities for women in traditionally male-stereotyped occupations and professional training programs. Each of these variables is salient for young men and women who are formulating their life goals and may in turn influence their expectations, educational and occupational aspirations, and family–life planning. How do high school girls and boys view their future roles?

In contrast to earlier studies on educational aspirations, recent research suggests that high school girls and boys are quite similar in their plans to attend a 4-year college (50–55% across various samples). Somewhat more boys than girls plan to attend vocational and/or professional schools, and slightly more girls anticipate only a 2-year college degree. Interestingly, both boys and girls report a similarly high commitment to career and work as a central focus of their future lives, but girls give higher priority to family and home and are more likely to say that they expect to modify their work for their family roles. Sex-role attitudes mediate these plans, however. Girls (but not boys) who hold traditional sex-role attitudes are more likely to value the parenting role, to choose homemaking over careers, to prefer doing the largest share of household tasks, and to have lower educational aspirations (Aneshensel & Rosen, 1980; Archer, 1985; Herzog & Bachman, 1980; Tittle, 1981).

Occupational plans reveal a restricted number of preferred choices for either girls or boys (about three choices each) but considerable segregation in job selection. Girls are still selecting, at a higher rate than boys, occupations in homemaking, service, clerical (secretarial or sales), and teaching. Boys select a wider range of jobs and are more likely to choose skilled or semiskilled occupations, technology, professional, and business–management. Girls tend to attribute more importance and value than boys to the altruistic and people-oriented aspects of the job and place more value on intrinsic interest and stimulation than on money and prestige. It is clear that sex-role socialization (mediated by parents, peers, teachers, and the broader culture) is still exerting a powerful effect on the vocational and career plans of contemporary high school girls and boys. Although trend analyses show an increase in female interest in professional and business careers, 70% of high school girls remain committed to traditionally female-stereotyped jobs, while 97% of males are interested in traditional male-dominated occupations (Block, Denker, & Tittle, 1981; Eccles & Hoffman, 1984; Herzog & Bachman, 1982).

Finally, we take a look at how today's adolescents view their future roles in relation to the division of marital child-care and household responsibilities. Studies reporting student attitudes between 1960 and 1975 tended to describe the high school senior as considerably conservative about marital and parental roles (see, for example, Angrist *et al.,* 1977; Christensen, 1961; Nelson & Goldman, 1969). More recently, there appear to be patterns of both conservative and liberalized attitudes about some sharing of both wage-earner and marital roles. On the traditional side, the vast majority of both boys and girls agree (about 85%) that sex-role reversal in employment patterns is undesirable, that is, husband working only part-time or remaining home and wife working full-time. In a similar vein, these students are in agreement that there will be marital and personal conflict if the wife should earn more than the husband, although, predictably, females were more open to this idea than were males. Typical responses to how a husband might feel if his wife were to earn more money than he did reflected traditional sex-role stereotypes: "He doesn't like it. He feels cheap. It doesn't make him feel like a man" (female view), and "Not good because he'd feel he's not succeeding. Feels like a dummy, because she supports him and that's not right" (male view) (Tittle, 1981, p. 199). In contrast, women were expected to accept the traditional wage-earner differences, with rationales that were consistent with some external reality: "He's earning more money, he has the better job," and "OK because the wife takes care of the kids more" (Tittle, 1981, pp. 199–201).

How do high school seniors anticipate juggling the dual roles of parent and wage earner? As indicated above, the position of the male is clearly to remain the major wage earner. Attitudes toward the working wife are relaxing, however. Only 13% of males and 4% of females consider it acceptable for a wife in a childless family to remain at home while the husband works. When young children are present, however, traditionalism prevails, and most agree that a mother should stay home full-time with the children. Only 14% feel it is desirable for the mother of young children to take on even half-time work (Herzog & Bachman, 1982; Herzog, Bachman, & Johnston, 1983). In each instance, again, women are more open to nontraditional alternatives than are men.

Finally, in the areas of childcare and household duties, we see a gradual shift in the direction of intended shared responsibilities. High school seniors believe that fathers, regardless of their wage-earner role, should not be relieved of child-care involvement and generally rank this task to be shared equally between spouses. In the area of household tasks, there is a large overlap in expectations for egalitarian role assumption, with 67% of males and 86% of females rating an egalitarian arrangement as either desirable or acceptable (Herzog & Bachman, 1982; Herzog *et al.*, 1983). These data stand in sharp contrast to current patterns of the division of household labor in dual wage-earner families, in which working women are still found to assume about 70–80% of both child-care and home management (Robinson, 1977). It may be that, as in other areas of our lives, behavioral changes lag behind attitudinal changes in sex-typed activities, or these findings may reflect a valid determination on the part of younger generations to do it differently than their parents. It will remain for future research to evaluate the congruence between words and deeds in the generation of parents ahead.

In summarizing these findings on life–career planning, four major conclusions are salient:

1. High school boys and girls are, on the whole, moving in the direction of increased equity in the life tasks ahead of them and view educational attainment, career development, and family responsibilities as equally important for adult women and men.

2. Both gender and sex-role attitudes influence these life–career decisions. Girls, more than boys, hold egalitarian views about their prospective life roles. Similarly, liberalized sex-role attitudes predict increased acceptance of equity between women and men in education, career, and family activities.

3. Stereotyped expectations have not entirely disappeared, however, and high school youth remain steadfastly traditional in many areas related to division of labor and success attainment by men and women. These traditional attitudes may be expected to influence the decisions that girls

and boys make about their high school curriculum and college plans, as well as their anticipations about the careers in which they believe they can be successful and their anticipations of the good life.

4. Finally, all these conclusions are moderated by variations in race, ethnic background, and socioeconomic status. Although a few of the studies reviewed above included minority samples for comparison, most did not. It would be a mistake to generalize from one cultural group to another. Professionals working with other than white, relatively middle-class samples need to take these possible differences into consideration.

Educational Implications

The literature on adolescent sex-typing contains mixed messages for professionals who deal with the adolescent on a daily basis. On one hand, we find considerable traditionalism in adolescent sex-typed personality traits, career aspirations, and beliefs about the other gender. High school seniors are still accepting a gender differential in their ideals of assertiveness and tenderness, in career choices that promise financial and advancement opportunities, and in the daily activities that they judge appropriate for females and males. In contrast, the recent literature also suggests that career and family plan are moving toward less traditional options. Most adolescents view career development, although a limited one, as normative for women and are accepting of increased participation of men in child-rearing and home maintenance tasks. Both traditional and alternative option trends appear to mirror the broad contemporary culture, and there is certainly evidence that revised social models are having an impact on adolescent aspirations and life–career planning.

Can schools therefore relax and let "natural" social consequences redirect the personal and career paths of the younger generation? Or should schools view with alarm both the continued tracking of females into low-paying career paths and the adolescent myth that males will somehow be psychologically harmed if their wives earn salaries as adequate as theirs? Do schools have any responsibility in fostering personal androgyny in view of the evidence concerning its association with psychological well-being in adolescence?

The extent to which schools should assume responsibility for encouraging high school youth toward new options in sex-role functioning is indeed a matter of values and policy development. If these values include issues of equity and excellence for all students, then interventions that target sex-typed behavioral attributes, attitudes toward future family roles, and vocational aspirations appear very appropriate to educational settings. Certainly, the responsibility lies not only in the educational system but with family, peers, and communities as well. We know that vocational aspirations and attitudes are more strongly influenced by family and friends than by schools (Eccles & Hoffman, 1984). However, families are generally less encouraging of achievement and career patterns for their adolescent girls than for their boys (Ihinger-Tallman, 1982; Peterson *et al.*, 1982), and thus they join with schools to maintain gender-segregated patterns of family and career expectations. Although schools should not be held accountable for producing these gender differences, they may be in a better position than families to initiate and implement effective programs for change.

Educational systems have responded to national legislation aimed at achieving equity in educational settings, through attempts to implement the requirements of Title IX of the Educational Equity Act and the Women's Equity Act of 1974, as well as by some attention to affirmative action programs. Recent evaluations of these efforts suggest, however, that school policies remain largely unresponsive to the imperative to encourage all students, regardless of gender, to develop themselves to their fullest vocational and personal potential. These policies are particularly evident in areas related to traditionalism in teacher and counselor behaviors and continued sex typing in curriculum, textbooks, and administrative arrangements (Brophy, 1985; Eccles & Hoffman, 1984; Morse & Handley, 1985; Tetreault & Schmuck, 1985). The foregoing review of the literature on adolescent sex-role development lends support to the need for more active policies within educational systems that address the needs of both women and men in a changing society. The targets that are minimally appropriate for intervention include teachers, counselors, and administrators.

Teachers and Counselors

Teachers and counselors are faced with two major tasks: Exploration and awareness of their own sex-role attitudes and behaviors, and active modeling and reinforcement of flexible behaviors for both their male and female students. In particular, teachers and counselors can give direct encouragement to girls, as well as to boys, to consider early career exploration, nontraditional career alternatives, and curriculum choices that match effective vocational goals (Fitzgerald & Crites, 1980). The highest priority is for all school personnel to deal honestly with their personal values and attitudes related to traditional sex-role behaviors. Unless teachers and counselors become sensitive to their own gender-related stereotypes, they are likely to continue to impose their views on students and will be less facilitative in helping students to explore new options and alternatives. Teacher–counselor awareness can be facilitated through teacher-training curricula (Worell & Stilwell, 1981), by means of planned in-service workshops (Remer & Ross, 1982) or by concentrated reading and self-study. Teachers and counselors can influence, in turn, the behaviors and attitudes of their students' parents by means of similar exposure to ideas that question and challenge traditional sex-role pre-scriptions.

Secondly, teachers and counselors can be influential in dealing directly with students to encourage excellence in both boys and girls and to explore attitudes toward equity between men and women. Of particular concern to the equitable career development of women has been the neglect of encouragement and participation of girls in advanced mathematics and the sciences. Both male and female teachers regard these disciplines as more important for boys, recommend boys more frequently for advanced math classes, and give boys more differential attention and reinforcement in these classes than they do for girls (Becker, 1981; Brophy, 1985; Eccles & Hoffman, 1984; Morse & Handley, 1985; Parsons, Kaczala, & Meece, 1982). In order to change traditional patterns of career expectation and choice, both teachers and counselors need to become more proactive in pointing out alternative career opportunities, selecting talented students of both genders for advanced scientific studies, and nurturing the creative efforts of girls in math and sciences especially. Some research suggests that such ambitious efforts pay off in increased participation of girls in nontraditional curricula (Casserly, 1979). An overriding concern in curriculum and career choice is the social fact that women, as well as men, will become major family providers of the future and need to prepare themselves with these realities in the forefront.

Administrative Policies

The efforts of individual school personnel to effect important changes in student attitudes and behaviors are influenced by the social organization of the school and its relationship to the surrounding community. As a complex social unit, the school itself is resistant to change. Major educational upheavals in recent years have come about mainly through external mandate (such as for PL94–142) or through internal collective effort (as in teacher unionization). Planned, orderly change, however, occurs in schools that are described as "the renewing schools," which contain the organizational vehicles for sensitive response to developing issues (Sarason & Klaber, 1985).

In view of the conflicting constituencies within any school system, changes in curriculum, textbook policies, and vocational and athletic programs that are incompatible with current community value systems are likely to flounder. Administrations within school and district units are in a sensitive position both to influence policies in these areas as well as to mediate between school personnel and the wider community. School administrations can support educational programs within their communities that emphasize the fullest utilization of student potential regardless of student gender. School districts can implement an affirmative action mandate that places more women in top administrative positions, such as high school principalships, as appropriate role models for both women and men. School administrations can also encourage continuing education programs that target dropout boys and girls (such as teenage parents) to remain in school. Administrative policy extends to vocational and athletic programs that ensure equity in opportunity to develop marketable skills and access to advanced educational training programs. The list of possibilities for effective improvement in gender-related education is extensive and well referenced (see, for example Hansen, 1978; Klein, 1985; *Resources for Educational Equity,* 1982; Stockard, Schmuck, Kempner, Williams, Edson, & Smith, 1980).

Conclusions

It has been the purpose of this chapter to examine the development of sex-role concepts and choice in adolescence, and to relate these developmental changes to educational intervention. Although developmental theory proposes a reciprocal model of personal–environmental progression over time, research evidence on modifications in sex-role ideation and behaviors supports the powerful influence of the social–historical context and changing social role expectations. The implications for educational institutions and personnel are conflicting. Schools can continue to educate for divergent work and family roles in society, and men and women will gradually adapt themselves to external demands in spite of their educational limitations. A preferred alternative, from the viewpoint of this author, is for schools to organize for equity and excellence in educational opportunity and experience for all students in preparation for new life–career roles in the future.

References

Ahammer, I. M. (1973). Social learning theory as a framework for the study of adults personality development. In P. B. Baltes & K. W. Schaie (Eds.), *Life-span developmental psychology: Personality and socialization* (pp. 253–284). New York: Academic Press.

Aneshensel, C. S., & Rosen, B. C. (1980). Domestic roles and sex differences in occupational expectations. *Journal of Marriage and the Family, 42,* 121–131.

Angrist, S. S., Mickelson, R., & Penna, A. N. (1976). Variations in adolescents' knowledge and attitudes about family life: Implications for curriculum design. *Adolescence,* **11,** 107–126.

Angrist, S. S., Mickelson, R., & Penna, A. N. (1977). Sex differences in sex-role conceptions and family orientation of high school students. *Journal of Youth and Adolescence,* **6,** 179–186.

Archer, S. L. (1985). Identity and the choice of social roles. In A. S. Waterman (Ed.), *Identity in adolescence: Processes and contents* (pp. 79–99). San Francisco: Jossey-Bass.

Ashmore, R. D., & Del Boca, F. K. (1984). *Toward a social psychology of male-female relations.* Paper presented at the first Nag's Head Invitational Conference on Sex and Gender, Nag's Head, NC.

Bandura, A. (1977). *Social learning theory.* Englewood Cliffs, NJ: Prentice Hall.

Bardwick, J. M. (1971). *Psychology of women.* New York: Harper.

Becker, J. (1981). Differential teacher treatment of males and females in mathematics classes. *Journal of Educational Psychology,* **72,** 119–132.

Bem, S. L. (1974). The measurement of psychological androgyny. *Journal of Consulting and Clinical Psychology,* **47,** 155–162.

Bem, S. L. (1976). Probing the promise of androgyny. In A. G. Kaplan & J. P. Bean (Eds.), *Beyond sex-role stereotypes: Readings toward a psychology of androgyny* (pp. 48–61). Boston: Little, Brown.

Bem, S. L. (1977). On the utility of alternative procedures for assessing psychological androgyny. *Journal of Consulting and Clinical Psychology,* **45,** 196–205.

Bem, S. L. (1979). Theory and measurement of androgyny: A reply to the Pedhauzer-Tetenbaum and Locksley-Colten critiques. *Journal of Personality and Social Psychology,* **37,** 1047–1054.

Bem, S. L. (1981). Gender schema theory: A cognitive account of sex typing. *Psychological Review,* **88,** 354–364.

Bem, S. L. (1984). Androgyny and gender schema theory: A conceptual and empirical investigation. In T. B. Sonderegger (Ed.), *Nebraska symposium on motivation: Psychology and gender* (Vol. 32, pp. 179–226). Lincoln, NE: University of Nebraska Press.

Block, J. H. (1973). Conceptions of sex roles: Some cross-cultural and longitudinal perspectives. *American Psychologist,* **28,** 512–525.

Block, J. H. (1976). Issues, problems, and pitfalls in assessing sex differences: A critical review of "The psychology of sex differences." *Merrill-Palmer Quarterly,* **22,** 284–308.

Block, J. H. (1978). Another look at sex differention in the socialization behaviors of mothers and fathers. In J. H. Sherman & F. L. Denmark (Eds.), *The Psychology of women: Future directions in research* (pp. 30–87). New York: Psychological Dimension.

Block, J. H. (1983). Differential premises arising from differential socialization of the sexes: Some conjectures. *Child Development,* **54,** 1135–1354.

Block, J., Denker, E. R., & Tittle, C. K. (1981). Perceived influences on career choices of eleventh graders: Sex, SES, and ethnic group comparisons. *Sex Roles,* **7,** 895–904.

Brophy, J. (1985). Interactions of male and female students with male and female teachers. In L. C. Wilkinson & C. B. Marrett (Eds.), *Gender influences in classroom interaction* (pp. 115–142). New York: Academic Press.

Brush, L. R., Gold, A. R., & Sprotzer, E. R. (1979). *The importance of a "same" category in research on sex-role stereotypes.* Paper presented at the bienniel meeting of the Society for Research in Child Development, San Francisco.

Bush, D. E., Simmons, R.G., Hutchinson, B., & Blyth, D. A. (1978). Adolescent perceptions of sec roles in 1968 and 1975. *Public Opinion Quarterly,* **41,** 459–474.

Bussey, K., & Perry, D. G. (1976). Shared reinforcement contingencies with a model: A social learning analysis of similarity effects in imitation research. *Journal of Personality and Social Psychology,* **34,** 1168–1176.

Casserly, P. L. (1979). Helping able young women take math and science seriously in school. In N. Colangelo & R. T. Zaffran (Eds.), *New voices in counseling the gifted* (pp. 346–369). Dubuque, IA: Kendall-Hunt.

Cate, R., & Sugarawa, A. I. (1986). Sex-role orientation and dimensions of self-esteem among middle adolescents. *Sex Roles,* **15,** 145–158.

Christensen, H. T. (1961). Lifetime family and occupational role projections of high school students. *Marriage and Family Living,* **23,** 181–183.

Deaux, K. (1984). From individual differences to social categories. *American Psychologist,* **39,** 105–116.

Deaux, K., & Major, B. (1987). Putting gender into context: An interactive model of gender-related behavior. *Psychological Review,* **44,** 369–389.

Della Selva, P. C., & Dusek, J. B. (1984). Sex role orientation and resolution of Eriksonian crises during late adolescent years. *Journal of Personality and Social Psychology,* **47,** 204–212.

Douvan, E., & Adelson, J. (1966). *The adolescent experience.* New York: Wiley.

Dusek, J. B., & Flaherty, J. F. (1981). The development of the self-concept during the adolescent years. *Monographs of the Society for Research in Child Development,* **46** (4, Serial No. 191). Chicago: University of Chicago Press.

Eagley, A. H. (1978). Sex differences in influenceability. *Psychological Bulletin,* **85,** 86–116.

Eagley, A., & Carli, L. L. (1981). Sex of researchers and sex-typed communications as determinants of sex differences in influenceability. A meta-analysis of social influence studies. *Psychological Bulletin,* **90,** 1–20.

Eccles, J. S., & Hoffman, L. W. (1984). Sex roles, socialization, and occupational behavior. In H. W. Stevenson & A. E. Siegel (Eds.), *Child development research and social policy* (Vol. I, pp. 307–420). Chicago: University of Chicago Press.

Eisenberg, N., & Lennon, R. (1983). Sex differences in empathy and related capacities. *Psychological Bulletin,* **94,** 100–131.

Elkind, D. (1967). Egocentrism in adolescence. *Child Development,* **38,** 1025–1034.

Emihovitch, C. A., Gaier, E. L., & Cronin, N. C. (1984). Sex-role expectations by fathers for their sons. *Sex Roles,* **11,** 861–868.

Emmerich, W. (1973). Socialization and sex-role development. In P. B. Baltes & K. W. Schaie (Eds.), *Life-span developmental psychology: Personality and socialization* (pp. 123–144). New York: Academic Press.

Emmerich, W. (1979). *Developmental trends in sex-stereotyped values.* Paper presented at the bienniel meeting of the Society for Research in Child Development, San Francisco.

Enright, R. D., Lapsley, D. K., & Shukla, D. A. (1979). Adolescent egocentrism in early and late adolescence. *Adolescence, 14,* 687–695.

Enright, R. D., Shukla, D. G., & Lapsley, D. K. (1980). Adolescent egocentrism-sociocentrism and self-consciousness. *Journal of Youth and Adolescence, 9,* 101–116.

Erickson, E. H. (1963). *Childhood and society.* New York: Norton.

Erickson, E. H. (1966). *Identity: Youth and crisis.* New York: Norton.

Etaugh, C., Levine, D., & Manella, A. (1984). Development of sex biases in children: 40 years later. *Sex Roles, 10,* 913–924.

Feather, N. T. (1984). Masculinity, femininity, psychological androgyny, and the structure of values. *Journal of Personality and Social Psychology, 47,* 604–620.

Feldman, S. S., & Nash, S. C. (1979). Changes in responsiveness to babies during adolescence. *Child Development, 50,* 942–949.

Feldman, S. S., Nash, S. C., & Cutrona, A. (1977). The influence of age and sex on responsiveness to babies. *Developmental Psychology, 13,* 675–676.

Fitzgerald, L. F., & Crites, J. O. (1980). Toward a career psychology of women: What do we know? What do we need to know? *Journal of Counseling Psychology, 27,* 44–62.

Garrett, C. S., Ein, P. L., & Tremaine, L. (1977). The development of gender stereotyping of adult occupation in elementary school children. *Child Development, 48,* 507–512.

Gilbert, L. A. (1981). Toward mental health: The benefits of psychological androgyny. *Professional Psychology, 12,* 21–38.

Guttentag, M., & Bray, M. (1976). *Undoing sex-role stereotypes.* New York: McGraw-Hill.

Guttentag, M., & Longfellow, C. (1977). Children's social attributions: Development and change. *Nebraska Symposium on Motivation.* Lincoln, NE: University of Nebraska Press.

Hanes, B., Prawat, R. S., & Grissom, S. (1979). Sexrole perceptions during adolescence. *Journal of Educational Psychology, 71,* 850–856.

Hansen, L. S. (1978). Promoting female growth through a career development curriculum. In S. L. Hansen & R. S. Rapoza (Eds.), *Career development and counseling of women* (pp. 425–442). Springfield, IL: Thomas.

Helmreich, R. L., Spence, J. T., & Gibson, R. H. (1982). Sex-role attitudes: 1972–1980. *Personality and Social Psychology Bulletin, 8,* 656–663.

Hemmer, J. D., & Kleiber, D. (1981). Tomboys and sissies: Androgynous children? *Sex Roles, 7,* 1205–1212.

Herzog, A. R., & Bachman, J. G. (1982). *Sexrole attitudes among high school seniors: Views about work and family roles.* Ann Arbor, MI: Institute for Social Research, University of Michigan.

Herzog, A. R., Bachman, J. G., & Johnson, L. D. (1983). Paid work, childcare, and housework: A national survey of high school seniors preferences for sharing responsibilities between husbands and wife. *Sex Roles, 9,* 109–135.

Hill, J. P., & Lynch, M. E. (1983). The intensification of gender-related role expectations during early adolescence. In J. Brooks-Gunn & A. C. Peterson (Eds.), *Girls at puberty: Biological and psychological perspectives* (pp. 201–230). New York: Plenum.

Hoffman, L. W. (1977). Changes in family roles, socialization, and sex differences. *American Psychologist, 32,* 644–657.

Hurtig, A. L., & Peterson, A. C. (1982). *The relationship of sex-role identity to ego development and self-esteem in adolescence.* Paper presented at the annual meeting of the American Psychological Association, Washington, DC.

Huston, A. C. (1983). Sex-typing. In P. H. Mussen (Ed.), *Carmichael's handbook of child psychology* (2nd ed.) (pp. 387–467). New York: Wiley.

Huston-Stein, A., & Higgens-Trent, A. (1978). Development of female role orientations. In B. P. Baltes (Ed.), *Life-span development and behavior* (Vol. 1, pp. 258–296). New York: Academic Press.

Hyde, J. S., & Phillis, D. E. (1979). Androgyny across the life span. *Developmental Psychology*, **15**, 334–336.

Ihinger-Tallman, M. (1982). Family interaction, gender, and status attainment value. *Sex Roles*, **8**, 543–557.

Kagan, J. (1964). Acquisition and significance of sex-typing and sex-role identity. In M. L. Hoffman & L. W. Hoffman (Eds.), *Review of child development research* (pp. 137–168). New York: Russell Sage Foundation.

Kaplan, A. G. (1976). Androgyny as a model of mental health for women: From theory to therapy. In A. G. Kaplan & J. B. Bean (Eds.), *Beyond sex-role stereotypes: Readings toward a psychology of androgyny* (pp. 352–362). Boston: Little, Brown.

Katz, P. (1979). The development of female identity. *Sex Roles*, **5**, 155–178.

Kelly, J. A., & Worell, J. (1977). New formulations of sex roles and androgyny: A critical review. *Journal of Consulting and Clinical Psychology*, **45**, 1101–1115.

Klein, S. (1985). *Handbook for achieving sex equity through education*. Baltimore: Johns Hopkins Press.

Kohlberg, L. (1966). A cognitive-developmental analysis of children's sex-role concepts and attitudes. In E. E. Maccoby (Ed.), *The development of sex differences* (pp. 82–173). Palo Alto, CA: Stanford University Press.

Kohlberg, L. (1969). Stages and sequences: The cognitive-developmental approach to socialization. In D. A. Goslin (Ed.), *Handbook of socialization theory and research* (pp. 347–480). Chicago: Rand McNally.

Konapka, G. (1976). *Young girls: A portrait of adolescence*. Englewood Cliffs, NJ: Prentice-Hall.

Lamke, K. (1982a). The impact of sex-role orientation on self-esteem in early adolescence. *Child Development*, **33**, 1530–1535.

Lamke, L. K. (1982b). Adjustment and sex-role orientation in early adolescence. *Journal of Youth and Adolescents*, **11**, 247–259.

Leahy, R. L., & Eiter, M. (1980). Moral judgment and the development of real and ideal androgynous self-image during adolescence and young adulthood. *Developmental Psychology*, **16**, 362–370.

Lerner, R. M., Sorell, G. T., & Brackney, B. E. (1981). Sex differences in self-concept and self-esteem of late adolescents: A time-lag analysis. *Sex Roles*, **7**, 709–722.

Livson, N., & Peskin, H. (1980). Perspectives on adolescence from longitudinal research. In J. Adelson (Ed.), *Handbook of adolescent psychology* (pp. 47–98). New York: Wiley.

Lueptow, L. B. (1984). *Adolescent sex roles and social change*. New York: Columbia University Press.

Maffeo, P. A. (1982). Gender as a model for mental health. In I. Alissa (Ed.), *Gender and psychopathology* (pp. 31–50). New York: Academic Press.

Marcia, J. E. (1966). Development and validation of ego identity status. *Journal of Personality and Social Psychology*, **3**, 551–558.

Marcia, J. E., & Friedman, M. L. (1970). Ego identity status in college women. *Journal of Personality*, **38**, 249–263.

Marini, M. M. (1978). Sex differences in adolescent aspirations: A review of research. *Sex Roles*, **4**, 723–753.

Martin, C. L., & Halverson, C. F. (1981). A schematic processing model of sex typing and stereotyping in children. *Child Development*, **52**, 1119–1134.

Mason, K. O., Czjaka, J. L., & Arber, S. (1976). Change in U.S. Women's sex-role attitudes, 1964–74. *American Sociological Review, 41,* 573–595.

Massad, C. M. (1981). Sex role, identity, and adjustment during adolescence. *Child Development, 52,* 1290–1298.

Morse, L. W., & Handley, H. M. (1985). Listening to adolescents: Gender differences in classroom interaction. In L. C. Wilkinson & C. B. Marrett (Eds.), *Gender influences in classroom interaction* (pp. 37–56). New York: Academic Press.

Mussen, P. H. (1969). Early sex-role development. In D. A. Goslin (Ed.), *Handbook of socialization theory and research* (pp. 707–732). Chicago: Rand-McNally.

Nash, S. C., & Feldman, S. S. (1981). Sex role and sex-related attributions: Constancy and change across the family life cycle. In M. Lamb & A. Brown (Eds.), *Advances in developmental psychology* (Vol. I, pp. 1–35). Hillsdale, NJ: Erlbaum.

Nelson, H. Y., & Goldman, P. R. (1969). Attitudes of high school students and young adults toward the gainful employment of married women. *Family Coordinator, 18,* 251–255.

Parsons, J. E., Kaczala, C., & Meece, J. (1982). Socialization of achievement attitudes and beliefs: Classroom influences. *Child Development, 54,* 322–339.

Paul, M. J., & Fischer, J. L. (1980). Correlates of self-concept among black early adolescents. *Journal of Youth and Adolescence, 9,* 163–173.

Perry, D. G., & Bussey, K. (1979). The social learning theory of sex differences: Imitation is alive and well. *Journal of Personality and Social Psychology, 37,* 1699–1712.

Peterson, A. C. (1980). Biopsychosocial processes in the development of sex-related differences. In J. C. Parsons (Ed.), *The psychobiology of sex differences and sex roles* (pp. 31–55). New York: McGraw-Hill.

Peterson, A. C., & Taylor, B. (1980). Biological change and psychological adaptation. In J. Adelson (Ed.), *Handbook of adolescent psychology* (pp. 117–155). New York: Wiley.

Peterson, G. W., Rollins, B. C., Thomas, L. K., & Heaps, L. K. (1982). Social placement of adolescents: Sex-role influences on family decisions regarding the careers of youth. *Journal of Marriage and the Family, 44,* 647–658.

Plumb, P., & Cowan, G. (1984). A developmental study of destereotyping and androgynous activity preferences of tomboys, nontomboys, and males. *Sex Roles, 10,* 703–712.

Remer, P., & Ross, E. (1982). The counselor's role in creating a school environment that fosters androgyny. *The School Counselor, 30,* 4–14.

Resources for Educational Equity (1982). Newton, MA: Educational Development Center.

Richmond, P. G. (1984). An aspect of sex-role identification with a sample of twelve-year olds and sixteen-year olds. *Sex Roles, 11,* 1021–1043.

Robinson, J. P. (1977). *How Americans use their time.* New York: Praeger.

Sarason, B. B., & Klaber, M. (1985). The school as a social situation. *Annual Review of Psychology, 36,* 115–140.

Scanzoni, J. H. (1975). *Sex role, life style, and child-bearing.* New York: Free Press.

Schaffer, K. F. (1980). *Sex-role issues in mental health.* Reading, MA: Addison-Wesley.

Schaie, K. W. (1965). A general model for the study of developmental problems. *Psychological Bulletin, 61,* 92–107.

Schlenker, B. R. (1980). *Impression management: The self-concept, social identity, and interpersonal relations.* Belmont, CA: Brooks/Cole.

Sherif, C. W. (1982). Needed concepts in the study of gender identity. *Psychology of Women Quarterly, 6,* 375–398.

Shichman, S., & Cooper, E. (1984). Life satisfaction and sex-role concept. *Sex Roles, 11,* 272–240.

Simmons, R. G., Blyth, D. A., & McKinney, K. L. (1983). The social and psychological effects of puberty on white females. In J. Brooks-Gunn & A. C. Peterson (Eds.), *Girls at puberty: Biological and psychosocial perspectives* (pp. 229–272). New York: Plenum.

Simmons, R. G., Blyth, D. A., Van Cleave, E. F., & Bush, D. M. (1979). Entry into early adolescence: The impact of school structure and early dating on self-esteem. *American Sociological Review*, **44**, 948–967.

Simmons, R. G., & Rosenberg, F. (1975). Sex, sex roles, and self-image. *Journal of Youth and Adolescence*, **4**, 229–258.

Small, A., Teagno, L., & Selz, K. (1980). The relationship of sex role to physical and psychological health. *Journal of Youth and Adolescence*, **9**, 305–314.

Sobol, S. B., & Russo, N. F. (Eds.) (1981). Sex roles, equality, and mental health. *Professional Psychology*, **12**, 1–189 (special issue).

Spence, J. T., & Helmreich, R. L. (19778). *Masculinity and femininity: Their psychological dimensions, correlates, and antecedents*. Austin: University of Texas Press.

Spence, J. T., Helmreich, R., & Stapp, J. (1975). Ratings of self and peers on sex-role attributes and their relation to self-esteem and conceptions of masculinity and femininity. *Journal of Personality and Social Psychology*, **32**, 29–39.

Spence, J., & Sawin, L. (1985). Images of masculinity and femininity: A reconceptualization. In V. E. O'Leary, R. K. Unger, & B. S. Wallston (Eds.), *Women, gender, and social psychology* (pp. 35–66). Hillsdale, NJ: Erlbaum.

Stericker, A. B., & Kurdick, L. A. (1982). Dimensions and correlates of third through eighth graders' sex-role self concepts. *Sex Roles*, **8**, 915–930.

Stockard, J., Schmuck, P. A., Kemper, K., Williams, P., Edson, S. K., & Smith, M. A. (1980). *Sex equity in education*. New York: Academic Press.

Tedeschi, J. T. (1981). *Impression management theory and social psychological research*. New York: Academic Press.

Tetlock, P. E., & Manstead, A. S. R. (1985). Impression management versus intrapsychic explanations in social psychology: A useful dichotomy? *Psychological Review*, **92**, 59–77.

Tetreault, M. K., & Schmuck, P. (1985). Equity, educational reform, and gender. *Issues in Education*, **3**, 45–65.

Tittle, C. K. (1981). *Careers and family: Sex roles and adolescent life plans*. Beverly Hills, CA: Sage.

Tobin-Richards, M., Boxer, A. M., & Peterson, A. C. (1983). The psychological significance of pubertal change: Sex differences in perceptions of self during early adolescence. In J. Brooks-Gunn & A. C. Peterson (Eds.), *Girls at puberty: Biological and psychosocial perspectives* (pp. 127–154). New York: Plenum.

Torgoff, I., Torgoff, L., & Ponder, M. (1979). *Life satisfaction of adolescents*. Paper presented at the bienniel meeting of The Society for Research in Child Development, San Francisco.

Unger, R. K. (1979). *Female and male: Psychological perspectives*. New York: Harper.

Urberg, K. A. (1979). Sex role conceptualizations in adolescents and adults. *Developmental Psychology*, **15**, 90–92.

Urberg, K. A., & Labouvie-Vief, G. (1976). Conceptualizations of sex roles: A life span developmental study. *Developmental Psychology*, **12**, 15–23.

Webster's New World Dictionary of the American Language (1978). Second college edition. Chicago: World Publ.

Wells, K. (1980). Gender-role identity and psychological adjustment in adolescence. *Journal of Youth and Adolescence*, **9**, 59–72.

Whitely, B. E., Jr. (1983). Sex role orientation and self-esteem: A critical meta-analysis review. *Journal of Personality and Social Psychology*, **44**, 765–778.

Worell, J. (1978). Sex roles and psychological well-being: Perspectives on methodology. *Journal of Consulting and Clinical Psychology,* **46,** 777–791.

Worell, J. (1979). *Changng sex roles.* Invited address presented at the Southeastern Psychological Association, New Orleans. (ERIC document reproduction service no. ED 170 066.)

Worell, J. (1981). Life-span sex roles: Development, continuity, and change. In R. M. Lerner & N. A. Busch-Rossnagel (Eds.), *Individuals as producers of their development* (pp. 313–347). New York: Academic Press.

Worell, J. (1982). Psychological sex roles: Significance and change. In J. Worell (Ed.), *Psychological development in the elementary years* (pp. 3–52). New York: Academic Press.

Worell, J., & Stilwell, W. E. (1981). *Psychology for teachers and students.* New York: McGraw-Hill.

Zanna, M. P., & Pack, S. J. (1975). On the self-fulfilling nature of apparent sex differences in behavior. *Journal of Experimental Social Psychology,* **11,** 583–591.

10

Are Adolescents People? Problems of Liberty, Entitlement, and Responsibility

Gary B. Melton

Infant, Adolescent, and Person as Legal and Moral Concepts

A chapter on legal issues in a book on adolescent development is anomalous in that the concept of adolescence is virtually foreign to the law. The term rarely appears in law or legal commentary (Wadlington, Whitebread, & Davis, 1983, p. 2; cf. Zimring, 1982). Rather a state of immaturity and dependency is generally assumed of *all* "infants" (a.k.a. "minors," "juveniles," or "children") who have yet to achieve the age of majority. Seventeen-year-olds are viewed in law as in need of care and protection by state and parents, but they are magically transformed from helpless infant to autonomous adult on their 18th birthday. In short, the law makes few distinctions on the basis of even gross developmental changes, other than the dichotomous distinction between minor and adult.

There is some evidence that, through the legal fiction of equating toddlers and teenagers, the law actually contributed to the invention of adolescence near the turn of the century. Social historians (Bakan, 1971; Kett, 1974, 1977; Platt, 1977) have generally concluded that the concept of adolescence was largely nonexistent until the creation of special legal institutions for the regulation of the lives of youth (e.g., juvenile courts, compulsory education, child labor laws). Through the elongation and formal confirmation of the period of de facto dependency, these legal measures served to increase social control over youth and to induce conflict—both direct and internalized—concerning their status. Adolescent *Sturm und Drang* is a product of neither evolution (cf. Hall, 1904) nor a pubescent surge in the strength of libido (cf. Blos, 1962). Rather, it is a reflection of the actual social ambiguity that adolescents confront.

In Western law, philosophy, and social norms, there has been persistent skepticism as to the personhood of children (Melton, 1983a, chaps. 1 and 9; Worsfold, 1974). At its roots, this view is a reflection of the historic economic role of children as chattel of their father. For example, Hobbes (1839–1945/1651) wrote, "There would be no reason why any man should desire to have children or to take care to nourish them if afterwards to have no other benefit from them than from other men" (p. 329). Even today, the definition of children in terms of their economic value is common in many parts of the world (see review in Melton, 1983a, pp. 194–200). In the more modern view, however, children lack the natural rights accorded persons because they lack the rationality required to participate in the moral community, the requisite for recognition of personhood (e.g., Moore, 1984). Therefore, the benevolent society must care for children and act on their behalf because they lack the capacity to act in their best interests. For the most part, the law reflects these assumptions; minors are generally unable to make contracts or otherwise act independently of their parents or those who act in loco parentis. Legally defined as children, adolescents are firmly within the legal and social status of nonpersons who are neither expected nor permitted to exercise responsible judgment. As Chief Justice Burger wrote in the majority opinion in *Parham v. J. R.* (1979), "Most children, even in adolescence, simply are not able to make sound judgments concerning many decisions, including their need for medical care or treatment. Parents can and must make those judgments" (p. 603).

Persuasive arguments can be made that the denial of personhood of children is philosophically unsound (Brown, 1982; Worsfold, 1974) and that, in any event, the assumption of unity of interests between parents and child is untenable (Melton, 1982). Regardless, the important point in this context is that, as I have argued elsewhere (Melton, 1983e), the usual arguments for failure to recognize personhood in children are simply inapplicable to adolescents. The evidence is overwhelming that in fact most adolescents do have the capacity to act as citizens of the moral community. Few would seriously claim that adolescents are unable to articulate moral preferences and reasons for these preferences. Indeed, for most decisions, adolescents do not differ from adults in their competence, whether determined by their understanding of alternatives, the rationality of their reasoning, or the reasonableness of their choices (Melton, Koocher, & Saks, 1983). Justice Stewart's denial of liberty to minors on the ground that "a child—like someone in a captive audience—is not possessed of that full capacity for individual choice which is the presupposition of First Amendment guarantees" (*Ginsberg v.*

New York, 1968, concurring opinion, pp. 649–650) can be properly applied to adolescents only as people who are de facto captive, not as people unable to make reasoned choices.

In short, adolescence is, and has been, frequently marked by a profound conflict between, on the one hand, psychological competence and moral personhood and, on the other, social captivity and legal status as a nonperson. In view of the historical and cultural relativity of adolescence, it is this role incongruity that is the most plausible explanation for the psychosocial conflicts endemic among adolescents in 20th-century industrialized societies. The psychological crisis around identity (cf. Erikson, 1968) can be understood as a direct reflection of the fact that the social–moral identity of adolescents *is* conflict-laden.

This conflict has found its way into legal thinking. Although in the late 1960s the Supreme Court finally recognized minors as persons within the meaning of the Constitution (*In re Gault*, 1967, p. 13; *Tinker v. Des Moines Independent School District*, 1969, p. 511), it has been less than forthright in the application of this principle. As suggested in the earlier quote from *Parham*, the Court has been reluctant to concede that adolescents can be competent decision makers, and it has frequently assumed that recognition of adolescents' liberty and privacy interests would result in great harm to the child, the family, and society. Most important, the Court has sometimes applied a lower level of scrutiny to abridgement of minors' constitutional rights than is applied to state intrusions upon adults' fundamental rights and, in so doing, has started with a *presumption* that age discrimination is constitutional. Rather than questioning whether the state has *compelling* interests (the usual standard) in infringement of minors' fundamental rights, the Court has frequently looked merely for *legitimate, significant,* or *rational* bases for limitations placed by the state on minors' exercise of constitutional rights (e.g., *City of Akron v. Akron Center for Reproductive Health, Inc.,* 1983, pp. 427–428, note 10; *Ginsberg v. New York,* 1968, pp. 641–643; *Planned Parenthood of Central Missouri v. Danforth,* 1976). In effect, the Court has answered Arthur's (1968) question, "Should children be as equal as people?," with "Not quite" (Melton, 1983b).

The Court's ambivalence about adolescence is also reflected in inconsistent holdings and dicta. Its assumptions, of both law and social fact, have often varied dramatically in cases involving children and youth, even in opinions announced the same day (for examples of such contradictions, see Melton, 1984, p. 454, note 34). Indeed, some commentators have questioned the Court's ability to adjudicate logically in family law cases (Melton, 1984; Perry & Melton, 1984; Wadlington *et al.,* 1983).

There are several reasons for the conflicts embedded in adolescents' legal status. First, there are divergent views of adolescence present in the social construct itself and the various schools of thought within the child advocacy movement (Melton, 1983a; Mnookin, 1978b; Rogers & Wrightsman, 1978; Skolnick, 1975). Second, the interests among child, family, and state are variously overlapping and contradictory (see generally Mnookin, 1978a; Wadlington *et al.,* 1983). These relationships are often complex and inadequately analyzed. Moreover, some of the interests potentially in conflict with adolescents' rights (e.g., family privacy) may themselves be constitutionally protected (*Merriken v. Cressman,* 1973, p. 918; *Roe v. Wade,* 1973, pp. 152–153). Third, it is not always clear how vindication of one sort of interest affects other aspects of adolescents' legal status. For example, does recognition of due process rights for juveniles accused of delinquency imply that juveniles should be viewed as fully responsible for their behavior and subject to adult criminal sanctions?

Some commentators (e.g., Moore, 1984) have argued that, for minors to qualify as persons, they must be full moral agents. In this view, the question of personhood determines *both* whether individuals are accountable for their behavior and whether individuals have rights. Just as the potential for rational action determines whether one is morally responsible, so it is argued, rights belong only to those who rationally can choose to exercise them. Moral persons are owed liberty in part because they are good practical reasoners, who have cognizable moral interests and the ability to calculate how to obtain both the good and their own self-interests (c. Mill, 1859/1947). Similarly, it is argued, positive rights (e.g., equal access to education) are owed persons because the morally relevant criterion for distribution of primary goods is personhood— autonomy and rationality (Moore, 1984, pp. 96–97). However, as will become clear over the course of this chapter, *liberty, entitlement,* and *responsibility* need not be grounded on the same moral premise. Thus, although I assume adolescents to be persons, I will consider these three issues separately. (For a similar conceptualization of legal policies affecting adolescents, see Zimring, 1982.)

Liberty and Privacy

Do Liberty and Privacy Matter to Adolescents?

Liberty and privacy are perhaps the most basic interests of individuals in our society. Recognition of these interests signals that one is indeed an autonomous *person* possessing cognizable boundaries that are generally inviolable by the state. Respect for persons demands the protection of self-determination (i.e., liberty) and control over one's body and mind, personal information, and personal space (i.e., privacy; see Melton, 1983d).

Few would seriously question the significance of the *right to be let alone* (cf. *Olmstead v. United States,* 1928, dissenting opinion of Justice Brandeis). Such a value is deeply embedded in the Anglo-American legal tradition. Nonetheless, there has been a persistent argument that the liberty and privacy of adolescents can be wantonly abridged because these interests are psychologically meaningless to them. Although the Supreme Court directly refuted "the assertion that a child, unlike an adult, has a right 'not to liberty but to custody'" when it announced minors' constitutional personhood (*In re Gault,* 1967, p. 517), the idea has continued to find its way into judicial opinions, including those of the Supreme Court. Recently, for example, the Court upheld preventive detention of juveniles accused of a delinquent offense, in part because juveniles' interest in freedom "must be qualified by the recognition that juveniles, unlike adults, are always in some form of custody" and because "society has a legitimate interest in protecting a juvenile from the consequences of his criminal activity" (*Schall v. Martin,* 1984, pp. 265–266). In other words, for juveniles, being incarcerated "in a facility closely resembling a jail" (*Schall,* 1984, dissenting opinion, p. 290) really differs little from being at home; regardless, juvenile respondents should be glad that they have been locked up while awaiting a hearing.

Using similar logic, a federal district court, affirmed by the Seventh Circuit Court of Appeals, upheld the constitutionality of dragnet canine searches of junior and senior high school students (*Doe v. Renfrow,* 1979). The court argued that pupils have no expectations of privacy:

> Students are exposed to various intrusions into their classroom environment. The presence of the canine team for several minutes was a minimal intrusion at best and not so serious as to invoke the protections of the Fourth Amendment [which protects "people" from "unreasonable searches and seizures"]. . . .
>
> [T]he students did not have a justifiable expectation of privacy that would preclude a school administrator from sniffing the air around the desks with the aid of a trained drug detecting canine. . . . Any expectation of privacy necessarily diminishes in light of a student's constant supervision while in school. Because of the constant interaction among student, faculty and school administrators, a public school student cannot be said to enjoy any absolute expectation of privacy while in the classroom setting. (*Doe v. Renfrow,* 1979, pp. 1020, 1022, citation omitted)

Whether rights to liberty and privacy are recognized should not be dependent upon subjective expectations. For example, an announcement by the FBI that it planned to do random searches of homes (and accompanying diminution of subjective expectations of privacy) would hardly legitimize such intrusions. Nonetheless, it is also clear that liberty and privacy *are* salient to adolescents and, indeed, to younger schoolchildren. Even for elementary schoolchildren, privacy (Parke & Sawin, 1979; Wolfe, 1979) and self-determination (Margolin, 1982; Melton, 1980) are psychologically meaningful. In view of developmentally appropriate concerns with individuation and separation, these interests are likely to have special significance for adolescents (Laufer & Wolfe, 1977; Melton, 1978; Wolfe, 1979).

Respect for personhood should be sufficient to guarantee recognition of adolescents' liberty and privacy. Even if it were not, there are utilitarian grounds for doing so (Melton, 1983c). Increased actual control of one's fate results, unsurprisingly, in increased perceived control (e.g., Rosen, 1977), which is related to psychological well-being (Perlmuter & Monty, 1979). Freedom of choice increases motivation and performance (Brehm, 1966; Melton, 1983c). Experiences of decision making and respect for one's liberty and privacy are also likely to enhance legal socialization and support for libertarian values (Melton, 1983c; Tapp & Levine, 1974; Tapp & Melton, 1983). Finally, respect for privacy may be important in solidifying a sense of identity (Wolfe, 1979).

Liberty, Privacy, and Education: The State of the Law

EDUCATIONAL DECISION MAKING

Although there may be important reasons to recognize adolescents' liberty and privacy, it is clear that such values have little support in the law regulating junior and senior high schools. Indeed, it is settled that the state's interest in preparation of children for exercise of citizenship and independent living is sufficiently compelling to require attendance in school and even prescription of the curriculum. All American jurisdictions have compulsory education laws (Wadlington *et al.*, 1983, p. 108). Moreover, while pupils are present, school officials have broad authority in regulating their behavior. These restrictions are said to be justified on the grounds that decorum is necessary for education, that the school's function is in part to socialize a sense of discipline, and that the school acts in loco parentis to protect youth from themselves.

Pupils' lack of standing in decisions about their education carries over to those instances in which the consequences may be the most profound. For example, although the Education for All Handicapped Children Act (1975) permits the inclusion of a pupil, "whenever appropriate," in the meeting to draft an individual educational plan (IEP), there is no requirement to include a pupil who wishes to have a say about whether he or she is placed in a particular special education program. Although the Department of Education (1981) has expressed a preference for participation by "older handicapped children," the decision as to whether the pupil will actually participate is left in the hands of the parent. The majority even of older adolescents (age 16 and older) do not participate in the formulation of their IEPs (Pyechia, 1979; Scanlon, Arick, & Phelps, 1981). Nonetheless, data from at least one special day school suggest that most students in special education, especially older adolescents, wish to be involved in planning their programs and feel that they are effective when they are allowed to do so (Taylor, Adelman, & Kaser-Boyd, 1983).

Pupils also have no control over the information in their school records. Although the Buckley Amendment (Family Educational and Privacy Rights Act, 1974) places substantial constraints on school officials' dissemination of information about individual pupils, it is parents who are vested with full authority over the information. Even in state in which minors can consent independently to psychotherapy, it is unclear that this right applies to school-based psychological services or that it guarantees confidentiality (Ehrenreich & Melton, 1983). Presumably parents have access to any counseling information in the school record.

FREEDOM OF EXPRESSION

ACCESS TO INFORMATION. There are also significant limitations on adolescents' freedom of expression in school, although *some* freedom is recognized. The limitations exist despite the fact that freedom of expression is clearly related to educational purposes. This relationship is closest with the right of access to information and opinion. For example, in a 5–4 decision in which seven opinions were filed, the Supreme Court held that school boards cannot remove books that they find politically objectionable from the libraries of junior and senior high schools (*Board of Education, Island Trees Union Free School District No. 26 v. Pico*, 1982). A plurality of the Court found that suppression of ideas by school officials adversely affects students' First Amendment interests in two ways. First, the right to distribute literature inherently subsumes the right to receive it. Otherwise, the *sender's* freedom of expression is empty. Second, "the right to receive ideas is a necessary predicate of the *recipient's* meaningful exercise of his own rights of speech, press, and political freedom" (p. 867). Restriction of access to ideas in the school library chills the student's efforts to test or expand ideas presented in or out of the classroom. Thus, the suppression of ideas through library censorship is inconsistent with schools' basic purpose of promotion of intellectual inquiry.

POLITICAL EXPRESSION.   *Island Trees* is the progeny of the leading case
on students' civil liberties, *Tinker v. Des Moines Independent School
District* (1969), which dealt with direct expression of political ideas. In
Tinker, the Supreme Court held that Des Moines school authorities had
violated the First Amendment by suspending students who wore black
armbands in protest of the Vietnam War. The majority opinion, written by
Justice Fortas, is filled with strong words about the application of
constitutional protections to students. "It can hardly be argued," the
Court said, "that either students or teachers shed their constitutional
rights to freedom of speech or expression at the schoolhouse gate"
(p. 506). In still stronger language, the Court added:

> In our system, state-operated schools may not be enclaves of totalitarian-
> ism. School officials do not possess absolute authority over their students.
> Students in school as well as out of school are "persons" under our
> Constitution. They are possessed of fundamental rights which the State must
> respect, just as they themselves must respect their obligations to the State. In
> our system, students may not be regarded as closed-circuit recipients of only
> that which the State chooses to communicate. They may not be confined to
> the expression of those sentiments that are officially approved. (p. 511)

However, when *Tinker* is examined closely, the seemingly clear
confirmation of students' rights becomes quite ambiguous. First, the
Court emphasized that the First Amendment must be "applied in the
special circumstances of the school environment" (p. 506), and that it
does not protect conduct that "materially disrupts classwork" (p. 513).
Thus, speech that provokes disruptions *by others* in the school who
disagree may not fall within the scope of the First Amendment. Second, it
is not clear whose rights were vindicated in *Tinker*. One of the Tinker
children was only 8 years old, and their parents were antiwar activists.
Tinker may stand more for *parents'* rights against the state than children's
rights. A clearer and more interesting case would have been presented if
the students had expressed political views independent of their parents or
even contrary to their parents' wishes.

The ambiguous message of *Tinker* is reflected in conflicting judgments
as to high school students' freedom to distribute uncensored newspapers,
especially alternative or "underground" publications. Some courts have
upheld sanctions against students for failing to submit newspapers to
school authorities for review or simply distributing the newspapers (e.g.,
Graham v. Houston Independent School District, 1970; *Schwartz v.
Schuker*, 1969; *Sullivan v. Houston Independent School District*, 1973).
On the other hand, several courts have struck down systems of prior
restraint on student pubications (e.g., *Bright v. Los Angeles Unified
School District*, 1976, and cases cited therein).

RELIGIOUS EXPRESSION. Nowhere is the potential conflict of interests between parent and child clearer than in the series of cases and controversies about the relationship between church and state in education. Consider, for example, the recent highly publicized confrontations between officials of Christian schools and state education authorities (e.g., *State ex rel. Douglas v. Faith Baptist Church,* 1981; discussed in Moshman, 1985). Is the state's interest in socialization of children demonstrably furthered by requiring teachers in religious schools to be certified? Regardless, who better represents the interests of the children: the state, which seeks to establish minimum standards for children's education, or the parents, who argue the supremacy of their religious freedom? Can the child's interest in religious freedom be assumed to be synonymous with that of the parents? How would the calculus change if a child sought to enroll in a Christian school against parental wishes?

These issues were most starkly raised in the Supreme Court by *Wisconsin v. Yoder* (1972), although all but Justice Douglas chose to avoid them. In *Yoder,* the Court overturned the convictions of several Amish parents for failing to cause their 14- and 15-year-old children to attend school until age 16. The state's interest in the children's attending school for a year or two more was found to be insufficient to countervail the parents' right to direct the religious upbringing of their children. In an impassioned dissent, Justice Douglas argued that the Court was permitting parents to run roughshod over the religious liberty and right to education of their adolescent children, whose interests were key.

The complexity of interests among parent, child, and state is also illustrated by the contemporary debate over the introduction of prayer and other religious exercises into the public schools. Critics have argued, of course, that voluntary prayer in the school is never really voluntary in that children with unorthodox religious views—or whose parents have unorthodox religious views—may be unlikely to feel comfortable in standing aside during the prayer. On the other hand, should the state be able to restrain religious expression by students who wish a forum for their views? This question is particularly acute if, as *Tinker* (1969) implies, students have at least some freedom to express other kinds of beliefs in school. Indeed, the Supreme Court has held that state universities may not prohibit meetings by religious groups in university facilities if other campus organizations are able to meet there (*Widmar v. Vincent,* 1981).

Although its decision was ultimately reversed on procedural grounds (*Bender v. Williamsport Area School District,* 1986), the Third Circuit Court of Appeals has held that the *Widmar* rule does not apply to high school students who wish to hold religious meetings during activity periods (*Bender v. Williamsport Area School District,* 1984). The court determined that the students' free-speech right to a forum was subordinate to the establishment clause because of "the special circumstances inherent in a high school" (p. 552). The majority argued that students, whose attendance in school is compelled, might perceive the state as endorsing religion, especially because the school required that all activities be monitored by a school-approved adult.

Similar arguments led the Supreme Court to overturn a state statute requiring public schools to observe a daily period of mediation or prayer (*Wallace v. Jaffree*, 1985). In testimony in federal court on a similar West Virginia law (Melton, 1986), I argued that young children would be unable to distinguish between prayer and meditation and that they would not perceive themselves as having a right not to participate. Thus, as a practical matter, the law would be perceived as a requirement to pray and thus would be in effect a promotion of religion.

PRESERVATION OF PRIVACY

PRIVACY OF INFORMATION. There are at least two separate privacy interests at stake for adolescents in school: protection of (1) private information against compelled disclosure and (2) one's person, clothing, automobile, desk, locker, and other effects against search and seizure. With respect to the former, adolescents usually have no control over records, as noted earlier. However, privacy of information is implicated not only in release of information collected by the school. It is also relevant when participation is sought or compelled in discussions of sensitive topics in classes and other school functions. Interestingly, the controversies in this area have typically been framed in terms of *family* privacy, not the personal privacy of the student.

Protection of family privacy has been a particular theme in recent years of conservative political and religious groups that have been concerned about the introduction of materials they find objectionable into the public schools. In particular, they watch for instruction that seems to be based upon, or to espouse directly, "humanist" values contrary to those taught at home. Battles over textbooks have been highly publicized (e.g., Billings & Goldman, 1983). The Hatch Amendment (1978) gives a federal imprimatur to such surveillance by permitting parental access to any materials used in experimental curricula. The Hatch Amendment also requires parents' consent for psychological or psychiatric examination or treatment, "in which the primary purpose is to reveal information" about a number of topics of concern of the family; for example, "political affiliations"; "mental and psychological problems potentially embarrassing to the student or his family"; "sex behavior and attitudes"; "critical appraisals of other individuals with whom respondents have close family relationships"; "income." The regulations pursuant to the Hatch

Amendment (Department of Education, 1984) are so broad as to require parental consent anytime that a teacher administers a "psychological test" by, for example, asking a question about politics.

Consistent with the emphasis on family privacy is *Merriken v. Cressman* (1973; for commentary, see, e.g., Bersoff, 1983; Melton, 1983d), one of the few reported cases about school overreaching in collection of information. In *Merriken*, a Pennsylvania junior high introduced, without parental or student consent, a two-step program to deal with drug abuse. In the first phase, a personality test would be administered to screen potential drug abusers. The second phase would entail compulsory intervention, including confrontational group therapy, for students so identified.

The *Merriken* court was especially disturbed by the content of the test:

> These questions go directly to an individual's family relationship and his rearing. There probably is no more private a relationship, excepting marriage, which the Constitution safeguards, than that between parent and child. This Court can look upon any invasion of that relationship as a direct violation of one's Constitutional right to privacy. (p. 918)

PROTECTION AGAINST UNREASONABLE SEARCHES. The most direct tests of a students' independent privacy rights have come in cases concerning the propriety of searches and seizures by school officials (Gardner, 1980; Melton, 1983d). These cases have arisen in two contexts. In one series of cases, students have sued school officials for violation of civil rights after the students were subjected to dragnet searches (*Doe v. Renfrow*, 1979; *Horton v. Goose Creek Independent School District*, 1982; *Jones v. Latexo Independent School District*, 1980) or other searches without particularized, reasonable cause (e.g., *Bilbrey v. Brown*, 1984). In the second series of cases, students have sought to exclude evidence obtained through warrantless searches and seizures by school officials from delinquency or criminal proceedings (e.g., *In re Ronald B.*, 1978; *State v. Mora*, 1975; *State v. Walker*, 1974; *State v. Young*, 1975).

These cases raise at least three major issues beyond the usually hoary questions of what constitutes a "search" under the Fourth Amendment (cf. Amsterdam, 1974; Slobogin, 1981; Weinreb, 1974). First, is the Fourth Amendment applicable at all to students? Do they have any cognizable expectation of privacy (compare *Doe v. Renfrow*, 1979, and *Jones v. Latexo Independent School District*, 1980)? Second, assuming that the Fourth Amendment applies, should the *probable cause* standard applicable to police searches also apply in school searches? (The majority of courts have adopted a *reasonable suspicion* standard; see Wadlington *et al.*, 1983, pp. 295–297.) Third, are school officials government agents for purposes of Fourth Amendment analysis, or do they act in loco parentis (e.g., *People v. Overton*, 1967; *State v. Walker*, 1974; *State v. Young*, 1975)?

The Supreme Court (*New Jersey v. T.L.O.*, 1985) has concluded that the Fourth Amendment does apply to students and that school officials act as government agents. However, the Court failed to reach the corollary question that it had been asked to address: whether the exclusionary rule applies to evidence illegally obtained by school officials.[1] Instead, the Court focused on the standard to be used in determining the "reasonableness" of a search under the Fourth Amendment. The Court adopted a standard for school searches of *reasonableness, under all the circumstances,* instead of probable cause.

Analogous to the standard for "stop-and-frisk" searches by police for weapons (*Terry v. Ohio*, 1968), school searches may be sufficiently special to warrant an exception to the probable cause standard. School officials have a duty to protect law-abiding students—who, after all, have no choice in whether to remain in attendance—from the dangerous or disorderly acts of other students. Some might also argue that there is a duty to protect wayward students from themselves.

However, a lowered standard (i.e., reasonable cause) is far different from no standard at all. Just as we tolerate some hiding of contraband by adult offenders so that the state cannot run roughshod over the privacy of adult citizens, it must be acknowledged that protection of the privacy of junior and senior high school students will sometimes have the effect of shielding illicit behavior. On balance, though, this social cost is justified by the protection of personhood. Preservation of personal integrity requires that private zones remain invulnerable to unreasonable intrusions.

Moreover, the state's interest in socialization of citizens—the raison d'être of compulsory education—is facilitated by respect for personal privacy. Consider, for example, Justice Brennan's dissent from the Supreme Court's denial of certiorari (refusal to consider the appeal) in *Doe v. Renfrow* (1981):

> We do not know what class petitioner was attending when the police and dogs burst in, but the lesson the school authorities taught her that day will undoubtedly make a greater impression than the one her teacher had hoped to convey. I would grant certiorari to teach petitioner another lesson; that the

---

[1] The exclusionary rule is the doctrine in criminal procedure that bars the admission of illicitly obtained evidence. It is intended in part as a deterrent against misconduct by the police and other state authorities.

Fourth Amendment protects "the right of the people to be secure in their persons, houses, papers, and effects, against unreasonable searches and seizures," and that before police and local officers are permitted to conduct dog-assisted dragnet inspections of public school students, they must obtain a warrant based on sufficient particularized evidence to establish probable cause to believe a crime hs been or is being committed. Schools cannot expect their students to learn the lessons of good citizenship when the school authorities themselves disregard the fundamental principles underpinning our constitutional freedoms. (pp. 1027–1028)

Entitlement

The Parens Patriae Power and Duty

The discussion thus far has focused on whether adolescents' autonomy is, or should be, equal to adults'. In this section, the question is whether adolescents are owed more rights than adults. Irrespective of the level of freedom from state intrusion to which adolescents have just claim, do they have positive rights to special entitlements?

The basic assumption that immature persons have a special claim on the resources of the community (e.g., education, nutritious food) is relatively uncontroversial, although there is little consensus as to the legitimate breadth of the claim. Illustrative of the level of agreement as to the root concept is the unanimity with which the United Nations (1959) Declaration of the Rights of the Child was adopted. The Declaration proclaims a potpourri of positive entitlements: a name and nationality; social security; special education, when needed; adequate nutrition, housing, and recreation; "an atmosphere of affection and of moral and material security"; priority for disaster relief; freedom from harmful labor, and so forth.

The concept of special entitlements for children is rooted in the state's parens patriae (the sovereign as parent) authority. According to this doctrine, control of the lives of dependent persons is vested ultimately in the state. In the past century, the parens patriae power has been used primarily to "save" children and youth (Platt, 1977). Within this framework, the state's interest in socializing children is conceptualized as coextensive with the child's interests; the state acts as benevolent parent.

However, this supposedly child-centered purpose may be an illogical extension of the historical underpinnings of the parens patriae power (*In re Gault*, 1967, pp. 16–17). In English common law, parens patriae doctrine provided authority for the sovereign to take control of a dependent person's estate so that the individual's wealth—and the taxes to be paid on it—would not be squandered. Thus, historically there was no pretense that exercise of the parens patriae power was really on behalf of the child; the exchequer was the primary intended beneficiary.

Assuming, though, that the state's contemporary purpose in use of the parens patriae power is benevolent, the parens patriae doctrine represents a duty as well as a power. Because immature persons are thought to be unable to care adequately for themselves, the humane society is obligated to protect the welfare of minors, who are perceived as vulnerable and lacking in autonomy. In other words, the legal authority is based at present on a moral imperative to protect those unable to protect themselves (pursuant to the principle of beneficence). Under such a theory, the work on liberty and privacy discussed earlier raised serious questions about whether the duty remains applicable to adolescents, who are typically capable of making reasonable judgments.

However, recognition of adolescents' full personhood does not necessarily negate the premises underlying the parens patriae power. First, even if adolescents have the capacity for reasoned choice, they are usually de facto dependent, whether by law or social custom. Insofar as the state enforces this social ordering, it is arguable that the state owes special protection to those who are at least indirectly oppressed by it.[2] Second, the state has a clear interest in facilitating adolescents' integration into the work force and electorate. Thus, there are utilitarian reasons in a society that is both technologically sophisticated and democratic for providing adolescents with entitlements (e.g., right to education) beyond those that may be claimed by all persons. Third, persons qua persons are owed primary goods (e.g., liberty necessary for human dignity; see Rawls, 1971). A corollary to this principle is that society owes persons the resources necessary to take advantage of these goods (Brown, 1982). Thus, acquisition of skills necessary for economic independence is an important requisite for true self-determination. Therefore, society may be

---

[2] Strict scrutiny is required when discrimination takes place by the government against a suspect class—a group "saddled with such disabilities, or subjected to such a history of purposeful unequal treatment, or relegated to such a position of political powerlessness as to command extraordinary protection from the majoritarian political process" (*San Antonio Independent School District v. Rodriguez,* 1973, p. 28). A strong argument can be made that minors constitute such a group (Melton, 1984; Tribe, 1975), especially in view of the age segregation officially supported by the state.

At the same time, care must be taken to avoid a quid pro quo basis for entitlements for adolescents. Morally unjustifiable actions are no less intolerable because the victims are given rewards for their victimization—all the more so when the rewards are undesired by the recipients and for their own good. The history of juvenile justice is illustrative. The law long accepted unfair treatment of respondents in delinquency proceedings on the theory that they were receiving rehabilitative services.

morally obligated to provide adolescents with the resources necessary for full participation in the community.

There is a potential conflict, though, between recognition of personhood and *broad* application of the parens patriae power. Protection of adolescents from exploitation and provision of resources necessary for self-protection are consistent with personhood. However, protection of adolescents from themselves is obviously inconsistent with preservation of liberty. Self-determination includes the freedom to make unwise or unconventional decisions.

Indeed, the parens patriae power may often be exercised more to protect the social order than to enhance the interests of youth. It is a perverse twist of logic to incarcerate an adolescent in a juvenile correctional facility in his interests. Similarly, the application of quasi-criminal sanctions against adolescents for many behaviors not prohibited for adults cannot be coherently justified on the ground that "it's good for them." The task for the community must be to preserve entitlement to *opportunities* for adolescents to fulfill human needs, not to use the parens patriae power to enforce disrespect for adolescents' personhood.

At the same time, though, it must be recognized that rejection of paternalism and respect for personhood will sometimes require tolerance of adverse decisions. Consider the distinction between universal *access* to education—an entitlement consistent with adolescents' personhood—and *compulsory* education—a deprivation of liberty justified by adolescents' immaturity. Recognition of adolescents' autonomy—in this instance, the right to choose education—may have significant personal and social costs. So too may bad business decisions by adults, but respect for personal autonomy demands that they be allowed to do so.

Positive Rights in Education

The current state of entitlements in education can best be described as a mixed picture. Throughout this century, the United States has supported universal public education. However, the Supreme Court has found that education is neither implicitly nor explicitly guaranteed by the Constitution (*San Antonio Independent School District v. Rodriguez*, 1973). Writing for the Court, Justice Powell, a former school board member, concluded that the rights to speak and to vote do not "guarantee to the citizenry the most *effective* speech or the most *informed* electoral choice" (*San Antonio Independent School District v. Rodriguez*, 1973, p. 36). The courts have also generally refused to recognize a tort of educational malpractice that might, in effect, guarantee an adequate education through threat of civil damages (e.g., *Donahue v. Copiague Union Free School District*, 1979; *Helm v. Professional Children's School*, 1980;

Hoffman v. Board of Education of City of New York, 1979; *Hunter v. Board of Education*, 1981; *Peter W. v. San Francisco Unified School District*, 1976).

Although there is, of course, substantial authority for equality of opportunity in *access* to education (e.g., *Brown v. Board of Education*, 1954; *Pennsylvania Association for Retarded Children v. Commonwealth*, 1971/1972), the state's affirmative duties to provide quality education are limited. The most ambitious federal attempt to create such duties was the Education for All Handicapped Children Act of 1975 (EAHCA), popularly known among educators as Public Law 94–142. The EAHCA guarantees a "free appropriate public education" to handicapped children aged 3 to 21. However, the Supreme Court has interpreted this statute narrowly to require only an "individualized educational program developed through the Act's procedures [and] reasonably calculated to enable the child to receive educational benefits" (*Hendrick Hudson District Board of Education v. Rowley*, 1982, p. 207). The program need not be optimally related to a student's needs; *some* educational benefit is enough. There is, analogously, a requirement that the school provide those "related services" (e.g., nursing services, psychological services) "necessary to aid a handicapped child to benefit from special education" (*Irving Independent School District v. Tatro*, 1984, p. 894). Presumably, there is no obligation under the EAHCA to provide psychological services to maximize a child's openness to education. Families found it difficult to vindicate even these limited rights, in that the Supreme Court held that litigants bringing suit to remedy violations of the EAHCA were not entitled to award of attorney's fees (*Smith v. Robinson*, 1984), a ruling that was later overturned by congressional action.

Although the *legal* right to an education, as provided by statute, may be limited to *some* education, the *moral* right to education may be more extensive. As noted earlier, there is arguably a natural right to whatever education is necessary to acquire the primary goods owed members of the moral community. For example, Bikson (1978) has discussed "intellectual rights" that she believes require "creative or critical independent approaches to learning" (p. 80). Bikson argues that autonomy is facilitated by teaching of skills in critical inquiry. She also contends that there is a need for "dialogical inquiry" in order to educate students as to their place in the community of autonomous inquirers (i.e., persons). In short, irrespective of whether adolescents sufficiently resemble "persons" to warrant self-determination, society should—arguably, *must*—provide advanced levels of education to enhance their participation in the kind of critical thinking necessary for autonomous moral reasoning.

Responsibility

Responsibility for Criminal Behavior

The question of the criminal responsibility of youth is one that lay dormant in this country for most of this century. In the common law, children under the age of 7 were considered morally blameless for illicit conduct; children between the ages of 7 and 14 were presumed incapable of forming criminal intent unless the state was able to show otherwise. The *defense of infancy* thus served to prevent punishment of children who might be unable to reason soundly about moral problems. However, for all practical purposes, infancy ceased to be a defense when juvenile courts were erected across the United States during the period between 1899 and 1925. The juvenile court was thought to act *for,* not against, youth accused of delinquent offenses. Its stated raison d'etre was exclusively rehabilitative. In such a context, questions of culpability were irrelevant.

Issues of responsibility (i.e., punishability for misconduct) were enlivened in 1967, when the Supreme Court (*In re Gault,* 1967) concluded that the juvenile court had been a mere "kangaroo court" that had deprived respondents of the rudiments of due process while subjecting them to deprivation of liberty in quasi-penal facilities—all in the name of treatment. Although *Gault* transformed juvenile courts into courts of *law,* it did not result in wholesale rejection of the rehabilitative ideal. Most states retain offender-based (rather than offense-based) dispositions, and the question of amenability to treatment remains the overarching issue in juvenile cases (Mulvey, 1984). Nonetheless, the trend, notably exemplified by the Juvenile Justice Standards Project (Morse & Whitebread, 1982), has been toward a just deserts model in which the traditional purposes of the criminal law, including retribution and incapacitation, are applied to juvenile courts. Some commentators have argued that this trend serves not only to protect society, but to guarantee that juvenile offenders are "punished for what they have done, not to be treated for what someone else thinks they are" (Fox, 1974, p. 6; see also Gardner, 1982).

In the new juvenile court, questions again arise of whether wayward juveniles deserve punishment and, if so, whether they are as blameworthy as adults who have committed the same offenses. Some commentators contend that the conclusion of personhood implies full moral responsibility (Moore, 1984); if adolescents are owed liberty, they are also responsible for their conduct. However, this syllogism is somewhat faulty. As Zimring (1982) has argued, the age of responsibility might legitimately be higher than the age of autonomy. The risk to the individual is greater when society errs in not finding autonomy when it is present and in finding responsibility when it is absent. Therefore, respect for human dignity would seem to demand errors in opposite directions when the age of majority is set for these two purposes. The risk of error in retribution and the moral desirability of benevolence might suggest the desirability of a kind of second-chance theory of disposition for youthful offenders.

Similarly, while, as previously discussed, utilitarian concerns might suggest the need for recognition of autonomy even of incompetent youth in some circumstances, the ill effects of punishment might support utilitarian arguments for shielding adolescents from the full force of the criminal law even if they are fully blameworthy. Also, the one area of research that indicates relative incompetence of adolescents in decision making is with respect to defending oneself in delinquency proceedings (Grisso, 1981). Juveniles, especially under age 16, are less likely than adult defendants to understand their rights and to reason well about whether to waive them. They are also less likely to understand attorney–client privilege and to comprehend the implications of the adversary defense. Therefore, due process may be different for juveniles, even if we recognize their right, as persons, to fundamental fairness in the adjudication of their cases (Rosenberg, 1980). Special procedural protections may be necessary if juveniles are to avail themselves of their rights and assist in their defense.

In short, recognition of the personhood of adolescents need not imply full accountability for their conduct. It does, however, enliven the question of the degree of culpability of wayward youth.

Responsibility and Education

At first glance, the conflicts about the purpose of juvenile law seem clearly misplaced in discussions of education. The socializing function of education appears on its face to have little to do with the retributive, deterrent, and incapacitative functions of criminal law. When a teacher or an administrator punishes a student, the punishment is ostensibly for the purpose of fostering a sense of discipline, not obtaining retribution. Assessment of whether the student is responsible for his actions—worthy of punishment—is therefore largely irrelevant.

However, this conclusion may be too pat. Basic concepts of justice apply in the assistant principal's office, just as in the juvenile court. It would be unjust to punish a kindergarten-age child for an error in judgment, or a student of any age who is not provided an opportunity to rebut the accusation of misconduct. Almost anyone's sense of justice would be offended by imposition of a severe punishment (e.g., expulsion) for a minor offense (e.g., chewing gum in class). When such examples are given, it becomes clear that retribution is in fact a deeply embedded purpose in punishment inflicted by school authorities; punishment, even when administered by the assistant principal, should fit the offense.

In at least tacit recognition of this fact, the Supreme Court held in *Goss v. Lopez* (1975) that school officials must exercise due care in punitive deprivation of education and its concomitant property value. However, perhaps reflecting its ongoing ambivalence about whether adolescents are really full-fledged persons, the Court in *Goss* required only the most rudimentary procedural safeguards before a student could be suspended for 10 days. The "hearing" may be immediate and need consist only of a description of the allegation and an opportunity for the student to tell his or her side of things. Moreover, four justices in *Goss* dissented from the finding that the Constitution requires *any* procedural due process in school suspensions.

Indeed, the Court has been reluctant to characterize punishment as punishment when the recipients are schoolchildren. Although acknowledging that corporal punishment is no longer acceptable punishment for prisoners, the Court has held, 5–4, that even *severe* paddlings— to the point a student requires medical attention—are not prohibited by the Eighth Amendment's bar of cruel and unusual punishments (*Ingraham v. Wright*, 1977). The Court concluded, contrary to both empirical data and common sense (Bersoff & Prasse, 1978; Melton, 1980–1981), that students do not *need* constitutional protection because "the public school remains an open institution" (*Ingraham*, p. 670), with pupils supposedly free to leave.

Even granting the questionable assumption of openness, it is, as the dissenters noted, irrelevant: "If a punishment is so barbaric and inhumane that it goes beyond the tolerance of a civilized society, its openness to public scrutiny should have nothing to do with its constitutional validity" (*Ingraham*, p. 690). Moreover, corporal punishment, even when administered in the name of school discipline, is still undeniably punitive:

> No one can deny that spanking of schoolchildren is "punishment" under any reasonable reading of the word, for the similarities between spanking in public schools and other forms of punishment are too obvious to ignore. Like other forms of punishment, spanking of schoolchildren involves an institutionalized response to the violation of some official rule or regulation prescribing certain conduct and is imposed for the purpose of rehabilitating the offender, deterring the offender and others like him for committing the violation in the future, and inflicting some measure of social retribution for the harm that has been done. (dissenting opinion, pp. 685–686)

At root, the courts', and the schools', failure fully to acknowledge the retributive aspects of school discipline is probably based on their ambivalence about the personhood of children and adolescents. To recognize the reality of punishment would imply a moral necessity for *justice,* for giving students their due. Otherwise, the rigors of due process are unnecessary; the student loses nothing of substance when he or she is "disciplined." The schools may have a vested interest in failing to permit the full exercise of responsibility by students; to do so would create an obligation of *reciprocality.* As it is, though, public schools are essentially unaccountable to their students.

The bottom line is that many adults may not *want* youth to be held responsible for their actions, especially in the schools. Responsibility is fundamentally inconsistent with the concept that adolescents are uncivilized savages (cf. Hall, 1904) who must be controlled by the authorities. To acknowledge responsibility is clearly to acknowledge personhood and to accept the duty to respect the autonomy and privacy of youth.

The persistence of the concept of adolescent as savage is well illustrated by Justice Black's dissent in *Tinker* (1969), in which he attacked his Brethren for fostering "a new revolutionary era of permissiveness" (p. 518) by recognizing some measure of freedom of speech:

> Change has been said to be truly the law of life but sometimes the old and the tried and true are worth holding. The schools of this Nation have undoubtedly contributed to giving us tranquility and to making us a more law-abiding people. Uncontrolled and uncontrollable liberty is an enemy to domestic peace. We cannot close our eyes to the fact that some of the country's greatest problems are crimes committed by the youth, too many of school ages. School discipline, like parental discipline, is an integral and important part of training our children to be good citizens—to be better citizens. . . . Turned loose with lawsuits for damages and injunctions against their teachers as they are here, it is nothing but wishful thinking to imagine that young, immature students will not soon believe it is their right to control the schools rather than the right of the States that collect the taxes to hire the teachers for the benefit of the pupils. This case, therefore, . . . subjects the public schools in the country to the whims and caprices of their loudest-mouthed, but maybe not their brightest, students. . . . I wish . . . wholly to disclaim any purpose on my part to hold that the Federal Constitution compels the teachers, parents, and elected school officials to surrender control of the American public school system to public school students. (pp. 524–526)

Clearly, for Justice Black the key aspect of public education was *control.* It is probably safe to assume that he viewed "discipline" as socializing, not punitive. For him, there was no real question of responsibility; students had none. Nor was there any question of autonomy; an authoritarian style was a necessary aspect of the socialization of youth, who would otherwise destroy domestic tranquility.

Public Education and Respect for Persons

Beyond a mischaracterization of the nature of students, Justice Black also missed the point of public education and maybe even democracy itself. A "good citizen" is not a submissive citizen. Rather, the democratic process is dependent upon citizens' understanding their role as law creators. Development of this concept requires experience with decision making and exercise of responsibility (Tapp & Levine, 1974; Tapp & Melton, 1983). It is further enhanced by education that teaches, both didactically and through experience, that the student is a valued person who both owes and is owed respect. In short, beyond the ethical and legal issues discussed in this chapter, it is important to emphasize that respect for the personhood of adolescents is instrumental in the public schools' fulfillment of their mission of preparation of the electorate.

At the same time, it should be recognized that there is an inherent paradox in the purposes of public education. This dilemma is illustrated well by the *Board of Education, Island Trees* (1982) case briefly discussed earlier. The schools have a clear goal of fostering intellectual exercise; library censorship is obviously incompatible with such inquiry. On the other hand, as the dissenters in *Island Trees* emphasized, the public schools also have indoctrination functions; they are intended to inculcate the values of the community. At first glance, library censorship appears to be congruent with the latter goal.

However, on closer examination, the paradox of purposes is not such a conundrum after all. Perhaps the most basic values in our political system are respect for the dignity of the individual and equality under the law. However, these values, while enduring, have been perpetually fragile. Although Americans have long given lip service to civil liberties, most Americans still fail to perceive these rights as applicable to themselves in everyday situations or as justly exercised by unpopular groups (McClosky & Brill, 1983). Perhaps the most significant pedagogical problem in public education is educating the citizenry in the morality of the Bill of Rights (Melton & Saks, 1985). In the long run, therefore, the inculcation of community values and support for the autonomy of adolescents are completely compatible. If the schools are to fulfill their mission of political and legal socialization, educators must also recognize that their students are *persons*, legally and morally.

References

Amsterdam, A. (1974). Perspectives on the fourth amendment. *Minnesota Law Review,* **58,** 349–477.

Arthur, L. G. (1968). Should children be as equal as people? *North Dakota Law Review,* **45,** 204–221.

Bakan, D. (1971). Adolescence in American: From idea to social fact. In J. Kagan & R. Coles (Eds.), *Twelve to sixteen: Early adolescence* (pp. 73–89). New York: Norton.

Bender v. Williamsport Area School District, 741 F.2d 538 (3rd Cir. 1984).

Bender v. Williamsport Area School District, 106 S.Ct. 1326, *reh. denied,* 106 S.Ct. 2003 (1986).

Bersoff, D. N. (1983). Children as participants in psychoeducational assessment. In G. B. Melton, G. P. Koocher, & M. J. Saks (Eds.), *Children's competence to consent* (pp. 149–177) New York: Plenum.

Bersoff, D. N., & Prasse, D. (1978). Applied psychology and judicial decision making: Corporal punishment as a case in point. *Professional Psychology,* **9,** 400–411.

Bikson, T. K. (1978). The status of children's intellectual rights. *Journal of Social Issues,* **34,** 69–86.

Bilbrey v. Brown, 738 F.2d 1462 (9th Cir. 1984).

Billings, D. B., & Goldman, R. (1983). Religion and class consciousness in the Kanawha County school textbook controversy. In A. Batteau (Ed.), *Appalachia and America: Autonomy and regional dependence* (pp. 68–85). Lexington: University Press of Kentucky.

Blos, P. (1962). *On adolescence: A psychoanalytic interpretation.* New York: Free Press.

Board of Education, Island Trees Union School District, No. 26 v. Pico, 457 U.S. 853 (1982).

Brehm, J. W. (1966). *A theory of psychological reactance.* New York: Academic Press.

Bright v. Los Angeles Unified School District, 18 Cal.3d 450, 134 Cal. Rptr. 639, 556 P.2d 1090 (1976).

Brown, P. G. (1982). Human independence and parental proxy consent. In W. Gaylin & R. Macklin (Eds.), *Who speaks for the child? The problems of proxy consent* (pp. 209–222). New York: Plenum.

Brown of Board of Education, 347 U.S. 483 (1954).

City of Akron v. Akron Center for Reproductive Health, Inc., 462 U.S. 416 (1983).

Department of Education (1981). Individualized education programs. *Federal Register,* **46,** 5460–5474.

Department of Education (1984). Student rights in research, experimental activities, and testing. *Federal Register,* **49,** 35318–35322.

Doe v. Renfrow, 475 F. Supp. 1012 (N.D. Ind. 1979), *aff'd in part, remanded in part,* 631 F.2d 91 (7th Cir. 1980), *reh'g and reh'g en banc denied,* 635 F.2d 582 (7th Cir. 1980), *cert. denied,* 451 U.S. 1022 (1981).

Donohue v. Copiague Union Free School District, 47 N.Y.2d 440, 418 N.Y.S.2d 375, 391 N.E.2d 1352 (1979).

Education for All Handicapped Children Act of 1975, 20 U.S.C. §§ 1401–1461 (1982).

Ehrenreich, N. S., & Melton, G. B (1983). Ethical and legal issues in the treatment of children. In C. E. Walker & M. C. Roberts (Eds.), *Handbook of clinical child psychology* (pp. 1285–1317). New York: Wiley.

Erikson, E. H. (1968). *Identity: Youth and crisis.* New York: Norton.

Family Educational and Privacy Rights Act of 1974, 20 U.S.C. § 1232g (1982).

Fox, S. J. (1974, August). The reform of juvenile justice: The child's right to punishment. *Juvenile Justice*, pp. 2–9.

Gardner, M. R. (1980). Sniffing for drugs in the classroom: Perspectives on fourth amendment scope. *Northwestern Law Review, 74*, 803–853.

Gardner, M. R. (1982). Punishment and juvenile justice: A conceptual framework for assessing constitutional rights of youthful offenders. *Vanderbilt Law Review, 35*, 791–847.

Ginsberg v. New York, 390 U.S. 629 (1968).

Goss v. Lopez, 419 U.S. 565 (1975).

Graham v. Houston Independent School District, 335 F. Supp. 1164 (S.D. Tex. 1970).

Grisso, T. (1981). *Juveniles' waiver of rights: Legal and psychological competence*. New York: Plenum.

Hall, G. S. (1904). *Adolescence: Its psychology and its relations to physiology, anthropology, sociology, sex, crime, religion, and education*. New York: Appleton.

Hatch Amendment of 1978, General Education Provisions Act, § 439(b), 20 U.S.C. § 1232h (1982).

Helm v. Professional Children's School, 103 Misc.2d 1053, 431 N.Y.S.2d 246 (App. Term. 1980).

Hendrick Hudson District Board of Education v. Rowley, 458 U.S. 276 (1982).

Hobbes, T. (1839–1845). *Leviathan* (Molesworth ed., Vol. 3). London: J. Bohn. (Original work published 1651.)

Hoffman v. Board of Education of City of New York, 49 N.Y.2d 121, 424 N.Y.S.2d 396, 400 N.E.2d 317 (1979).

Horton v. Goose Creek Independent School District 690 F.2d 470 (5th Cir. 1982), *reh'g denied*, 693 F.2d 524 (1982).

Hunter v. Board of Education, 47 Md.App. 709, 425 A.2d 681 (1981).

In re Gault, 387 U.S. 1 (1967).

In re Ronald B., 61 A.D.2d 204, 402 N.Y.S.2d 544 (1978).

Ingraham v. Wright, 430 U.S. 651 (1977).

Irving Independent School District v. Tatro, 468 U.S. 883 (1984).

Jones v. Latexo Independent School District, 499 F. Supp. 223 (E.D. Tex. 1980).

Kett, J. F. (1974). The history of age grouping in America. In J. S. Coleman (Ed.), *Youth: Transition to adulthood* (pp. 9–29). Chicago: University of Chicago Press.

Kett, J. F. (1977). *Rites of passage*. New York: Basic Books.

Laufer, R. S., & Wolfe, M. (1977). Privacy as a concept and a social issue: A multidimensional developmental theory. *Journal of Social Issues, 33* (2), 22–42.

Margolin, C. R. (1982). A survey of children's views on their rights. *Journal of Clinical Child Psychology, 11*, 96–100.

McClosky, H., & Brill, A. (1983). *Dimensions of tolerance: What Americans believe about civil liberties*. New York: Russell Sage Foundation.

Melton, G. B. (1978). Children's right to treatment. *Journal of Clinical Child Psychology, 7*, 200–202.

Melton, G. B. (1980). Children's concepts of their rights. *Journal of Clinical Child Psychology, 9*, 186–190.

Melton, G. B. (1980–1981). Legal policy and child development research. *Child and Youth Services, 3* (3–4), 1, 13–20.

Melton, G. B. (1982). Children's rights: Where are the children? *American Journal of Orthopsychiatry, 52*, 530–538.

Melton, G. B. (1983a). *Child advocacy: Psychological issues and interventions*. New York: Plenum.

Melton, G. B. (1983b). Children's competence to consent: A problem in law and social science. In G. B. Melton, G. P. Koocher, & M. J. Saks (Eds.), *Children's competence to consent* (pp. 1–18). New York: Plenum.

Melton, G. B. (1983c). Decision making by children: Psychological risks and benefits. In G. B. Melton, G. P. Koocher, & M. J. Saks (Eds.), *Children's competence to consent* (pp. 21–40). New York: Plenum.

Melton, G. B. (1983d). Minors and privacy: Are legal and psychological concepts compatible? *Nebraska Law Review, 62,* 455–493.

Melton, G. B. (1983e). Toward "personhood" for adolescents: Autonomy and privacy as values in public policy. *American Psychologist, 38,* 99–103.

Melton, G. B. (1984). Developmental psychology and the law: The state of the art. *Journal of Family Law, 22,* 445–482.

Melton, G. B. (1986). Populism, school prayer, and the courts: Confessions of an expert witness. In D. Moshman (Ed.), *Children's intellectual rights* (pp. 63–73). San Francisco: Jossey-Bass.

Melton, G. B., Koocher, G. P., & Saks, M. J. (Eds.). (1983). *Children's competence to consent.* New York: Plenum.

Melton, G. B., & Saks, M. J. (1985). The law as an instrument of socialization. In G. B. Melton (Ed.), *Nebraska Symposium on Motivation* (Vol. 33, pp. 235–277). Lincoln: University of Nebraska Press.

Merriken v. Cressman, 364 F. Supp. 913 (E.D. Pa. 1973).

Mill, J. S. (1947). *On liberty.* Arlington Heights, IL: AHM Publishing. (Original work published 1850)

Mnookin, R. H. (1978a). *Child, family, and state: Problems and materials on children and the law.* Boston: Little, Brown.

Mnookin, R. H. (1978b). Children's rights: Beyond kiddie libbers and child savers. *Journal of Clinical Child Psychology, 7,* 163–167.

Moore, M. S. (1984). *Law and psychiatry: Rethinking the relationship.* London & New York: Cambridge University Press.

Morse, S. J., & Whitebread, C. (1982). Mental health implications of the Juvenile Justice Standards. In G. B. Melton (Ed.), *Legal reforms affecting child and youth services* (pp. 5–27). New York: Haworth.

Moshman, D. (1985). Faith Christian v. Nebraska: Parent, child, and community rights in the educational arena. *Teachers College Record, 86,* 553–578.

Mulvey, E. P. (1984). Judging amenability to treatment in juvenile offenders: Theory and practice. In N. D. Reppucci, L. A. Weithorn, E. P. Mulvey, & J. Monahan (Eds.), *Children, mental health and the law* (pp. 195–210). Beverly Hills, CA: Sage.

New Jersey v. T.L.O., 469 U.S. 325 (1985).

Olmstead v. United States, 277 U.S. 438 (1928).

Parham v. J. R., 442 U.S. 584 (1979).

Parke, R. D., & Sawin, D. B. (1979). Children's privacy in the home: Developmental, ecological and child-rearing determinants. *Environment and Behavior, 11,* 84–104.

Pennsylvania Association for Retarded Children (PARC) v. Pennsylvania, 334 F. Supp. 1257 (E.D.Pa. 1971) and 343 F. Supp. 279 (E.D.Pa. 1972).

People v. Overton, 20 N.Y.2d 360, 283 N.Y.S.2d 22, 229 N.E.2d 596 (1967).

Perlmutter, L. C., & Monty, R. A. (Eds.). (1979). *Choice and perceived control.* Hillsdale, NJ: Erlbaum.

Perry, G. S., & Melton, G. B. (1984). Precedential value of judicial notice of social facts: *Parham* as an example. *Journal of Family Law, 22,* 633–676.

Peter W. v. San Francisco Unified School District, 60 Cal.App.3d 814, 131 Cal.Rptr. 854 (1976).

Planned Parenthood of Central Missouri v. Danforth, 438 U.S. 52 (1976).

Platt, A. M. (1977). *The child savers: The invention of delinquency* (2nd ed.). Chicago: University of Chicago Press.

Pyechia, J. (1979). *A national survey of individualized education programs (IEPs) for handicapped children* (draft report). Research Triangle Park, NC: Research Triangle Institute.

Rawls, J. (1971). *A theory of justice.* Cambridge, MA: Harvard University Press.

Roe v. Wade, 410 U.S. 113 (1973).

Rogers, C. M., & Wrightsman, L. S. (1978). Attitudes toward children's rights: Nurturance or self-determination. *Journal of Social Issues,* **34** (2), 59–68.

Rosen, C. E. (1977). The impact of an Open Campus program upon high school students' sense of control over their environment. *Psychology in the Schools,* **14,** 216–219.

Rosenberg, I. M. (1980). The constitutional rights of children charged with crime: Proposal for a return to the not so distant past. *UCLA Law Review,* **27,** 656–721.

San Antonio Independent School District v. Rodriguez, 411 U.S. 1 (1973).

Scanlon, C. A., Arick, J., & Phelps, N. (1981). Participation in development of the IEP: Parents' perspectives. *Exceptional Children,* **47,** 373–374.

Schall v. Martin, 467 U.S. 253 (1984).

Schwartz v. Schuker, 298 F. Supp. 238 (E.D.N.Y. 1969).

Skolnick, A. (1975). The limits of childhood: Conceptions of child development and social contexts. *Law and Contemporary Problems,* **39,** 38–77.

Slobogin, C. (1981). Capacity to contest a search and seizure: The passing of old rules and some suggestions for new ones. *American Criminal Law Review,* **18,** 387–418.

Smith v. Robinson, 468 U.S. 992 (1984).

State *ex rel.* Douglas v. Faith Baptist Church, 207 Neb. 802, 301 N.W.2d 571, *appeal dismissed,* 454 U.S. 803 (1981).

State v. Mora, 307 So.2d 317 (La. 1975).

State v. Walker, 19 Or.App. 420, 528 P.2d 113 (1974).

State v. Young, 234 Ga. 488, 216 S.E.2d 586 (1975).

Sullivan v. Houston Independent School District, 475 F.2d 1071 (5th Cir. 1973), *cert. denied,* 414 U.S. 1032 (1974).

Tapp, J. L., & Levine, F. J. (1974). Legal socialization: Strategies for an ethical legality. *Stanford Law Review,* **27,** 1–72.

Tapp, J. L., & Melton, G. B. (1983). Preparing children for decision making: Implications of legal socialization research. In G. B. Melton, G. P. Koocher, & M. J. Saks (Eds.), *Children's competence to consent* (pp. 215–233). New York: Plenum.

Taylor, L., Adelman, H. S., & Kaser-Boyd, N. (1983). Perspectives of children regarding their participation in psychoeducational decisions. *Professional Psychology: Research and Practice,* **14,** 882–894.

Terry v. Ohio, 392 U.S. 1 (1968).

Tinker v. Des Moines Independent School District, 393 U.S. 503 (1969).

Tribe, L. (1975). Childhood, suspect classifications, and conclusive presumptions: Three linked riddles. *Law and Contemporary Problems,* **39,** 118–143.

United Nations (1959). *Declaration of the rights of the child.* Resolution adopted by the General Assembly.

Wadlington, W., Whitebread, C. H., & Davis, S. M. (1983). *Children in the legal system: Cases and materials.* Mineola, NY: Foundation Press.

Wallace v. Jaffree, 472 U.S. 38 (1985).

Weinreb, L. L. (1974). Generalities of the fourth amendment. *University of Chicago Law Review*, **42,** 47–85.

Widmar v. Vincent, 454 U.S. 263 (1981).

Wisconsin v. Yoder, 406 U.S. 205 (1972).

Wolfe, M. (1979). Childhood and privacy. In I. Altman & J. F. Wohlwill (Eds.), *Human behavior and environment: Advances in theory and research* (Vol. 3, pp. 175–222). New York: Plenum.

Worsfold, V. L. (1974). A philosophical justification for children's rights. *Harvard Educational Review*, **44,** 142–157.

Zimring, F. E. (1982). *The changing world of legal adolescence.* New York: Free Press.

Index

J/